EDUCATION
AND THE
FEDERAL
GOVERNMENT

EDUCATION
AND THE
FEDERAL
GOVERNMENT

A Historical Record

AMERICO D. LAPATI
THE CATHOLIC UNIVERSITY OF AMERICA

NEW YORK 1975

Library of Congress Cataloging in Publication Data

Lapati, Americo D
    Education and the Federal Government.

    Bibliography: p.
    Includes index.
    1. Educational law and legislation--United States.
2. Educational law and legislation--United States--
History. I. Title.
KF4119.L35   344'.73'07   75-4696
ISBN 0-88405-105-6

Contents

Introduction   1

PART I: CONGRESS AND EDUCATION   5

   1. Office of Education   7
   2. Elementary and Secondary Education   14
   3. Higher Education   48
   4. Vocational Education, Rehabilitation, and the Handi-
      capped   96
   5. International Education   126

PART II: THE SUPREME COURT AND EDUCATION   139

   6. The Financing and Control of Public Education   141
   7. Private and Religious Schools   150
   8. Religious Teaching and Activities in Public Schools
      197
   9. Teachers   219
  10. Students   244
  11. Integration   266
  Notes   310
  Selected Bibliography   373
  Index   377

Introduction

The state, as well as the home and the church is considered as a sponsoring agent of schools by philosophers of education.[1] Jacques Maritain defines the state as "that part of the body politic especially concerned with the maintenance of law, the promotion of the common welfare and public order, and the administration of public affairs."[2] Political scientist Harold Laski has described the state as "a public service corporation."[3] And education is considered among the services needed to promote the common welfare of the members of a particular state. Citizens have looked to the state as their civil governing authority with both a protective and a promotive function in regard to education.[4] The state's protective function insures the rights of parents to choose schools for and to educate their children. These schools need not be sponsored by the state; they can be either privately sponsored or under the immediate supervision of a particular religious denomination. The state's promotive function is to provide educational opportunities for all its members. This includes a public school system in which parents may enroll their children should they neither desire nor be able to afford a private school education. Not to establish a free public school system would lead to restricting educational opportunity solely to those financially able and to those whose religious denomination affords the opportunity.

But when speaking of the state as a sponsor of education in the United States, a special problem arises. This problem would not exist if a national system of education existed, as in many European countries. In the United States, the state authority can be either the federal, state or local government. And the matter is made more complex by the fact that today American education is sponsored by the state on all levels, through both control and financing.

1

The Constitution of the United States, as framed by the Constitutional Convention and by subsequent amendments, makes no mention of education. Before and after the ratification of the Constitution, education was and had been either under private sponsorship or provided by local communities. The passage of the Tenth Amendment to the Constitution convinced many Americans who were more concerned with states' rights than with a strong federal government that education was a right reserved to the states: "The powers not delegated to the United States by the Constitution, nor prohibited by it to the States, are reserved to the States respectively, or to the people." And in May, 1776, the Continental Congress urged the states "to adopt such government as shall, in the opinion of the representatives of the people, best conduce to the happiness and safety of their constituents in particular and America in general."[5] From 1776 to 1798 eleven states provided explicitly in their constitutions for the legislature or general assembly to establish schools for the instruction of their youth.[6]

Yet education never was strictly a state or local matter. The federal government, even before the adoption of the Constitution in 1789, undertook effective steps in the direction of material assistance to education by means of land grants.[7] Practically each Congress in the nineteenth century passed a measure that proceeds from the sale of land be used for education.[8] A well-documented study of higher education reports that before the enactment of the Land-Grant College Act of 1862 numerous, although "piecemeal," efforts were made by the federal government to aid colleges and universities.[9] Henry Barnard's words of 1868 confirm the opinion of many students of government that education was "included in the first clause of the enumerated powers of Congress 'to levy taxes and to provide for the common defense and general welfare of the United States.' "[10]

Whatever the arguments offered for or against federal aid to education[11]—especially the argument that federal aid leads to federal control—the federal government has been involved in both the support and control of education. The support by grants and loans to states, educational institutions, private organizations, and individuals has been made possible by the laws enacted by Congress. Furthermore, although respecting local control of education, Congress exerts control over the use of funds granted in specifying the purpose for which these funds may be used. Presidents, as leaders of their political parties, have often initiated educational programs and measures; they have used the prestige and power of their office for the enactment of legislation by Congress.

In addition to federal laws pertaining to education, the federal government through its judicial branch insures the protection of the educational rights of its citizens—whether parents, teachers, or students—and of educational institutions and local and state governments. The many decisions of the U.S. Supreme Court dealing with education led one member of the Court to warn that "to allow zeal for our own ideas of what is good in public instruction is to induce us to accept the role of a super board of education for every school district in the nation."[12] But a unanimous Court, in a case dealing with desegregation, clarified and justified its proper role in education:

> It is, of course, quite true that the responsibility for public education is primarily the concern of the States, but it is equally true that such responsibilities, like all other state activity, must be exercised consistently with federal constitutional requirements as they apply to action. The Constitution created a government dedicated to equal justice under law.[13]

In a matter involving religion and education, the Court defined its own limitations in settling educational problems:

> Judicial interposition in the operation of the public school system of the Nation raises problems requiring care and restraint. Our courts, however, have not failed to apply the First Amendment's mandate in our educational system where essential to safeguard the fundamental values of freedom of speech and inquiry and of belief. By and large, public education in our Nation is committed to the control of state and local authorities. Courts do not and cannot intervene in the resolution of conflicts which arise in the daily operation of school systems and which do not directly and sharply implicate basic constitutional values.[14]

The purpose of this book is to present a historical record of the federal government's role in education through the acts of Congress and the decisions of the Supreme Court. It is not a legal work in the sense that it presents the law in educational matters. Rather, it traces the historical development of the federal government's involvement in different areas of education. The chapters on the role of Congress are divided into levels and kinds of education to afford a clearer and more comprehensive historical development for each. The chapters on the role of the Supreme Court are divided so as to center upon decisions affecting the rights of groups and individuals. These decisions represent some of the most important thinking on American education and merit a place in the history of American educational thought.

This book has been written in an effort to gather in one volume a concise analysis of the historical record of congressional legislation and Supreme Court decisions dealing with education. Similar efforts to offer a historical record were made by Hollis P. Allen in 1950,[15] Truman M. Pierce in 1964,[16] Hsien Lu in 1965,[17] Sidney W. Tiedt in 1966,[18] AND Homer D. Babbidge, Jr., and Robert M. Rosenzweig in 1962 (writing about higher education).[19] The latest work on educational decisions of the Supreme Court was by Clark Spurlock in 1955.[20] The present volume covers all major and minor legislative enactments by Congress to the end of 1973, and all major and minor decisions of historical significance up to the first few months of 1974. The background of these laws and decisions is presented in order to give more meaning to the historical record.

PART I

CONGRESS AND
EDUCATION

1
Office of Education

Although he regarded education as primarily a state function, Henry Barnard, once secretary of the school commission of Connecticut, saw the need for the federal government to have a role in education. Seeking to ascertain facts regarding the alarming problem of illiteracy in the nation, he went to Washington in 1838. Since no agency of the federal government could offer him any reliable information, he emphasized the need and the value of a central national agency to collect statistics and information on education. He subsequently called for "the establishment at Washington of a permanent statistical bureau charged with the decennial census, which should present an annual report on the educational statistics and progress of the country."[1]

At first, Barnard's call was not answered by the federal authorities. But then he began to generate interest in, and support for, his idea by delivering speeches throughout the country. He influenced leaders of the American Institute of Instruction, the Association for the Advancement of Education, and the National Teachers' Association.[2] S. H. White of Illinois urged action on Barnard's proposal at the 1864 meeting of the National Teachers' Association, as did S. S. Greene of Rhode Island and A. J. Rickoff of Ohio at the 1865 meeting of the NTA. The meeting adopted a resolution urging all educational leaders to circulate petitions among the people to convince Congress of the need for a national agency of education.[3]

It was at the annual meeting of the National Association of State and City School Superintendents, held in Washington, D.C., in February, 1866, that action of immediate consequence took place. A committee of three—E. E. White, state commissioner of common schools of Ohio; Newton Batement, state superintendent of public instruction, Illinois; and J. S. Adams, secretary of the state board of

7

education, Vermont—prepared and issued a statement outlining the need for, value, and role of a national bureau of education.[4] The committee further entrusted Congressman James A. Garfield of Ohio (later elected president of the United States) to commence work for passage of such a measure in the House of Representatives. On February 14, 1866, Garfield introduced the bill, largely the work of E. E. White. It was not until the following year that the bill received the approval of both houses of Congress and was signed into law by President Andrew Johnson on March 2, 1867.[5] Although the bill specified a Department of Education headed by a commissioner, the department was without cabinet status. Fittingly, Henry Barnard was appointed its first commissioner.

The Department of Education functioned as an independent governmental agency until June 30, 1869, when it was designated as the Office of Education, with a commissioner as its chief officer, and placed in the Department of the Interior.[6] A year later the office was renamed the Bureau of Education, and in 1929, it was again renamed the Office of Education.[7] On July 1, 1939, under a government reorganization plan, the Office of Education was transferred from the Department of the Interior to the Federal Security Agency, which also directed such federal activities as public health and social security.[8] It was not until April 11, 1953, that the Office of Education, with a commissioner in charge, was placed within the newly created cabinet Department of Health, Education, and Welfare.[9]

Efforts to create a Department of Education with a secretary at its head and as a member of the cabinet failed to achieve congressional approval. Some seventy such bills, the best known being the Smith-Towner bill, were stopped in congressional committees between October 10, 1918 and March 4, 1925.[10] Since these bills also sought to equalize educational opportunities throughout the country by the use of federal funds, they engendered much opposition from various groups, most notably Roman Catholics, who felt that their own schools were being ignored, and southerners, who feared an infringement upon states' rights.[11]

Although the original function of the Office of Education was restricted to the collection of statistics and facts and the promotion of the cause of education, the passage of the Morrill Land-Grant College acts in 1862 and 1890 expanded the scope of the office. The secretary of the interior, assigned with the proper administration of these laws, delegated the duty to the commissioner of education.[12]

A similar delegation took place in 1884 with reference to an act providing educational opportunities for children in the Territory of Alaska.[13] In 1905, the Office of Education had jurisdiction only over the Eskimo and Indian children; the white children were provided for in a new school system under the direction of the governor of Alaska as superintendent of instruction.[14] The information section of the office was called upon by Congress in 1896 to publish bulletins on the condition of the various levels and kinds of education in the country and educational activities in the world that were deemed of value and interest to the United States.[15] In 1928, the office was authorized to make an annual inspection of Howard University,[16] for which Congress had begun making annual appropriations in 1879. Congress passed in 1892 an act providing that library facilities of the office be made available to students in higher educational institutions incorporated under the laws of Congress or the District of Columbia.[17] In 1901 the library provision was broadened to include qualified individuals, students, and graduates of institutions in the states, territories, and the District of Columbia.[18]

The growing concern for education during the time of the depression led Congress to appropriate for the commissioner of education the sum of $205,000 for a nationwide survey specifically concerning secondary education, teacher training, and school financing.[19] The commissioner also reorganized the office to meet more effectively the educational needs of the country.

With increased participation of the federal government in education through the establishment of many programs involving loans and grants, it became the responsibility of the Office of Education to administer these funds. Some eighty programs are now under the office's direction and they affect every level and area of educational activity. Moreover, they require the services of approximately three thousand employees, most of whom are in Washington but some of whom are in regional offices.[20] The accompanying chart illustrates the present organization of the office with its manifold divisions and activities.

The General Education Provisions Act, enacted January 2, 1968, and amended on October 16, 1968, and on April 13, 1970, delineates and elaborates upon the duties of the Office of Education and of the commissioner of education under the secretary of health, education, and welfare.[21] The HEW secretary is entrusted with the overall function of presenting to the respective committees of Con-

EDUCATION DIVISION'S

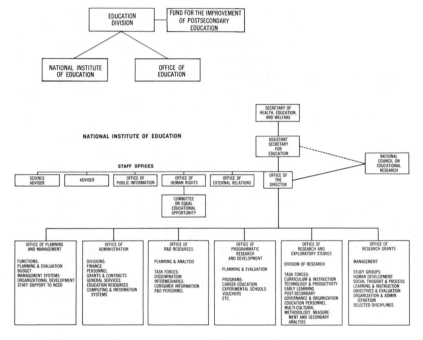

Source: 10 *American Education* (Jan.-Feb. 1974), pp. 30–31

ORGANIZATION CHARTS

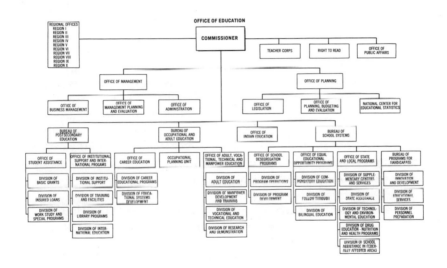

gress reports, evaluations, and planning of all contracts and grants for federal educational programs. He also informs what appropriations and advance funding are available to educational agencies and institutions receiving federal funds.[22] The commissioner's authority is specified. He may delegate any of his functions under any applicable program to any officer or employee of the Office of Education and is authorized to utilize the services and facilities of any agency of the federal government or of any public or nonprofit agency or institution to expedite federal educational programs. The traditional role of the commissioner is to collect and disseminate information through reports and studies published by the Office of Education. He is charged with providing technical assistance to all agencies and institutions requesting information and advice, including the parents of children who are involved in any federal program. The commissioner must withhold funds from any agency or institution that fails to comply with other provisions of federal law, especially Title VI of the Civil Rights Act of 1964 which calls for desegregation of schools. The commissioner must include in his annual reports the recommendations and proceedings of the meetings of the various advisory councils established by Congress to aid the commissioner in different educational programs and areas.[23]

Despite the power that invariably flows from the managing of funds for education by the federal government, in 1970 Congress specified as part of the General Education Provisions Act a prohibition against federal control of education by forbidding:

> any department, agency, officer, or employee of the United States to exercise any direction, supervision, or control over the curriculum, program of instruction, administration, or personnel of any educational institution, school, or school system, or over the selection of library resources, textbooks. or other printed or published instructional materials by any educational institution or school system, or to require the assignment or transportation of students or teachers in order to overcome racial imbalance.[24]

The education amendments of 1972 established the National Institute of Education within the Office of Education, as a division of the Department of Health, Education, and Welfare. While reaffirming that the education system remains primarily the responsibility of state and local governments, Congress viewed the federal government as having "a clear responsibility to provide leadership in the conduct and support of scientific inquiry into the educational process." With the objective of providing an equal opportunity for every American to receive an education of high quality, Congress saw the need for "far more dependable knowledge about the processes of learning and education that now exists or can be expected from present research and experimentation in this field"; hence the need for the National Institute of Education.[25] The institute would seek to improve education by helping to solve or to alleviate the problems, and to achieve the objectives, of American education; advancing the practice of education as an art, science, and profession; strengthening the scientific and technological foundations of education; and building an effective education research and development system.[26]

A council of fifteen members, appointed by the president with the approval of the Senate, is entrusted with the overall supervision of the institute; a director, however, would be in charge of the immediate implementation of the institute's objectives.[27] Congress appropriated the aggregate sum of $550 million for the institute for the period beginning July 1, 1972, and ending June 30, 1975.[28]

2

Elementary and Secondary Education

LAND GRANTS TO THE STATES

Although it appears that education became a function primarily of the states at the adoption of the Constitution, the concern of federal government for education was not necessarily wanting. The Continental Congress agreed on the ordinance of 1785, which decreed that "there shall be reserved the lot No. 16 of every township for the maintenance of public schools, within the said township."[1] And the ordinance of 1787, which established the Northwest Territory (comprised of the present states of Ohio, Indiana, Illinois, Michigan, Wisconsin, and part of Minnesota), provided that "Religion, morality, and knowledge, being necessary to good government and the happiness of mankind, schools and the means of education shall be forever encouraged."[2]

Both of these ordinances have educational significance. The ordinance of 1785 marked a precedent on the part of the federal government, putting into motion a policy for the survey and sale of public lands to which all sections of the country would agree. The reservation of a particular section for education was considered primarily an inducement to attract settlers.[3] The ordinance of 1787 contained no land grants for education, but it did enunciate the principle of encouraging the means of education, which the federal government chose to do by making land grants for education.[4] It did not become a national policy, however, until 1802.

The Enabling Act of Ohio in 1802 became the first act of Congress to establish the national policy of land grants for education:

"Section number sixteen in every township, and where such section has been sold, granted or disposed of, other lands equivalent thereto and most contiguous to the same, shall be granted to the inhabitants of such township for the use of schools."[5] Grants of land for educational purposes to the states by the federal government extended not only to states of the Northwest Territory but to almost every new state admitted to the Union after 1802.[6] It has been estimated that the total of these land grants for schools has amounted to 94,164,284 acres.[7] The federal government, however, did not manage the school lands but placed control in the hands of state and local authorities; the details for expenditure were a state concern as long as a state carried out the general purposes of the grant from the federal government.[8] Despite the insuring of local control, the policy of land grants from the federal government to the states is said to have led to further involvement of the federal government in the field of education. Writing in 1922, H. C. Taylor concluded in his study of the early federal land grants that

> the most interesting educational tendency that has grown out of the early land grants for schools is the present-day policy of making national money grants out of the United States treasury for education, as exemplified by the Smith-Hughes act. The transition from land grants for education to grants of money out of the proceeds from the sale of public lands was natural and easy. The transition from money grants out of the general revenue of the national government is no more difficult. This tendency appears to be leading towards national supervision and control of education.[9]

PLANS FOR A NATIONAL SYSTEM OF EDUCATION

Despite the fact that the Constitution was silent on education, plans for a national system of education were being devised from 1786 to 1799.[10] Basic to all the plans was the promotion of a national culture to express the principles of the republican form of government, the freeing of the American mind from European traditions, and a source of unity through an education that would emphasize a common national outlook and character.[11] So Benja-

min Rush in his plan argued: "Our schools of learning, by producing a general, and more uniform system of education, will render
the mass of the people more homogeneous."[12] After describing the
public schools of the time as "in every respect completely despica-
ble, wretched and contemptible," and judging equal educational
opportunity to be at the root of equal representation in government, the principle for which the American Revolution was fought,
Robert Coram urged a tax-supported national system of education
available to all.[13] James Sullivan, mindful that many forces that
plagued the loosely united colonies continued to operate even after
the Constitution had been adopted and the federal government had
been established, called for a national system of education as a
means of national integration to solve "the dreadful apprehension
of a disunion of, and controversy among the states."[14] Nathaniel
Chipman, in a speech before the Vermont state convention urging
ratification of the federal constitution, proposed national leadership
in education because state control of education would be confined
to "narrow limits" and "local prejudices."[15] Educator Noah Webster also envisioned a national system of education as the only
adequate means for forming a national character.[16]

In 1796 the American Philosophical Society offered a prize for
a plan of education that would incorporate "the genius of the Government of the United States." The prize was divided between
Samuel H. Smith and Samuel Knox, who both advocated a national
system of education. Smith's essay emphasized the liberal philosophy of the sponsoring society in advocating a system of education
free from the limitations of local, racial, and religious prejudices.[17]
Also within the framework of nineteenth-century liberal thought
was Knox's proposal for a system of national education. A national
university "connected with every branch or seminary of the general
system," was deemed necessary to make such a scheme effective. It
would be "the fountainhead of science, that centre to which all
literary genius of the commonwealth would tend, and from which,
when matured by its instructive influence, would diffuse the rays of
knowledge and science to the remotest situations of the united
government." Of all the proponents of a national system of education, Knox was the only one who expressed doubt about the adoption of a national educational plan, largely because of "the manner
in which the subject of instituting a *National University* passed
through the legislative council of the nation." He noted the great

admiration Americans had for George Washington as one who "has never been treated even with the appearance of disrespect, save in his liberal endeavors to cherish into maturity and perfection the all important object of an uniform national education."[18]

These plans for a national system of education evoked little response; the extent of their circulation has been questioned.[19] They were, furthermore, issued at a time when the states hesitated to relinquish in any degree their sovereignty, with small states fearing domination from the larger states, and all states hesitant of resting too much authority in a potentially oppressive strong central government.[20] But more significantly, Americans were not yet convinced of the importance of free public education. Thomas Jefferson's "Bill for the More General Diffusion of Knowledge," which proposed a system of free public schools from the elementary and secondary school levels to the university, failed to pass the Virginia legislature in 1779. The idea of a common public school, taken for granted today, was opposed even on state and local levels in the early years of the American republic. It was not until the 1830s that the movement for free public schools began to make headway under such leaders as Horace Mann, Henry Barnard, James Carter, Calvin Wiley, and Caleb Mills. The struggle to secure public support for common schools took place in every state of the nation, however, as has been concluded by eminent educational historians, it was not until 1865 that "enough of a general development had taken place to say that the *principle* of public support for common schools had definitely taken root and that the American people were definitely committed to it."[21] If Americans had been convinced a century earlier, it may have been possible to gather support for a national system of education. Until the middle of the nineteenth century, public education was supported almost entirely by religious organizations, benevolent societies, and private individualist groups—not by the states, and certainly not by the federal government. As to the historical significance of the plans for a national system of education, the following comment of Bernard Bailyn is worthy of note: "Such writings undoubtedly helped promote the idea that public enlightenment was a political necessity in the new nation; but the most striking fact about them is the absolute nullity of their practical effects. Not one such proposal, not even those endorsed by the heroes and statesmen of the Revolution, came close to realization."[22]

BLAINE AMENDMENT

President Ulysses S. Grant urged the enactment of a constitutional amendment that would affect education. In his annual message to Congress on December 7, 1875, he asked that

> a constitutional amendment be submitted to the legislatures of the several States for ratification making it the duty of each of the several States to establish and forever maintain free public schools adequate to the education of all children in the rudimentary branches within their respective limits, irrespective of sex, color, birthplace, or religion; forbidding the teaching in said schools of religious, atheistic, or pagan tenets; and prohibiting the granting of any school funds, or school taxes, or any part thereof, either by legislative, municipal or other authority for the benefit or in aid, directly or indirectly, of any religious sect or demomination, or in aid or for the benefit of any other object of any nature or kind whatever.

Grant further went on to suggest "the taxation of all property equally, whether church or corporation, exempting only the last resting place of the dead, and possibly, with proper restrictions, church edifices."[23]

The call for a constitutional amendment to forbid the receipt of financial aid by any religious denominational school came in a period of anti-Catholicism in American history.[24] The Protestant churches had already largely relinquished the elementary schools under their direct sponsorship and accepted the common public school system.[25] The Roman Catholics, however, opposed the public schools, either for their strong indifference to religion or for their Protestant influence in teachers, textbooks, hymns, and the reading of the King James version of the Bible.[26] In some states and communities there were instances of Roman Catholic schools receiving some type of financial aid, and requests were being made to begin or increase aid in other states and communities.[27] Much opposition arose against these efforts; in some states constitutional provisions against aid to denominational schools were sought.[28] In a political speech on September 29, 1875, President Grant reflected the anti-Catholic feelings in many parts of the country.[29]

James G. Blaine introduced a resolution proposing a constitutional amendment in the House of Representatives on December 14, 1875, one week after Grant's formal recommendation to Congress. On August 4, 1876, the House, with a vote of 180 in favor, 7 against, and 80 not voting, passed the following as a constitutional amendment:

> No State shall make any law respecting an establishment of religion or prohibiting the free exercise thereof; and no money raised by taxation in any State for the support of public schools, or derived from any public fund therefor, nor any public lands devoted thereto, shall ever be under the control of any religious sect or denomination; nor shall any money so raised or lands so devoted be divided between religious sects or denominations. This article shall not vest, enlarge, or diminish legislative power in Congress.[30]

The Senate then began consideration of what has come to be known as the "Blaine Amendment." Where the wording of the House version forbade the use of public money reserved for education, but not the use of public money from a general fund to aid religious institutions, the Senate version made no such distinction.

> No State shall make any law respecting an establishment of religion, or prohibiting the free exercise thereof; and no religious test shall ever be required as a qualification to any office or public trust under any State. No public property and no public revenue of, nor any loan of credit by or under the authority of the United States, or any State, Territory, District, or municipal corporation shall be appropriated to or made or used for the support of any school, educational or other institution under the control of any religious or antireligious sect, organization, or denomination, or wherein the particular creed or tenets of any religious or antireligious sect, organization, or denomination shall be taught. And no such particular creed or tenets shall be read or taught in any school or institution supported in whole or in part by such revenue or loan of credit, and no such appropriation or loan of credit shall be

made to any religious or antireligious sect, organization, or
denomination, or to promote its interests or tenets. This
article shall not be construed to prohibit the reading of the
Bible in any school or institution; and it shall not have the
effect to impair rights of property already vested. Sec. 2.
Congress shall have power, by appropriate legislation, to
provide for the prevention and punishment of violations of
this article.[31]

But when the Senate voted on its own version of the Blaine Amendment, the required two-thirds vote was not obtained, with 28 voting
for, 16 against; 29 senators were absent. Most of the senators opposing the amendment based their decision on the ground that the
states would be denied their traditional rights in education. Although similar legislation has been introduced in Congress some
twenty times since 1876, none has been referred out of committee
for discussion on the floors of Congress.[32]

LANHAM ACT (1941) AND IMPACT LAWS (1950)

In 1941 Congress passed the Lanham Act, an emergency war
measure, to aid communities that had been financially overbur-
dened by increased school enrollments because of their proximity
to war factories and military installations.[33] From 1941 to June 30,
1947, an estimated $187 million was spent on programs for school
construction and equipment, school maintenance and operation,
and child care.[34] The justification for such expenditures was that
workers in the new essential industries often had to move to be near
their jobs, causing sudden relocations of families. Local communities were not in a financial position to meet the sudden and heavy
expenses connected with this mass movement. Nursery schools
were also needed to enable mothers to work in war industries. The
Lanham Act has been extended to include postwar national defense-
incurred situations on the basis of the same rationale as when it was
first enacted. Because of the Korean War, Congress enacted two
laws in 1950: Public Law 815 for the construction of school buildings, and Public Law 874 for funds to cover the operating costs of
school districts.[35] These laws have been known as the "impact
laws," and payments under them have been regarded as in lieu of

taxes, since the federal government has a responsibility to provide money for community services, and federal property is not taxable by local communities. In 1958, 25 percent, or 7.5 million, of all students in public elementary and secondary schools were affected by these two laws, with funds allocated to 316 of 437 congressional districts.[36] These laws have been amended, extended, and expanded since they were originally enacted in 1950. Title I of the Elementary and Secondary Education Act of 1965, entitled "Financial Assistance to Local Educational Agencies for the Education of Low-Income Families," subsumed Impact Law 874.[37] The Impact Aid program was amended by Congress in 1968 to ensure "that federal support will be independent of state education funding and not in partial substitution thereof."[38] In 1970 Congress added the "comparability" requirement to the use of funds under Title I of ESEA so that federal funds would not supplant expenditures of local educational agencies.[39] The present federal impact laws thus include school construction costs and costs of operating schools for both the areas affected by federal activity and the areas whose student bodies come from families of exceptionally low incomes (estimated at less than $3,000 per year in 1970). The federal impact laws have been judged as "among the most successful laws in educational legislation," even favored by the strongest opponents of federal aid to education.[40]

SCHOOL LUNCH PROGRAM

In 1946 Congress enacted the National School Lunch Act; although programs for school lunches were already in existence, both on a federal and local basis. In the desire to improve the physical well-being of children, efforts to provide adequate lunch programs were made by local government and charitable agencies as early as the mid-nineteenth century. Lunch programs were considered a purely local responsibility until 1932, when loans were allotted to a few communities for partial support of school lunch programs through the Reconstruction Finance Corporation and for certain school lunches in programs provided by the Works Progress Administration (WPA) and the National Youth Administration (NYA).[41]

Greater federal efforts in this area were made in 1935 and 1936.

Public Law 320 encouraged the secretary of agriculture to encourage "the domestic consumption of such commodities or products by diverting them, by the payment of benefits or indemnities or by any other means, from the normal channels of trade and commerce. . . ."[42] This 1935 law was interpreted as authorization for furnishing food for school lunches, and any doubt was clarified by Public Law 461 in 1936, when Congress designated the Federal Surplus Commodities Corporation as the federal administering agency to direct food for school lunches.[43] In 1940 the Penny Milk Program was advanced by the secretary of agriculture to aid both dairy interests and needy children. The Department of Agriculture and milk handlers contracted to sell milk at one cent per half pint to selected schools; by 1943 milk was included in some school lunch programs. World War II brought on emergency administrative changes in the distribution and cooperative efforts between the federal government, the states, and the schools. The Food Distribution Administration of the War Food Administration was entrusted with the administrative responsibility.[44]

In 1946 all federal efforts were regularized by the National School Lunch Act.[45] The purposes of the act were "to safeguard the health and well-being of the nation's children and to encourage the domestic consumption of nutritious agricultural commodities and other foods . . . through grants in aid and other means, in providing an adequate supply of foods and other facilities for the establishment, maintenance, operation, and expansion of non-profit school lunch programs." Placed under the authority of the secretary of agriculture, the act provided for an appropriation of $75 million for 1947, with an added deficiency appropriation of $6 million. An additional $10 million was authorized for providing nonfood assistance, such as equipment used on school premises for storing, preparing, or serving food for school children. Apportionment of funds to the states would be based on (1) the number of school children from five to seventeen years of age inclusive and (2) the need for assistance in the state as indicated by the relation of the per capita income in the country to the per capita income in the state. A significant feature of the act was that both public and nonprofit private schools could share in the program, the latter made possible under the child-benefit theory of aid directly to the children, with only an incidental benefit to the nonpublic schools. Through the acts of 1960 and 1961 schools could receive surplus foods if, in their training of students in home economics courses, college students could be allowed to use the same facilities and instructors as the high school students.[46] Positive inclusion of milk in the program was made in 1949 with the Special Milk Program, deemed to be "in the public interest" under the Agricultural Act of 1949.[47] Numerous amendments have since been made to the school lunch program, largely of an administrative and technical nature.[48]

A significant change in the school lunch program was made by the 1970 amendments: Any child at poverty level is to receive a free or reduced-price lunch, and priority for free lunches is to be given to the neediest children. Rather than allow local school authorities to establish maximum prices for reduced price lunches, in 1970 Congress set a ceiling of twenty cents for any reduced-price lunch. Furthermore, the Department of Agriculture was authorized to promulgate regulations designed to implement these amendments.[49] Failure to comply with the regulations concerning the 1970 amendments, especially with regard to establishing school lunch programs in the neediest schools and to providing free lunches to the neediest children, led to a successful civil rights action against state officials in Rhode Island.[50]

On the basis of findings that the volume and variety of federal food donations to the school lunch program were significantly below the amounts programmed and budgeted for the fiscal year ending June 30, 1973, Congress enacted emergency legislation on March 30, 1973, to ensure that federal financial assistance would be maintained to allow schools participating in the program to obtain sufficient supplies of the foods required to meet the nutritional standards established by law.[51]

In April, 1974, the Department of Agriculture announced that, effective June 30, it would begin a "phase-down year" of buying surplus foods for distribution to the schools. The principal reason offered was that surplus food was getting scarce. Some government and educational leaders felt that unless the situation could be remedied the National School Lunch Program would be in jeopardy.[52]

EDUCATION OF CONGRESSIONAL AND SUPREME COURT PAGES

In 1946 Congress enacted legislation that provided for the education of congressional and Supreme Court pages in the public school system of the District of Columbia. The district school system would be reimbursed for any additional expenses incurred in carrying out such an arrangement. The act also provided for pages to "elect to attend a private or parochial school of their own choice." The amount of the expenses in this case could not, however, exceed the amount that would be paid for the education of a page in a public school.[53]

LIBRARY SERVICES AND CONSTRUCTION ACT, 1956

One of the chief goals of the American Library Association when it was founded in 1876 was to lead in library development and cooperation between schools and local libraries. Educators before 1876 had labored for such a cooperation with the hope of making the school "a vestibule of the public library." Yet, at the seventy-fourth annual meeting of the American Library Association in 1955, its head claimed that twenty-seven million Americans "had no access whatever to a local public library."[54] This fact, plus inadequate facilities in numerous areas of the country, led to the enactment of the Library Services and Construction Act on June 19, 1956: "It is the purpose of this Act to promote the further extension by the several States of public library services to areas without such services or with inadequate services, to promote interlibrary cooperation, and to assist the States in providing certain specialized State library services."[55]

The commissioner of education was directed by this act to appropriate to states, on the basis of a prescribed formula, funds for the further extension of public library services to areas without or with inadequate services. For the fiscal year ending June, 1971, the total sum was $75 million.[56] Additionally, federal funds were made available for actual construction of public libraries in areas without library facilities. For the year 1971 alone, the sum allowed for construction purposes was $80 million.[57] Besides providing aid to state plans for interlibrary cooperation, funds would also be allotted for specialized state library services. These services included providing books and other library materials and services to (1) inmates, patients, or residents of penal institutions, reformatories, orphanages, residential training schools, and hospitals substantially run by the state and (2) students in residential schools for the handicapped under state sponsorship.[58]

Libraries of educational institutions have received special attention in major educational legislation, such as the National Defense Education Act, the Elementary and Secondary Education Act, and Higher Educational Facilities Act.

NATIONAL COMMISSION ON LIBRARIES AND INFORMATION SCIENCE ACT

On July 20, 1970, Congress enacted the National Commission on Libraries and Information Science Act.[59] Established as an independent agency within the executive branch, and in cooperation with the Department of Health, Education, and Welfare, Congress saw in the creation of such a body the fulfilling of the need for more effective coordination and utilization of the vast, growing amount of knowledge in all fields of study. A central federal agency to cooperate with state and local governments and public and private agencies was seen as "assuring optimum provisions of such services."[60] The commission was entrusted with such functions as advising the president and Congress on the implementation of national policy through appropriate statements and reports; conducting surveys, studies, and analyses of the library and informational needs of the country, especially in deprived areas, and deciding how these needs could be met by educational institutions and by both public and private libraries; developing plans for meeting national library and informational needs on all levels of government; and promoting research that would improve such services.[61]

NATIONAL DEFENSE EDUCATION ACT

The National Defense Education Act of 1958 (NDEA) affected both elementary and secondary education and higher education. The act is discussed more completely in the chapter on higher education. Elementary and secondary education benefited from NDEA's titles which sought to strengthen instruction in science, mathematics, and modern foreign languages.[62] Secondary education benefited further from the grants made available to improve guidance, counseling, and testing programs.[63]

The NDEA has produced a nationwide impact on elementary and secondary education. Where in 1959 some 55,000 students were pursuing technical training in 355 schools, two years later the amount had almost tripled to 150,000 in 870 schools.[64] Private schools spent almost $4 million, through low-interest loans, for equipping science laboratories, installing language laboratories, and acquiring mathematics teaching devices.[65] More counseling and testing services, improved methods of teaching mathematics, science, and foreign languages, and a college student loan program which made higher education possible for many more young Americans, are seen as the results of the NDEA. Sixty-six percent of those in the fifth grade in 1956 completed high school in 1963; but between 1956 and 1963 the number of high school graduates rose by 30 percent, a 35 percent increase in first-time college students, and a 39 percent increase in the total enrollment of students attending college.[66] The study of foreign languages shifted from a mere reading knowledge to a more extended goal of writing and speaking; Russian and Chinese were taught, as well as the more common languages of French, German, and Spanish. The number of language laboratory installations rose from a mere forty-six in 1958 to more than seven thousand in 1965.[67] More lower-class youths could obtain a college education than ever before.[68] Centers have been established to demonstrate all types of educational communications media.[69] The administration and implementation of the act alone by the federal government necessitated the hiring of more than two hundred to staff the U.S. Office of Education.[70] As a matter of fact, the assignment of many new duties required a major reorganization of the office.[71]

Enacted independently, although related to the NDEA and *Sputnik*, a law was passed to foster, encourage, and assist the establishment of clubs for boys and girls interested in science.[72] Enacted on September 2, 1958, the act appropriated an annual sum of $50,000 "to strengthen future scientific accomplishment in our Nation by assisting in the development of a body of boys and girls with a special interest in science." The display of youngsters' scientific works and projects through science fairs was a means suggested for creating interest. The commissioner of education, through the personnel and facilities of the Office of Education, was directed to administer the provisions of this act.

"PROJECT HEADSTART" AND "FOLLOW-THROUGH"

Among the concerns of the Economic Opportunity Act of 1964 was the effect of poverty in contributing to the social, economic, and cultural impact upon children. Numerous studies in the early 1960s have demonstrated that the disadvantaged preschool child is not ready to learn to read, too often lacks ambition, and is not ready for the school environment.[73] Thus was enacted in 1964 a program to be known as "Project Headstart," the purpose of which is to provide culturally and socially deprived children with a "head start" through enriched preschool programs. Focusing upon children who have not reached the age of compulsory school attendance, the program provides comprehensive health, nutritional, education, social, and other services that will aid socially and culturally deprived children to attain their full potential.[74] Headstart serves children through three basic programs: full year, part day; full year, full day; and short summer programs. Some of the activities employed seek to arouse curiosity, develop language skills, improve the child's self-image, and provide experiences that are enjoyed by children of more affluent home environments. There is also heavy emphasis on parental involvement.[75]

The Office of Education officials realized, however, that headstart programs were not in themselves a panacea; one to three years of preschool programs were not sufficient to crystallize gains and overcome previous social and cultural disadvantages.[76] Thus was added in 1967 a program known as "Follow-Through," designed to build upon the gains enjoyed by children in headstart programs. This newer program begins with the first year of school, either the kindergarten or first grade, and continues to extend the headstart objectives and services as the child advances through the early elementary school grades.[77]

Through an amendment in 1969, Congress permitted children from families above the poverty line to participate in headstart programs. Payment for the services in whole or in part would be made where the family's income was in excess of the eligibility standards.[78] In 1973, the general eligibility requirement for participation was raised.[79]

CIVIL RIGHTS ACT OF 1964

On the occasion of the centennial of Lincoln's Emancipation Proclamation on February 28, 1962, President Kennedy sent to Congress a message on civil rights. In it he vowed to continue efforts to bring about the end of all discrimination and to provide equal opportunity for all, for "through these long 100 years, while slavery has vanished, progress for the Negro has been too often blocked and delayed. Equality before the law has not always meant equal treatment and opportunity." He expressed pleasure at the progress made toward desegregation in education since the *Brown* decision which "represented both good law and good judgment— it was both legally and morally right." But progress had also been "too slow, often primarily so," Kennedy pointed out. He therefore promised that in all areas of racial discrimination "the executive branch will continue its efforts to fulfill the constitutional objective of an equal nonsegregated, educational opportunity for all children. . . . That the full authority of the Federal Government should be placed behind the achievement of school desegregation, in accordance with the command of the Constitution." He thereby called for "the enactment of effective civil rights legislation and the continuation of effective executive action."[80]

Congressional action on the civil rights bill was, however, slow. President Kennedy therefore sent a special message to Congress on this matter on June 19, 1963. So urgent did he consider the passage of this legislation that he proposed that

The Congress stay in session this year until it has enacted . . . the most responsible, reasonable and urgently needed solutions to this problem, solutions which should be acceptable to all fair-minded men. This bill would be known as the Civil Rights Act of 1963, and would include—in addition to the aforementioned provisions on voting rights and the Civil Rights Commission—additional titles on public accommodations, employment, Federally assisted programs, a community relations service, and education. . . . In addition, I am requesting certain legislative and budget amendments designed to improve the training, skills and economic opportunities of the educationally distressed and discontented, white and Negro alike. . . . I therefore ask every Member of Congress to set aside sectional and political ties, and to look at this issue from the viewpoint of the Nation. I ask you to look into your hearts, not in search of charity, for the Negro neither wants nor needs condescension, but for the one plain, proud, and priceless quality that unites us all as Americans: a sense of justice.[81]

But Congress adjourned without passing the recommended civil rights legislation of the president. Five days after President Kennedy's assasination, on November 27, 1963, President Johnson addressed the nation and a joint session of Congress. In an emotionally charged speech, Johnson recalled the dreams Kennedy had for America, among which "and above all, the dream of equal rights for all Americans, whatever their race or color—these and other American dreams have been vitalized by his drive and by his dedication. And now the ideas and ideals which he so nobly represented must and will be translated into effective action."[82] And again, in his State of the Union message on January 8, 1964, Johnson charged the Congress: "Let this session of Congress be known as the session which did more for civil rights than the last hundred sessions combined. . . . It can be done by this summer." Partisanship and sectional differences were asked to be cast aside in passing the bill for civil rights as a memorial to the late President Kennedy.[83] On July 2, President Johnson signed the Civil Rights Act of 1964.

In the field of education one of the main purposes of the act was to accelerate the pace of desegregation in public educational institutions. Title IV defined desegregation as "the assignment of students to public schools and within such schools without regard to their race, color, religion, or national origin, but 'desegregation' shall not mean the assignment of students to public schools in order to overcome racial imbalance."[84] The attorney general of the United States was empowered to institute civil action against local school boards denying equal rights to students. Any educational institution which participates in any federal financial assistance program cannot deny a student admission because of race, national origin, religion, or color. The act empowered the commissioner of education to award grants to education officials and teachers studying the problems connected with desegregation. Colleges and universities were also afforded grants to establish training institutes to help interested education personnel deal effectively with special educational problems occasioned by desegregation.[85]

Title VI of the Civil Rights Act, entitled "Nondiscrimination in Federally Assisted Programs," insists that all programs receiving federal assistance must end racial discrimination in order to qualify for future federal aid. Each federal department and agency empowered to extend federal financial assistance to any program or activity by way of grant, loan, or contract is to insure, moreover, compliance with the law.[86]

As regards busing to achieve desegregation, the act stated "that nothing herein shall empower any official or court of the United States to issue any order seeking to achieve a racial balance in any school by requiring the transportation of pupils or students from one school to another or one school district to another in order to achieve such racial balance, or otherwise enlarge the existing power of the court to insure compliance with constitutional standards."[87] The Supreme Court in *Swann* maintained that through default by school authorities of their obligation to proffer acceptable remedies, federal district courts had the power to fashion a remedy that would assure a unitary school system, and such power was not restricted by public education provisions of the federal Civil Rights Act of 1964.[88] In response to those who argued that the equity powers of federal district courts have been limited by Title IV of the 1964 Act, the Court held that the title

> was enacted not to limit but to define the role of the Federal Government in the implementation of the Brown I decision. . . . On their face, the sections quoted purport only to insure that the provisions of Title IV . . . will not be read as granting new powers. The proviso . . . is in terms designed to foreclose any interpretation of the Act as expanding the *existing* powers of federal courts to enforce the Equal Protection Clause. There is no suggestion of an intention to restrict those powers or withdraw from courts their historic equitable remedial powers. The legislative history of Title IV indicates that Congress was concerned that the Act might be read as creating a right of action under the Fourteenth Amendment in the situation of so-called "de facto segregation," where racial imbalance exists in the schools but with no showing that this was

brought about by discriminatory action of state authorities. In short, there is nothing in the Act that provides us material assistance in answering the question of remedy for state-imposed segregation in violation of Brown I. The basis of our decision must be the Fourteenth Amendment.[89]

However, Title VIII of the education amendments of 1972 substantially reaffirmed the proviso of Section 407a of the Civil Rights Act: "No funds appropriated for the purpose of carrying out any applicable program may be used for the transportation of students or teachers (or for the purchase of equipment for such transportation) in order to overcome racial imbalance in any school or school system, or for the transportation of students or teachers . . . in order to carry out a plan of racial desegregation of any school or school system, except on the express written voluntary request of appropriate local school officials."[90] The whole matter of the extent of busing to achieve racial desegregation in schools, however, awaits further Supreme Court decisions.[91]

The act has led to the adoption of "guidelines" by the U.S. Office of Education to ensure the meeting of minimum requirements for achieving desegregation. A "freedom of choice" plan was adopted in the guidelines by permitting a child to request attendance at a school of his own choosing. The plan did not work, however, because white children did not request attendance at predominantly "black" schools and black children were frequently denied admission to "white" schools for reasons such as inadequate facilities. It was also generally agreed that, considering the hostile feelings toward integration, black children would prefer to choose black schools; thus, the status quo was maintained. Racial imbalance continued, notwithstanding the limitations imposed by the Civil Rights Act.[92]

Both the courts and the Office of Education, however, decided on plans for desegregation by assigning racial quotas. A federal court gave indirect approval to racial balance.[93] The Office of Education adopted guidelines for the 1969–70 school year. The guidelines called for a single, integrated public school system, thus eliminating "white" or "black" schools.[94] The Supreme Court affirmed these guidelines in the *Holmes* and subsequent decisions.[95] A more recent move by federal courts to ensure compliance with Supreme

Court decisions on desegregation and the Civil Rights Act has been the withdrawal of federal funds from school districts not complying with integration rules and guidelines of the Office of Education.[96]

ELEMENTARY AND SECONDARY EDUCATION ACT–1965

John F. Kennedy campaigned for the presidency with a party platform that stressed education and the necessity of action on the part of the federal government to aid state and local governments in their educational efforts.[97] Promising a "New Frontier" in his campaign, he called for federal aid to education in many areas, including school construction. He sought to resolve doubts about federal control by granting to the states themselves the choice of the manner of distributing federal grants. He stressed the need for scientists and engineers, as Russia was producing them at a rate twice that of ours. He expressed concern over the lack of educational opportunities for the black child, the need for more trained medical and dental personnel, and the fact that 35 percent of the nation's brightest students graduating from high school are unable to attend college, more often because of financial reasons.[98]

In his inaugural message President Kennedy stressed the nation's educational needs,[99] and on February 20, he presented to Congress a special message on education. After pinpointing the major educational problems, he announced "our twin goals must be: a new standard of excellence in education—and the availability of such excellence to all who are willing and able to pursue it." He recommended to Congress a three-year program which called for: general federal assistance for public elementary and secondary classroom construction and teachers' salaries; extension of the college housing loan program; a low-interest loan program for construction and modernization of college academic facilities, such as classrooms, laboratories, and libraries; establishment of state-administered scholarships for talented and needy young people to supplement already existing programs; and a review and evaluation of the federal vocational education programs so as to improve and redirect them.[100]

An elementary and secondary school education bill, the Public School Assistance Act of 1961, was introduced in both the Senate and the House.[101] A three-year program of $2.3 billion was authorized for school construction and teachers' salaries. Funds were to be paid to the states, which were required to set aside 10 percent for payment of experimental projects and pilot demonstrations in connection with special school problems. But the bill encountered much opposition. Catholic education leaders wanted aid for their parochial schools. In a news conference on March 1, 1961, President Kennedy was asked why, in view of the criticism that had occurred, he did not recommend federal aid to private and parochial elementary and secondary schools. The president emphatically replied that such aid was clearly unconstitutional and was so declared by the Supreme Court in the *Everson* case.[102] A proponent of federal aid, and desirous of helping the nonpublic schools and their financial burdens, Senator Wayne Morse, during the Senate hearings, requested the secretary of health, education, and welfare for a legal brief on the constitutionality of aid to nonpublic schools. The department replied that federal grants to primary and secondary schools under sectarian sponsorship was unconstitutional, whether the grants were applied for general educational purposes, construction of school facilities, or teachers' salaries. Even low-interest loans to them would be unconstitutional "inasmuch as they would provide measurable economic benefit to religious institutions."

A question was raised as to the constitutionality of federal programs that would render incidental benefits to religious schools. These benefits, it was believed, would probably be permissible if not directly connected with religion. The brief also suggested the inclusion of a judicial review provision in the bill to permit the creation of a case or controversy enabling the courts to review the proposed aid and decide upon its constitutionality.[103]

In addition to a discussion of the religion issue, there arose determined opposition to any federal aid bill that would help states and communities with racially segregated schools. Adam Clayton Powell, chairman of the House Education and Labor Committee, warned that he would oppose any educational legislation that did not specifically clarify this point. He would insist on adding the Powell Amendment: no federal assistance to segregated schools.[104]

The Senate's Labor and Public Welfare Committee voted the bill out for floor action on May 11 and the Senate passed it on May 25 with minor changes. Several amendments to the bill were defeated in the Senate: Senator Strom Thurmond's proposal to withhold funds because of racial segregation; Senator Prescott Bush's condition of allotting funds only to states working toward ending segregation; and Senator Barry Goldwater's provision for loans for the construction of private schools.[105]

Although the House Education and Labor Committee voted the bill out for floor action at the end of May, on June 20 the Rules Committee voted to withhold action temporarily, and on July 18 decided to withhold all action on educational bills during the first session. An attempt to vote the bill out of the Rules Committee to the floor of the House failed overwhelmingly; that was the end of the Public School Assistance Act of 1961.[106]

In his second year in the presidency, Kennedy made another attempt for legislation aiding elementary and secondary schools. In his "Special Message to the Congress on Education" on February 6, 1962, he characterized the elementary and secondary schools as "the foundation of our education system" and that "our crucial needs at this level have intensified and our deficiencies have grown more critical. We cannot afford to lose another year in mounting a national effort to eliminate the shortage of classrooms, to make teachers' salaries competitive, and to lift the quality of instruction."[107] But the Kennedy administration, in view of the bitter debates and its failure in 1961, concentrated its efforts on the college aid bill, instead of attempting an all-out effort for elementary and secondary school aid.

In 1963 President Kennedy's "Special Message to Congress on Education" reiterated his previous views and hopes for federal aid for strengthening public elementary and secondary education.[108] He recommended a four-year program to provide $1.5 billion which would assist the states in improving salaries for teachers, constructing classrooms, initiating pilot, experimental, and demonstration projects to meet special educational problems, especially in slums and depressed areas; extend the National Defense Education Act programs to improve the quality of elementary and secondary education; and continue federally affected area laws. The Kennedy administration's strategy in 1963 was unlike that of previous years. Instead of presenting the elementary and secondary school aid bill separately, the administration included it with other educational proposals for higher education, vocational and special education, "impacted areas" aid program, and a plan for improving and expanding opportunities for adult education, all in an omnibus educational bill, the National Education Improvement Act of 1963. But the administration's strategy failed; many objected to this manner of enacting educational legislation. Congressman Powell announced in May that his House Education and Labor Committee would not consider the bill in an omnibus fashion, but would divide it into four categories, one of which would be elementary and secondary education. The Senate eventually concurred with Powell's decision.[109] As a result, Congress passed the Higher Educational Facilities Act, the Vocational Education Act, and "impacted areas" aid program, and extended the National Defense Education Act, but only after Kennedy's death and Lyndon B. Johnson had become president. Congress did not act on elementary and secondary education school aid during 1963–64.

Astute in political matters and sensitive to congressional behavior, President Johnson waited for a more favorable climate of opinion before pressing Congress for a broader program of federal aid to elementary and secondary school education. The qualitative improvement of education was surely included, however, in the goals of the "Great Society" he sought to establish during his presidency. To solicit support for education, he convened the White House Conference on Education held on July 20–21, 1965. The nation's most influential educators and government leaders united in their demand for federal aid to what President Kennedy had referred to as "the foundation of our educational system." Congress therefore passed the Elementary and Secondary Education Act of 1965.[110] ESEA represented a shift in federal government policy toward aid-to-education bills, as it provided for general aid rather than a specific purpose or type of instruction, as were science and mathematics under NDEA or vocational education under the Smith-Hughes Act. Most significantly, ESEA allowed nonpublic schools, including religious, to receive federal aid.

ESEA sought to achieve the overall goal of strengthening and improving "educational quality and educational opportunities in the Nation's elementary and secondary schools" through five titles:

Title I authorized approximately $1 billion to help local school districts broaden and strengthen public school programs where there are concentrations of educationally disadvantaged children from low-income families. The local educational agency could use its own discretion as to the use of funds for both public and nonpublic schools.

Title II authorized $100 million to the states for school library resources, textbooks, and other instructional materials, such as periodicals, magnetic tapes, and phonograph records. The allotments were to be distributed according to the number of children enrolled in public and nonpublic elementary and secondary schools within each state.

Title III authorized $100 million for supplementary educational centers and services, such as mobile libraries, science and language laboratories, audiovisual aids, educational television, programmed materials, specialized guidance and counseling. A state's allotment was to be determined by considering both the school-age population and the total population of the state. These supplementary services would be equally available to public and nonpublic school pupils, but local school authorities would be required to own and administer the materials.

Title IV provided for educational research and training and amended and supplemented the Cooperative Research Act of 1954. One hundred million dollars over a five-year period was authorized for construction of national and regional research facilities, expansion of established programs of research and development, and a new program for training researchers in education.

Title V authorized $25 million for grants to strengthen state departments of education. For the first two years the federal funds were to be unmatched, but thereafter the states would be required to match one-third to one-half of the federal government's contribution.

Since its initial passage in 1965, new titles have been added to ESEA and amendments have been made. The nature of the amendments have dealt largely with administrative changes, mostly with Title I, and increasing the original appropriations to implement the bill. The administration of ESEA by the Office of Education, in cooperation with local agencies, met with many problems in organization, staffing, and implementation of regulations and guidelines.[111] Establishing a proper balance between federal and state efforts and authority was a main issue. But as a study of the problem has shown, this was resolved through practice and legislative action when "initiative as to program content and character was left with the states and localities."[112] The local school districts, after identifying educationally disadvantaged children from low-income families, now design the programs to meet their needs. State departments evaluate and approve them before referral to the Office of Education for final approval. An analysis of the allocation of responsibility in administering Title I has been set forth as follows:

> Title I provides influence for each level of government, but at the same time sets limits. The USOE by-passes the state departments of education in determining the allocation of grants and establishes basic criteria which must be met by local districts, but it has no operating control over the projects. The states have the responsibility for approving projects but they must apply federal criteria in carrying out this responsibility. Local districts have access to earmarked funds and latitude in designing projects, circumscribed only by the effectiveness of state supervision and federal criteria. Thus, even on paper, the local school districts had the greatest say in how Title I funds were to be spent.[113]

In 1966, Title VI was added to ESEA: Education of Handicapped Children, which is treated in this work in a special chapter.[114] In 1968, Title VII, Bilingual Education Programs, was added.[115] Also known as the Bilingual Education Act, this title recognized the special educational needs of large numbers of children with limited English-speaking ability. It therefore sought to provide financial assistance to local educational agencies to develop and carry out "new and imaginative elementary and secondary school programs designed to meet these special educational needs" of children who come from environments where the dominant language is other than English.[116] Priority of funds (as high as $40 million for the fiscal year ending June 30, 1970) was to be given to those states having the greatest need for bilingual education programs, with special consideration for the number of children of limited English-speaking ability between the ages of three and eighteen. Applications for grants to the U. S. commissioner of education and his Advisory Committee on the Education of Bilingual Children could be made for establishment, maintenance, and operation of these programs, including acquisition of necessary teaching materials and equipment for such activities as:

1. bilingual education programs
2. programs designed to impart to students a knowledge of the history and culture associated with their languages
3. efforts to establish closer cooperation between the school and the home
4. early childhood educational programs related to the purposes of this title and designed to improve the potential of children for profitable learning activities
5. adult education programs related to the purpose of this title, particularly for parents of children participating in bilingual programs
6. programs designed for dropouts or potential dropouts having need of bilingual programs
7. programs conducted by accredited trade, vocational, or technical schools
8. other activities which meet the purposes of this title.[117]

The effect of ESEA on American education has been considered as "the beginning of a stream of legislative enactments that will have more impact on the future of education than any previous legislation in the history of the country."[118] ESEA has also been called "the first step toward a new face for American education," since it was designed "to stimulate innovation, to strengthen the states, to link research with the schools, and to make the problems of the poor the nation's number one education priority."[119] Educational historian James D. Teller regards the act as "probably the most significant federal aid to education program ever enacted by the Congress" and accountable for more than one-third of all federal appropriations to education.[120]

ESEA's effect on church-state relations has been termed "enormously significant"[121] for private religious schools became eligible for federal aid. But the constitutionality of these provisions for private religious schools has been both affirmed and denied. On the basis of the child-benefit theory, some feel that the church-state issue has been reconciled.[122] A more extensive study of the constitutional question has reasoned:

As long as public education is primarily a public responsibility, not all legislation at all levels of government should be based on the child-benefit theory. Public school construction and salary legislation will always be necessary. But the possibility of structuring some kinds of future legislation on the child-benefit concept so that all students and the whole community may benefit has now been established. The Elementary and Secondary School Act of 1965 may be viewed as a temporary ceasefire in the century-old religious and educational struggle over the schools. If it is successful, future federal aid legislation based on the child-benefit theory might prove to be a permanent treaty of peace.[123]

But despite the above assessment, Title I of ESEA has been challenged as violating the First Amendment's establishment clause.[124] In January, 1974, the U.S. Supreme Court heard an appeal from a circuit court's ruling that federal aid from Title I be provided for parochial school students not only on public school premises but also in parochial schools. On June 10, 1974, the Court handed down its decision favoring aid to the educationally deprived in non public schools.[125]

ENVIRONMENTAL EDUCATION ACT

On October 20, 1970, Congress enacted the Environmental Education Act. The act was in response to the findings from hearings conducted on the pressing issue of the dangers to the environment. Congressmen were made aware of the deterioration of the quality of the nation's environment and of the ecological imbalance posing a serious threat to the nation's environmental resources.[126] The act declared that its purpose was

to encourage and support the development of new and improved curricula to encourage understanding of policies, and support of activities designed to enhance environmental quality and maintain ecological balance; to demonstrate the use of such curricula in model educational programs and to evaluate the effectiveness thereof, to provide support for the initiation and maintenance of programs in environmental education at the elementary and secondary levels; to disseminate curricular materials and

other information used in educational programs throughout the nation; to provide training programs for teachers,
other educational personnel, public service personnel, and
community, labor, and industrial and business leaders and
employees, and government employees at State, Federal,
and local levels; to provide for the planning of outdoor
ecological study centers; to provide for community education programs on preserving and enhancing environmental quality and maintaining ecological balance; and to provide for the preparation and distribution of materials by
mass media in dealing with the environment and
ecology.[127]

Environmental education was defined in this act as "the educational process dealing with man's relationship with his natural and
manmade surroundings, and includes the relation of population,
pollution, resource allocation and depletion, conservation, transportation, technology, and urban and rural planning to the total
human environment."[128] The commissioner of education was authorized to award grants to, and contract with, institutions of higher
education, state and local educational agencies, regional educational research organizationɔ, libraries, and museums to support
research, demonstration, and pilot projects that would advance the
stated purposes of the act. An advisory council on environmental
education would assist and advise the commissioner on setting up
criteria and implementing programs and projects according to the
act's purposes. An initial annual authorization of $5 million for the
fiscal year ending June 30, 1971, was made, allowing for an increase
of up to $25 million for 1973.[129]

DRUG ABUSE EDUCATION ACT

The growing use of drugs by Americans, including those who
have just reached school age, prompted Congress to enact the Drug
Abuse Education Act on December 3, 1970.[130] The act's "statement
of purpose" summarizes much of the discussion that led to the
legislative proposal made necessary by the abuse of drugs.

The Congress hereby finds and declares that drug abuse
diminishes the strength and vitality of the people of our

nation; that such abuse of dangerous drugs is increasing in urban and suburban areas; that there is lack of authoritative information and creative projects designed to educate students and others about drugs and their abuse; and that prevention and control of such drug abuse require intensive and coordinated efforts on the part of both governmental and private groups.

It is the purpose of this Act to encourage the development of new and improved curricula on the problems of drug abuse; to demonstrate the use of such curricula in model educational programs and to evaluate the effectiveness thereof; to disseminate curricular materials and significant information for use in educational programs throughout the Nation; to provide training programs for teachers, counselors, law enforcement officials and other public service and community leaders; and to offer community education programs for parents and others, on drug abuse problems.[131]

Appropriations of $5 million for the fiscal year beginning July 1, 1970, double that amount for 1971, and up to $14 million for 1972, were authorized for drug abuse education projects. Grants to, and contracts with, educational institutions on all levels and research organizations could be awarded for such projects as developing curricula, training programs for teachers, counselors, and parents through workshops, institutes, and conferences, as well as formal course offerings. Similar appropriations were also made for community education projects dealing largely with imparting information about drug abuse and drug dependency problems. These included the establishment of "peer group" leadership programs, which were of special value because of the "generation gap" and the likelihood of young persons to more readily discuss such a topic with their own peers.[132]

EMERGENCY SCHOOL AID ACT

Cognizant of the many administrative problems brought on by the Supreme Court's order to desegregate the nation's public schools, Congress passed the Emergency School Aid Act as part of the education amendments of 1972. The act's purpose is threefold:

to meet the special needs incident to the elimination of minority group segregation and discrimination among students and faculty in elementary and secondary schools; to encourage the voluntary elimination, reduction, or prevention of minority group isolation in elementary and secondary schools with substantial proportions of minority group students; and to aid school children in overcoming the educational disadvantages of minority group isolation.[133]

The act called for compliance with already existing federal laws, especially Title VI of the Civil Rights Act of 1964, and Section 182 of the elementary and secondary education amendments of 1966. Violation of these laws would necessitate the withdrawal of funds from school districts not complying with integration rules. Federal courts have ordered the Department of Health, Education, and Welfare to cut off federal aid to school systems in seventeen states that have failed to comply with desegregation requirements. HEW has even been judged as "not [having] properly fulfilled its obligation" to eliminate segregation in the nation's public schools through better enforcement procedures in school districts not in compliance with federal law.[134] The Emergency School Aid Act unequivocally states the policy that the two mentioned federal laws, as well as the new 1972 provisions, "be applied uniformly in all regions of the United States in dealing with conditions of segregation by race whether de jure or de facto in the school of the local educational agencies of any state without regard to the origin or cause of such segregation."[135]

Funds appropriated by the act amount to $1 billion yearly and are apportioned to the states based largely on the number of minority group children aged five to seventeen inclusive. The term "minority group" extends beyond blacks to include American Indians, Spanish-surnamed Americans (Mexican, Puerto Rican, Cuban, or Spanish origin or ancestry), Portuguese, Orientals, Alaskan and Hawaiian natives.[136]

The act authorizes the following activities for which financial assistance can be provided: (1) remedial services, including student-to-student tutoring; (2) additional staff members, including the training and retraining in problems incident to desegregation and elimination of minority group isolation; (3) utilization and training of teacher aides, with preference given to parents of children in schools assisted by this act; (4) inservice teacher training in institutions of higher education; (5) comprehensive guidance, counseling, and other personal services; (6) development and use of new curricula and instructional methods and techniques, including instruction in the language and cultural heritage of minority groups; (7) educational programs using shared facilities for career education; (8) innovative interracial educational programs or projects; (9) community activities, including public information efforts; (10) administrative services to facilitate activities under this act; (11) planning, evaluation, and dissemination of information of activities; and (12) repair or minor remodeling of existing school facilities for these activities, including instructional equipment. Creative special programs and metropolitan area projects are also encouraged, but need approval from federal authorities. The use of educational television is also encouraged, and funds provided for the cost of "development and production of integrated children's television programs of cognitive and effective educational value."[137]

A National Advisory Council on Equality of Educational Opportunity, consisting of fifteen members, at least one-half of whom shall be representative of minority groups, shall be appointed by the president. The council shall advise on the operation of this act, set forth criteria for approval of applications, review and evaluate the operation, and submit reports to Congress.[138]

ETHNIC HERITAGE PROGRAM

A distinctive feature of American society has been its cultural pluralism. Regarded as the "melting pot" of the world, the United States has become the home of peoples of all races, colors, and creeds from practically every part of the world. Assimilation into a new land with its own customs, usages, and manners has often produced problems of adjustment. But the American ideal of unity in diversity has also been an assurance to many "foreigners" that they can hold on to cherished traditions while pledging allegiance to a new country. Much of America's history has been characterized by the process of acculturation, a process which seeks a blending of cultures, not their destruction.[139]

Sensitive to the diverse ethnic origins of Americans, the Education Amendments of 1972 added a new title to the Elementary and Secondary Education Act of 1965, the Ethnic Heritage Program. A statement of policy was declared.

In recognition of the heterogeneous composition of the
Nation and of the fact that in a multiethnic society a greater
understanding of the contributions of one's own heritage
and of those of one's fellow citizens can contribute to a
more harmonious, patriotic, and committed populace, and
in recognition of the principle that all persons in the educational institutions of the Nation should have an opportunity to learn about the differing and unique contributions to the national heritage made by each ethnic group,
it is the purpose of this title to provide assistance designed
to afford to students opportunities to learn about the nature of their own cultural heritage, and to study the contributions of the cultural heritages of the other ethnic groups
of the Nation.[140]

As a result of this legislation, the commissioner of education
was authorized to award grants to public and private educational
agencies, institutions, and organizations to plan, develop, establish,
and operate ethnic heritage studies programs. All levels of education could participate in the use of curriculum materials designed
to present the cultures of the ethnic groups and their contributions
to the American heritage. Training for specialized persons and cooperation with persons and organizations involved in ethnic heritage programs and activities were also provided. An appropriation
of $15 million for fiscal year 1973 was authorized to carry out the
provisions of the program. A National Advisory Council of fifteen
members appointed by the secretary of health, education, and welfare would assist the commissioner of education in implementing
the program.[141]

INDIAN EDUCATION

Up to 1824 the Department of War took charge of all matters
dealing with the American Indians, while they were considered
"wards of the federal government." From 1824 to 1832, they were
governed by a separate Office of Indian Affairs, and from 1832 to
1849, by the Office of the Commissioner of Indian Affairs which, in
1849, was made a bureau in the Department of the Interior.[142]

The first step toward educational arrangements for the Indians was made in 1819, when Congress authorized an appropriation of $10,000 to assist the Indians in agriculture and to train their children in basic academic skills; these funds could be used to subsidize the efforts of organizations and individuals involved in the education of the Indians. Prior to any federal aid, a number of Indian tribes had established their own schools. A more concentrated effort was inaugurated after the Civil War, when the federal government liberalized its appropriations for Indian education.[143] It is at this time that Cubberly affirms that "the real development of Indian education began."[144] In 1897, Congress declared that it shall be the "settled policy of the Government to hereafter make no appropriation whatever for education in any sectarian school" for Indians. The U.S. Supreme Court in 1908 upheld the use of funds taken from treaty funds on the request of Indians, as these did not come within the scope of the 1897 act.[145]

Four different classes of schools for Indian children have been identified: (1) day schools, which are located in Indian villages or near Indian settlements, largely dealing with elementary education; (2) reservation boarding schools, located within the territory reserved for Indian tribes, which also stress elementary education; (3) non-reservation boarding schools, stressing secondary and vocational education; and (4) contract schools, which include federal government contracts with private groups or, as it has become more common, with public day schools. The latter arrangement, fostered by the federal government, gradually led to the establishment of public schools as the more popular means for education of Indian children.[146] The Johnson-O'Malley Act of 1934 explicitly provided for federal funds to be turned over to "any State or Territory, or political subdivision thereof" or to "any State university, college, or school" or "any appropriate State or private corporation, agency, or institution" for Indian education.[147]

Congress has passed many laws affecting the education of Indian children since 1819.[148] A valuable service of the education amendments of 1972 was to synthesize and update these laws in Title IV, also known as the "Indian Education Act." The Impact Areas Program of Public Law 874 was amended so as to explicitly include financial assistance to local educational agencies for the education of Indian children. A declaration of policy was set forth: "In recognition of the special educational needs of Indian students in the United States, Congress hereby declares it to be the policy of the United States to provide financial assistance to local educational agencies to develop and carry out elementary and secondary school programs specially designed to meet these special educational needs." The commissioner of education was entrusted to set up a program of making grants, which included the determination of sums, procedures and requirements for application and the conditions for approval.[149]

In addition to accustomed educational services, the 1972 amendments provided for special programs and projects to improve educational opportunities for Indian children. Among these would be included:

1. innovative programs related to the educational needs of educationally deprived children
2. bilingual and bicultural education programs and projects
3. special health and nutrition services and other related activities which meet the special health, social, and psychological problems of Indian children
4. coordinating the operation of other federally assisted programs which may be used to assist in meeting the needs of such children.[150]

In accordance with Title VIII of the Elementary and Secondary Education Act of 1965, educational services not available to Indian children in sufficient quantity or quality would also be provided, such as remedial and compensatory instruction, comprehensive academic and vocational instruction, instructional materials and equipment, counseling and testing services, special education programs for the handicapped, preschool programs, and the encouragement of new and innovative approaches, methods, and techniques designed to enrich programs of elementary and secondary education. For conducting these programs more effectively, grants would be authorized to institutions of higher learning to prepare trained personnel, such as teachers, teacher aides, and social workers, or to improve the qualifications of such persons working with Indian children. Special programs would also be established for the improvement of employment and educational opportunities for adult Indians. Among such programs would be the creation of basic literacy opportunities to all nonliterate Indian adults and the chance to qualify for a high school equivalency certificate.[151]

The 1972 act established a National Advisory Council on Indian Education, composed of fifteen Indian and Alaskan members. The president would appoint the council members from among nominees recommended by Indian tribes and organizations, and they were to represent diverse geographic areas of the country. The council has been entrusted with the responsibility of reviewing applications for financial assistance, evaluating programs and projects, and providing technical assistance to educational agencies involved in Indian education. Additionally, the council would advise the deputy commissioner of Indian education who would direct the Office of Indian Education under the U.S. commissioner of education.[152]

The ultimate aim, however, of Indian communities is community control of education.[153] After two years of intensive study, the Special Subcommittee of Indian Education supported this aim in 1969.[154] In 1970, President Nixon stated in agreement that "we believe every Indian community wishing to do so should be able to control its own Indian schools."[155] It is believed that the Indian Act of 1972 was a result of recognition of this movement for community control. And so Indian education is in a "renaissance," reacting to the coercive assimilation imposed upon Indian communities through education, but now not only demanding but actually receiving an education "relevant to their needs, their culture, and their language."[156]

3
Higher Education

PLANS FOR A NATIONAL UNIVERSITY

At the federal convention of 1787, Charles C. Pickney, a delegate from South Carolina, proposed on May 29 a "Plan of a Federal Constitution" in which one of the powers of Congress would be "to establish and provide for a national university at the seat of government of the United States."[1] When the convention received drafts of the powers of the proposed new Congress, no power referring to education was included. On August 18, James Madison offered as an additional power "proper to be added to these of the general legislative" the power "to establish a University."[2] Pickney immediately proposed his own suggestions for legislative powers, among which were "to establish seminaries for the promotion of literature, and the arts and sciences" and "to establish public institutions, rewards, and immunities, for the promotion of agriculture, commerce, trades, and manufactures." Both Madison's and Pickney's propositions were referred to the Committee of Detail which had prepared the report on the powers of the federal legislature.[3] As the list presented to the convention on September 14 did not include any powers concerning education, Madison and Pickney moved to insert a power "to establish a university, in which no preferences or distinctions should be allowed on account of religion." James Wilson of Pennsylvania supported the motion but Gouverneur Morris, also of Pennsylvania, differed: "It is not necessary. The exclusive power at the seat of government will reach the object."[4] When they voted on the motion of Madison and Pickney, 6 states voted for, 4 states voted against, and 1 state was divided. Thus, no power explicitly referring to education was granted to Congress. Morris's reply was that this power was already implied in the powers of Congress.

Because no further mention or action was taken on this point, it is questionable to agree with Burke A. Hinsdale's conclusion that "although it may not have been expressed . . . the proposition was an invasion of the proper jurisdiction of the State authority."[5]

Four of the first six presidents of the United States perceived the need for, and value of, a national university. It is highly doubtful that they would have made such a proposal if it were contrary to the directives of the federal Constitution. This is especially true of Madison who has been called by a constitutional expert "unquestionably the leading spirit" of the federal convention and whose *Notes* remain "the standard authority for the proceedings of the Convention."[6] Chief Justice of the U.S. Supreme Court Charles Evans Hughes has remarked that Madison's was "the most direct approach to the intention of the makers of the Constitution."[7]

George Washington is said to have expressed the desire for a national university in the nation's capital while he was encamped with troops in October, 1775.[8] In his first annual message as president on January 8, 1790, Washington reaffirmed his interest:

> Nor am I less persuaded, that you will agree with me in opinion, that there is nothing which can better deserve your patronage than the promotion of science and literature. Knowledge is in every country the surest basis of public happiness. In one, in which the measures of government receive their impression so immediately from the sense of the community, as in ours, it is proportionably essential. To the security of a free constitution it contributes in various ways; by convincing those who are intrusted with the public administration that every valuable end of government is best answered by the enlightened confidence of the people, and by teaching the people themselves to know and to value their own rights; to discern and provide against invasions of them; to distinguish between oppression and the necessary exercise of lawful authority, between burthens proceeding from a disregard to their convenience and those resulting from the inevitable exigencies of society; to discriminate the spirit of liberty from that of licentiousness, cherishing the first and avoiding the last, and uniting a speedy but temperate vigilance against encroachments, with an inviolable respect to the laws.

Whether this desirable object will be the best promoted
by affording aids to seminaries of learning already established, by the institution of a national university, or by any
other expedients, will be well worthy of a place in the
deliberations of the legislature.[9]

Congress, however, appears to have ignored Washington on this
matter.

In 1785, the legislature of Virginia voted to give Washington,
as a testimonial to his contributions to the country, shares in the
Potomac Company and in the James River Company. The gift
caused him much embarassment. But he accepted with the understanding that the shares of the James River Company would be "for
the use and benefit of Liberty Hall Academy" in Virginia, while
those of the Potomac Company would be intended for a national
university in the nation's capital. Washington desired to make an
appeal for a national university in his farewell address, but Alexander Hamilton advised that it would be more appropriate to do so
at the opening of a legislative session. Hence, Washington's only
reference to education was: "Promote as an object of primary importance institutions for the general diffusion of knowledge. In
proportion as the structure of government gives force to public
opinion, it is essential that public opinion be enlightened." In his
last annual message to Congress on December 7, 1796, however,
Washington did refer to the university. Again there was no response
from Congress, even though a proposition in the form of a
memorial calling for the founding of a university had been presented to it during the same year. Nor was there any action on the
part of Congress to execute Washington's wish to apply the Potomac stock towards the hoped-for university, as set forth in his last
will and testament.[10]

There is no record of John Adam's public advocacy of a national university during his presidency, but it has been assumed that
he was in sympathy with the idea and that no constitutional provisions could restrain its adoption.[11]

Thomas Jefferson earned renown as an educational leader
prior to his election as president. In 1779, he had proposed to the
Virginia Assembly a "Bill for the More General Diffusion of Knowledge," advocating a system of public elementary and secondary
schools. He had, moreover, also offered a plan for reconstructing

the traditional curriculum of William and Mary College in 1779.[12] Such a champion of education could render the prestige of his office and of his experience to the cause of a national university. But when Jefferson discussed the subject in his sixth annual message to Congress on September 2, 1806, he questioned not its value but rather its constitutionality. Foreseeing a surplus in the federal treasury, he felt that the American people would prefer to use it for "great purposes," among which would be public education.[13] Jefferson's questioning of the constitutionality of a national university, because such a power was not explicitly granted to Congress in the powers enumerated in the Constitution, reflects his political philosophy of a strong state government as opposed to Hamilton's advocacy of a strong federal government. Thus, Jefferson followed the view that the Tenth Amendment placed education among the rights reserved to the states; a constitutional amendment would be required for the national government to enter the field of education. In commenting on Jefferson's political philosophy, Allen Oscar Hansen has noted: "The idea that Jefferson was opposed to centralized control is probably a mistaken conception. It is known that he believed in a high degree of centralization. For instance, in 1785 in a letter to Colonel Monroe he advocated the regulation of trade by Congress, and in the same letter opposed a 'plan of opening our land offices, by dividing them among the States, which ought to be made joint in every possible instance, in order to cultivate the idea of our being one nation, and to multiply the instances in which the people shall look up to Congress as their head.' Jefferson represented the democratic element of the back country, and he always worked on the principle of expedience. It was probably for this reason that the system of education which he recommended was largely based upon local control. It was expedient to offer such a system as would appeal to his clientele."[14]

During Jefferson's administration, Joel Barlow, upon returning to the United States after serving as minister to France, proposed in 1806 a "Prospectus of a National Institution to be Established in the United States." The plan was introduced into the Senate, and referred to a committee where it died, despite favorable reaction from many administration leaders.[15]

As president, James Madison included the subject of a national university in his second annual message on December 5, 1810,[16] his seventh annual message on December 15, 1815,[17] and his last annual message on December 3, 1816, in which he called upon members of the national legislature to direct "their attention to the expediency of exercising their existing powers."[18] Madison believed, as he had for the last twenty years, that the establishment of a national university was within the powers of Congress. Twice the issue came before congressional committees during Madison's administration. In 1811, a committee appointed by Congress ruled that a university established by the national legislature was unconstitutional as to its founding, endowing, and controlling.[19] Another committee of Congress studied the subject in 1816 and arrived at the same conclusion.[20]

However, President James Monroe followed Jefferson's political philosophy and, although favoring a national university, recommended in his first message to Congress on December 2, 1817, an appropriate amendment to the Constitution: "I think proper to suggest, also, in case this measure is adopted, that it be recommended to the States to include in the amendment sought a right in Congress to institute, likewise, seminaries of learning, for the all-important purpose of diffusing knowledge among our fellow-citizens throughout the United States."[21]

President John Quincy Adams, in his first annual message to Congress on December 6, 1825, suggested the erection of an astronomical observatory in connection with the national university. He saw no constitutional restriction.[22]

Although the first six presidents of the United States favored a national university, only two deemed necessary any change in the Constitution.

The issue of the national university was heard again in connection with the James Smithson bequest. President Andrew Jackson informed Congress on December 17, 1835, that the intent of the bequest was "for the purpose of founding at Washington an establishment under the name of the Smithsonian Institution, for the increase and diffusion of knowledge among men."[23] Jackson, believing that "the Executive having no authority to take any steps for accepting the trust and obtaining the funds," referred the matter to Congress, and each branch referred the problem to a committee, the Senate to the Committee on the Judiciary, and the House to an appointed select committee, in which former President John Quincy Adams, now a member of Congress from Massachusetts, was included. Upon favorable reports from both branches, Congress voted to accept the bequest on July 1, 1836, allowing for expenses necessary to fulfill the technicalities of law.[24] On December 6, 1838, President Martin Van Buren informed Congress that the Smithson bequest had been executed and deposited with the Department of the Treasury. He asked Congress to determine the manner with which the terms of the bequest could best be complied.[25] Among the suggestions offered in Congress and by scientists and educators was a national university. When the idea was presented in the form of a bill in the Senate on February 25, 1839, John C. Calhoun echoed the strongest objection: "This is a bill making provision for the common benefit of all mankind; but we are restricted in our powers. The question whether we have the power to establish a university or not was a subject of consideration at an early stage of our Government, and President Washington decided that Congress had the power. But the question was voted down and never revived. And now what do we do? We accept a fund from a foreigner, and would do what we are not authorized to do by the Constitution. We would enlarge our grant of power derived from the States of this Union. Sir, can you show me a word that goes to invest us with such a power? I not only regard the measure proposed as unconstitutional, but to me it appears to involve a species of meanness which I can not describe, a want of dignity wholly unworthy of this Government."[26]

It was not until August 10, 1840, that Congress agreed on "an act to establish the *Smithsonian Institution* for the increase and diffusion of knowledge among men," primarily by facilitating and promoting scientific research and publication.[27] Responsible to Congress, the Smithsonian has embraced under its charge the National Museum, the National Gallery of Art, the National Zoological Park, the International Exchange Service, the Astrophysical Observatory, and the Bureau of American Ethnology.

Proponents for a national university, despite their defeat in regard to the Smithson bequest, continued their interest and efforts. In 1869 John W. Hoyt urged its creation in an address to the National Teachers' Association, which organized a committee to study and work on such a project. The committee, whose name was later changed to the National Educational Association, reported favorably and prepared a bill for introduction in Congress in 1872. President Ulysses S. Grant, in his message to Congress in 1873, recommended "the establishment of an institution of learning or university of the highest class, by the donation of lands . . . [and] there is no place better suited for such an institution than the national capital."[28] Although the bill had been passed favorably by the House Committee on Education on March 3, 1873, Congress adjourned without taking action. Efforts were renewed, more bills were introduced and revised, and hearings were held in Congress but with no results. Not conceding defeat, the NEA in 1898 appointed another committee, whose report in 1901 spelled out the consensus of feeling of the nation's leading educators. In view of the fact that so many American universities afforded adequate opportunities for advanced research in all areas of knowledge, the committee saw no special need for a national university. All the facilities of educational and scientific research sponsored by the government in Washington were available to all students and scholars through private or individual auspices without requiring "the creation of a statutory, degree-conferring university." In view of the Constitutional aspects of the problem, the committee concluded that the federal government ought not "to control the educational instrumentalities of the country" and that a university in the nation's capital was not a requirement of government.[29] This line of reasoning on the part of educators is particularly significant because Congress had already passed the two Morrill acts in 1862 and in 1890. The educators distinguished between grants of land and money from the federal government to education and actual control of educational facilities by the federal government. Every other subsequent attempt since to establish a national university has failed.[30]

THE SERVICE ACADEMIES

That the federal government has the right to establish service academies for the armed forces has not been questioned. In 1802 Congress established the Military Academy at West Point, the first educational institution under direct control of the federal government. It was during the War of Independence that the need for a national military academy was perceived. In September, 1776 the Continental Congress established a committee to inquire into the state of the army in New York. The committee's investigation, having found a lack of capable commanders and too many poorly disciplined soldiers, recommended "that the board prepare a continental laboratory and a military academy, and provide the same with officers."[31] A second committee of the Continental Congress requested a plan for a military academy.[32] In 1783 the Continental Congress appointed Alexander Hamilton as chairman of a committee to prepare a plan for training an army. Hamilton consulted General George Washington, whose chief recommendation was to establish a military school at West Point. Washington made the same recommendation as president in his annual message of 1793.[33] But it was not until 1802 that Congress passed the act to establish the Military Academy at West Point.[34]

The Department of the Navy was established by Congress in 1798. No provisions were made for the formal training of midshipmen; they depended on on-the-job training. Several small naval schools were set up at suitable ports for instructing midshipmen while off regular duty. In 1845 these four small naval schools—at New York, Philadelphia, Boston, and Norfolk, Virginia—had an annual maintenance cost of $28,200.[35] It was not until 1845 that the United States Naval Academy was established on the same level as that of the Military Academy.[36] Fort Severn, an old army post at Annapolis, became and has remained the site of the naval academy, with the exception of the years 1861 to 1865, when the academy was located at Newport, Rhode Island, because of the Civil War.

By an act of July 31, 1876, Congress established a two-year program for the training of officers for the Coast Guard.[37] The schooner *Dobbin* was overhauled and fitted as a school ship with formal classes and training beginning on May 25, 1877. It was called the U.S. Revenue Cutter Service School of Instruction.[38] A new cadet training ship, the *Chase,* replaced the *Dobbin* in the summer of 1878 and except for a period of four years (1890–94) served as the Coast Guard's school ship. In 1900 the *Chase* made its winter headquarters at Arundel Cove, near Baltimore, Maryland. A few frame buildings were converted for classroom use.[39] The training program in 1903 was extended to three years. A permanent shore academy was established at New London, Connecticut,[40] in 1910 and the name changed to the U.S. Coast Guard Academy in 1915. The increase of cadets and the need for better academic facilities led to the construction of the present facilities in 1929, and the training program was extended to four years in 1930.[41]

The passage of the Merchant Marine Act of 1936 led to the establishment of the U.S. Merchant Marine Cadet Corps on March

15, 1938.[42] As in the case of the Coast Guard, training was first given aboard merchant ships and later at temporary shore establishments until the U.S. Merchant Marine Academy was completed in 1943 at Kings Point, New York. The present four-year program was not instituted until the end of World War II in August, 1945.[43] Unlike graduates of the other service academies, graduates of the Merchant Marine Academy become employees of steamship companies rather than of the U.S. government.[44]

The emerging importance of air power was recognized when with the passage of the National Security Act of 1947 the Army Air Forces became the autonomous U.S. Air Force.[45] As with the other service branches, the Air Force also sought its own academy, which was established at Colorado Springs, Colorado, in 1954, with classes beginning in 1955.[46]

RESERVE OFFICERS TRAINING CORPS PROGRAMS

The Morrill Land Grant Act of 1962 offered to each state tracts of federally controlled public lands. The funds derived from their sale were to be devoted to "the endowment, support, and maintenance of at least one college where the lending object shall be, without excluding other scientific and classical studies, and including military tactics, to teach such branches of learning as are related to agriculture and the mechanic arts."[47] The state colleges established under this act gave different interpretations as to the military instruction to be given. Disagreement existed as to both the number of hours of instruction per week and the number of required years; a few colleges did not even require it at all. The implementation of the military provisions was left to be worked out through cooperative efforts between the colleges and the War Department.[48] Seeking uniformity for these military training programs in the land-grant colleges, Congress, in enacting the National Defense Act of 1916— "an act for making further and more effective provision for the national defense, and for other purposes"—placed these programs under the ROTC system.[49] Thus, the Reserve Officers Training Corps became a means of providing a steady supply of young college-trained reserve officers and was regarded by army leaders as "a feasible alternative" to expanding the military academy at West Point.[50]

The 1920 National Defense Act provided for the establishment of ROTC programs at colleges and universities other than the land-grant institutions.[51] In both private and public institutions students could thus take military training as part of their academic courses under the supervision of the War Department in a government-sponsored scholarship program. In 1925, the Navy inaugurated a similar ROTC program in conjunction with both public and private universities.[52] While still under the War Department, the Air Force in 1946 established ROTC units similar to the Army's and the Navy's on college campuses.[53]

In addition to the service academies and ROTC programs in colleges, the Defense Department operates specialized schools and training programs for leadership in the armed forces.[54]

HOWARD UNIVERSITY

Although not a national university according to the accepted understanding of its purpose and function, the Howard University in Washington, D.C., is regarded as a "unique instance of federal support of higher education."[55] On November 20, 1866, the original proposal for Howard was for a theological seminary to train black preachers.[56] At a subsequent meeting on December 4, 1866, it was recommended that the name of the proposed institution be changed from the Howard Theological Seminary to the Howard Normal and Theological Institute for the Education of Teachers and Preachers. The change of name and purpose was credited to Senator Samuel C. Pomeroy of Kansas, one of its trustees, who believed that the addition of a normal school would increase its chances of obtaining approval from Congress.[57] But the trustees also began to envision a broader scope of education to embrace the liberal arts and sciences and thus sought incorporation on January 23, 1867, as the Howard University.[58] Although Howard's charter states its goal as "the education of youth," the university was intended primarily, but not necessarily and exclusively, for blacks. Private donations were its main means of support until financial difficulties were encountered. In 1879, Congress began annual appropriations which have since continued and increased.[59] In 1899, Congress stipulated that no government appropriations be used, directly or indirectly, for the support of the theological department or for any religious sectarian instruction. Congress also required federal inspection and supervision of funds appropriated to the university.[60] In 1891, Congress directed in an appropriations act an annual report to the secretary of the interior as to the expenditures of government funds.[61]

On December 13, 1928, Congress amended Section 8 of the Act of Incorporation of Howard and authorized annual appropriations from and inspection by the U.S. Office of Education—thus placing the university in the category of a semifederal educational institution.[62] In September, 1961, Congress, in establishing a teaching hospital for Howard, transferred Freedmen's Hospital to the university.[63] Freedmen's Hospital had been established by Congress on March 3, 1865, as part of a program to meet the health needs of blacks.[64]

MORRILL ACTS

In an effort to meet the needs of improved techniques in agriculture a number of schools were founded in the first half of the nineteenth century. The Gardiner Lyceum in Maine was regarded as "America's first agricultural school."[65] Although privately established, it received state aid, but with the loss of this aid in 1832, the school was forced to discontinue instruction in agriculture and to change its role to that of an academy.[66] A similar attempt by the Agricultural Seminary in Derby, Connecticut, lasted but a year.[67] Rensselaer Institute, founded in 1824, included the study of agriculture among its courses in applied science, but did not continue such instruction beyond its formative years.[68] Other short-lived projects in agricultural education in the 1830s and 1840s have been noted, such as the Cream Hill Agricultural School in West Cromwall, Connecticut, the Farmer's College near Cincinnati, Ohio, and the school and experimental farm of James J. Mapes near Newark, New Jersey.[69] Projects such as Simeon De Witt's agricultural college, Harrison Howard's People's College in New York, and a farm school in Virginia went unrealized.[70]

In 1838, Charles L. Fleischman, a graduate of the Bavarian Royal Agricultural Society urged in a memorial to Congress the establishment of schools specializing in agricultural, mechanical, and veterinary education, modeled after successful schools in

Europe. The following year Fleischman suggested that the Smithson bequest be utilized for this purpose, as did the Agricultural Society of the United States in 1842 when it called for a national agricultural school, library, and experimental garden "that should bear and be worthy of the name of Smithson."[71] Among other suggestions were those offered by Professor Edwin D. Sanborn of Dartmouth College, Professor Jonathan B. Turner of Illinois College, and Congressman John Wentworth of Illinois. They suggested either a national agricultural school or pro rata appropriations to each state for its own schools or a combination of such efforts. Not only did individuals present memorials to Congress for agricultural education but to state legislatures as well.[72]

Despite this agitation for action by the federal government on the matter of aid for agricultural education, it was not until December 14, 1857, that the first bill on the subject was introduced to the House of Representatives by Justin S. Morrill of Vermont. The bill granted 6,340,000 acres of the public land, with each state receiving 20,000 acres for each senator and representative in Congress according to the 1850 census. The bill passed the House by a scant 105 to 100 vote, but the Senate, in a 28 to 20 vote, voted to defer further immediate consideration.[73] When the bill finally passed Congress in February, 1859, President James Buchanan vetoed it for the following reasons: an increased strain on the federal treasury at a time when the government was having difficulty in meeting its expenses; the danger of speculation in regard to the purchase of the lands required; the beginning of a bad precedent in having the states receive aid from the federal treasury; the creation of competition for existing colleges that already taught agriculture; and, most of all, the unconstitutionality of the bill by going beyond the power of Congress to use public lands for purposes not enumerated in the Constitution. An attempt by Morrill to override the presidential veto failed; states' rights were the most pressing reason for the bill's defeat.[74]

After the election of Abraham Lincoln as president, Morrill reintroduced his bill on December 16, 1861.[75] With a new Congress and the absence of the seceded Southerners, the bill, now allowing for 30,000 acres instead of 20,000 on the basis of the 1860 census, was passed by Congress in June, 1862, approved by President Lincoln, and became a law on July 2, 1862. Instruction in military science and tactics was also a new feature of the bill. The constitu-

tional issue remained in the background and an era of federal cooperation with the states in the field of education had begun. Public
lands had been granted to private corporations for the encouragement of building railroads; the amount of lands granted for the
purpose of education constituted a small fraction in comparison to
those received by railroad corporations. Lincoln and the Congress
concentrated their concern on the educational benefits to the states
and the nation at large and thus each state that accepted land-grants
would obligate itself "to the endowment, support, and maintenance
of at least one college, where the leading object shall be, without
excluding other scientific and classical studies, and including military tactics, to teach such branches of learning as are related to
agriculture and the mechanic arts, in such manner as the legislatures
of the States may respectively prescribe, in order to promote the
liberal and practical education of the industrial classes in the several
pursuits and professions in life."[76]

Because of misconceptions as to the aims and implementation
of the Morrill Act and the more urgent concern over the Civil War
and the resulting problems of Reconstruction, a number of states
delayed taking advantage of the federal funds available. Subsequently, Congress amended the act of 1862 on July 23, 1866, and
allowed all the states an additional three years to acknowledge their
acceptance of the provisions of the Morrill Act and five additional
years after acceptance thereof for the actual establishment of a
college of agriculture and mechanical arts. Moreover, seceded
states, as well as new states admitted to the Union, would be entitled
to the bill's benefits.[77]

As a result of the different interpretations of the Morrill Act, the
course of agricultural education throughout the country did not
follow a uniform pattern, either educationally or financially.[78] Fifteen states incorporated the land-grant institution into their already
established state universities. Twenty-eight states established independent "A. and M." (agricultural and mechanical) colleges. In a
few states the grant was entrusted to a private institution. Since the
states themselves had the obligation, their legislatures, through
boards and committees, were to determine the character of the
college. The result was a struggle by financially difficult colleges
with no previous interest or involvement in agriculture and by small
institutions—public, private, sectarian—to obtain federal funds.[79]
The curricula and caliber of agricultural and mechanical training

varied considerably, from the concept of a mere trade school to the university type of scientific education, because of the uneven quality of teachers and students.[80] Financially, most of the colleges mismanaged their land grants, often selling them below the usual price per acre. Funds were not always wisely invested and additional funds were sought, as President Buchanan had earlier predicted.[81]

Requests and efforts for further aid for agricultural education were therefore not surprising; they culminated in a convention called by the U.S. commissioner of agriculture in February, 1872. Composed of "delegates of Agricultural Colleges, State societies and boards, to take such action regarding the interests of agriculture as they shall deem expedient," the convention sought further congressional land grants, the establishment of experiment stations, changes in the instruction of military training, and more effective cooperation between the colleges and the Department of Agriculture.[82] In introducing a bill for further aid, Morrill referred to the "convention of high character, and [of whose delegates] hardly ever surpassed in this country for their intelligence."[83] Other more pressing business prevented discussion of the bill even though it had been favorably received by the Committee on Education and Labor. At the next session, on December 5, 1872, Morrill again introduced his bill. Extensive debate followed; opponents emphasized their fear that a national system of education would encroach upon the rights of the states, With the House and the Senate in disagreement as to certain aspects of the bill and the House unwilling to agree to a conference committee to iron out the disputed points, the bill was killed. Morrill renewed his efforts in the next session on December 15, 1873, but the bill never emerged from committee. A similar fate befell the bills Morrill introduced on January 25, 1875, and on January 25, 1876. Senator Ambrose Burnside of Rhode Island introduced a bill on December 9, 1880, with Morrill taking the lead for its passage on December 15; with amendments the bill passed the Senate but the House refused to take any action. Efforts on December 5, 1881, and on January 24, 1882, to reintroduce the bills failed. Morrill did not renew efforts again until May 1, 1888; again he was unsuccessful in even having the bill heard.[84]

In 1890, however, Morrill met with success. He had learned the pulse of the Congress as it had defeated the Hoar proposal for a national system of education and the Blair proposals for support of the common public schools.[85] He therefore asked that the states receive annual appropriations from the sales of federal public lands and from receipts on the debts owed from the land-grant railway companies. The annual appropriations were to be equal and fixed for each state, beginning at $15,000, increasing $1,000 yearly, and stopping at $25,000. The debates on what has come to be known as the Second Morrill Bill were lengthy in the Senate and a one-day affair in the House. Although the bill called for federal money to ensure "the more complete endowment and maintenance of colleges for the benefit of agriculture and the mechanic arts," actual control of the colleges remained with the states; the federal government, however, had more responsibility for proper administration of the funds. That the funds be distributed for instruction in agriculture and the mechanic arts and the various branches of sciences necessary to them became a *sine qua non* for House approval of the bill. The bill gave major consideration to blacks: Any state making a distinction between race or color in the admission of students would be deprived of federal funds; the establishment and maintenance of separate colleges for white and black students, however, would be acceptable. Thus, following the southern philosophy of "equal but separate" educational facilities, the act in effect led to the establishment of seventeen black land-grant colleges.[86] In 1907, through the Nelson Amendment, Congress raised the annual appropriation to $35,000, with another $5,000 added each year until $50,000 would become the annual appropriation to the land-grant colleges. This amendment stipulated that the "colleges may use a portion of this money for providing courses for the special preparation of instructors for teaching the elements of agriculture and the mechanic arts."[87]

The land-grant colleges received further support for their resident instruction programs with the passage of the Bankhead-Jones Act in 1935. It specifically granted the sum of $980,000 for this purpose, and after increments the total appropriations in 1940 amounted to $2,480,000. While the initial amount under this act was distributed equally among the states, further distributions were apportioned on the basis of their total population.[88]

Despite the long struggle for eventual passage of the Second Morrill Act, the agricultural colleges were not left solely with the funds provided for them in the First Morrill Act of 1862. In 1887 the Hatch Act, or the Agricultural Experimental Station Act, was adopted by Congress. Reports from European institutions had emphasized the value of model farms or experiment stations in connection with agricultural education; several such efforts had proven successful in the United States.[89] Delegates from agricultural colleges gathered in a convention at Washington in 1883 in connection with a bill that had been introduced in Congress to seek federal aid for the establishment of experimental stations. In 1885, at the request of the commissioner of agriculture, the delegates met again and adopted a resolution "that the condition and progress of American agriculture require national aid for investigation and experimentation in the several states and territories."[90] The bill introduced on December 10, 1885, although favorably reported from the Senate Committee on Agriculture and Forestry, became entangled in parliamentary procedures and was dropped; but introduced again on December 20, 1886, the bill received extensive attention. Taking into consideration the usual fear of federal control, the experimental stations were to be state institutions under immediate control of the land-grant colleges or their departments of agriculture; the role of the federal commissioner of agriculture was merely advisory. The sum of $15,000 to each state was determined as the annual appropriation. On January 27, 1887, the Senate passed the bill, followed by the House two days later under the leadership of Representative Henry Hatch, and signed by the president on March 2, 1887. Although Senator James Z. George introduced the bill and was its chief spokesman in the Senate, the speedy passage of the bill in the House through the efforts of Hatch led to the latter's name being attached to the bill.[91]

The research encouraged by the Hatch Act led to many improvements in such areas as the dairy industry, animal breeding, crop improvement, and farm management.[92] "The stations," according to Ross's evaluation, "brought system and gave direction to the land-grant colleges, and assured their continuation more than any other factor."[93] The request for increasing the annual appropriation was therefore looked upon favorably by Congress, which passed in 1906 the Adams Amendment to the Experimental Station Act. The annual appropriation was raised to $20,000, with an additional $2,000 yearly until the total of $30,000 was reached.[94] The Purnell Act of 1925 further increased the annual appropriation to $50,000, with $10,000 yearly increases until a total of $90,000 would be reached in 1930. The Purnell Act extended the areas of investigation by the experimental stations to include production, manufacture, preparation, use, distribution, and marketing of agricultural products and including such scientific researches as have for their purpose the establishment and maintenance of a permanent and efficient agricultural industry, and such economic and sociological investigations as have for their purpose the development and improvement of the rural home and rural life.[95]

Title I of the Bankhead-Jones Act of 1935 substantially aided the experimental stations by authorizing $1 million in the first year with a similar amount each year to total $5 million annually. Of that amount, however, only 60 percent was relegated to the experimental stations; 40 percent was for research by the U.S. Department of Agriculture. Funds were allocated to the states in proportion to the rural population and had to be matched dollar for dollar.[96]

Another large increase to the experiment stations came with the passage of the Research and Marketing Act of 1946. By 1951 the total annual appropriation would reach $20 million, 20 percent of which was to be equally divided among the states, 26 percent to be distributed in proportion to the rural population, 26 percent to be distributed in proportion to the farm population, 25 percent to be for cooperative research between two or more state agricultural experiment stations, and 3 percent for administrative expenses incurred by the Department of Agriculture. By 1950 an additional $6 million could be appropriated for "cooperative research with the state agricultural experiment stations and such other appropriate agencies as may be mutually agreeable to the Department of Agriculture and the experimental stations concerned." By 1951 an additional $20 million could be appropriated for conducting research and service work pertaining to the marketing of agricultural products; the secretary of agriculture was empowered to allot funds to state agencies and experiment stations for this function. By 1951 an additional $15 million could be used for research concerned with agricultural commodities and products in laboratories under the direction of the U.S. Department of Agriculture or contracted with private or other public agencies, as the state experiment stations.[97]

THE NATIONAL YOUTH ADMINISTRATION

The depression years of the 1930s, in causing a high unemployment rate, led to the disruption of the education of many American youths. A partial answer to this problem was the establishment in 1935 of the National Youth Administration (NYA). The purpose of NYA was to provide needy students with part-time employment so that they might continue their education.[98] President Franklin D. Roosevelt expressed the hope that NYA would "extend the educational opportunities of the youth of the country."[99] From 1935 to 1943, students in the age group of sixteen to twenty-five could be engaged in work projects under the direction of the school authorities of their educational institutions, which received federal funds to maintain part-time employment for needy students. Students in colleges, universities, graduate schools, and even in high schools were included in the NYA. The usual work load was about forty hours a month for those in higher education and twenty hours a month for high school students. The hourly wage varied according to the minimum wage in different parts of the country. The total cost of NYA was approximately $100 million a year.[100] NYA's aid to college students has been characterized as "motivated more by temporary economic considerations than by any purposeful plan to give federal aid to college students."[101] But it did afford many youths the opportunity to obtain or continue their education in a period of American history when many of their own parents were unemployed or unable to aid their children with an education beyond high school.

STUDENT WAR LOAN PROGRAMS

During World War II most American colleges adopted accelerated programs that eliminated summer vacations. Students opting for professions in scientific fields were also deferred from military service. In 1942 Congress authorized $5 million for loans in such areas as medicine, dentistry, pharmacy, engineering, chemistry, and physics. Furthermore, students had to be within two years of graduation, before they could receive loans of up to $500 a year, at an annual interest rate of 2.5 percent. The student, moreover, had to agree to accept employment upon graduation at the direction of the War Manpower Commission.[102]. An estimated loan total of $3,327,601 was granted to over eleven thousand students in 286 colleges for the years 1942–44.[103]

G.I. BILL OF RIGHTS

Concern over the education of American youth whose education was either interrupted or who could not continue beyond high school because of military service in World War II led to a speedy passage by Congress of the Servicemen's Readjustment Act of 1944, more commonly known as the G.I. Bill of Rights.[104] The act provided tuition, books and supplies, counseling services, and subsistence allotments for the veteran and his dependents. Extensive latitude was permitted as to choice of course in college or training school. The period of benefits under the bill was determined by the length of service of the veteran: one year plus the number of months spent in the service, but not to exceed a total of forty-eight months. At first the federal government made payment directly to the educational institution, but the Veteran's Readjustment Assistance Act of 1952 provided for payments directly to the veteran.[105] In 1951, when the deadline for training under the G.I. Bill was reached, an estimated eight million veterans of World War II had received benefits, with a total cost of about $14 billion.[106]

Abuses rose in respect to the G.I. Bill when many profit-making schools were founded to catch the G.I. trade. The law provided no method whereby either the federal or state government approved training courses not sponsored by recognized colleges and schools. Some veterans also received grants for sport flying, ballroom dancing, hobby photography—not for vocational training but for avocational or recreational purposes.[107] This latter abuse was corrected by the 1949 Supplemental Independent Offices Appropriation Bill which Congress passed in June, 1948.[108] In 1952 the same educational benefits of the G.I. Bill were extended to veterans of the Korean War.[109] An estimated twenty-three million Korean veterans received benefits.[110] In 1966 Congress passed, and liberalized in 1967, a permanent G.I. Bill extending benefits not only to veterans of the war in Vietnam but also to all men and women who had been honorably discharged after six or more months of service in the Army, Navy, Marine Corps, Air Force, and Coast Guard since the original G.I. Bill expired on January 31, 1955.[111] In December, 1973, Congress passed emergency legislation to cover benefits for veterans attending educational institutions which may, because of the fuel energy crisis, extend normal Christmas vacations or delay the start of the spring semester or quarter.[112] The legislation was necessary because the veterans involved receive monthly assistance payments only during an "ordinary school year," which is generally nine months.[113]

Despite the costs and some abuses of the G.I. benefits, "the general consensus was that this was a tremendous educational undertaking at federal expense and of untold benefit to the veterans, to the educational institutions concerned, and to the country as a whole."[114]

WAR ORPHANS' EDUCATIONAL ASSISTANCE ACT

A special kind of G.I. benefit was passed by Congress in 1956: the War Orphans' Educational Assistance Act to provide aid for the education of children of deceased or permanently and totally disabled veterans as a result of a service-connected injury or disease. The act extends as far back as to cover children of Spanish-American War veterans. Eligibility begins on a child's eighteenth birthday or upon successful completion of high school, and ends on his twenty-sixth birthday. Only educational institutions in the United States or its territories can be chosen under this act. While enrolled in an approved educational institution, the veteran's child is entitled to a monthly allowance of $175 if a full-time student and $81 per month if a part-time student. This monthly allowance is for living expenses, tuition, books and supplies, and other educational costs. Each eligible person shall be entitled to educational assistance for a period not in excess of thirty-six months, or the usual four academic nine-month years, or the equivalent of part-time educational training.[115]

COOPERATIVE RESEARCH PROGRAM

In 1954 Congress enacted into law the Cooperative Research Act by which the U.S. commissioner of education is authorized to "enter into contracts or jointly financed cooperative arrangements with universities and colleges and state educational agencies for the conduct of research, surveys, and demonstrations in the field of education." Working with the Bureau of Educational Research and Development within the Office of Education, the authorized agency receives most, if not all, of the funds necessary to conduct the research projects with complete independence, except for auditing of funds and periodic consultation with the Office. A research advisory council reviews, evaluates, and decides whether to accept or reject all research proposals. The overriding criterion for all proposals is the contribution of the research to education; for example, one proposal contracted for the establishment of an educational television library.[116]

This act was amended and supplemented by the Elementary and Secondary Education Act of 1965 and its amendments and by the education amendments of 1972.[117]

NATIONAL SCIENCE FOUNDATION ACT

World War II made necessary the pooling and utilization of the nation's scientific resources by the federal government. Even before the end of the war, the Senate Subcommittee on War Mobilization had begun intensive study on the important role of the federal government in financing scientific research activities during the war; the subcommittee also envisioned problems of reconversion of these activities after the war. Whether it was war or peace, the promotion of science and the encouragement of present and future scientists were deemed essential.[118]

In 1945 Vannevar Bush, the director of the Office of Scientific Research and Development, issued his study, *Science, The Endless Frontier,* as a report to the president on a program for postwar scientific research. Bush analyzed the nation's manpower and the country's basic scientific needs in time of peace; he urged the creation of a national research foundation.[119]

Both studies led to the introduction of legislation for a national science foundation, and hearings commenced in early 1945. The Senate hearings found about one hundred scientific and educational leaders almost unanimous in their support for a foundation.[120] However, between 1945 and 1950, when the National

Science Foundation Act was enacted, much debate arose as to the justification for such a legislation. Few questioned the major purposes of the proposed act as support for basic scientific research, the promotion of manpower talent through scholarships and fellowships, and the dissemination of scientific information. But disagreements as to the structure and control of the foundation, policy for patents, and the addition of study in the social sciences as well, caused delay in legislative action. When a bill was passed in 1947, President Harry S Truman felt obliged to exercise his veto because of the objections to the administrative structure of the foundation.[121] When differences were finally resolved in the spring of 1950, Congress passed the National Science Foundation Act with the president's approval.

Viewing the intimate connection between science and national welfare, the foundation's goals were "to promote the progress of science; to advance the national health, prosperity, and welfare; to secure the national defense; and for other purposes." Pertaining to education, the foundation's goal was specifically "to develop and encourage the pursuit of a national policy for the promotion of basic research and education in sciences; to initiate and support basic and scientific research in the mathematical, physical, medical, biological, engineering, and other sciences . . . [and] to award . . . scholarships and graduate fellowships" in the above-mentioned fields. As the first of these educational functions was open to broad interpretation, legislators sought to make "explicit the foundation's authority to support programs designed to stimulate improved scientific teaching and to encourage the undertaking of careers in science."[122] Therefore in 1959, an amendment to the act of 1950 was incorporated which called for support of "programs to strengthen scientific research potential . . . by making contracts and other arrangements . . . to support such scientific activities."[123]

A National Science Board with a director and twenty-four members was placed in charge of the foundation. The foundation was looked upon by Congress as an independent agency in the executive branch. The board was given authority over all policy decisions and approval of all grants and contracts, and further empowered to create whatever divisions, commissions, and advisory groups were required to execute the purposes of the foundation. Education in the sciences, engineering, and mathematics have been strengthened by fellowship programs, research participation programs for under-

graduates, summer programs for secondary school students, in cooperation with science departments of colleges and universities,
postdoctoral fellowships, summer traineeships for graduate teaching assistants, and grants for independent research.[124]

The National Defense Education Act of 1958 directed the National Science Foundation to establish a Science Information Service
in order to provide, or arrange for the provision of, indexing, ab-
stracting, translation, and other services leading to a more effective
dissemination of scientific information, and to undertake programs
to develop new or improved methods, including mechanized systems, for making scientific information available.[125]

NATIONAL SEA GRANT COLLEGE AND PROGRAM ACT

In 1966, Congress placed under the National Science Foundation the administration of the provisions of the National Sea Grant
College and Program Act of 1966. A national council on marine
resources and engineering development would advise and provide
policy guidance to the foundation in regard to this act. No specific
educational institution was to be established, but any public or
private institution which had major programs devoted to increasing
the country's utilization of the world marine resources could get aid
for programs or research for this purpose. Congress was authorized
to appropriate as much as $5 million for 1967 and $15 million for
1968; subsequent yearly appropriations depended on the sums that
Congress would specifically authorize. Thus, in encouraging scientific endeavors in oceanography and oceanology, and developing,
conserving, and utilizing the physical, chemical, geological, and
biological resources of the nation's seas, oceans, and lakes, the act
sought to regard aquaculture, as well as agriculture on land, as a
means to benefit substantially "the United States, and people of the
world, by providing greater economic opportunities, including expanded employment and commerce; the enjoyment and use of our
marine resources; new sources of food; and new means for the
development of marine resources."[126] In 1973 Congress extended
this act with increased appropriations.[127]

NATIONAL FOUNDATION ON THE ARTS AND THE HUMANITIES ACT

Many educators objected to the overemphasis being given to science by the federal government, and urged similar support for the arts and the humanities. Thus, the National Foundation on the Arts and the Humanities Act was passed in 1965, patterned after the very successful National Science Foundation Act of 1950. Educators were glad to hear, in the words of the 1965 act, "that the encouragement and support of national progress and scholarship in the humanities . . . is also an appropriate matter of concern to the Federal Government . . . that a high civilization must not limit its efforts to science and technology alone but must give full value and support to the other great branches of man's scholarly and cultural activity . . . that democracy . . . foster and support a form of education designed to make men masters of their technology and not its unthinking servant . . . it is necessary and appropriate for the Federal Government to help create and sustain not only a climate encouraging freedom of thought, imagination, and inquiry but also the material conditions facilitating the release of this creative talent."[128]

A federal council on the arts and the humanities would be set up to ensure coordination between the National Endowment for the Arts and the National Endowment for the Humanities, each foundation having its own council to advise on policies and programs and review applications for financial assistance. The arts endowment would provide matching grants to nonprofit organizations, to state and other public organizations, and to individuals involved in the creative and performing arts for artistic activity, including the construction of facilities. States would be provided special grants to support such organizations within their own states. States having no arts council could receive a $25,000 grant for the purpose of establishing arts councils. The humanities endowment would provide for nonmatching grants and loans for research, award fellowships and grants to institutions or individuals for training, the publication of scholarly works, the interchange of information, and the fostering of understanding and appreciation of the humanities. Both endowments would be authorized to receive annual appropriations of $5 million from 1966 to 1968. Within this three-year period the Office of Education would also be authorized to distribute $500,000 to state and local educational agencies for loans to private elementary and secondary schools. This could be used for purchasing equipment and for minor remodeling related to the arts and humanities. Likewise, a sum of $500,000 could be used for training institutes to strengthen the teaching of the arts and humanities in elementary and secondary schools.[129] The act was amended on June 18, 1968, to delineate the manner of payments to states and again on October 16, 1968, by continuing the appropriations to both endowments.[130]

NATIONAL DEFENSE EDUCATION ACT

The successful launching of Russia's *Sputnik* in 1957 created an almost quasi-hysterical situation in American education. That the United States could not be first in the launching of a satellite into space was largely due, according to many critics, to the inability of American science education to keep pace with Russian science education. But *Sputnik* should be considered more of a catalyst, since some of the provisions of the National Defense Education Act (NDEA) had been suggested long before the Russian scientific achievement.[131] The 1955 White House Conference on Education, suggested by President Eisenhower in his state of the union message on January 7, 1954, and the cost of which was defrayed by congressional passage of Public Law 530, had highlighted some of these problems in education and had recommended federal assistance to the states.[132] The report of the committee for the conference had emphasized: "The schools have fallen far behind both the aspirations of the American people and their capabilities."[133]

However, the impact of *Sputnik* can be seen in the passage of the National Defense Education Act in 1958 which declared the existence of an "educational emergency." It stated: "To meet the present emergency requires additional effort at all levels of government. It is therefore the purpose of this Act to provide substantial assistance in various forms to individuals, and to States and their subdivisions, to insure trained manpower of sufficient quality and quantity to meet the national defense of the United States."[134] Accordingly, Congress made available $900 million in a four-year period "to education for programs which are important to our defense." Specifically to be expanded and improved on were the equipping and remodeling of classrooms and laboratories in science, mathematics, and foreign languages. Guidance and counseling services were to be improved, and student loans for colleges were to be made more easily available. Provision was made for private nonprofit elementary and secondary schools to obtain low-interest loans to strengthen instruction by purchasing equipment and materials, equipping science laboratories, and installing language laboratories; testing programs were to be made available to students in nonpublic secondary schools. A brief summary of the provisions of NDEA follows title by title:

I Although the federal government provides "substantial assistance," federal control of curriculum programs of instruction, administration, or school personnel under NDEA programs is prohibited.

II Provides long-term, low-interest loans to college students, with up to 50 percent cancellation of loans to students who opt to teach in public elementary and secondary schools.

III Strengthens instruction in science, mathematics, and modern foreign languages by providing laboratory equipment, audio-visual materials, minor remodeling of facilities, and state supervisory services.

IV Offers graduate fellowships for earning doctorates to those interested in a teaching career in institutions of higher education.

V Authorizes grants to state educational agencies to establish and maintain guidance, counseling and testing programs in secondary schools, and grants to present and future counselors for study in guidance institutes operated by colleges and universities.

VI Seeks improvement and extension of instruction in modern foreign languages at all educational levels through language and area centers, fellowships, research, and studies.

VII Provides a two-year program for the acquisition of data in reference to the utilization of and the means of disseminating knowledge about the educational use of communications media, such as television, radio, motion pictures and related media, and printed and published materials.

VIII Amends and makes permanent the George-Barden Act by authorizing $15 million a year to train highly skilled technicians for occupations requiring scientific knowledge; the states, however, must match federal funds.

IX   Authorizes the National Science Foundation to establish a Science Information Service and a Science Information Council.

X   Allots grants to states (up to $50,000 a year if matched by state funds) for improving statistics on education.[135]

After NDEA became effective, opposition arose over the provision requiring the signing of a "loyalty oath" by students requesting college loans under Title II. Some colleges and universities would not cooperate with the loan program unless this section of the act was repealed; over fifty higher educational institutions formally protested against it while following its requirements.[136] On January 29, 1959, Senators John F. Kennedy and Joseph Clark introduced a bill that would repeal this controversial section of NDEA. Kennedy regarded the affidavit condition to receiving funds as "an insupportable invasion of educational autonomy, which has grave implications for the integrity of our educational system."[137] Although the bill was reported favorably after committee hearings, the Senate voted to recommit it.

In January, 1960, Senators Kennedy and Clark again introduced a similar bill, calling this time only for the repeal of the affidavit requirement, but not the oath of allegiance.[138] Kennedy pointed out that the non-Communist affidavit was unnecessary because the oath of allegiance affirmed the student's loyalty; a Communist would have no scruples about signing any document, thus the provision would not ensure its desired effect. The affidavit also invited opposition from some outstanding universities and rendered a discriminatory aspect to education, since other recipients of government funds—such as farmers, businessmen, veterans—were not compelled to sign an affidavit. Although the bill was passed by the Senate with amendments, the House took no action.

As president, Kennedy had the opportunity to sign a bill he had worked for as a legislator. On October 16, 1962, P.L. 87–835 was enacted into law; it repealed the disclaimer affidavit provision in both the National Defense Education Act of 1958 and the National Science Foundation Act of 1950. The oath of allegiance was maintained, but it was considered a crime for a member of a Communist organization even to apply for a loan or fellowship under either act and it required an applicant's disclosure of any criminal record.[139]

Commissioner of Education Lawrence G. Derthick rendered a favorable report after the first year of NDEA in operation:

> The several programs . . . offer a challenging opportunity to share the responsibility and creative cooperation among public and private agencies, individuals and institutions. The provisions of the Act are of such scope that the positive effects upon education in America will greatly surpass the immediate defense objectives and thereby strengthen and enrich our educational and cultural heritage.[140]

Derthick's successor, Sterling M. McMurrin, also concluded favorably as to the act's scope and purpose and saw in NDEA a partnership "in which the Federal Government assists state educational agencies and institutions of higher education with programs —pioneering new ones as well as strengthening existing ones . . . The Office [of Education] has continued to operate in a spirit of leadership without domination and assistance without interference."[141]

The promotion of scientific research was further encouraged on September 6, 1958, by the enactment of an act "to authorize the expenditure of funds through grants for support of scientific research, and for other purposes." The act provided that the head of any agency of the federal government could enter into contracts for basic scientific research at nonprofit institutions of higher education or at nonprofit organizations whose primary purpose is the conduct of scientific research. Government heads thereby received discretionary authority to enter into contracts or award grants for basic or applied scientific research; the use of funds for this purpose would have to be reported to appropriate committees of both houses of Congress.[142]

The overall qualitative improvement in education resulting from NDEA led to its extension in 1964 with amendments, the more important of which included: the addition of English, reading, history, geography, methods of teaching disadvantaged youth, and educational media to the existing curriculum of mathematics, foreign languages, and sciences; the expansion of guidance, counseling, and testing programs; the liberalization of loans to college students, including those attending foreign universities; and the inclusion of teachers in armed forces schools in the special repayment feature for teachers.[143]

Title IV, Part D, of the Higher Education Act of 1965 provided further amendments to NDEA, as did also the higher education amendments of 1966 and 1968.[144] The International Education Act of 1966 extended the provisions for the study of modern foreign languages and of international affairs.[145]

HIGHER EDUCATION FACILITIES ACT OF 1963

In campaigning for the presidency in 1960, John F. Kennedy stressed the need for federal aid for more facilities in higher education: "On the college level, our need for new buildings in the next ten years will equal all the structures built on all United States campuses since the American Revolution. By a system of loans and matching grants, not only dormitory facilities, but laboratories must be provided."[146] As president, Kennedy asserted in his first state of the union message on January 30, 1961, that "The war babies of the 1940s, who overcrowded our schools in the 1950s, are now descending in the 1960s upon our colleges—with two college students for every one, ten years from now—and our colleges are ill prepared. . . . One-third of our most promising high school graduates are financially unable to continue the development of their talents. . . . Federal grants for higher education can no longer be delayed."[147]

On February 20, 1961, President Kennedy submitted his special message on education to Congress. In addition to his recommendations for vocational education and assistance to public elementary and secondary schools, he urged passage of legislation that would: (1) extend the already existing college housing loan program with a five-year, $250 million-a-year program for residential housing for students and faculty; (2) establish long-term, low-interest loans for five years to assist in the construction, as well as renovation, rehabilitation, and modernization, of classrooms, laboratories, libraries, and other educational facilities; and (3) establish a five-year program with an initial authorization of $26,250,000 for state-administered scholarships for talented and needy young people as a supplement to existing financial assistance programs.[148]

On March 7, 1961, Kennedy sent to the presiding officers of

Congress an administration bill for higher education construction and college housing which he deemed necessary "to relieve both the students and the universities from impossible financial burdens."[149] Among the many supporters of the higher education bill was the American Council on Education, which offered numerous recommendations similar to Kennedy's for strengthening federal aid in higher education.[150] Following congressional hearings, the House version of the bill provided grants and loans for the construction of academic facilities, and the Senate version, loan assistance for construction and aid for public junior colleges; both branches recommended scholarship aid. On July 18, the House Rules Committee, however, refused to act on all education legislation during the first session. That was the end of Kennedy's higher education bill for 1961.[151]

On January 11, 1962, Kennedy's second state of the union address again stressed the need for higher education legislation.[152] And in his second education message to Congress he urged: "We must find the means for financing education—another $20 billion a year for expansion and improvement—particularly in facilities and instruction which must be of the highest quality if our nation is to achieve its highest goal."[153] The different versions approved by the House and Senate in 1961 became the basis for 1962 congressional action and were forwarded to a conference committee of both branches. The House rejected the conference report largely because of the nonreimbursable aspect of some student scholarships and the distinction between grants and loans for both public and private colleges. A bill for higher education was again defeated.

In his third special message on education to Congress on January 29, 1963, Kennedy charged that the federal government had not met its responsibilities to education and proposed a comprehensive program in an omnibus bill entitled the National Education Improvement Act of 1963, covering all aspects of education on every level.[154] Congress, however, was not enthusiastic about the Kennedy omnibus approach. Although hearings were held, the bill was at a standstill until May, when Adam Clayton Powell, chairman of the House Education and Labor Committee, announced that his committee would consider the bill in categories, one of which would be higher education; the House college bill achieved passage on August 14. The Senate, deciding to concentrate also on separate education bills, passed its own on October 21. Disputes over the vocational education bill were used by senators in the conference committee to stall agreement on the higher education bill in early November.[155] Upon his succession to the presidency in late November, Lyndon B. Johnson obtained compromises on the disputed aspects of both bills, and on December 16, 1963, he signed into law the Higher Education Facilities Act.[156]

The 1963 act is divided into four titles. Title I establishes a five-year program of grants for the construction of undergraduate academic facilities, beginning with the sum of $230 million for the 1964 to 1967 fiscal years, with Congress determining the appropriations thereafter. Of these funds, 22 percent must be allotted to the states for public community colleges and public technical institutes, on an allotment ratio determined by the number of high school graduates and the income per person in each state. Provisions are also included for nonpublic community colleges and technical institutes from state funds, but grants for these institutions would be limited only to structures designed for instruction or research in the natural or physical sciences, mathematics, modern foreign languages, and engineering, or for use as a library. The law delineated the procedures for a state's participation by establishing a state commission which recommends all plans for approval by the U.S. commissioner of education.

Title II provides grants for the construction of graduate academic facilities, beginning with the sum of $25 million for 1964, $60 million from 1965 to 1967, with subsequent appropriations to be determined by Congress. The federal share of graduate facilities shall not, however, exceed one-third of the development cost of any construction project.

Title III provides for loans for the construction of academic facilities, with no state receiving more than 12.5 percent of the total funds provided. For 1964 to 1966 inclusive, the sum of $120 million was appropriated for such loans; after 1967 Congress was to determine the sum that could be authorized. Not less than one-fourth of a facility's development cost is to be financed from nonfederal sources; elaborate and extravagant designs and materials must be avoided. All loans whose interest rate approximate 3⅝ percent (according to the calculation suggested in the act), are to be repaid in a period of no more than fifty years.

Title IV, entitled "General Provisions," defines the terms used within the act. Of importance are certain exclusions from the act, such as athletic or recreational activities; medical and related public health activities (which are covered by the Public Health Service Act); and facilities to be used for sectarian instruction or religious worship, or programs for training ministers of religion or teachers of theology. The federal government was to maintain an interest in these facilities for a period of twenty years after completion of their construction. The *Tilton* decision of 1971 declared this provision of the act (Section 404) unconstitutional and in violation of the establishment of religion clause of the First Amendment. It removed the twenty-year limit as to the use of federally constructed academic facilities, thus ensuring no religious use of them.[157]

The act was well received by leaders in higher education. It met the pressing need for more facilities and made possible a college education for students who would have been denied such an opportunity because of lack of facilities.[158] The American Library Association especially noted the assistance the act afforded college libraries.[159] The *Christian Century* praised the overall purposes of the act but regretted the giving of aid to religious institutions, as it weakened the wall of separation between the church and the state.[160]

HIGHER EDUCATION ACT OF 1965

The Higher Education Facilities Act of 1963 was basically a "bricks and mortar" act: it had met the desperate need for improving and expanding the facilities necessitated by increasing enrollments. President Johnson viewed education as a part of his hope to create "the Great Society," and he declared in his state of the union message on January 4, 1965, that "every child must have the best education that this nation can provide. . . . For the college years we will provide scholarships to high school students of the greatest promise and greatest need and guaranteed low interest loans to students continuing their college studies."[161] On January 12, 1965, in an education message to Congress, he elaborated: "Over 100,000 of our brightest high school graduates each year will not go to college—and many others will leave college—if the opportunity for higher education is not expanded." He singled out the achievements of the 88th Congress in providing legislation for badly needed facilities in higher education, as well as the availability of more loans, but he urged the extension of "the commitment still further" so that "every child must be encouraged to get as much education as he has the ability to take. . . . Higher education is no longer a luxury, but a necessity." He, therefore, sought to extend the opportunity for higher education more broadly among lower- and middle-income families by expanding programs of scholarships and work-study for college students. In addition, he recommended aid to smaller and less developed colleges, more support for college library resources and university extension programs concentrating on problems of the community, and special manpower needs for more professional librarians and teachers for handicapped children.[162]

Congresswoman Edith Green introduced into the House Johnson's proposals for higher education as did Senator Wayne Morse in the Senate. The House passed the bill by a 367 to 22 vote on August 26, and the Senate by a 79 to 3 vote on September 2, 1965.[163] President Johnson issued special statements of approval on the action of each house.[164] The versions went to a conference committee which resolved the differences, such as length of time—three or five years—for authorization for most of the programs; specifics as to the creation of a national teachers corps; and distinctions between fellowships, direct scholarships, and educational opportunity grants. On October 20, 1965, the Senate unanimously, and the House by a vote of 313 to 63, adopted the conference committee's report. President Johnson signed the bill at his alma mater, Southwest Texas State College, on November 8, 1965, and noted that "this bill that I am signing will help our colleges and our universities add grasp to their reach for new knowledge and enlightment. . . . From this act will come a new partnership between campus and community, turning ivory towers of learning into the allies of a better life in our cities. . . . It insures that college and university libraries will no longer be the anemic stepchildren of federal assistance."[165]

Title I of the Higher Education Act of 1965[166] calls for the enlargement of community service and continuing education programs, and appropriated for this purpose $25 million for fiscal year 1966, $50 million for 1967 and 1968, with Congress to determine subsequent appropriations. Thus, the partnership of educational institutions enable them "to assist in the solution of community problems such as housing, poverty, government, recreation, employment, youth opportunities, transportation, health, and land use." A state desiring federal funds would have to designate an agency to ensure the carrying out of the purposes of the act. A national advisory council on extension and continuing education, appointed by the president, would be set up to advise the commissioner of education on general regulations and policies regarding administration of this title and guidelines for approving state plans.

Title II provides grants for library materials, for which $50 million was appropriated for 1966, and $15 million for the training of library personnel. Library materials include not only books but periodicals, documents, magnetic tapes, phonograph records, audiovisual materials, and even necessary binding. Small and poorly supported colleges could receive double or triple the funds available for library development. Institutions must, however, continue to maintain library expenditures from its own funds and match federal funds on a one-to-one basis. Although the maximum annual basic grant to each institution would be $5,000, supplemental grants not exceeding $10 per full-time student can be awarded for additional library resources. The commissioner of education must set up an advisory council on college library resources to set forth criteria for establishing the supplemental grants. The second part of this title, recognizing the need for more and better trained librarians, authorizes grants for training in all aspects of librarianship.

Title III encourages the strengthening of developing institutions, which are usually small colleges hampered by lack of finance and are struggling to survive. Up to $55 million were appropriated to these institutions in 1966, 78 percent for four-year, and 22 percent to two-year, colleges. Accreditation or reasonable progress toward it is required. National teaching fellowships are offered to encourage highly qualified graduate students and junior faculty members of larger colleges and universities to teach at developing institutions. An advisory council on developing institutions would be established in the Office of Education with the commissioner as chairman to carry out the provisions of this title.

Provisions for student assistance are made in Title IV through educational opportunity grants, federally subsidized loans, and work-study programs. The amount of $70 million was appropriated from 1966 to 1969, and authorization for further appropriations left to the discretion of Congress. The first-year grants ranged from $200 to $800, with an equal amount provided from the institution's loan and scholarship funds, including NDEA loans and state or private financial aid programs. A student ranking in the upper half of his class for his remaining three years in college can have his amount increased by as much as $200. In addition to grants, the title also provides for federally subsidized loans to college students of up to $1,500. These low-interest insured loans do not have to be repaid until five or ten years after graduation, with payments beginning nine months after graduation. The work-study program inaugurated under the Economic Opportunity Act of 1964 was transferred to the office of the commissioner of education. Although preference is to be granted to students from low-income families, the act seeks to promote part-time employment of students in need of earnings to pursue higher education. The NDEA of 1958 was amended to include nonaccredited colleges working satisfactorily towards accreditation; make loan adjustments for part-time students; increase the loan cancellation for teachers from 10 to 15 percent for each complete academic year; add economics to subjects of instruction receiving financial assistance; and establish institutes to improve the teaching, and supervision of the training, of teachers of economics, civics, and industrial arts.

Besides establishing an Advisory Council on Quality Teacher Preparation in the Office of Education to review all federal assistance programs involving teacher training, Title V creates a National Teacher Corps. Appropriations of $36 million for 1966 and $64,715,000 for 1967 were authorized to encourage the training of teachers for children in areas with a concentration of low-income families. Both experienced and inexperienced teacher-interns possessing a bachelor's degree can be included in this special program for a period of two years, within which time a master's degree can be earned. Additionally, fellowships are authorized to institutions of teacher-training for interested and for potential teachers on a graduate level in preparation for careers in elementary and secondary education.

Title VI provides financial assistance for the improvement of undergraduate instruction by the purchase of teaching equipment and the minor remodeling of facilities. Grants of $145 million were authorized for fiscal years 1966 to 1968. Federal grants must be matched, however, with an equal amount by the institution. Faculty development programs in the use of specialized educational media through workshops and institutes were encouraged by $5 million appropriations for 1966 to 1968, with Congress deciding the sums to be appropriated for 1969 and 1970.

Title VII contains amendments to the Higher Education Facilities Act of 1963. Restrictions on the use of grants to only certain academic facilities were removed. Appropriations for certain titles were increased and extended for more years. Title VIII clarifies certain definitions, specifies method of payment, and insures against federal control of education.

The *Journal of Higher Education* regarded the act as "a measure of very great importance" with its provisions touching every college and university in America and enlarging educational opportunity for many.[167] The American Association of University Professors' organ praised the significant improvements the act could make in higher education but noted that the nature of the improvement for many programs would depend upon the funds made available to implement the bill's provisions.[168]

HIGHER EDUCATION AMENDMENTS OF 1966

On November 3, 1966, Congress passed the higher education amendments of 1966, amending the Higher Education Facilities Act of 1963, the Higher Education Act of 1965, and the National Defense Education Act of 1958. The main features of these amendments were: extension of the grants for construction of undergraduate academic facilities; modification of allotments to the states for providing academic facilities for public community colleges and technical institutes; extension of grants and increase of appropriations for the construction of graduate academic facilities; extension of the amount of loans available for the construction of academic facilities; the requirement that federal funds granted under the Higher Education Facilities Act of 1963 be used to comply with standards devised by the secretary of health, education, and welfare for facilities "accessible to and usable by handicapped persons"; authorization to the District of Columbia to establish a loan insurance program; and provision for loan cancellation for those teaching handicapped children.[169]

EDUCATION PROFESSIONS DEVELOPMENT ACT

On June 29, 1967, Congress enacted the Education Professions Development Act to amend and extend Title V of the Higher Education Act of 1965.[170] The purpose of this act is to improve the quality of teaching and to help meet critical shortages of adequately trained personnel by (1) developing information on the actual needs for educational personnel, both present and long range; (2) providing a broad range of high quality training and retraining opportunities, in response to changing manpower needs; (3) attracting a greater number of qualified persons into the teaching profession; (4) attracting persons who can stimulate creativity in the arts and other skills to undertake short-term or long-term assignments in education; and (5) helping to make educational personnel training programs more responsive to the needs of the schools and colleges.[171]

The act calls for a national advisory council on education professions development, appointed by the president, for the purpose of reviewing the operation of this title and of all federal programs related to the training and developing of educational personnel, and for advising the secretary of health, education, and welfare and the commissioner of education on policy matters pertaining to the administration of this title.[172]

A means of attracting young people to the field of education adopted in 1965 was extended and is now known simply as the Teacher Corps instead of National Teacher Corps. The appropriations for this program were increased from the original $36 million in 1966, rising annually up to $56 million in 1970. The provisions for the Teacher Corps remain substantially the same as in the 1965 act.[173]

An endeavor to attract and qualify teachers to meet critical teacher shortages became a new addition to the 1965 act. A program was called for whereby the commissioner of education could award grants to states to enable them to support efforts of local communities experiencing critical teacher shortages. These grants would attract to the field of teaching those persons in the community who have been otherwise engaged, and provide them, through short-term intensive training programs and subsequent in-service training, with the qualifications necessary for a successful career in teaching, and also obtain the services of teacher aides who would be provided with the necessary training to increase the effectiveness of classroom teachers. The sums of $50 million for 1969 and $65 million for 1970 were authorized to states offering plans to participate in this program.[174]

The 1965 Teacher Fellowship Program for Elementary and

Secondary Education was extended and the 1967 act includes graduate education fellowships for preschool and adult and vocational education personnel. Fellowships may be granted for up to $2,500 per academic year for tuition and nonrefundable fees.[175] Advanced training and retraining of teachers other than in higher education are encouraged by grants to, and contracts with, colleges and universities in cooperation with state and local educational agencies. Special emphasis is suggested for programs and projects which meet the needs of the socially, culturally, and economically disadvantaged, special education for the handicapped, the needs of exceptionally gifted students, and the preparation of craftsmen and homemakers to teach or assist in teaching vocational subjects.[176] Colleges and universities can receive federal funds for programs seeking to train persons who have, or are preparing to undertake, teaching or administrative responsibilities in institutions of higher education, or the responsibilities of an educational specialist in such institutions.[177]

HIGHER EDUCATION AMENDMENTS OF 1968

On October 16, 1968, Congress passed the higher education amendments of 1968, amending the Higher Education Act of 1965, the National Defense Education Act of 1958, the National Vocational Student Loan Insurance Act of 1965, and the Higher Education Facilities Act of 1963.[178] Five titles comprised this act seeking to update and revise previous legislation concerning higher education: Title I–student assistance; Title II–amendments to other provisions of the Higher Education Act of 1965; Title III–amendments to other provisions of the National Defense Education Act of 1958; Title IV–amendments to Higher Educational Facilities Act of 1963; and Title V–miscellaneous.

Student assistance was a major concern of Congress, as student costs at both public and private colleges had been constantly increasing. The educational opportunity grant program begun in 1965 was extended and annual appropriations were increased 40 percent. The maximum amount of an educational opportunity grant was placed at $1,000, which could include any compensation paid under a work-study program.[179] Grants to and contracts with educational agencies could be made for three special programs: (1) "Talent Search" programs, designed to identify and to encourage qualified youths of financial or cultural need with an exceptional potential for post high school training and education; (2) "Upward Bound" programs, designed to generate skills and motivation necessary for educational success beyond school for students who come from low-income backgrounds and who may have an inadequate high school preparation for further training and education; and (3) "Special Services for Disadvantaged Students," designed for students with a deprived educational, cultural, or economic background, or physical handicap, and who could receive remedial, counseling, and career guidance services for developing academic potential to continue or enter higher education programs. Similar provisions contained in the Economic Opportunity Act of 1964 would be transferred to the office of the commissioner of education.[180]

The insured student loan program under the Higher Education Act of 1965 was extended and nonfederally insured loans for higher education were to be guaranteed by the federal government. The federal government would continue to pay interest charges on loans to students who were still in college, provided the adjusted annual gross income of their families was below $15,000. Death or permanent disability exempted an individual or family from loan repayment. The maximum permissible interest rate was raised to 7 percent. The National Vocational Student Loan Insurance Act and Higher Education Act loans were merged into one program and a set of uniform standards established for maximum size of loans and for the terms of repayment as a means of simplifying administrative procedures. Loan payment may now be deferred while students are in the military service, VISTA, or Peace Corps service. Special arrangements are made for students who cannot qualify for state loan programs because of state residency requirements.[181]

The Work-Study Program, inaugurated under the Economic Opportunity Act of 1964, was transferred to the Higher Education Act of 1965 with increased appropriations. Students in postsecondary vocational institutions are now eligible to participate in such a program, for which the federal government's share may not exceed 80 percent of a student's compensation. The forty hours per week maximum applies only to those weeks when the student is enrolled in regular classes. A college may receive as much as $75,000 a year for up to three years to plan and develop cooperative education programs whereby students can alternate between full-time study and full-time employment.[182]

The cancellation provision in NDEA for teachers of up to 50 percent of their loans was extended to 1970. The cancellation privelege was also applied to teachers in low-income schools, but in this latter case up to as much as 100 percent of their loans. A low-income school would be defined as any school in any state where more than 50 percent of the students come from families whose income is less than $3,000 per year.[183]

Title II contains a number of amendments to other provisions of the 1965 Higher Education Act. The federal government will share the cost of community service programs sponsored by higher educational institutions for up to 66 ⅔ percent of the costs. The college library assistance and library training and research programs were extended and now include branch institutions located in different communities (a matter of special help to statewide college systems). The share of funds for junior colleges was increased to 23 percent. Retired professors from regular colleges and universities would become eligible for grants if they were willing to apply their expertise to developing institutions. The Education Professions Development Act was extended, and state education agencies could receive funds for recruiting teachers and teacher aides. School administrators could receive fellowships of up to $3,500 per year in pursuing programs under the Education Professions Development Act. Institutions could enter into cooperative programs and still apply for single equipment and materials in consultation with the National Science Foundation.[184]

A new concept of cooperation was introduced for higher education by the expression "networks of knowledge." Colleges and universities were encouraged "to share to an optimal extent, through cooperative arrangements, their technical and other educational and administrative facilities and resources" such as faculties, library collections, scientific equipment, closed-circuit television or equivalent transmission facilities, and electronic computer materials and equipment.[185]

Education in public service to prepare students for entrance into state, local, or federal governments received prominent attention. Higher education institutions could receive grants and contracts for developing or expanding such programs, including the training and retraining of faculty. Fellowships of up to three years of study in public service graduate programs were established. The improvement of graduate programs in all areas other than medical was encouraged by appropriations and grants applicable for strengthening faculties, acquiring equipment and materials, and improving graduate school administration. Law schools could receive as much as 90 percent of costs for establishing clinical experience programs for students of law. Preference was given to programs that provide actual experience in preparation for and trial of cases.[186]

NDEA's program for equipment and materials for elementary and secondary education was extended, including equipment for the needs of educationally deprived children. Nonpublic school children must receive an equitable share of the benefits of equipment purchased. A new set of rules was set up for grant application of local educational agencies desiring to participate in a better equalization of funds both within and among the states.[187] The NDEA fellowship program continues to authorize seventy-five hundred new fellowships a year, with the length increased from three to four years. A more equitable distribution of these fellowships is sought for areas of the nation in need of more highly qualified persons to teach in higher education institutions. Both short-term training programs for guidance counselors and language development programs are to be continued.[188]

Amendments to the Higher Education Facilities Education Act of 1963 include: the broadening of eligibility criteria for construction grants not only to schools with expanding enrollments, but also to schools with enrollments that would decrease if construction were not permitted; eligibility of student health facilities to receive grants up to 50 per cent of construction costs; and annual interest grants to help cover the cost of nonfederal financing of construction.[189]

A significant, and possibly debatable, provision concerns eligibility for student assistance. Students involved in campus disturbances which "prevent officials or students from engaging in their duties or pursuing their studies" must be denied federal assistance. Notice and opportunity for a hearing must be given to a student and his participation must have been of a "serious nature" and contributing to "substantial disruption" of the administration of the educational institution.[190]

EMERGENCY INSURED STUDENT LOAN ACT

In 1969 Congress enacted the Emergency Insured Student Loan Act to be made part of Title IV–B of the Higher Education Act of 1965. Congress felt it necessary, because of economic conditions, to ensure that students would have reasonable access to loans for financing their education and, therefore, permitted incentive payments on insured student loans. However, Congress would not extend any payments to lending institutions that discriminate against particular classes or categories of students on the basis of sex, color, creed, or national origin.[191] This act was extended by the education amendments of 1972.[192]

EDUCATION AMENDMENTS OF 1972

Some two-thirds of the education amendments of 1972 enacted by Congress on June 23, 1972, deal with higher education. Practically all programs initiated under the Higher Education Act of 1965 and subsequent amendments were continued, with increased appropriations until the fiscal year ending June 30, 1975. A few new programs and sections have been added by these 1972 amendments.

The community service and continuing education programs previously established were continued with increased appropriations. A new section was added to these entitled "Special Programs and Projects Relating to National and Regional Problems." Grants to and contracts with institutions of higher education can be made by the commissioner of education to carry out programs and projects designed to seek solutions to national and regional problems related to technological and social changes and environmental pollution.[193]

The college library programs begun in 1965 and amended in 1968 were continued. Increased funds are available for the acquisition of library resources and encouraging research and training persons in librarianship. Grants are now included for law library resources and law librarianships. Grants are to be continued to institutions of higher education and library organizations or agencies for fellowships and traineeships with stipends.[194]

The strengthening of developing institutions was again emphasized. Previously established programs and projects were continued with increased appropriations. Of special concern in this section is the provision of emergency assistance for institutions of higher education. The nature of the assistance is "to enable them to determine the nature and causes of such (financial) distress and the means by which such distress may be alleviated, and to improve their capabilities for dealing with financial problems using, to the extent appropriate, assistance authorized under the Higher Education Act of 1965 and all other sources of financial assistance." Grants for this type of assistance are available to both public and private institutions and express the concern of the Congress not only for the continuance of an institution, but also any substantial curtailment of its academic program to the detriment of the quality of education available to students.[195]

The previously established student aid programs of grants, work-study, and subsidized loans were retained. A major change in student assistance programs was the addition of a program of Basic Educational Opportunity Grants. This new program was intended to guarantee a minimum amount of resources for every needy student who wished to continue into postsecondary education. These grants provide up to $1,400 per year; however, no grant may be more than half the cost of attending the particular institution where the student is enrolled or more than the difference between that cost and the expected family contribution, whichever is less. Funds from these grants are channeled directly to students rather than to or through the institutions. Furthermore, aid is targeted to low-income students, especially those from disadvantaged families. The programs "Talent Search" and "Upward Bound" were continued.[196]

A further strengthening of student assistance was made by the creation of the Student Loan Marketing Association. Previously, students could obtain a loan from a private financial institution. This loan would be protected against loss in case of the student's death, incapacity, or default by the federal government. However, despite this guarantee, many lenders often hesitated to make student loans because of the time element. No repayment was required until nine to twelve months after leaving school and further stay of the loan could be requested for three years while serving in the armed forces, Vista, or the Peace Corps. The marketing association would purchase students' notes from lenders or accept them as collateral as a means to encourage loans for students.[197]

The Education Professions Development Act of 1967 was extended and amended to include fellowships for those seeking to pursue careers in school nursing, and to include programs and projects for training teachers in education programs for children of migratory agricultural workers.[198]

Grants and loans for the construction of undergraduate and graduate academic facilities, inaugurated by the Higher Education Facilities Act of 1963, and made part of the Higher Education Act of 1965 in Title VII, were continued. Eligibility conditions, amounts, and terms of grants and loans were more clearly defined and updated.[199] Fellowship programs in graduate and professional education were also continued.[200]

A firm federal commitment was received in the 1972 act for the establishment and expansion of community colleges. A necessary prerequisite for obtaining federal assistance is for each state to develop a statewide plan for postsecondary education programs in community colleges as prescribed under Title X. Establishment and expansion grants are made to the states, as well as grants to lease facilities, for this purpose.[201] Of special importance is the interlocking of the programs of support for community colleges with the promotion of occupational education, through which the HEW secretary is to "encourage coordination." The definitions the law gives to a community college and postsecondary occupational education have significance. A community college is "any junior college, postsecondary vocational school, technical institute, or any other educational institution (which may include a four-year institution of higher education or a branch thereof)" which admits high school graduates or the equivalent, or those who are at least eighteen years old, provides a two-year postsecondary educational program leading to an associate degree or credits acceptable toward a bachelor's degree, is a public or nonprofit institution, is accredited or working for accreditation, and provides programs of postsecondary vocational, technical, occupational, and specialized education.[202] Postsecondary occupational education is defined as education, training, or retraining by a postsecondary institution that is "designed to prepare individuals for gainful employment as semiskilled or skilled workers, technicians, or subprofessionals in recognized occupations (including new and emerging occupations) or to prepare individuals for enrollment in advanced technical education programs." Specifically excluded are occupations "generally considered professional or which require a baccalaureate or advanced degree."[203] Both planning and program grants are made available for state occupational education programs. The planning grants may not be used to build or buy facilities, but may be used to remodel, renovate, or lease them. Grant-seeking state agencies involved in the planning of community colleges must include in their planning "the development of a long-range strategy for infusing occupational education . . . into elementary and secondary schools on an equal footing with traditional academic education, to the end that every child who leaves secondary school is prepared either to enter productive employment or to undertake additional education at the post-secondary level, but without being forced prematurely to make an irrevocable commitment to a particular educational or occupational choice."[204] Two new agencies within the Office of Education were created for the purpose of carrying out the 1972 act's directives pertaining to occupational education and community colleges: the Bureau of Occupational and Adult Education and the Community College Unit.[205]

In addition to the above two agencies, the 1972 act required the establishment of a state commission on postsecondary education. Such a commission was required for any state to receive federal assistance for education beyond high school. The state commission was to be composed of members representing the general public and public and private institutions of postsecondary education, which included "community colleges, junior colleges, postsecondary vocational schools, area vocational schools, technical institutes, four-year institutions of higher education and branches thereof." The state commissions were to make studies, surveys, and recommendations, or what the act generally called "comprehensive statewide planning."[206]

But statewide planning was not considered sufficient for the existing financial crisis in higher education. Congress, therefore, saw as necessary the establishment of a national commission on the financing of postsecondary education, an independent agency within the executive branch. The commission's purpose was "to give the States and the Nation the information needed to assess the dimensions of, and extent of, the financial crisis confronting the Nation's postsecondary institutions . . . [and] such study shall determine the need, desirability, the form, and the level of additional governmental and private assistance." Specifically, the commission's study was to recommend alternative models for long-range solutions to the problems of financing postsecondary education through the assessment of (1) previous related private and governmental studies and their recommendations; (2) existing state and local programs of aid; (3) the level of endowment, private sector support, and other incomes of postsecondary institutions, and the feasibility of using federal and state income tax credits for charitable contributions to postsecondary institutions; (4) the level of federal support through such programs as research grants and other general and categorical programs; (5) alternative forms of student assistance; and (6) suggested national standards for determining the annual per student costs of providing various types of postsecondary education.[207]

Congress had originally hoped for a report from the commission by April 30, 1973, but it extended the time to December 31, 1973, and the commission was to terminate on June 30, 1974. Congress reiterated the "need of indepth study" of postsecondary education and has deemed the answers to questions in regard to it "even more important."[208]

PROHIBITION OF SEX DISCRIMINATION

The education amendments of 1972 included an educational issue that was treated explicitly for the first time in federal legislation: the prohibition of sex discrimination. Title IX states: "No person in the United States shall, on the basis of sex, be excluded from participation in, be denied the benefits of, or be subjected to discrimination under any education program or activity receiving Federal financial assistance. . . ." Five exceptions were made, however. First, in regard to admissions to educational institutions, the only institutions to which the law applies are institutions of vocational education, profession education, and graduate higher education, and to public institutions of undergraduate higher education. Second, educational institutions in transition from single sex to coeducational status may have up to seven years to complete the process of transition in a plan approved by the U.S. commissioner of education. Third, institutions controlled by a religious organization are exempt if the application of the provisions of the title are inconsistent with the religious tenets of the controlling organization. Fourth, an institution whose primary purpose is the training of individuals for the military or merchant marine services of the United States is exempt. Fifth, traditionally single sex public undergraduate institutions are also exempt.[209]

Among other noteworthy provisions of Title IX are that no educational institution is prohibited from maintaining separate living facilities for the different sexes; all federal departments and agencies empowered to extend federal financial assistance to any education program or activity by grants, loans, or contracts must effectuate this title. Lack of compliance with this title can result in termination of federal assistance, with opportunity for judicial review, if desired.[210]

The passage of Title IX was in response to a growing concern over discrimination affecting women students, faculty, and administrators. The late 1960s witnessed increasing concern over discrimination of women.[211] Regarding discrimination against women in admissions a federal task force observed: "We believe it is not the case that opportunities exist for women which they simply decline to exercise. Rather, we find there are specific barriers which block their progress and which will not disappear without conscious effort."[212] The problem of discrimination against women should also be seen in the larger context of achieving the goal of equality of opportunity and the efforts of women's organizations to promote equal rights. The civil rights legislation and the federal programs for education in the 1960s were aimed at equality of opportunity. The report of the President's Commission on the Status of Women, created in 1961, with subsequent counterpart state commissions, further pointed out the inconsistencies of equal treatment of the sexes.[213] Women's academic organizations especially devoted themselves to the task of equality. Their efforts have been described as "indications . . . of the most potent forces to hit the academic world since SDS."[214]

Legislative enactments in the 1960s also took cognizance of discrimination against women. The Equal Pay Act of 1963 required that men and women doing equal work in the same establishment should receive equal pay.[215] The Civil Rights Act of 1964 contained a clause prohibiting discrimination in employment on the basis of sex, color, or national origin.[216] Women faculty members were not, however, covered by these acts.[217] Executive Order 11375, effective in October, 1968, prohibited federal contractors from discrimination in employment on the basis of sex.[218] The Department of Health, Education, and Welfare, in cooperation with the Department of Labor, applied this executive order to educational institutions holding federal government contracts.[219] HEW further announced in December, 1971, that programs for affirmative action must require educational institutions to take positive steps in the hiring of women.[220] In the light of these developments, women's academic organizations filed complaints against educational institutions and charged them with discrimination in admissions, employment, pay rates, promotion, and recruitment. By 1972, formal charges of sex discrimination were filed against 360 institutions of higher learning, including some of the most prestigious universities and college systems of four states.[221]

These developments led to the introduction of two legislative proposals prohibiting sex discrimination in higher education in the House of Representatives in 1970.[222] The proposals sought principally to prohibit discrimination on the basis of sex in any federally assisted program or activity. During June and July, 1970, hearings were held on these proposals, and documented discrimination against women in many educational matters, especially at the graduate and professional levels, were recorded.[223] No immediate legislative action followed these bills introduced in 1970. In 1971 similar proposals were again introduced in both the House and the Senate, followed by hearings.[224] When floor debate began in the Senate on August 4, 1971, on an omnibus education bill (S. 659) to be known later as the education amendments of 1971, no provision prohibiting sex discrimination in higher education was included. After repeated introductions of amendments and committee deliberations from August 7, 1971, to May 23, 1972, Title IX prohibiting sex discrimination in educational institutions became part of the legislation passed by the Senate on May 24, and by the House on June 8, as the education amendments of 1972.[225] HEW has been entrusted with issuing regulations concerning Title IX and its basic applicability to educational institutions.[226]

4

Vocational Education, Rehabilitation, and the Handicapped

SMITH-LEVER ACT AND SMITH-HUGHES ACT

One of the great benefits of the land-grant colleges and the agricultural experiment stations was the practical service they rendered to the farmer. Professor John A. Porter of Yale University had written in 1859 stressing the importance of the availability of agricultural information and of the utilization of new scientific equipment. He instituted the Yale agricultural lectures in 1860 for this purpose.[1] New ideas and suggestions were afforded the farmer by fairs and exhibits organized by state agricultural societies in cooperation with the land-grant colleges. Farm journals and bulletins were used, as well as institutes for farmers.[2] Enlargement and better organization of these activities in all states was recommended by a committee of the Association of American Agricultural Colleges and Experiment Stations at its annual conference in 1909 by calling for financial support from the federal government.[3]

Several bills were introduced in Congress with the aim of providing some kind of agricultural education for those not enrolled in formal college classes.[4] In 1914, Congress passed the Smith-Lever Act providing federal assistance to state agricultural colleges "to aid in diffusing among the people . . . useful and practical information on subjects relating to agriculture and home economics, and to encourage the application of the same" through agricultural extension work.[5] President Woodrow Wilson, who signed the measure,

96

called it "one of the most significant and far-reaching measures for the education of adults ever adopted by a Government."[6] The common working-day people could now share in the abundant research being done in the agricultural colleges and experiment stations— an advantage stemming from the legislation of the Morrill and the Hatch acts. The manner of distributing federal grants in the Smith-Lever Act differed from the earlier legislation, however, since a new policy of having the federal government match dollar for dollar state expenditures of up to $10,000 annually was adopted. The total federal expenditure of $480,000 was to be raised to $4 million through a series of annual increments, and was to be divided by the secretary of agriculture among the states in proportion of their rural population to that of the whole country; each state would still have to appropriate an amount equal to that of the federal government. Although the secretary of agriculture did exercise control over the appropriations, state officials enjoyed sufficient freedom to meet local needs. The special contribution of this act in sending teachers to the farmers was seen during World War I in the improved means of producing, conserving and distributing food, and effective measures of controlling the influenza epidemic.[7]

The Smith-Lever Act partially fulfilled the goals of agricultural and vocational education; colleges were the only educational institutions involved. Under the leadership of Senators Carrol S. Page and Hoke Smith, efforts were begun to extend federal grants to the secondary schools, not only for the specific area of agriculture, but for the whole area of vocational education, including the training of teachers for vocational subjects. What Senator Jonathan P. Dolliver had unsuccessfully sought in 1910 began to crystallize in 1913 when Congress established a federal Commission on National Aid to Vocational Education.[8] Realizing that less than 1 percent of the nation's workers had been able to acquire technical training for their jobs, the commission's report favored federal grants for vocational education for the following reasons:

(1.) There was a pressing need for vocational education.
(2.) The problem of vocational education was too extensive to be worked out except by a national agency.
(3.) The states were too poor to attempt a solution of the problem.
(4.) Federal grants would start an interest in, and stimulate

local effort in the direction of, vocational education.

(5.)   Federal grants in this case were constitutional on the basis of promoting general welfare.

(6.)   The mobility of the population, and of labor in particular, justified the application of federal resources to the problem.

(7.)   The training of teachers of vocational subjects was expensive, and teachers were migratory; both reasons justified federal aid for their training.

(8.)   A bureau should be maintained by federal appropriation to assemble and distribute information on vocational subjects.[9]

The Smith-Hughes bill was introduced in the House of Representatives on June 1, 1914, followed by the expected controversy over the possibility of a federally controlled system of education. But on the strength of the commission's report, the bill received congressional approval and was signed into law by President Wilson on February 23, 1917.[10]

The Smith-Hughes Act was by far the most comprehensive federal legislation dealing with education to date. It intended to provide for the promotion of vocational education; cooperation between the states and the trades and industries in the promotion of such education in agriculture; cooperation with the states in the preparation of teachers of vocational subjects; and the appropriation of money and the regulation of its expenditure. The salaries of teachers, supervisors, and directors of agricultural subjects would be entitled to federal grants, beginning with a total appropriation of $500,000 in 1918, and rising to $3 million by 1926. For the preparation of teachers, supervisors, and directors of both agricultural education and trade and industrial subjects, equal appropriations of $500,000 in 1918, and up to $1 million in 1921, would be allocated. As with the Smith-Lever Act, the states were to match the federal government's annual appropriation dollar for dollar. A federal Board for Vocational Education was established consisting of the secretaries of agriculture, commerce, and labor, the U.S. commissioner of education, and three appointees of the president to represent the interests of agriculture, commerce and manufacturing, and labor. The board would cooperate with the states in implementing the provisions of the bill and would conduct studies on various areas of vocational education stressed in the bill. Each state, after signifying its intent to accept the bill's provisions through its legislature, would create a board of three or more members to work with the federal board to supervise vocational education within its confines.[11] Through the Smith-Hughes Act, the federal government entered into the sphere of public vocational education below college level and in a manner of well-defined limits and restrictions as to the expenditure of federal monies. The National Resources Committee, in a report issued in 1936, considered the act one of the two federal grants-in-aid (the other being the National Guard) with the greatest degree of federal control.[12]

In 1929 the George-Reed Act granted an annual supplemental appropriation of $500,000, which was to increase to $2,500,000 by 1934, to the states and the territories of Alaska and Hawaii. Half of the money was designated for vocational education in agriculture and distributed on the basis of farm population; the other half was for vocational education in home economics and was distributed on the basis of rural population.[13] When the George-Reed Act expired in 1934, similar provisions were contained in the George-Ellzey Act, which provided an annual $3 million for three years, and included vocational education in the trades and industries to the previous act.[14]

In 1936 Congress passed the George-Deen Act, another in the series of acts continuing the Smith-Hughes Act; its annual appropriation of $14,480,000 almost doubled the amount appropriated in 1917, and widened the area of aid to vocational education by including the distributive occupations. Specifically, under the George-Deen Act, the annual appropriation would be $4 million each for agriculture, home economics, and the trades and industries; $1,200,000 for the distribution or selling occupations, including teacher education for this area; and $1 million for teacher education in the other three areas. To receive their share of federal monies, the states had to match half of their federal allotment until 1942, with increases in the matching ratios until 1947, when a state's contribution would have to equal the federal government's contribution. The proportionate amount of money to be allocated to each state was determined by the farm population for agricultural education, by rural population for home economics education, by nonfarm population for trade and industrial education, and by total population for both distributive occupational education and teacher education.[15]

In 1946 Congress enacted the George-Barden Act, also known

as the Vocational Education Act of 1946. It was meant to supersede the George-Deen Act while continuing to implement the Smith-Hughes Act by appropriating more than $28,850,000 annually for vocational education. As a result, the total annual sum for distribution in agriculture was increased to $13 million; for home economics, $8 million; for trades and industry, $8 million; and for distributive occupations, $2,500,000. No state or territory was to receive less than $15,000 annually for programs in distributive education, or less than $40,000 annually for each program in agriculture, home economics, and in trades and industry. The preparation for vocational teachers, supervisors, and directors was not specified as it was in the George-Deen Act; rather, funds for teacher training were to be included in general grants to the states for vocational education.[16] As had now become customary with the acceptance of federal funds, the states were to match them dollar for dollar; most states, however, expended more than the federal government, with a nationwide average of three times as much.[17] Although funds from the George-Barden Act were primarily designated for vocational education, the U.S. commissioner of education ruled that these funds could be utilized for certain guidance purposes, such as maintenance of a state program of supervision, reimbursement of salaries of counselor educators, research in the field of guidance, and reimbursement of salaries of local guidance supervisors and counselors.[18] The actual use of funds for vocational guidance had been recommended by the President's Advisory Committee on Education in 1936.[19] Acting upon the recommendations of this presidential committee, the Department of Labor established its Occupational Outlook Service, which was placed under the direction of the Bureau of Labor Statistics, while the U. S. Office of Education inaugurated the Occupational Information and Guidance Service, because "the vocational schools [are] vitally concerned with some kind of program of counseling and guidance, which will include as one of its major features an attack on the problems of occupational adjustment. In view of the foregoing, the Office of Education is now undertaking through cooperation with the states the promotion of a nationwide movement toward building up an effective program of occupational information and guidance."[20]

The immediate effects of the George-Barden Act were that "the availability of federal funds for the promotion and development of guidance services served to expand state guidance consultative staffs; encouraged expansion of professional opportunities in the field for counselors, administrators, and other educational personnel; led to an increased number of local guidance counselors and supervisors; and generally contributed to the improvement of guidance services at the secondary school level."[21] Even more importantly for the improvement of guidance services, this emphasis on vocational guidance came at a time when it was considered as being within the total framework of a student's personality, counseling theories were being defined, and psychologically rooted theories of vocational choice had begun to be developed.[22]

Title VIII of the National Defense Education Act in 1958 amended the George-Barden Act and made it permanent. Congress authorized $15 million a year to train highly skilled technicians for occupations requiring scientific knowledge as a means to alleviate the nation's shortage of such technicians. The states were required to match the federal government's funds and use them for programs of administration, supervision, teacher training, salaries and travel expenses of staff members of state and local educational agencies and of members of advisory committees or state boards, maintenance of instructional equipment, purchase of instructional supplies and teaching aids, transportation of students, planning and developing programs to train young persons not in school, and related apprenticeship instruction. Training could be acquired in preparatory curricula or in extension classes in secondary and postsecondary institutions which, however, had to be of less than college grade. Eligibility of applicants for such training required either completion of junior high school or being at least sixteen years old, as well as giving promise of successful completion of the desired program. Adults could be eligible if training was needed either to maintain their present jobs, advance to better jobs, or stay abreast of the latest developments in their particular fields.[23]

Agricultural extension was furthered in 1928 when Congress passed the Capper-Ketcham Act, which gave an additional $20,000 annually to each state, and a yearly sum of $500,000 to be distributed to the states in proportion to their rural population; the latter provision, however, required state matching funds.[24]

Title II of the Bankhead-Jones Act of 1935 further extended the annual appropriations for agricultural extension service by $8 million, with yearly increases of $1 million, until a total of $12 million would be reached. This act adopted a policy of appropriating federal funds that was different from the Smith-Lever and Capper-Ketcham acts: It did not require state matching funds and the distribution was to be made in proportion to the farm population instead of the rural population.[25]

In 1945 the Bankhead-Flanagan Act made more funds available for, and broadened the scope of, agricultural extension work by: (1) paying the expenses of cooperative extension work in agriculture and home economics, including technical and educational assistance to farm people in improving their standards of living; (2) developing individual farm and home plans; (3) better marketing and distribution of farm products; (4) working with rural youth in 4–H clubs and older out-of-school youths; (5) guiding farm people in improving farm and home buildings; (6) developing effective programs in canning, food preservation, and nutrition, and authorizing the necessary printing and distribution of information in connection with the foregoing. To provide for these activities, the act authorized an appropriation of $4,500,000, with two-year increments of $4 million each, until a total of $12 million would be achieved in 1948.[26]

FUTURE FARMERS OF AMERICA

On August 30, 1950, Congress passed an act to incorporate an organization to be called the Future Farmers of America. The purpose of the organization would be to create, foster, and assist chapters of students and former students of vocational agriculture in the states and territories of the country. Previously trained under the Smith-Hughes Vocational Act or the Vocational Act of 1946, these chapters would serve to foster leadership in the field of agriculture, to create more interest in the intelligent choice of farming occupations, to strengthen the confidence of farm boys and young men in themselves and their work, to encourage members in the development of individual farming programs, and to promote permanent establishment in farming. Prizes, awards, and financial assistance through loans or grants would serve to encourage deserving young farmers. The chapters would also cooperate with state boards for vocational education in securing employment. An official magazine and other publications would serve as a clearing house for information on agricultural trends and opportunities. Established as a corporation, the organization was bound by Congress with the usual restrictions placed on such bodies, especially with regard to control of and membership in the organization, and the regulations regarding the use of funds and maintenance of financial records. The corporation has a governing board chaired by the chief of the Agricultural Education Service of the Office of Education.[27]

SCIENCE CLUBS

On September 2, 1958, in response to the growing need for scientists in the country—again an influence of the Russian success with *Sputnik*—Congress appropriated $50,000 annually to enable the U.S. commissioner of education "to encourage, foster, and assist in the establishment in localities throughout the nation of clubs which are composed of boys and girls who have an especial interest in science." Encouraged by the success of the Future Farmers of America established in 1950, and following its organizational guidelines, these clubs would seek to: (1) develop an interest in science on the part of the young people of America; (2) provide an opportunity for the exchange of scientific information and ideas among members of the clubs; (3) encourage the promotion of science fairs at which members of the clubs may display their scientific works and projects; and (4) develop an awareness of the satisfaction to be derived from a career devoted to science.[28]

MEDICAL AND NURSING EDUCATION

President Kennedy's frustrating efforts for higher education, rewarded with the passage of legislation only after his death, were better known than his successful attempt to secure legislation in the areas of medical and nursing education. As a U.S. senator in 1955, he cited the report of the President's Commission on the Health Needs of the Nation, which declared a serious and growing shortage of physicians because of the lack of facilities for medical education.[29] His "Special Message to the Congress on Education" as president in 1962 reiterated a 1960 proposal, not only for medical construction facilities, but also for scholarships, to alleviate the heavy cost of medical training for needy but otherwise qualified students.[30] On September 24, 1963, two months before his assassination, Kennedy signed into law Public Law 88–129, the Public Health Service Act. Two of its titles dealt with medical and nursing education: Title VII–Health Research and Training Facilities, Training of Professional Health Personnel and Mental Retardation Research Facilities, and Title VIII-Nurse Training.[31]

Title VII authorized grants to assist in the construction of new teaching facilities, or to assist in the replacement or rehabilitation of existing facilities for the training of physicians, pharmacists, optometrists, podiatrists, veterinarians, professional public health personnel, and dentists. The surgeon general was at first empowered to act upon applications for grants, but this function was transferred to the secretary of health, education, and welfare in June, 1966. A National Advisory Council on Education for Health Professions was established by the act to supervise and advise on the regulations and policy matters arising from the administration of the provisions of the act, especially as to the eligibility of institutions to receive grants.[32]

A notable feature of Title VII was the establishment and operation of a student loan fund. The loan provisions made possible an amount not to exceed $2,500 a year for any student pursuing a full-time course of study in the health professions leading to a doctoral degree, with the exception of pharmacy which also included study for the bachelor's degree. Repayment of loans could be extended for a ten-year period, beginning one year after the student had completed his full-time course of study. Excluded in the ten-year period were up to three years spent on active military duty or service in the Peace Corps, and up to five years in advanced professional training such as internships and residencies. Payments were also made to schools to cover certain costs incurred in granting student loans from borrowed funds. Additionally, students of exceptional financial need could receive scholarship grants not to exceed $2,500 for any year. A National Advisory Council on Health Professions Educational Assistance would supervise and advise upon the administration of the scholarship funds.[33]

Educational institutions engaged in preparing applicants for the health professions could also apply for special project grants. These grants could be used for developing new programs and modifying old programs as to curricula, needs for meeting accreditation requirements, planning experimental teaching facilities, or improving and expanding programs to train future personnel in the health professions. The act focused attention on costs of trainee-ships for health service technicians, administrative and supervisory positions in medical institutions, and allied health profession specialties.[34]

Title VIII made similar provisions for nurse training: construction grants, grants for improvement of nurse training programs, grants for advanced training of professional nurses, establishment of a loan fund, and scholarship grants. A National Advisory Council on Nurse Training would supervise and advise upon the implementation of the provisions of the act. Educational agencies, organizations, and institutions could also apply for grants to aid in identifying qualified youths for nurse training and publicizing the existing forms of financial aid for nursing students.[35]

VOCATIONAL EDUCATION ACT OF 1963

Among the areas of education that President Kennedy desired to improve was vocational education. In his education message to Congress on February 20, 1961, a month after his inauguration, he characterized the basic purpose of the country's vocational education effort as "sound and sufficiently broad to provide a basis for meeting future needs." But he also stressed that the technological changes that had taken place in all occupations required "a review and re-evaluation" of previous legislation. He, therefore, requested Abraham Ribicoff, secretary of health, education, and welfare, to convene an advisory board to study and provide recommendations for improving and redirecting the goals and measures of support for vocational education.[36]

On January 29, 1963, President Kennedy reported to Congress the results of the review and evaluation of the federal government's vocational education laws and the recommendations for their modernization.

> The report of that committee shows the need for providing new training opportunities—in occupations which have relevance to contemporary America—to 21 million youth now in grade school who will enter the labor market without a college degree during the 1960's. These youth—

representing more than 80 per cent of the population between the ages of 16 and 21—will be entering the labor
market at a time when the need for unskilled labor is
sharply diminishing. It is equally necessary to provide
training or retraining for the millions of workers who need
to learn new skills or whose skills and technical knowledge
must be updated.[37]

Kennedy not only recommended funds to allow the doubling
of the number of workers trained under the Manpower Development and Training Act programs by increasing the 1964 budget,
but also recommended legislation that would "expand the scope
and level of vocational education programs supported through the
Office of Education by replacing the Vocational Education Act of
1946 with new grant-in-aid legislation aimed at meeting the needs
of individuals in all age groups for vocational training in occupations where they can find employment in today's diverse labor mar-
kets, and provide employment and training opportunities for unemployed youth in conservation and local public service projects."[38]
    Kennedy did not present his vocational education program as
a bill by itself; rather, he chose to incorporate all his legislation
proposals for education in an omnibus bill, the National Education
Improvement Act of 1963. He had hoped that such a strategy would
gather the widest possible support, would unite the various proponents of federal aid to education instead of having each special
group lobbying for its own interests, and would command greater
congressional support. His bills advocating aid to elementary and
secondary schools and to higher education had already been defeated in the two previous sessions of Congress.[39] The reluctance
with which the House Committee on Education and Labor began
hearings on the omnibus bill demonstrated the lack of enthusiasm
for much of Kennedy's educational legislation, and doubt as to its
eventual passage. In May, Congressman Adam Clayton Powell,
chairman of the Education and Labor Committee, announced that
the bill should be divided into four categories, one of which was
vocational education. This was reported favorably upon in June,
and passed by the House on August 6.[40] The Senate's Subcommittee on Education did not commence hearings on the omnibus bill
until spring, and eventually adopted the House's policy of considering and reporting on the education bill as separate acts. Early in

October, the Senate's Labor and Public Welfare Committee voted favorably on the vocational education bill, followed by similar action by the Senate on October 8.[41] Differences in the Senate and House versions caused further delay. Where the House wanted the funds distributed on the basis of population, the Senate preferred per capita income to be considered, in addition to population. Both sides remained stubborn on their positions, and the Senate held up the higher education bill pending a resolve of differences over the vocational education bill. Meanwhile, President Kennedy was assassinated on November 22. President Lyndon B. Johnson effectively secured a compromise between the House-Senate conferees. The Senate's version of per capita income and population was accepted as the basis for distribution, as long as no state would receive more than one and a half times more than any other state; differences as to the amounts to be allowed for vocational education grants and National Defense student loans were also resolved. The Vocational Education Act of 1963 was finally passed by Congress on December 16 and signed by the president on December 18.

The purpose of this latest act dealing with vocational education is

> to authorize Federal grants to States to assist them to maintain, extend, and improve existing programs of vocational education, to develop new programs of vocational education, and to provide part-time employment for youths who need earnings from such employment to continue their vocational training on a full-time basis, so that all persons of all ages in all communities of the State—those in high school, those who have completed or discontinued their formal education and are preparing to enter the labor market, those who have entered the labor market but need to upgrade their skills or learn new ones, and those with special handicaps—will have ready access to vocational training or retraining which is of high quality, which is realistic in the light of actual or anticipated opportunities for gainful employment, and which is suited to their needs, interests, and ability to benefit from such training.[42]

The act required matching grants from the states to build and improve vocational and technical schools. It provided funds for construction and improvement of vocational and technical education in specialized high schools, in high school departments providing education in five or more occupational fields, in technical or vocational schools, and in vocational divisions of community colleges or four-year colleges. State education agencies were entitled to grants to finance work-study programs associated with local or area vocational and technical education. Research and demonstration funds were allotted to universities, state and local education agencies, and qualified private nonprofit organizations.

The progress sought by the act was noticeable within a relatively short period of time. According to an evaluation of the U.S. Office of Education,

> Federal assistance through the Vocational Education Act is helping to provide non-college-bound youth with meaningful occupational education and training. Enrollment in the Nation's vocational and technical schools increased 30 percent over 1964 to nearly 5.8 million by the fall of 1965. . . . In the summer of 1965 the States reported 125 new vocational and technical schools under construction in 28 States and three territories; 209 additional schools planned in 27 States; and 62 educational institutions in 10 States designated as area vocational and technical training centers.[43]

The act also amended the National Defense Education Act of 1958 and the "impacted areas" aid programs by extending them to June 30, 1965.[44]

MANPOWER DEVELOPMENT AND TRAINING ACT

The changing patterns of living in the United States, especially the migration of families from rural to urban areas, and the increasing demand for more adequate training required by business and industry to keep pace with technological changes, have had their effect on the country's labor force. The total labor force has been estimated to have increased about 28 percent since 1950, and an additional 2 percent annual increase expected from 1960 to 1970. The number of women in the labor force has increased about 6 percent per year from 1950 to 1968. Their participation in the labor force is high in the late teens and early twenties, decreases with marriage and motherhood, but begins again at age thirty-five when children attain school age, and reaches a peak from ages forty-five to fifty-four. All of these factors, in addition to the usual economic cycles affecting employment, have produced periods of high unemployment rates, as in the 1960s.[45] The unemployment rate for the fourteen-to-twenty-four-year-old age group has been as high as 11.1 percent and for blacks, 11 percent of the total unemployment rate.[46]

In addition to the Vocational Educational acts, Congress enacted two laws in the early 1960s with the purpose of reducing the unemployment rate and the underemployment of disadvantaged persons. In 1961 the Area Redevelopment Act (ARA) was passed to enable the states, with the help of the federal government, to help areas with substantial and persistent unemployment and underemployment.[47] Federal assistance became available in four ways: (1) low-interest, long term loans to help industrial and commercial enterprises expand or to promote new ventures; (2) loans and grants to communities to help provide public facilities for new or existing firms; (3) technical assistance to communities for planning and implementing programs of economic development; and (4) programs to retrain workers in skills needed for new or expanding industries, and providing these workers with subsistence allowances while in training

The overall administration of the ARA program was assigned to the U.S. Department of Commerce, but other departments shared specific responsibilities. The Department of Labor determined the training or retraining needs of the unemployed and underemployed in consultation with the Departments of Commerce and Agriculture, authorized payments to the states for subsistence payments to trainees, and provided assistance for establishing apprenticeships and improving the quality of work through on-the-job training. The responsibilities for training were carried out through local and state employment and security offices. The Department of Health, Education, and Welfare was authorized to contract with both public and private educational institutions for needed services and facilities, such as the use of buildings, purchase of equipment and supplies, and training of personnel for teaching vocational education.

The ARA program was designed to establish programs for persons in depressed areas, but it was soon realized that the need for technical training was not confined to specific areas but, rather, was a national problem. In 1962 Congress enacted the Manpower Development and Training Act (MDTA).[48] The national administration of MDTA was assigned primarily to the secretary of labor, while the secretary of health, education, and welfare was placed in charge of conducting the training programs. Both the provisions and mechanics of ARA and MDTA are substantially the same. MDTA was amended in 1962, 1963, and 1968.[49] ARA training was absorbed into MDTA programs under the 1965 MDTA amendments.[50] In 1968 ARA was consolidated into MDTA, with emphasis on finding solutions to such problems as shortage of qualified workers, need for more and better trained workers in vital job classifications, outdated skills of some workers, and the anticipated rapid growth of the labor force.[51] Through the offices of state employment and security, programs for testing, counseling, and selecting workers for training were established, as well as cooperation with government and industry for the placement of newly trained or retrained workers. More than a million trainees are estimated to have been trained under MDTA from 1963 through 1968. Some 30 percent received on-the-job training and 70 percent attended institutional programs.[52] The programs have been considered "an important extension of this Nation's commitment to the fullest possible creative use of its human resources."[53]

In 1973, the Manpower and Development and Training Act was subsumed under the updated Comprehensive Employment and Training Act of 1973.[54]

ECONOMIC OPPORTUNITY ACT OF 1964

Part of the "Great Society" envisioned by President Johnson included a war on poverty: "We are citizens of the richest and most fortunate nation in the history of the world. . . . [Yet] there are millions of Americans—one-fifth of our people—who have not shared in the abundance which has been granted to most of us, and on whom the gates of opportunity have been closed."[55] Although the Economic Opportunity Act of 1964 was not per se and primarily an educational act, Johnson noted that "exits from poverty" can be made through the doors of education.[56] Thus, this bill has important sections dealing with education. Title I establishes the Job Corps within the Office of Economic Opportunity. Residential and/or nonresidential centers would be established for low-income, disadvantaged youth who need employment to continue their high school or college education, as well as to help unemployed or low-income persons, young and old alike, to improve their employability through special training programs. Youths in school could not work more than fifteen hours per week. An initial sum of $412.5 million was appropriated for the Job Corps.[57] In Title II, the act also provides for urban and rural community action programs with "the goal of enabling low-income families, and low-income individuals of all ages . . . to attain the skills, knowledge, and motivations and secure the opportunities needed for them to become fully self-sufficient." An allocation of $340 million was authorized for the first year, with the federal government paying up to 90 percent of the cost of projects in such fields as job training, vocational rehabilitation, and health and welfare, with special emphasis on programs to ensure literacy training and basic education for adults.[58] Due partly to the success of the Peace Corps, Title VIII establishes a domestic volunteer service program popularly known as VISTA, Volunteers in Service to America. The volunteers will be "required to make a full-time personal commitment to combating poverty . . . to live among and at the economic level of the people served, and to remain available for service without regard to regular working hours, at all times during their term of service, except for authorized periods of leave."[59] Thus, VISTA workers would be engaged on Indian reservations, in mental hospitals, in migratory farm camps, and poverty-stricken areas.

Amendments to the act consisting of increased appropriations to those initially authorized were passed in 1966. The act, known as the Economic Opportunity Amendments of 1966, was "to provide for continued progress in the Nation's war on poverty."[60] Amendments were again offered in 1967; they too dealt with increased appropriations and the power of the comptroller general in checking on the efficiency of the administration of the programs and activities by the Office of Economic Opportunity.[61] Similar action was taken by Congress in 1969 and 1972.[62] In 1973, Congress transferred Title I–A, "Job Corps," of the Economic Opportunity Act to Title VI of the Comprehensive Employment and Training Act of 1973.[63]

APPALACHIAN REGIONAL DEVELOPMENT ACT

President Johnson's war on poverty through education continued in certain features of the Appalachian Regional Development
Act of 1965. Counties in thirteen states comprising the Appalachian
Region were found by Congress to be "lag[ging] behind the rest of
the Nation in its economic growth and that its people have not
shared properly in the Nation's prosperity." Supported by findings
of the President's Appalachian Regional Commission, the act seeks
to assist the region in meeting its special problems, to promote its
economic development, and to establish federal and state efforts to
meet these needs on a coordinated and concerted regional basis.
The act aids vocational education by facilitating the construction of
facilities and the purchase of equipment for such facilities, without
regard to the provisions relating to appropriation authorization
ceilings, or to allotments to be distributed among the states according to the Vocational Education Act of 1963. Because of the region's
inability to provide matching funds necessary to participate in federal grant-in-aid programs, the act allocates funds without ceilings
to the grant-in-aid provisions of the Vocational Education Act of
1963, the Library Services Act of 1956, the Higher Education Facilities Act of 1963, and the National Defense Education Act of 1958.[64]

NATIONAL VOCATIONAL STUDENT LOAN INSURANCE ACT OF 1965

In 1965 Congress passed the National Vocational Student Loan
Insurance Act.[65] This act established a system of loan insurance and
a supplementary system of direct loans to assist students to attend
postsecondary business, trade, technical, and other vocational
schools. The act was repealed by the higher education amendments
of 1968.[66] Vocational students are now eligible for insured loans
under the Insured Student Loan Program of the Higher Education
Act of 1965.[67]

VOCATIONAL EDUCATION AMENDMENTS OF 1968

Whatever favorable evaluation was given to the 1963 Vocational Act was short-lived; it has been judged as "permissive in

tone," resulting in only a few changes in the old routines, not adjusting vocational courses to meet local job opportunities, and not providing for the vocational needs of the handicapped.[68] A May, 1966, study found twelve states with no vocational programs in operation for students with special needs: the handicapped and the academically and economically disadvantaged. The investigators for the study identified only seventy-nine programs throughout the nation that provided vocational education for students with special needs. Many of these programs eliminated students who otherwise could benefit from vocational training by requiring such qualifications as minimum level of ability. The U.S. Office of Education reported that in 1966 less than 1 percent of the persons enrolled in vocational programs were persons with special needs; furthermore, in the 1965–66 school year, only 1 percent of such funds were utilized for them. The report also pointed out that those with special needs comprised 10 percent of the school population.[69]

The 1963 act had authorized the establishment of a National Advisory Council which, however, was not appointed until 1966. In January, 1968, the council issued its first report, "Vocational Education—The Bridge Between Man and His Work." Its recommendations helped lead members of Congress to question the effectiveness of the 1963 act in meeting vocational educational problems. Upon studying this report, the House General Subcommittee on Education concluded that the five following ideas must be taken into consideration for any improvement of vocational educational possibilities:

(1) any dichotomy between academic and vocational education is outmoded; (2) developing attitudes, basic educational skills, and habits appropriate for the world of work are as important as skill training; (3) prevocational orientation is necessary to introduce pupils to the world of work and provide motivation; (4) meaningful career choices are a legitimate concern of vocational education; (5) vocational programs should be developmental, not terminal, providing maximum options for students to go on to college, pursue postsecondary vocational and technical training, or find employment.[70]

Congressional hearings in 1966 and 1967 on provisions for vocational education resulted in no affirmative action.[71] But in 1968 the Johnson administration offered a proposal entitled "Partnership for Learning and Earning Act of 1968," upon which the House subcommittee opened hearings in February, 1968. Illinois Congressman Roman Pucinski, who introduced the bill in the House, stated: "I commend the administration for this proposal, but I believe that this bill should serve as a basis for a very intensive investigation of the present state of vocational education in this country."[72] Testimonies from the National Education Association, the Study Committee on Vocational Education for the Handicapped of the Council for Exceptional Children, and the American Vocational Education Association were among those groups urging clearer delineated recommendations for federal assistance in vocational education, especially for the handicapped.[73] In addition to the administration proposal, five other similar bills were introduced. Hearings continued until May, with the final bill being a composite of those introduced. Senate and House differences were resolved in conference during the first week of October and the bill received passage in both houses without a dissenting vote.[74] President Johnson signed the act into law on October 16, 1968.

The purpose of the act was broad and comprehensive enough to allow persons of all ages from throughout all the states to take advantage of opportunities for vocational training or retraining, according to their needs and capacities. All previous vocational education acts were absorbed and extended. The Smith-Hughes Act of 1917, however, remained, although appropriations under this act had to be in conformity with the terms of the 1968 law.[75] The federal government was authorized to extend grants to the states, beginning with $355 million for 1968, and gradually reaching $565 million in 1972 and thereafter. Funds were to be distributed to the states through formulas considering the number of persons in various age groups requiring vocational education, and the per capita income of the particular state of which the persons were residents. Funds could also be used for the construction of facilities, purchase of equipment, research, and training of needed personnel.

More specifically, states can use federal funds for these purposes:

(1) programs for high school students, including those designed to prepare them for advanced or highly skilled postsecondary training;

(2) programs for those who have completed or left high school and are preparing to enter the labor market;

(3) education for those in the labor market who need it to achieve stability or advancement (except those already benefiting from one of the manpower development laws);

(4) programs for those who are handicapped and need special training;

(5) vocational guidance and counseling for those in the above four categories;

(6) construction of area vocational education school facilities;

(7) provision of vocational training through arrangements with private institutions where it can be efficiently done; and

(8) ancillary services such as teacher training, program evaluation, special demonstrations, development of materials, and improved administration.[76]

Numbers 2 and 4 of the above purposes were to receive more emphasis than in the 1963 act. A minimum of 15 to as much as 25 percent of a state's annual allotment is to be used for the benefit of young unemployed high school graduates or dropouts. A minimum of at least 10 percent of each state's allotment is to be used only for the vocational education of the handicapped. Where the 1963 act included handicapped children under the broad category of "academic, socioeconomic, and/or other handicaps," the 1968 act provides a definition more consonant with those utilized by authorities in the Bureau for the Handicapped. The term "handicapped" has been broadened to embrace "persons who are mentally retarded, hard of hearing, deaf, speech impaired, visually handicapped, seriously emotionally disturbed, crippled, or other health impaired persons who by reason thereof require special education and related services."[77]

The 1968 act established new vocational education programs: exemplary programs and projects or "new ways to create a bridge between school and earning a living for young people who are either still in school, have left school either by graduation or by dropping out, or are in a postsecondary program of vocational preparation, and to promote cooperation between public education and manpower agencies";[78] consumer and homemaking education, which includes education and preparation for dual homemaking and wage-earning roles, especially in economically depressed areas;[79] cooperative vocational education programs, such as plans for alternate full-time study and full-time jobs;[80] curriculum development, especially for improvement in and dissemination of existing vocational educational materials, and the development of curricula for new and changing occupations.[81] Two programs, established by previous laws but which never received the funds to become operative, were again authorized: work-study programs for vocational education students[82] and residential vocational schools for youths from fifteen to twenty-one,[83] with the possibility of including the Job Corps within this program.[84]

An important item in the 1968 law was the establishment of the National Advisory Council on Vocational Education, consisting of twenty-one members appointed by the president. It was clearly specified that members must represent the many diversified aspects of vocational education; one-third of the membership should represent the general public, including parents and students. The council must meet at least four times a year and its duties are: (1) to advise the commissioner of education on policy concerning regulations and guidelines; (2) to make an annual report based on a review of the administration and operation of the act; and (3) to conduct independent evaluations and to publish its findings.[85]

In order to be granted federal funds, each state must establish an advisory council on vocational education. State council members are to be appointed by the governor or by elected state boards of education; they must reflect all elements in the community acquainted with occupational problems.[86]

The state vocational council's duties deal largely with advising on policy, preparation of annual and long range plans, and evaluation of programs and publication of the findings thereof. The act calls for aggressive leadership by the states, a weak point of the 1963 act. Therefore, the state council must ensure that vocational plans are elaborately specified, give evidence of consultation and cooperation with all interested groups and agencies in the community, fully publicize policies and procedures as to the distribution of funds, provide for hearings of dissatisfied groups and agencies, update plans without denying funds to local districts too poor to provide their matching share, consider the needs of students in nonprofit private schools, and furnish all data for reports required by the commissioner of education.[87]

The first annual report of the National Advisory Council on Vocational Education was submitted on July 15, 1969, and it indicated that the 1968 act "created a statutory framework under which substantial federal appropriations could be directed toward the prevention of increases in unemployment and underemployment."[88] But the report did point out that schools were failing to educate to the level of employability approximately one-fourth of the eighteen-year-olds each year, that inadequate education had brought on much unrest and unemployment, that the government on all levels was spending more for higher education than for vocational education, that students should be provided with a multiple choice of courses in high schools with both academic and vocational offerings, including supervised work experience, and that adults should be afforded vocational programs through adult schools and community colleges.[89] That Congress reacted favorably to the progress made under the 1968 act can be seen in the extension of the provisions of the 1963 act, its absorption within the 1968 act, and in the extension of the provisions of the education amendments of 1972 to July 1, 1975,[90] with emphasis on a new nexus between community colleges and occupational education.[91]

COMPREHENSIVE EMPLOYMENT AND TRAINING ACT OF 1973

Since 1961, manpower programs in the United States have grown into a complex system of programs funded under different statutory authorities and aimed at different client groups. Excessive duplication and overcentralization of program administration at the national level have led to an increasing awareness of the need for manpower reform. The Select Subcommittee on Labor of the House began hearings on the need for a reorganized comprehensive manpower system on December 10, 1969. Congress did enact in 1972 the Emergency Employment Act, but still felt that the patchwork of programs often overlapping one another made it impossible to establish an effective federal-state-local partnership. Further hearings in both House and Senate Committees on Labor led to the passage in December, 1973, of the Comprehensive Employment and Training Act.[92]

The purpose of this 1973 legislation was to provide a new and up-to-date charter for the manpower programs which were previously operated under the authority of the Manpower Development and Training Act, the Economic Opportunity Act, and the Emergency Employment Act. With the goal of being more responsive to the diversity of local needs, the bill would make grants available to about 550 local and state agencies who would plan and operate their programs to meet local needs. While providing for decentralization, the bill reaffirms the role of the federal government in assuring that manpower programs are operated according to federal policy. The Job Corps, previously under the Economic Opportunity Act, was transferred to the Comprehensive Employment and Training Act of 1973.[93]

VOCATIONAL REHABILITATION

The employment problems of the disabled veterans of the World War I were met by the Smith-Sears Vocational Rehabilitation Act, passed by Congress on June 27, 1918.[94] With an initial appropriation of $2 million, the act sought to provide an extensive national plan not only for medical, surgical, and mental treatment, but also for vocational rehabilitation of those disabled while in military service. As a result of this act, many returning servicemen received grants for tuition at existing schools, colleges, and technical institutions, and all received guidance in choosing an occupation with which they could sustain themselves. While in the process of reestablishing himself, the disabled veteran continued to receive his military pay and family allowance. The act was placed under the direction of the United States Veterans' Bureau. Expenditures under the act reached their peak in 1921–22, with $178,809,861 spent for vocational rehabilitation.[95] Of the act it has been commented that "The work represents another new phase of national educational effort, and the most costly of any educational work the Government has so far undertaken."[96]

The philosophy and practical value of vocational rehabilitation as begun in the 1918 act led only two years later to the enactment of the Smith-Bankhead, or the Federal Vocational Rehabilitation, Act.[97] It extended vocational rehabilitation to "persons disabled in industry or otherwise, and their return to civil employment." The administration of this program was placed under the charge of the

Federal Board of Vocational Education, which collaborated with the state boards of vocational education as they had been established under the Smith-Hughes Act. In 1933 the U.S. Office of Education took charge of the program of vocational rehabilitation until 1943, when the Office of Vocational Rehabilitation was established as a unit of the Federal Security Agency.[98] A first-year appropriation of $750,000 was granted, but subsequent annual appropriations amounted to $1 million; each state was required to match the federal funds it requested. From 1933 to 1937 the program received supplemental funds from the Federal Emergency Relief Administration. In 1939 an amendment to the Social Security Act of 1935 authorized the increase of the annual appropriation to $3,500,000.[99]

The Vocational Rehabilitation Act of 1943 continued the provision for vocational rehabilitation as begun under the Smith-Sears Act of 1918 and the Smith-Bankhead Act of 1920. In superseding these two previous acts, it sought to provide for the vocational rehabilitation of war-disabled civilians and other disabled civilians by means of plans devised by the states and approved by the Federal Security Administration. The federal government would reimburse the states for the "necessary costs" of the vocational rehabilitation of those disabled by war, and for "one-half of necessary expenditures" of other disabled persons; administration expenses incurred by the states would, however, be excluded. Among the services that the states could provide and could receive reimbursement for would be medical and surgical care, hospitalization, prosthetic devices, occupational equipment, and vocational education and guidance, including training in accredited schools, colleges, and technical institutes. The secretary of the treasury would make the actual disbursements to the states upon the approval of the Federal Security Agency, which was empowered to withhold funds if the states did not administer the program according to approved specifications. The state boards for vocational education were authorized to administer the program in their respective states.[100]

In 1954, amendments for vocational rehabilitation provided provisions to improve financing, and included authorization for research, demonstration, and training activities to advance state rehabilitation programs as well as voluntary programs. The financing provisions were changed to provide a system for allotting more federal funds to states with relatively small per capita incomes.

Project grants were awarded for extending and improving services to the states, with federal matching of up to 75 percent, so that states could develop new aspects of their programs and extend their services to additional disability groups.[101]

In 1965, amendments were designed to expand and enlarge the public program to effect the rehabilitation of a much larger number of handicapped individuals. Congress liberalized federal financing to encourage states to provide greater matching appropriations. Provisions to improve, strengthen, and assist in workshops and rehabilitation centers, and to construct new facilities were made.[102]

In 1967, amendments extended and expanded the basic support grants to the states for rehabilitation services. Provisions were enacted to establish a national center for deaf-blind youths and adults, and to extend services to disabled migrants and their families. Additionally, state vocational rehabilitation services were required to provide services to handicapped individuals without regard to their place of residence.[103]

In the 1968 amendments, Congress increased the federal share of basic support grants to 80 percent, and a minimum allotment to the states of $1 million was established. Grants were allowed for recruiting and training handicapped persons for public service employment and for encouraging individuals to enter rehabilitation work. Grants were also made available for projects with private industry to train handicapped individuals for gainful employment. Congress further broadened and defined rehabilitation services to include: (1) follow-up services; (2) services which promise to contribute to the rehabilitation of a group of individuals; (3) services to families; (4) establishment and construction of rehabilitation facilities; and (5) new employment opportunities for the handicapped. Rehabilitation services were so defined as to include centers, workshops, and other facilities established for the primary purpose of providing vocational rehabilitation services to, or gainful employment for, handicapped individuals.[104]

The Rehabilitation Act of 1973, while not substantially changing any of the previous legislation, updated and synthesized efforts of the federal government in this area. A Rehabilitation Services Administration headed by a commissioner appointed by the president was established within the HEW. The secretary of HEW and the heads of the Civil Service Commission and the Veterans Administration were to comprise the nucleus of an Interagency Committee on Handicapped Employees, the purpose of which was to develop and recommend procedures and policies to facilitate the hiring, placement, and advancement of handicapped individuals who have received rehabilitation services from both federal and state agencies. One of the main features of the 1973 act is the specification that requirements for receiving federal funds be met by the states. Innovation and expansion grants to states can make up 80 percent of costs, while grants for construction can amount to 90 percent. Greater encouragement is given through appropriations for planning and conducting research and training to increase the number of skilled rehabilitation personnel, and for improving the existing skills of such personnel. The act also requires efforts to eliminate architectural and transportation barriers confronting handicapped individuals, especially in federally controlled or regulated areas.[105]

PROVISIONS FOR THE HANDICAPPED

In 1856, Amos Kendall, a former postmaster general of the United States, founded a school in the District of Columbia for the deaf, dumb, and blind. On February 16, 1857, Congress incorporated the Kendall School as the Columbia Institution of the Deaf, Dumb, and Blind. Needy students in the school were provided for by federal funds. Edward Miner Gallaudet, son of Thomas Hopkins Gallaudet, the founder of the first school for the deaf in the United States and a leading educator for the deaf, became its superintendent.[106] Gallaudet succeeded in making the institution a national college for the deaf in 1864, when Congress approved the collegiate division of the institution as the National Deaf-Mute College. In 1865, because of limited resources, both the college and the school were forced to restrict themselves to the education of the deaf only. In 1894 the college division was named Gallaudet College in honor of Thomas Hopkins Gallaudet, and in 1954, Congress changed the name of the entire institution to Gallaudet College.[107]

A recipient of federal funds from its institution, the 1954 act authorized the appropriation of whatever sums would be needed for the administration, operation, maintenance, and improvement of Gallaudet College, as well as sums for student aid, research, and the construction of new facilities. The board of directors of Gallaudet would report annually to the secretary of health, education, and welfare on the use of federal funds.[108] In 1966, Congress authorized the establishment of a model secondary school for the deaf, to be operated by Gallaudet College, to serve residents of the District of Columbia and of nearby states.[109] In 1970, Congress modified and enlarged the authority of Gallaudet College to maintain and operate the Kendall School as a demonstration school for the deaf, serving primarily the national capital region.[110]

Provisions for a college education for the deaf through federal funds were not limited to the District of Columbia. In 1965, Congress established the National Technical Institute for the Deaf. Any institution of higher education could enter into an agreement with the secretary of health, education, and welfare for creating special programs for deaf students. Funds could be received for the construction and/or remodeling of facilities and equipment for this purpose. A National Advisory Board on the Establishment of the National Technical Institute for the Deaf would review and approve all proposals of institutions desirous of creating such programs.[111]

In 1963, as a means of providing assistance in combating mental retardation, Congress enacted the Mental Retardation Facilities and Community Mental Health Centers Construction Act. Two of the act's titles dealt directly with education. Title III concerned itself with the training of teachers of mentally retarded and other handicapped children. The commissioner of education was empowered to make grants to states, state or local educational agencies, and public and nonprofit institutions of higher learning, for conducting research, surveys, or demonstrations relating to education for the mentally retarded, hard of hearing, deaf, speech impaired, visually handicapped, seriously emotionally disturbed, crippled, or health impaired children.[112] Title V authorized appropriations for the training of physical educators and recreation personnel for mentally retarded and other handicapped children.[113] In 1958, Congress had already authorized grants to public and nonprofit institutions for higher learning that would establish training programs for teachers of handicapped children.[114]

In 1958, Congress established within the Department of Health, Education, and Welfare a loan service of captioned films for the deaf, as a means for enriching their cultural and educational experiences. The act also provided for the educational advancement of handicapped persons by promoting research in the use of instructional media for the handicapped, the ways of producing and distributing these media, and the training of persons in the use of educational media in the instruction of the handicapped.[115] In 1968, Congress passed the Handicapped Children's Early Education Assistance Act. Thus, preschool and early education programs for handicapped children became eligible for federal funds. The act stressed cooperation and effective coordination of these programs with similar programs in the schools of the community, and the participation of parents of handicapped children in such programs.[116]

On November 3, 1966, Congress enacted Public Law 89-750, which amended the Elementary and Secondary Education Act of 1965 by adding Title VI which provided for the education of handicapped children. The commissioner of education was authorized to approve plans by the states, and to supervise the allotment of funds "for the purpose of assisting the States in the initiation, expansion, and improvement of programs and projects (including the acquisition of equipment and where necessary the construction of school facilities) for the education of handicapped children . . . at the preschool, elementary and secondary school levels."[117]

To improve the education of handicapped children, the commissioner could award grants or enter into contracts for the establishment of regional resource centers. Thus, within particular regions of the country, one or more local educational agencies, institutions of higher learning, state educational agencies, or any combination of these agencies or institutions, could cooperate in forming these centers with federal money. The centers would be expected to (1) provide testing and evaluation services to determine the special needs of handicapped children referred to such centers; (2) develop educational programs to meet those needs; and (3) assist schools and other appropriate agencies in providing educational programs which would include consultation with parents and teachers of handicapped children, and periodic examination and evaluation of the programs and services. The commissioner was also empowered to arrange for similar centers and services for deaf-blind children. Such centers would be assigned the task of designing programs "to develop and bring to bear upon such children, beginning as early as feasible in life, those specialized, intensive professional and allied services, methods and aids that are found to be most effective to enable them to achieve their full potential for communication with and adjustment to the world around them, for useful and meaningful participation in society, and self-fulfillment."[118]

In recognition of the need for trained personnel in this field of education, the act authorized the commissioner of education to make grants or to enter into contracts with agencies and institutions, with the purpose of encouraging students and professional personnel to work in various fields of education of handicapped children, through the publicizing of such careers, and the existing forms of financial aid for pursuing them. A need was also seen for disseminating information about programs, services, and resources for the education of the handicapped, especially to parents and teachers; funds to meet this need were provided.[119] To implement the features of this new title for ESEA, and to coordinate all other government activities in this educational area, a bureau of education and training of the handicapped would be established within the Office of Education. Furthermore, a national advisory committee on handicapped children in the same office would advise and recommend on the present and future effectiveness of laws and means in the education of handicapped children.[120]

On April 30, 1970, Congress enacted the Education of the Handicapped Act. Effective July 1, 1971, this act replaced Title VI of the Elementary and Secondary Education Act of 1965, and superseded the Handicapped Children's Early Education Assistance Act of 1965, Grants for Teaching in the Education of Handicapped Children enacted in 1963, Titles III and IV of the Mental Retardation Facilities and Community Mental Centers Construction Act of 1963, and the act dealing with instructional media for handicapped children in 1958. However, the main provisions of all these acts have been maintained in the new 1970 act and with increased appropriations.[121]

AMERICAN PRINTING HOUSE FOR THE BLIND

On March 3, 1879, "an act to promote the education of the blind" was passed by Congress in answer to a petition representing the interests of over thirty thousand blind persons in the United States.[122] The legislation was urged by the Association of the American Instructors of the Blind at a convention in 1876. "Embossed books and tangible apparatus" were then considered as special needs of the blind. The association recommended that Congress aid the education of the blind by appropriating funds to the American Printing House for the Blind in Louisville, Kentucky, which had been established by the cooperative efforts of the states of Kentucky, New Jersey, and Delaware, and which several other states had been helping through financial appropriations. The 1879 act appropriated the sum of $250,000 as a perpetual fund, the interest of which would be used to distribute freely printed materials to the blind.

The act was amended on June 25, 1906, to increase the funds allotted in 1879, and further amended later to insure that adequate appropriations beyond the initial sum could fulfill its purpose.[123]

5

International Education

Government-sponsored international education did not begin in the United States until the passage of the Fulbright Act on August 1, 1946. But international education in the United States is as old as the American republic and, in the history of education, dates back to ancient and biblical times.[1] The staunch nationalism of the newly founded American nation, seeking not only a political but a cultural identity of its own, feared foreign educational influence on young Americans.[2] The 1830s exemplified a change of attitude toward foreign education, since American educators, most notably Horace Mann, Henry Barnard, Calvin Stowe, all of them leaders in the movement for the common public school system, had been to Europe to study its educational systems and published reports of their observations.[3] Many of the annual reports of the U.S. commissioner of education have included analyses and comparative studies of foreign education.[4] Even before World War I, but more especially after it, programs of international exchange of teachers, scholars, and students were developed.[5] These programs, however, were sponsored by philanthropic foundations, such as the Rockefeller Foundation, the Carnegie Endowment for International Peace, and the Guggenheim Foundation, and learned and professional groups, such as the American Association of University Women and the Institute of International Education, established in 1919 by Elihu Root, Nicholas Murray Butler, and Stephen P. Duggan.[6]

THE FULBRIGHT LEADERSHIP

Government sponsored and directed international education was adopted under the leadership of Senator J. William Fulbright,

126

a former university president, law school professor, and Rhodes scholar at Oxford University, England. Fulbright saw in international education a means for improving international relations through cultural exchange.[7] On September 7, 1945, Fulbright introduced an amendment to the Surplus Property Act of 1944: "Mr. President, I ask unanimous consent to introduce a bill for reference to the Committee on Military Affairs, authorizing the use of credits established abroad for the promotion of international good will through the exchange of students in the fields of education, culture and science." The parent bill, of which the Fulbright Act became a part, authorized the "orderly disposal" of surplus war material located outside of the United States to be sold at a fair value, with the Department of State as the directing agency. The Fulbright proposal received favorable endorsement from the Commission of the American Council on Education, representatives of the National Education Association, and former President Herbert Hoover, well versed in the value of international exchange largely because of his relief work during World War I. The Senate unanimously passed the bill, and the House, assured that international education would not deprive domestic education of its primary support, gave it overwhelming approval.[8] President Harry S Truman signed the act on August 1, 1946. A *New York Times* editorial expressed the typical reception of the act by most Americans.

> In the tangled skein of contemporary international relationships, it is often difficult to see the ordered system of a better future. Therefore there is something definitely heartening about the Fulbright Act, signed recently by the President. In the midst of confusion and wrangling this is a constructive forward-looking step that seems certain to improve international understanding.[9]

The Fulbright Act[10] entrusted the general administration of the program to the Department of State. A Board of Foreign Scholarships, appointed by the president, would select students and educational institutions qualified to participate in the program and supervise the exchange program. The board, composed of ten members, without compensation, would be "representatives of cultural, educational, student and war veteran groups, and including representatives of the United States Office of Education, the United States

Veterans Administration, state educational institutions, and privately endowed educational institutions." Preference to applicants with military service was suggested, as well as representative geographical distribution. Financing of the Fulbright program was to be done by the selling of American war property in foreign countries, with $1 million a year the maximum amount to be spent for programs in any one country. Estimated expenditures for the first year of the program amounted to $5 million for thirteen hundred grants in nine countries.[11]

The Fulbright program, although speedily passed by Congress, was not without its problems. A rival claimant for funds derived from the sale of surplus war property in foreign countries was an act passed on July 25, 1946, the Foreign Buildings Act.[12] Despite the assurance of continuation of funds, there were frequent delays and uncertainties. Learning about the brief history of the program, Senator Fulbright obtained approval from Congress to include in the Mutual Security Act of 1952 an amendment to the Fulbright Act that would authorize the use of foreign currencies and credit arising from any source, not just war surplus sales, for the international study program.[13] Despite a more liberal authorization of funds, the flexibility of, and the long-term planning for, the program was jeopardized by the passage of the "Rabout Amendment" (named after Congressman Louis Rabout who introduced it) to the Supplemental Appropriation Act of 1953, which specified that foreign credits owed to or owned by the United States would not be available for expenditure unless authorized annually in appropriation acts.[14] By executive action, President Dwight D. Eisenhower directed that the Fulbright Program be exempted from the Rabout Amendment for the 1953–54 fiscal year.[15] In August, 1954, Congress authorized the reservation of certain portions of available foreign currencies or credits for financing the program.[16] The program was also aided by a new source of revenue: currencies accruing from the sale of surplus agricultural commodities.[17] The passage of these subsequent modes of financing ensured the continuation and the extension of the Fulbright Program.

Besides its financial problems, the Fulbright Program was plagued by attacks from Senator Joseph R. McCarthy, who claimed that the State Department was infested with Communists. In the hearings on the Supplemental Appropriation Act of 1954 before the Senate's Government Operations Committee, McCarthy charged that the Board of Foreign Scholarships had selected, despite required clearance procedures, Communist students and professors, or at least those with Communist leanings and sympathies. Senator Fulbright successfully defended the program, and the act bearing his name, against the charges which McCarthy was unable to substantiate.[18] All in all, the Fulbright Program (as well as other international cultural and educational programs) survived the passing fad of McCarthyism.[19]

On January 27, 1948, Congress passed the Smith-Mundt Act, the Information and Educational Exchange Act of 1948.[20] With a broad and all-embracing scope, the act provided for "an information service to disseminate abroad information about the United States, its people, and policies . . . an educational exchange service to cooperate with other nations in: (a) the interchange of persons, knowledge, and skills; (b) the rendering of technical and other services; (c) the interchange of developments in the field of education, the arts, and sciences." Basically, the Smith-Mundt Act did differ from the Fulbright Act. It dealt with the exchange of persons, teachers and students in the same academic fields and in the same countries, and covered more countries. Cognizant of this similarity of purpose, the Smith-Mundt Act provided that "all provisions in this Act regulating the administration of . . . educational exchanges provided herein shall apply to all such international activities under jurisdiction of the Department of State." It, however, clearly distinguished between three bodies established by Congress to have jurisdiction over international education and exchange programs. Smith-Mundt programs were supervised by the United States Advisory Commission on Educational Exchange which the act created, while the Fulbright Act was administered through a Board of Foreign Scholarships within the Department of State. The Smith-Mundt Act was financed by funds appropriated annually by Congress within the budget, rather than by agreements based on foreign currency settlements through the Department of State, for international information and educational exchange activities.

In addition to the Fulbright and Smith-Mundt Acts, Congress passed other legislation dealing with specific types of international education and cultural exchange. The Finnish Exchange Act of 1949[21] and the India Emergency Food Aid Act of 1951[22] provided grants to American-sponsored schools abroad, including funds for books and equipment. The Humphrey-Thompson Act, or the International Cultural Exchange and Trade Fair Participation Act of 1956, constituted a distinct program in the performing arts.[23] Furthermore, the National Science Foundation, the National Institutes of Health, and the U.S. Office of Education sponsored international fellowship programs. The National Defense Education Act of 1958 laid great stress on the preparation of teachers for developing programs in foreign languages, including in the countries where the language was spoken. Programs of intercultural exchange also existed with the Organization of American States. Under the G.I. Bill of Rights, American veterans could study in foreign, as well as American, colleges and universities. The U.S. Information Agency (USIA) maintained public information programs in foreign countries. The Agency for International Development (AID) placed increasing emphasis on the role of education in lending technical assistance to the less developed countries of the world. When the United States joined UNESCO in 1946, the U.S. National Commission for the United Nations Educational, Scientific, and Cultural Organization was established to promote collaboration between nations in the exchange of knowledge and ideas.[24] The American commitment to international education and cultural exchange had not only become broad and comprehensive, but also so involved that the coordination and clarification of the programs and agencies concerned were required. Senator Fulbright and members of the Senate Foreign Relations Subcommittee on Overseas Information Programs of the United States had suggested in 1953 separate administrations of the educational exchange and the mass media programs.[25] In 1956 J. L. Morrill, a former chairman of the U.S. Advisory Commission on Educational Exchange, studied the problem and presented a proposal for coordinating international education activities.[26] A Committee on the University and World Affairs of the Ford Foundation issued a report suggesting coordination, inasmuch as present intergovernmental relations in the field of international education were "limited, sporadic, uncoordinated and ill-supported."[27] On March 2, 1961, Senator Fulbright introduced into the Senate an obviously needed bill to consolidate in one legislation act the many existing legal provisions affecting international education and cultural exchange, and to authorize increases in the size and scope of these programs. "The approach to the international scene of the 1940s," he said, "is not good enough for the 1960s."[28]

Public hearings on the new Fulbright bill began on March 29,

1961, in the Senate and on May 25 in the House, where Congressman Wayne Hays had earlier introduced the bill. In the hearings, outstanding leaders in international education from the government and the academic world gave their support to the Mutual Educational and Cultural Exchange Act of 1961, or the Fulbright-Hays Act, as it has come to be more popularly known.[29] Typically characteristic of the testimony offered in favor of the new and extended Fulbright program was that of the National Grange, which praised the "total program of exchanges as a highly effective instrument in the strengthening of peaceful and friendly relations between peoples of different lands and different customs."[30] The Kennedy administration had also expressed its approval for expanding and coordinating international education, especially in accordance with the report that the Board of Foreign Scholarships had presented to the president on February 27, 1961.[31]

The bill received the Senate's approval by a vote of 79 to 5, and the House's by 329 to 66. Minor differences on the bill were ironed out in a conference committee. The House had especially emphasized the effectiveness of the programs for foreign students as to activities, services for them, and visa requirements, as well as assurance of security clearance, the use of funds for dependents of American participants, and nondiscriminatory administration of the programs as to race, creed, or color.[32] A few days after final approval by both House and Senate, the bill was signed into law by President Kennedy on September 25, 1961.

The Fulbright-Hays Act repealed the Fulbright Act, the Finnish Educational Exchange Act, the International Cultural Exchange and Trade Fair Participation Act, and the Smith-Mundt Act's provisions for educational exchange.[33] All of these acts dealing with international educational and cultural exchange programs were now to be not only coordinated but consolidated. President Kennedy, by an executive order, aided the proper delineation of these activities by establishing the new position of assistant secretary of state for educational and cultural affairs, whose duties would be administering and exerting leadership in this field of government. For all practical purposes, Congress gave the program a "blank check" by authorizing contracts for exchanges, visits, and activities in advance of appropriations, and by reserving foreign currencies in the amounts determined to be required for providing the authorized programs. For participants in the programs, tax exemption of the grants was liberalized, and members and their families were granted the same types of visas. The act permitted the creation of binational and multinational commissions in and with foreign countries to facilitate exchange activities, thus insuring mutuality of cooperation and agreement among the nations involved.

The Board of Foreign Scholarships, increased from ten to twelve members, was empowered with supervisory jurisdiction over all educational exchange activities; the board continued its duty of selecting participants in the program. Also established was the U.S. Advisory Commission on International and Cultural Affairs, composed of nine members whose duty was to formulate and recommend policies and report on the evaluation of the programs. Additionally, the act created an Advisory Committee on the Arts to assist the advisory commission in matters pertaining to the role of the arts in international education and cultural exchange.

The Fulbright-Hays Act was evaluated a few years later as "fostering cooperative effort in the sensitive field of education and scholarship, it also helped build up the kind of respect and confidence among peoples that is prerequisite to friendship and cooperation among governments."[34] Senator Fulbright has looked upon international cultural exchange not solely from its educational advantages but from the dimension of fostering world peace: "In our quest for world peace, the alteration of attitudes is no less important, perhaps more important, than the resolution of issues. It is in the minds of men, after all, that wars are spawned; to act upon the human mind, regardless of the issue or occasion for doing so, is to act upon the course of conflict and a potential source of redemption and reconciliation."[35]

THE PEACE CORPS

A new dimension to mutual understanding and cooperation among nations was added by the Peace Corps, advocated by President John F. Kennedy as an essential part of the New Frontier. During the campaign for the presidency, Kennedy promised:

> I would explore thoroughly the possibility of utilizing the services of the very best of our trained and qualified young people to give from three to five years of their lives to the cause of world peace by forming themselves into a Youth

Peace Corps, going to the places that really need them and doing the sort of jobs that need to be done. Such an example of young Americans helping nations to pioneer new fields on the world's underdeveloped frontiers . . . would be not only a great assistance to such nations and a great example to the world, but the greatest possible growing experience of the new generation of American leadership which must inevitably lead the free world coalition.[36]

Kennedy presented the idea of the Peace Corps as a challenge to college students, to "all Americans, of whatever age" to serve as "ambassadors of peace . . . dedicated to freedom . . . able to be missionaries, not only for freedom and peace, but to join in a worldwide struggle against poverty and disease and ignorance"; to "counter to the flood of well-trained and dedicated Communist technicians now helping . . . nations help themselves, to show them modern agriculture, public health, road building, government and other skills."[37] After his election as president, Kennedy announced his intent to establish a national peace corps.[38]

Not all Americans responded favorably to the idea, however. The project was called a "juvenile experiment" and even labeled as "Kennedy's Kiddie Korps." Extreme caution was urged for its adoption, and if adopted, it was to be permitted only on an experimental basis with restricted funds.[39]

In view of the criticism and doubt as to its success, Kennedy engaged a task force to develop its mechanics, and decided to establish an experimental and tentative pilot plan under the direction of Sargent Shriver, his brother-in-law. On March 1, 1961, he issued an executive order establishing the Peace Corps on a "temporary pilot basis," and allotted $1.6 million from the foreign aid contingency fund for financing it.[40] On the same day, he also sent to Congress a plan for a permanent Peace Corps. In his message to Congress, Kennedy announced that the idea had been receiving "strong support from universities, voluntary agencies, student groups, labor unions and business and professional organizations," as well as from members of Congress. He also pointed out that congressional studies had demonstrated that "the Peace Corps is feasible, needed, and wanted by many foreign countries."[41]

Kennedy offered examples of specific programs in which members of the Peace Corps would be engaged:

teaching in primary and secondary schools, especially as part of national English language teaching programs; participation in the worldwide program of malaria eradication; instruction and operation of public health and sanitation projects; aiding in village development through school construction and other programs; increasing rural agricultural productivity by assisting local farmers to use modern implements and techniques. The initial emphasis of these programs will be on teaching. Thus the Peace Corps members will be an effective means of implementing the development programs of the host countries—programs which our technical assistance operations have helped to formulate.[42]

Members of the Peace Corps would be made available to developing nations through private voluntary agencies carrying on international assistance programs, overseas programs of colleges and universities, assistance programs of international agencies, assistance programs of the United States government, and new programs developed by the Peace Corps as needs and requests arise.[43]

Kennedy explained the process and standards for selecting volunteers to the program. He insisted not only on the possession of abilities to participate in a specific program, but also on "personal qualities which will enable them to represent the United States abroad with honor and dignity." A recruit would be required to undergo a six weeks to six months training and orientation period to learn the language and culture of the country in which he would serve, and training to insure adequacy for his specialized field. A period of service would usually range from two to three years. The corpsmen would receive no salary, but an allowance sufficient to meet their basic needs and would live under the same conditions as the people among whom they would work.[44]

The bill to establish the Peace Corps was introduced in the first session of the 87th Congress as S.2000 and H.R. 7500. Upon its passage by both branches of Congress separately and with minor variations, several conferences were held to smooth out differences, after which it was sent to the president who signed it on September 22, 1961.[45] After Congress passed the Peace Corps bill, President Kennedy expressed gratitude at the bipartisan effort and support by which the bill was discussed and enacted into law.[46]

For the fiscal year 1962 Congress appropriated a sum not to exceed $44 million for Peace Corps expenses. The program would be immediately under a director appointed by the president with the consent of the Senate; the secretary of state, however, was empowered with "continuous supervision and general direction" of the programs so that they could be effectively integrated with American foreign policy. Regarded as employees of the United States government, the volunteers would be allowed the necessary living and travel expenses to participate in the program, a termination payment not to exceed $75 for each month of satisfactory service, prescribed health and disability benefits. Voluntary leaders, so-called because of supervisory or special responsibilities, would receive termination payments of $125 a month, with consideration for their spouses and minor children in regard to living, travel, housing, and health care. Provisions were also made for those Peace Corps employees who would be required to carry out the details of the program in the United States. The act also included provisions for the training of volunteers and volunteer leaders, as well as for the utilization of foreign nationals to help train volunteers. Security investigations were required of all participants in the Peace Corps. Service in the program did not exempt them from the military service obligation. A Peace Corps National Advisory Council of twenty-five persons, representing a broad spectrum of life concerned with the program, was established "to advise and consult with the President with regard to policies and programs designed to further the purposes" of the act; experts and consultants required by the various programs were to be called upon and compensated for their services. The Internal Revenue Code and Social Security Act were amended to provide for the problems arising from the taxation of allowances and coverage for social security.[47]

The response to the Peace Corps was enthusiastic. Over 3,000 applied for the first Peace Corps examination in May, 1961, with some 750 already actively participating in the program by the end of the first year. At the end of 1962 the number of participants had reached over 4,200.[48] The amount increased rapidly to approximately 7,000 in 1963 and 10,000 in 1964. Over seventy nations of the world have requested Peace Corps volunteers. Each year Congress has authorized increased appropriations and the number of volunteers.[49]

President Nixon, on June 30, 1971, issued an executive order declaring the continuance and administration of the Peace Corps as an agency of the executive branch to be known as "ACTION." The basic features of the original act, however, remain the same. The National Voluntary Action Program was established by an executive order on May 26, 1969 and transferred to ACTION. This latter program seeks to "encourage and stimulate more widespread and effective voluntary action for solving public domestic problems."[50]

An interesting by-product of the American effort to help the underdeveloped nations is the "reverse Peace Corps." Begun in the summer of 1967 with some one hundred volunteers from Africa, Asia, and Latin America, foreign teachers and students came to the United States to teach their own culture and languages in American schools and international understanding programs.[51]

INTERNATIONAL EDUCATION ACT OF 1966

The latest legislative endeavor to promote international education was the International Education Act of 1966. President Johnson, speaking on September 16, 1965, at the bicentennial celebration of the founding of the Smithsonian Institution, urged a broadening of the country's role in international education, and announced the appointment of a task force to recommend "a broad and long-range plan of worldwide educational endeavor."[52] Congressman John Brademas was designated chairman of the Task Force on International Education under the direction of the House Committee on Education and Labor. On February 2, 1966, President Johnson sent a special message to Congress dealing with international education and health. He stressed what he termed certain self-evident truths: "Ideas, not ornaments, will shape our lasting prospects for peace. The conduct of our foreign policy will advance no faster than the curriculum of our classrooms. The knowledge of our citizens is one treasure which grows only when it is shared." In a spirit of free exchange and full collaboration with all interested nations, he proposed by further legislation "to strengthen our capacity for international cooperation, to stimulate exchange with students and teachers of other lands, to assist the progress of education in developing nations, to build new bridges of international understanding."[53]

On the same day of the presidential message, the International

Education Act of 1966 was introduced in Congress by Senator Wayne Morse in the Senate, and by Congressmen Adam Clayton Powell and John Brademas in the House. Hearings were heard in the House in late March and early April and House approval was won on June 2, 1966. In the Senate, hearings were held in August and September, and approval won on October 13, 1966.[54]

The ease with which the bill won approval owes much to the publication "in one convenient volume [of] some of the best published and unpublished material on international education," prepared by the Task Force on International Education. Congressman Powell described the volume as "a comprehensive and substantive compilation of searching and instructive treatises on a broad spectrum of problems and issues in international education."[55] Powell's urging of the passage of the act reflected the academic community's hope for "the opportunity for many and, hopefully, all educational institutions to broaden the vision of every phase of their curriculums, precisely to achieve the necessary international and universal perspective indicated in this volume. The role of the Federal Government in supporting international education—education to function effectively in a multi-cultural universe—is aimed primarily at enabling our schools and universities to carry forward the essential training and research in international studies."[56] Prominent educators and leaders in international education appraised the results of the past and suggested qualitative improvements for the future.

The prime purpose of the International Education Act is "to provide for the strengthening of American educational resources for international studies and research." The first title authorized grants to colleges and universities and other agencies involved in international education for the purpose of expanding and strengthening the teaching of international affairs. Specific proposals were made for undergraduate programs in international studies; these included training of faculty members in foreign countries, supervised student work-study-travel opportunities, exchange of faculty members with foreign institutions, and improvement in teaching, research, and curriculum development. The secretary of health, education, and welfare would be in charge of the distribution of grants to institutions and persons qualified to carry out the suggested proposals of the act. A national advisory committee on international studies of no more than fifteen members would be established, with the assistant secretary of health, education, and welfare for education as chairman to assist in carrying out the provisions of the act. Title II of the act amended Title VI of the National Defense Education Act of 1958 by increasing the number of programs in foreign languages to include new languages and more liberal financial support of language area centers. Provision was also made for the establishment of International Affairs Institutes for secondary school teachers, who could participate in in-service training programs under the sponsorship of institutions of higher education. Amendments to the Mutual Educational and Cultural Exchange Act of 1961, through the 1966 International Education Act, dealt with regulating the exchange of foreign currencies for those students and teachers involved in exchange programs.[57]

The International Education Act of 1966 has been extended by the higher education amendments of 1968[58] and the education amendments of 1972 until 1975 with increased appropriations.[59]

PART II

THE SUPREME COURT
AND EDUCATION

6

The Financing and Control of Public Education

Education in colonial America was regarded as a prerogative of local communities, with much individual and group efforts, largely under religious auspices. After the adoption of the federal Constitution, virtually every state, either in its original constitution or subsequently, included provisions for education.[1] Despite these state constitutional provisions, the states have manifested their concern for education primarily through aid and encouragement to the local schools rather than by exercising authority over them. State legislatures have enacted laws governing many aspects of education, such as powers of local school boards, length of school year, compulsory attendance, certification requirements for teachers, minimum standards for school buildings and facilities, but for the most part, the states have respected local autonomy in matters educational. Edward Bolmeier has assessed the extent of state control over local communities in regard to schools as follows:

> Local initiative with respect to education is so highly regarded in our democratic society that the state legislatures have not unduly exercised their constitutional powers to the extent of denying local communities the right to participate in the management of the schools. On the contrary, most states have enacted legislation which permits, delegates, or requires considerable local school management. In so doing the states have not surrendered their prerogatives, but have merely determined the machinery by which the state function shall be performed.[2]

141

THE FINANCING OF PUBLIC SCHOOLS

State concern for education in the twentieth century has extended to increasing financial support, with state funds distributed
to local school districts and communities. Because of great differences in wealth and in efforts to improve school buildings and
programs on the part of local school systems, states have had to
divert some of their revenue to supplement the customary source
of the local communities' means to pay for educational expenses—
the local property tax. The ability of local communities to provide
quality education depended largely on this one source of income.
Only Hawaii, where the entire state is a single school district, spends
the same amount on each pupil. Inequality of revenue received in
different communities, coupled with resistance of taxpayers to
higher rates on property taxes, has led to large differentials in per
capita pupil expenditure in communities within the same state, and
even more so in comparison with communities in other sections of
the nation. Such inequality in educational expenditures and their
consequence on educational facilities and programs were demonstrated by studies in 1948 and 1951.[3]

The inequities in education brought on by racial segregation
were one aspect of the problem, since expenditures per black pupil
were far less than those in districts that were predominantly white.
One estimate made was that the per pupil expenditure for black
students was 40 to 70 percent of the per pupil expenditure for white
students in the Deep South.[4] Supreme Court decisions highlighted
the unequal educational facilities for black students.[5] One case,
Hobson v. *Hansen*, evoked much publicity although it did not reach
the Supreme Court. The federal district court not only declared the
"track" system of pupil assignment in Washington, D.C., schools as
discriminatory, but also noted a $100 per pupil difference in ex-
penditure between predominantly black elementary schools ($292)
and the predominantly white elementary schools ($392).[6]

But the situation was not restricted to blacks alone. Communities limited by local taxable wealth found themselves handcuffed in
the amounts that could be allotted to education. Studies in the
1960s, among the best known of which is the Coleman Report,
revealed disturbing facts: Poor children, mostly from minority
groups in our society, attend the most outmoded schools, are the
least motivated to learn, are taught by the least competent teachers,

and their level of achievement is too often inferior to children educated in "richer" schools.[7] The need for the equalization of educational expenditures was seen as a serious and pressing problem in American public education.

In 1970, as a means to solving this problem, John E. Coons, a law professor at the University of California, offered a legal theory that would transform the financing of American public schools.[8] Arguing on the basis of the "equal protection" clause of the Fourteenth Amendment that education, like voting and a fair trial, was a fundamental right of citizens, Coons maintained that the inequalities in local school spending violate equality of opportunity. These inequalities result from the differences in private wealth of school districts because of the local property tax base. Richer communities, having a stronger tax base, can provide more for educational expenses than poorer communities; the result is inequality of educational opportunity for students residing in poor communities. An example offered to demonstrate this inequality was the comparison of Baldwin Park, a Los Angeles, California, suburb with a $700-a-year-per-child expenditure from a meager tax base, with nearby Beverly Hills which spent $1,000 per child, with a property tax rate half that of Baldwin Park. Lawyers at the Western Center on Poverty Law, a federally financed project, and psychiatric social worker John A. Serrano became influenced by Coons' thesis; with Serrano as the lead plaintiff, a case testing the system of financing public schools by means of the property tax was brought to court.[9]

The California State Supreme Court upheld Coons' theory and declared that the quality of education ought not be a function of local wealth. To avoid inequalities in educational expenditures, the taxable assets of rich school districts should become available for the support of the education of all children within a given state.[10] The *Serrano* decision led to the filing of other suits; in seven other states—Michigan, Kansas, Wyoming, Arizona, New Jersey, Minnesota, and Texas—the courts ruled against the method of financing local public schools through property taxes because of the inequities in many communities.[11] The Texas case, *Rodriguez* v. *San Antonio Independent School District*, was appealed to the U.S. Supreme Court, as the federal district court had concluded that the substantial interdistrict disparities in school expenditures throughout the state of Texas violated the equal protection clause of the federal Constitution.[12]

On March 21, 1973, the Supreme Court reversed the lower court's decision by a 5 to 4 vote.[13] Speaking for the majority, Associate Justice Lewis F. Powell, Jr., acknowledged the fact that partial reliance on local property taxes did result in broad disparities in expenditures on a per pupil basis for education. But he maintained that the equal protection clause was not violated, for he found no facts to substantiate the assumption that the poorest people were concentrated in the poorest districts. Rather, oftentimes the poor are clustered around industrial and commercial areas, which provide "the most attractive sources" of property tax income for school districts. Moreover, since equal protection does not require "absolute equality of precisely equal advantages," lack of equal spending for education may have resulted in only a poorer quality education and not the absence of public education.[14] The Court asserted, furthermore, that it is an "unsettled and disputed" question whether the quality of education can be judged by the amount of money spent for it. Thus the Court saw no discrimination against the poor who, because of their poverty, were not completely unable to pay for a desired benefit, and who thereby sustained no absolute deprivation of a meaningful opportunity to enjoy the benefit of education.[15]

Although the Court reiterated its "historic dedication" to public education, it did not consider education a "fundamental" right for equal protection purposes, for the right to education is neither explicitly nor implicitly guaranteed by the Constitution. Even though the Court has zealously protected the individual's right to speak and to vote against unjustifiable government interference, the Court has not been able to guarantee the most effective speech or the most informed electoral choice. So in education, since no charge can be made that each child is not provided with an opportunity to acquire the basic minimal skills, the Court is not expected to guarantee a higher quality of education.[16]

The Court insisted that it was not placing its "judicial imprimatur on the status quo." Local communities have depended on the property tax too long and too heavily for funding their schools, but "the consideration and initiative of fundamental reforms with respect to state taxation and education are matters reserved for the legislative processes of the various states."[17] If the Court were to require equal expenditures for all local community services provided by the revenue derived from property taxes, then this concept of equality would have to be extended to other necessary and customary services provided from the same source, such as local police and fire protection, health and sanitary services, as well as education. The Court clearly maintained that education is a state and local responsibility, with "each locality . . . free to tailor local programs to local needs."[18]

In a minority opinion, Justice Thurgood Marshall, with whom Justice William O. Douglas concurred, called the majority decision a "retreat from our historic commitment to equality of educational opportunity" and a denial of the "right of every American to an equal start in life." Waiting for local "political" solutions to the problem only continues an inferior education unjustifiably for countless children.[19] Justice Byron White's dissenting opinion, with which Justice William J. Brennan, Jr., concurred, noted "an invidious discrimination against the Equal Protection Clause" because the states, in permitting school districts to rely on the property tax, do not "maximize" local initiative by state funds equally distributed, since in districts where property tax bases are so low there is little opportunity for rich or poor parents to augment school district revenues.[20]

Commenting on the *Rodriquez* decision, Coons observed that the Supreme Court has legalized a system of taxation that favors rich school districts, and that the movement to reform the financing of public schools through federal litigation would remain stalled until membership in the present Court changes. Hope for more immediate change can come only from state legislatures and courts, which must establish that "education—like voting—is a specially protected right."[21] Legal scholars are seeking alternatives to *Rodriguez* so that the inequities caused by present school financing can be eliminated.[22] Stephen Browning of the Lawyers' Committee for Civil Rights Under Law, which serves as coordinator of school-finance litigation throughout the country, announced continued efforts for school-tax reform in state courts.[23]

The U.S. Supreme Court has also dealt with two cases closely related to *Rodriguez*. In 1969, the Court in the *McInnis* case affirmed a federal district court's decision to dismiss a suit which charged that various Illinois state statutes dealing with the financing of the public school system violated Fourteenth Amendment rights to equal protection and due process because they permitted wide variations in expenditures per student.[24] In 1971, the Court in the *Hargrave* case remanded for further proceedings a federal district court's decision declaring a Florida statute unconstitutional.[25] The statute, known as the "Millage Rollback Act" and passed in 1968, provided that any county that imposes on itself more than ten mills in ad valorem property taxes for educational purposes would not be eligible to receive state minimum foundation program funds for the support of its public education system.[26] The Court held the statute contrary to the equal protection clause which requires uniform treatment of persons standing in the same relation to governmental action questioned or challenged.[27]

It is unlikely that the problem of school financing can be solved with equal per pupil expenditure, as many educators have questioned whether equality of expenditures insures equality of educational opportunity. Bowles has claimed that "equality in the resources devoted to the education of different racial groups will not achieve equality of educational opportunity."[28] Kirp has maintained that a state's obligation to provide equal educational opportunity can be satisfied "only if each child, no matter what his social background, has an equal educational outcome, regardless of disparities in cost or effort that the state is obligated to make in order to overcome such differences."[29] Jenks's much publicized study, *Inequality,* has concluded that quality of education has little, if any, effect on the future income of students, and that schools do little to close the gap between the rich and the poor.[30] Even the Coleman report has suggested that a far more important influence on a child's achievement than the school is his socioeconomic status; home environment and influences apart from formal education have much to bear on general educational opportunity for the disadvantaged.[31] In view of the importance of the socioeconomic backgrounds of children, Sorgen *et al* have reasoned that "efforts to enhance the equality of opportunity among children of diverse backgrounds could be achieved, if at all, either (a) by influencing the socioeconomic status (SES) of the parents of the disadvantaged child to a point of accomplishing substantial equality with his wealthier peers, or, (b) by some form of remedial schooling, designed to offset the disadvantages of a low socioeconomic status."[32] While Congress has built into the Economic Opportunity Act and the Elementary and Secondary Education Act special provisions to meet the needs of disadvantaged youngsters from low-income families,[33] Kurland has observed that "ideally, disadvantaged youth should receive more than average funds, rather than equal expenditures, so their potential can be fully developed. A rule coercing equal expenditures for all, especially if raised to a constitutional plane, would completely frustrate this ideal."[34] The *Rodriguez* decision has summed up the problem succinctly: "Indeed, one of the hottest sources of controversy concerns the extent to which there is a demonstrable correlation between educational expenditures and the quality of education."[35]

SCHOOL BOARD MEMBERSHIP AND VOTING IN SCHOOL ELECTIONS

In May, 1967, the U.S. Supreme Court upheld a practice in the state of Michigan whereby delegates from local school boards elect a county school board. A group of Kent County, Michigan, voters had claimed that such a system violates the principle of "one man, one vote" and produces inequities by giving one vote to every local school board, irrespective of population. The Court saw no violation of the Fourteenth Amendment. As for the decision's implication for education, it held that where a county school board is an administrative, and not a legislative, body, its members need not be elected.[36]

According to Section 2012 of the New York Education Law (Supp. 1968), certain New York school district residents, who are otherwise eligible to vote in state and federal elections, may vote in the school district election only if they own or lease taxable real property within the district, or are parents or custodians of children enrolled in the local public schools. A bachelor fulfilling neither of the law's requirements challenged its constitutionality. Unsuccessful in the lower courts, he appealed to the U.S. Supreme Court. On June 16, 1969, Chief Justice Warren saw in the New York law a violation of the equal protection clause of the Fourteenth Amendment: "Statutes granting the franchise to residents on a selective basis always pose the danger of denying some citizens any effective voice in the governmental affairs which substantially affect their lives." To the argument offered that only those "primarily interested" or "primarily affected" should be entitled to vote, Warren questioned whether all those excluded to vote in the school district elections are "in fact substantially less interested or affected than those the statute includes."[37]

Missouri residents of the Kansas City School District, one of eight school districts constituting the Junior College District of Metropolitan Kansas City, claimed that their right to vote was unconstitutionally diluted in violation of the equal protection clause of the Fourteenth Amendment. Their claim was based on the fact that their district contained approximately 60 percent of the total apportionment basis of the entire Junior College District, while the state statutory formula allowed them to elect only 50 percent of the trustees from their district. Unsuccessful in Missouri courts, the appellants brought the case to the U.S. Supreme Court.[38] Justice Black, in writing the opinion of the Court, based his decision on the "one man, one vote" principle previously expounded by the Supreme Court.[39] He concluded that the Fourteenth Amendment requires that "the trustees of this junior college district be apportioned in a manner that does not deprive any voter of his right to have his own vote given as much weight as far as is practicable, as that of any voter in the junior college district."[40] And he further explained: "If one person's vote is given less weight through unequal apportionment, his right to equal voting participation is impaired just as much when he votes for a school board member as when he votes for a state legislator."[41]

Black residents of Taliaferro County, Georgia, challenged the constitutionality of a system employed in many counties of Georgia to select juries and school boards. In reference to the applicability of this case to education, the county board of education consisted of five "freeholders," or owners of real estate. The board was selected by the grand jury, which in turn was drawn from a jury list selected by the six-member county jury commission, whose members were appointed by the judge of the state superior court for the circuit in which the county is located. Although blacks comprised about 60 percent of the county's residents, and although all the students in the county school system were blacks (inasmuch as every white pupil had transferred elsewhere), the board of education consisted entirely of white people who had been selected by a predominantly white grand jury, which in turn had been selected by jury commissioners, all of whom were also white. The blacks, therefore, alleged a lack of sensitivity to the educational problems of their children and sought representation on the county school board.[42]

On January 19, 1970, the U.S. Supreme Court, in addition to dealing with the entire scheme of selecting juries and commissioners, struck down the Georgia statute which enabled only owners of real estate to become members of the county school board. Eliminating the question of race as a direct issue in this case, the Court claimed that all citizens have a federal constitutional right to be considered for public service "without the burden of invidiously discriminatory disqualifications." For "the State may not deny to some the privilege of holding public office that it extends to others on the basis of distinctions that violate federal constitutional guarantees."[43] The Court could not conceive of "any rational state interest" behind the property requirement.

> It cannot be seriously urged that a citizen in all other respects qualified to sit on a school board must also own real property if he is to participate responsibly in educational decisions, without regard to whether he is a parent with children in the local schools, a lessee who effectively pays the property taxes of his lessor as part of his rent, or a state and federal taxpayer contributing to the approximately 85% of the Taliaferro County annual school budget derived from sources other than the board of education's own levy on real property. Nor does the lack of ownership of realty establish a lack of attachment to the community and its educational values.[44]

7

Private and Religious Schools

DARTMOUTH COLLEGE CASE

In 1819, the Supreme Court of the United States rendered its first decision involving education in the *Dartmouth College* case. The English crown had granted a charter to Dartmouth in the colony of New Hampshire in 1769. Like many colleges in colonial America, it was founded as a private institution under religious sponsorship, in this case the Congregationalists. Dartmouth's president, John Wheelock, in aligning himself politically with the Presbyterians and Republicans, antagonized the board of trustees, composed mostly of Congregationalists and Federalists. The trustees retaliated by firing Wheelock in 1815. When the Republicans became the majority party the following year, they annulled the colonial charter and placed the college under state control, with the trustees appointed by the governor of the state. The legislature's action was upheld in 1815 by the New Hampshire Court of Appeals which maintained that since Dartmouth had become a public institution, the state legislature had the right to modify its charter.[1]

The ousted trustees appealed to the U.S. Supreme Court in 1818; Daniel Webster, an alumnus of Dartmouth, pleaded the case. Chief Justice John Marshall handed down the Court's decision which invalidated the action of the New Hampshire legislature as it violated the federal Constitution (Article I, Section 10): "No state shall pass any bill of attainder, ex post facto law, or law impairing the obligation of contracts." The Court upheld the colonial charter as a contract and restored control of the college to the board of trustees duly chosen under the provisions of that charter.[2]

The decision in the *Dartmouth College* case ended serious efforts to change privately established colleges into state institutions

150

through legislative action. With the exception of Brown, Princeton, and Rutgers, attempts were made to place colonial colleges under state control; Columbia and Pennsylvania had been so placed for a short period of time, while William and Mary, Howard, and Yale did consent to state membership in their boards of control.[3]

The *Dartmouth* decision's effect upon education has received varied interpretations. Educational historian Cubberly has concluded that "it guaranteed the perpetuity of endowments" for private educational institutions, but not that "the great period of private and denominational effort now followed" as a result.[4] Other reasons, such as the desire for the benefits of a college education, population growth, and denominational pride, fostered the growth of religious and private educational institutions.[5] Nor was the movement for state-sponsored colleges necessarily affected by the decision.[6] The movement toward founding state universities received its greatest stimulus with the passage of the Morrill Act in 1862. The *Dartmouth* decision dealt a serious blow to Jefferson's proposal of a unitary state system of education he had advocated for his native state of Virginia, and to the ideas of the French enlightenment on state-sponsored education.[7] Following the trend of the growing common public elementary, and later secondary, school system of the nineteenth century, a university president wished to extend the nonsectarian, state-controlled concept of education to the colleges and universities: "Nearly all our colleges are . . . the creations of the different religious denominations which divide our people. They are regarded as important instrumentalities, through which the peculiarities of doctrine which distinguish their founders are to be maintained, propagated, or defended."[8] The *Dartmouth* decision did, however, make the denominational colleges "secure from popular storms"; if the states wanted to sponsor public colleges, they then had to establish such public colleges, instead of converting church colleges into secular public institutions by revoking their charters without the consent required by American law.

Guarantee by law of private educational institutions was also ensured by decisions rendered in the Girard College case, which assured donors and testators that their endowments could not be changed, and in the *Oregon School* case and *Myers* v. *Nebraska*, by confirming the right of parents to send their children to nonpublic schools.

GIRARD CASE

The death of Stephen Girard in 1831, leaving an estate of approximately $6 million, $2 million of which was earmarked for the establishment of a college in Philadelphia, Pennsylvania, led to another decision from the U.S. Supreme Court following the contesting of the will by relatives.[9] Girard's will provided for a college for "poor, male, white orphans" and

> that no ecclesiastic, missionary, or minister of any sect whatsoever, shall ever hold or exercise any station or duty whatever in the said College; nor shall any such person ever be admitted for any purpose, or as a visitor, within the premises appropriated to the purposes of the said College. In making this restriction, I do not mean to cast any reflection upon any sect or person whatsoever; but, as there is such a multitude of sects, and such a diversity of opinion amongst them, I desire to keep the tender minds of the orphans . . . free from the excitement which clashing doctrines and sectarian controversy are so apt to produce; my desire is, that all the instructors . . . shall take pains to instill into the minds of the scholars the purest principles of morality.[10]

The contesters of the will argued that the bequest was an invalid charity under both common law and the constitution of the state of Pennsylvania, and that it, furthermore, was contrary to a Christian state by making orphan boys "the victims of a philosophical speculation." In a unanimous opinion written by Justice Joseph Story, the Court upheld Girard's will for the establishment of a college according to the provisions of the bequest. Story maintained that "we are satisfied that there is nothing in the devise establishing the college, or in the regulations and restrictions contained therein, which are inconsistent with the Christian religion, or are opposed to any known policy of the State of Pennsylvania."[11]

As in the *Dartmouth College* case, the Court upheld a legally valid contract, assuring donors and testators the execution according to the conditions of their wishes, even if they excluded sectarian instruction in the designated institution of the bequest. Although the free exercise of religion as guaranteed by the First Amendment of the federal Constitution was not at issue, Spurlock has concluded that "very likely, the decision had the effect of fixing more firmly for the whole nation the concept of religious freedom."[12] In a democracy with no established religion and no preferential treatment for any religion, the rights of conscience dictate as much respect and guarantee for the rights of a particular sectarian religion, nonsectarianism, or even atheism.

THE BEREA COLLEGE CASE

The *Berea College* case is considered from two points of view: (1) as a chartered private school, and (2) as an institution which did not practice segregation of white and black students. As a private, nondenominational institution founded in the 1850s in Kentucky, Berea College admitted both white and black students without discrimination to its manual training programs. In 1904, however, the legislature of Kentucky enacted a law which declared that "it shall be unlawful for any person, corporation or association of persons to maintain or operate any college, school or institution where persons of the white and negro races are both received as pupils for instruction." In the same year of the law's passage, Berea College was charged with violating the law and penalized $1,000 as the law prescribed. Kentucky's Court of Appeals upheld the decision of the lower state court, and Berea College appealed to the U.S. Supreme Court.[13]

The Supreme Court, following the then legal precedent of "separate but equal" rights of the races set by *Plessy* v. *Ferguson* in 1896, upheld the state statute. "The decision by a state court," the Supreme Court reasoned, "of the extent and limitation of the powers conferred by the State upon one of its own corporations is of a purely local nature. In creating a corporation a State may withhold powers which may be exercised by and cannot be denied to an individual. It is under no obligation to treat both alike. In granting corporate powers the legislature may deem that the best interests of the State would be subserved by some restriction, and the corporation may not plead that in spite of the restriction it has more or greater powers because the citizen has."[14]

Unlike the *Dartmouth* decision of 1819, when the Court upheld the original charter of an educational institution, and the *Girard* case of 1844, when the Court respected the provisions of a will requiring nonsectarian educational influence, the *Berea* decision regarded the charter as a grant of right or privilege resting "entirely in the discretion of the State, and, of course, when granted, may be accompanied with such conditions as its legislature may judge most befitting to its interest and policy."[15]

By its decision, the Court trampled upon a serious and fundamental question of educational philosophy: who has the right to educate? As a private school, sponsored by private citizens sharing a similar policy—in this instance, the teaching of students without racial discrimination—private citizens were deprived of their right by state legislation and upheld by the Supreme Court. It was not until the subsequent cases of *Myers* v. *Nebraska* and *Pierce* v. *Society of Sisters* that the Court acknowledged the constitutional right of private education, and the *Brown* decision of 1954 which declared segregation unconstitutional. Spurlock has maintained that the "separate but equal" doctrine of *Plessy* was not involved in *Berea,* but the case did deal with segregation, although not in public education, and the rights of citizens to choose the kind of education they desired were infringed upon.[16]

RIGHTS OF CORRESPONDENCE SCHOOLS

The failure of an enrollee, Mr. Pigg, to remit the contracted fee in a correspondence course with the International Text-Book Company, led to legal action. As a resident of Kansas, Mr. Pigg maintained that according to the laws of his state the textbook company, a Pennsylvania corporation, could not bind him as the corporation did not submit a detailed annual report to Kansas. The Kansas courts judged in favor of the defendant, but when appealed to the Supreme Court, the lower court's decision was reversed in favor of the textbook company. The Court considered correspondence instruction by mail a matter of interstate commerce, and cited and applied the doctrine it enunciated in a previous interstate commerce case: "It is not only the right, but the duty, of Congress, to see to it that *intercourse* among the states and the *transmission of intelligence* are not obstructed or unnecessarily encumbered by state legislation."[17]

Thus, commercial correspondence schools could function legally both intrastate and interstate. If the Court had ruled against the International Text-Book Company, then only intrastate home study courses would be allowed, unless a correspondence school incorporated itself in every state.

TEACHING OF FOREIGN LANGUAGES IN PRIVATE SCHOOLS

The existence of private schools conducted in a foreign language were threatened as a result of the growth of nationalism spurred on by World War I, as well as by the fact that a large percentage of draftees were unable to speak or understand the English language. One-fourth of the states had passed laws prohibiting the instruction of children in private schools in any language other than English.[18] The Supreme Court became involved in an important decision through the challenge of a law passed by the state of Nebraska on April 9, 1919. The law was entitled "An Act Relating to the Teaching of Foreign Languages in the State of Nebraska," and it declared:

> Section 1. No person, individually or as a teacher, shall, in any private, denominational, parochial or public school, teach any subject to any person in any language other than the English language.
> Section 2. Languages, other than the English language, may be taught as languages only after a pupil shall have attained and successfully passed the eighth grade as evidenced by a certificate of graduation issued by the county superintendent of the county in which the child resides.[19]

Meyer, a teacher in a parochial school sponsored by the Zion Evangelical Lutheran Congregation, was charged with teaching German reading to a youth who had not yet passed the eighth grade. As the courts of Nebraska sustained the state law, Meyer appealed to the Supreme Court, which reversed the lower courts' ruling. The Supreme Court went beyond the narrow issue of whether a state can forbid the teaching of a foreign language in nonpublic schools. It insisted upon respect for "certain fundamental rights," of protecting "those who speak other languages as well as those born with

English on the tongue." In stressing fundamental rights, the Court
also recognized the freedom of a foreign language teacher to teach
and the freedom of parents to engage teachers of their own choosing to instruct their children: "Plaintiff . . . taught this language in
school as part of his occupation. His right thus to teach and the right
of parents to engage him so to instruct their children, we think, are
within the liberty of the Amendment [Fourteenth]." The right of
parents to select the school and teachers of their children, other
than just public schools, was affirmed again, in greater length, in the
Oregon school case, *Pierce* v. *Society of Sisters*. But in *Meyer* the Court
recognized the authority of the state "to compel attendance at some
school and to make reasonable regulations for all schools, including
a requirement that they shall give instructions in English . . . [yet]
no emergency has arisen which renders knowledge by a child of
some language other than English so clearly harmful as to justify its
inhibition with the consequent infringement of rights long freely
enjoyed."[20]

RIGHT OF ATTENDANCE AT FOREIGN LANGUAGE SCHOOLS

With legislative acts in 1920, 1923, and 1925, the Territory of
Hawaii sought to restrict foreign language schools. Of such schools,
7 were Chinese, 9 Korean, and 147 were Japanese. About 12,400
pupils and 192 teachers were involved, with school property valued
at about $250,000 and support coming from some five thousand
persons.

The law of 1925 sought to limit the students attending foreign
language schools to those who were in regular attendance at a
public school or at a territorially approved private school, or who
had completed the eighth grade, or were over fourteen years of age.
In addition, the textbooks used in the primary grades had to be
approved. The parents of the Japanese children contested the law
as it deprived them of their liberty and property without due process
and was thus in violation of the Fifth Amendment which protected
such rights of residents of a territory. The Court, as in *Meyer* v.
Nebraska, upheld the rights of the parents.

> Enforcement of the act probably would destroy most, if not
> all, of them; and certainly, it would deprive parents of fair

opportunity to procure for their children instruction which they think important and we cannot say is harmful. The Japanese parent has the right to direct the education of his own child without unreasonable restrictions; the Constitution protects him as well as those who speak another tongue.[21]

After World War II, the legislature of the Territory of Hawaii sought to prevent the teaching of a foreign language before a child had completed the fourth grade at school. The law was advocated because educators in Hawaii found that children instructed in a foreign language in their early years were hindered in their progress of learning. District court judges, in the light of *Meyer* v. *Nebraska,* upheld the rights of parents to have their children taught in a foreign language, but the governor of Hawaii appealed their judgment to the Supreme Court, which denied hearing it on procedural grounds.[22] Thus, Hawaiian children in the first four grades of schooling could freely attend foreign language schools.

RIGHT OF ATTENDANCE AT NONPUBLIC SCHOOLS

On November 7, 1922, the legislature of the state of Oregon enacted a law, to become effective in 1926, that all children between the ages of eight and sixteen years, with certain exceptions, must attend the public school of their district; instruction by nonpublic school teachers would have to have the approval of the county superintendent of schools. Fearing the possible destruction of nonpublic schools, the sponsors of a parochial school, the Sisters of the Holy Names of Jesus and Mary, and the sponsors of a private school, Hill Military Academy, successfully obtained injunctions against Governor Pierce and Oregon state officials from putting the law into effect as it violated the Fourteenth Amendment. The state officials appealed to the Supreme Court.

The Court based its reasoning on the doctrine enunciated in *Meyer* v. *Nebraska* and claimed that the Oregon act "unreasonably interferes with the liberty of parents and guardians to direct the upbringing and education of children under their control."[23] The Court issued what has been termed a Magna Carta for private and parochial education.

The fundamental theory of liberty under which all governments in this Union repose excludes any general power of the State to standardize its children by forcing them to accept instruction from public teachers only. The child is not the mere creature of the State; those who nurture him and direct his destiny have the right, coupled with the high duty, to recognize and prepare him for additional obligations.[24]

The Court insisted that it did not place private and parochial schools above or beyond educational laws passed by the state. The state could "reasonably regulate all schools," and thus pass laws regarding the inspection, supervision, and examination of these schools, their teachers and students. The state could enact legislation requiring attendance at some school, designating age and length of time to be spent in school, qualities and minimum qualifications for teachers, the teaching of certain subjects, or what expressly comes within the purview of the state to ensure the common good of all its citizens.

The First Amendment was not directly at issue in this case, as a nondenominational private school was not concerned with religious instruction. However, the Court did indirectly support the guarantee of religious liberty by maintaining the right of parents to choose a denominational school in preference to a public school. Neither the growth of the Roman Catholic parochial school system nor of schools of other religious denominations were helped by the decision, but it did free them from potentially unwarranted or excessive interference by states or local school districts unfavorably disposed to nonpublic education.

Constitutional lawyers have given strong support to the Court's *Pierce* decision; the few dissenting analyses have stressed states' rights and the need of the public school as America's "melting pot."[25] Some leading American educators, however, have urged for a reconsideration of the Oregon decision. John L. Childs of Teachers College, Columbia University, advocated that all children spend at least half of their education in public schools, because he believes that attendance at nonpublic schools prevents the public school "from giving American children the richest possible experience of community."[26] In an address to the American Association of School Administrators in 1952, James B. Conant, then president of Harvard University, although not questioning the right of private and parochial schools to exist, pointed out the divisive spirit they caused by their isolation from the whole of American society into religious and social class groups.[27] Dean Hollis L. Caswell of Teachers College, Columbia University, looked upon attendance at the common public schools as essential to the preservation of American unity.[28] Theodore Brameld, noted philosopher of education, emphasized the divisions among children and asked Americans to "recall the profoundly hostile conceptions of reality that divide Catholic parochial schools from American public schools." Moreover, he extended the concept of divisiveness even to released-time religious programs with which some public school systems cooperated, and concluded that a "most conspicuous effect [of these programs] is to separate children of various faiths from one another and to accentuate group differences at the very time when a culture-in-crisis needs to concern itself seriously with strengthening intergroup solidarities."[29]

Despite these criticisms of nonpublic education, private and parochial schools have a constitutional guarantee to exist. Cultural diversity is a necessary corollary of America's free and pluralistic society. When parents must surrender the right to educate their children, even for the sake of enforced cultural unity, then the danger of state monopoly of education will exist. The Supreme Court has explicitly cited the Oregon case as a legal precedent in cases dealing with the rights of parents to educate their children according to the dictates of their consciences, and in cases dealing with nonpublic schools.[30]

The latest case affirming the basic, natural right of parents to educate their children involved members of the Old Order Amish religion and the Conservative Amish Mennonite Church. The Amish were accused of violating Wisconsin's compulsory school attendance law, which requires a child to be enrolled in a public or private school until graduation from high school or until he becomes sixteen years of age.[31]

The three Amish children in the case, Frieda Yoder and Barbara Miller, both aged fifteen, and Vernon Yutzy, fourteen, had completed the eighth grade of public school and were no longer enrolled in any school. Their parents were therefore fined for violating the compulsory education law. The Amish claimed that the Wisconsin law interfered with rights guaranteed by the First and Fourteenth amendments. Arguing on the basis of religious convictions (not questioned by the state of Wisconsin as insincere), the Amish claimed that their children's attendance at high school was contrary to their religion and way of life. Their beliefs, stemming from the Swiss Anabaptists of the sixteenth century, emphasized a simple Christianity. Salvation for them requires living separately and apart from the modern world's stress and material success. Members of an Amish religious community make their living from farming or closely related activities. High school education fosters values contrary to their religious views by emphasizing intellectual and scientific achievements, competitiveness, and worldly success. A high school education takes Amish children physically and emotionally away from their community environment during an important formative stage in their lives. At such a time, the commitment to Amish ideals is also most favorably developed, especially through stress of the importance of manual work. Beyond the basics of learning in elementary school, education by "doing" rather than learning in the classroom prepares an Amish for entrance into their religious community.[32]

With *Pierce* as important legal precedent, the Supreme Court upheld the case of the Amish. Granting to the state both the power and the responsibility for establishing "reasonable regulations" pertaining to education, it affirmed "the values of parental direction of the religious upbringing of their children in their early and formative years [as having] a high place in our society." For "a State's interest in universal education, however highly we rank it, is not totally free from a balancing process when it impinges on other fundamental rights and interests, such as those specifically protected by the Free Exercise Clause of the First Amendment and the traditional interest of parents with respect to the religious upbringing of their children. . . ."[33]

The Court's upholding of the Amish was based solidly on respect of the right to follow one's conscience in religious matters. The decision of the Amish not to conform to contemporary society is not a philosophical or personal one, as was Henry David Thoreau's rejection of the social values of his day and subsequent isolation at Walden Pond, but a matter of "deep religious conviction," based on their interpretation of the Bible. Therefore, the Court maintained:

The conclusion is inescapable that secondary schooling, by exposing Amish children to worldly influences in terms of attitudes, goals and values contrary to beliefs, and by substantially interfering with the religious development of the Amish child and his integration into the way of life of the Amish faith community at the crucial adolescent state of development, contravenes the basic religious tenets and practice of the Amish faith, both as to the parent and the child . . . the unchallenged testimony of acknowledged experts in education and religious history, almost 300 years of consistent practice, and strong evidence of a sustained faith pervading and regulating respondents' entire mode of life support the claim that enforcement of the State's requirement of compulsory formal education after the eighth grade would gravely endanger if not destroy the free exercise of respondents' religious beliefs.[34]

Thus the Court saw in the long-established program of informal vocational education provided by the Amish for their children a reasonable substitute for one or two additional years of formal high school education. The Court further accepted testimony of educational experts that the Amish system of learning by doing was preparing Amish children for life as adults in the Amish community; the visible results of their education have, moreover, provided "productive and law-abiding members of society."[35]

Justice Douglas dissented largely because two of the three children involved in the case did not testify. He felt strongly that "the education of the child is a matter on which the child will often have decided views"—including the desire to break from the Amish tradition, as some Amish children have done.

It is the future of the student, not the future of the parents, that is imperilled in today's decision. If a parent keeps his child out of school beyond the grade school, then the child will be forever barred from entry into the new and amazing world of diversity we have today. The child may decide that that is the preferred course, or he may rebel. It is the student's judgment, not his parent's, that is essential if we are to give full meaning to what we have said about the Bill of Rights and of the right of students to be masters of their own destiny.[36]

Despite this 1972 Supreme Court ruling, Pennsylvania Attorney General Israel Packel ruled on January 25, 1973, that the state can require Amish children to attend school beyond the eighth grade. While Packel admitted that they could not be forced to attend the ordinary public or private school, they could meet state school requirements by pursuing special academic, agricultural, and home-making courses on their farms.[37] The *Yoder* decision took note of the Pennsylvania plan for the education of Amish children of high school age, but the Wisconsin state superintendent of public instruction had rejected such a substitute proposal because it would not afford Amish children a "substantially equivalent education" to that offered in schools to children of the same area in Wisconsin. Programs similar to Pennsylvania have been instituted in Indiana, Iowa, and Kansas.[38]

PUBLIC FUNDS FOR INDIAN RELIGIOUS SCHOOLS

The Northwest Ordinance of 1787 not only deemed "religion, morality and knowledge" as "necessary to government and the happiness of mankind," but also encouraged schools to carry out this purpose by setting aside lot number 16 of every township to be used exclusively for the support of schools which, at that time, were predominantly religiously controlled. Ohio, governed under this ordinance until admitted as a state, provided in its constitution of 1802 (twelve years after the adoption of the First Amendment) that

> The laws shall be passed by the legislature which shall secure to each and every denomination of religious societies in each surveyed township which now is or may hereafter be formed in the State, an equal participation, according to their number of adherents, of the profits arising from the land granted by Congress for the support of religion, agreeably to the ordinance or act of Congress making the appropriation.[39]

In 1789 the secretary of war, Henry Knox, recommended with the approval of President Washington that Congress appropriate funds for the support of those missionaries among the Indians: "The object of this establishment would be the happiness of Indians, teaching them the great duties of religion and morality, and to inculcate a friendship and attachment to the United States."[40] The policy of the federal government of aiding religion and religious education was continued in 1803 with President Jefferson's request to ratify a treaty with the Kaskosia Indians. The treaty said in part:

> And whereas the greater part of said tribe have been baptized and received into the Catholic Church, to which they are much attached, the United States will give annually, for seven years, one hundred dollars toward the support of a priest of that religion, who will engage to perform for said tribe the duties of his office, and also to instruct as many of their children as possible, in the rudiments of literature, and the United States will further give the sum of three hundred dollars, to assist the said tribe in the erection of a church.[41]

In acts passed by Congress in 1819, 1820, and in 1870, similar arrangements were made with various sectarian agencies for the education of Indians. Congress restricted this practice in 1895, when it would grant federal money to sectarian schools only when nonpublic schools were not available.[42] In 1897, however, Congress enacted the following: "And it is hereby declared to be the settled policy of the government to hereafter make no appropriation whatever for education in any sectarian school."[43]

In 1868, through a treaty with the Sioux Indians, the U.S. government agreed to provide free educational services for a period of twenty years in consideration of large cessions of land. Congress extended the educational obligation it assumed in 1899, so that thereafter every annual Indian appropriation contained a provision for continuing this educational arrangement.[44]

The 1908 Supreme Court case, *Quick Bear* v. *Leupp*, arose from a complaint on the part of Reuben Quick Bear, Ralph Eagle Feathers, and other members of the Indian Sioux Tribe. They sought to enjoin Charles E. Leupp, the commissioner of indian affairs, from paying out of tribal funds for the support of sectarian schools on their reservation, as the commissioner had entered into a contract with the Bureau of Catholic Indian Affairs. The Court, in upholding the action of the commissioner of indian affairs, classified the declaration of policy established by Congress in 1897 and the treaty obligations as "distinct and different in nature, and having no relation to each other, except that both are technically appropriations." The Court agreed with and quoted from the Court of Appeals which had previously heard the case:

> The "treaty" and "trust" moneys are the only moneys which the Indians can lay claim to as a matter of right; the only sums on which they are entitled to rely as theirs for education; and while these moneys are not delivered to them in hand, yet the money must not be provided, but be expended for their benefit, and in part for their education; it seems inconceivable that Congress shall have intended to prohibit them from receiving religious education at their own cost if they desire it; such an intent would be one to prohibit the free exercise of religion amongst the Indians, and such would be the effect of the construction for which the complainants contend.[45]

In providing funds for religious education in this case, the Supreme Court felt that the free exercise of religion on the part of the Indians would have been otherwise constrained. Spurlock has described the Court's reasoning as reflecting "a concept that the obligation to provide education transcended an obligation to maintain the wall between Church and State," and that the child-benefit theory, later developed by the Court in *Cochran* v. *Louisiana* "was heralded here."[46]

TEXTBOOKS FOR NONPUBLIC SCHOOL CHILDREN

Up to 1928, the practice of providing textbooks for children in parochial schools was generally considered as contrary to state constitutional requirements or statutes forbidding the use of public funds for religious denominational schools. The decision of the Ohio Supreme Court in 1901 that the equal protection clause of both the federal and Ohio state constitutions was not violated when a school district furnished free textbooks to public school children, and not to those in religious denominational schools, was looked upon as a legal precedent in this matter.[47] In 1928, however, the state legislature of Louisiana passed a law which allowed the granting of free textbooks "to the children of the state" from the proceeds of the severance tax fund. The state board of education so interpreted and applied the law to include children in nonpublic schools, even though private schools were not mentioned in the law. The practice of furnishing free textbooks to parochial school children in the city of Ogdensburg, New York, was declared unconstitutional by the appellate division of the New York state supreme court in 1922.[48] The New York court had argued that such an arrangement would constitute a grant directly to the schools and not to the pupils. Even if a statute were so designed as to furnish books to the pupils, an indirect aid would be involved which the state court would also consider unconstitutional. Donald F. Boles maintains that it was in this New York case that "the issue of the child-benefit theory began to materialize."[49]

In Louisiana, a group of citizens contested the legality of the school board's interpretation of the law on the grounds that public property was being diverted for private use; this violated the Fourteenth Amendment, for children in private and religious schools which were not part of the public educational system of the state, were also being furnished free textbooks as the children in the public schools. The Louisiana State Supreme Court upheld the board's interpretation and application of the law as being opposed neither to the state nor to the federal Constitution.

After hearing the appeal to the U.S. Supreme Court Chief Justice Charles E. Hughes sustained the Louisiana statute and the Louisiana Supreme Court, which he quoted:

One may scan the acts in vain to ascertain where any money is appropriated for the purchase of school books for the use of any church, private, sectarian, or even public school. The appropriations were made for the specific purpose of purchasing school books for the use of the school children of the state free of cost to them. It was for their benefit and the resulting benefit to the state that the appropriations were made. True, these children attend some school; public or private, the latter, sectarian or nonsectarian, and that the books are to be furnished them for their use, free of cost, whichever they attend. The schools, however, are not the beneficiaries of these appropriations. They obtain nothing from them, nor are they relieved of

a single obligation because of them. The school children
and the state alone are the beneficiaries. It is also true that
the sectarian schools, which some of the children attend,
instruct their pupils in religion, and books are used for that
purpose, but one may search diligently the acts, though
without result, in an effort to find anything to the effect that
it is the purpose of the state to furnish religious books for
the use of such children. . . . What the statutes contemplate
is that the same books that are furnished children attending public schools shall be furnished children attending
private schools. This is the only practical way of interpreting and executing the statutes, and this is what the state
board of education is doing. Among these books, natu-
rally, none is expected [to be] adapted to religious instruction.[50]

The distinctions emphasized in the *Cochran* case are significant:
The children receive the books, not the sectarian schools; books are
furnished, but not religious books. The Court, in so distinguishing,
offered the child-benefit theory of public aid. Spurlock has suggested that it would be difficult to see "that no benefit was conferred
upon the private schools by the fact that such schools could avail
their children of free textbooks."[51] He fails to note, however, that
most private schools require students to purchase their own textbooks. The state's lending of textbooks to private school children
was a savings not to the private schools but to the children and their
parents, who also supported public schools through taxation. As a
result of the *Cochran* decision, as many as eight states have provided
textbooks in secular branches of knowledge to nonpublic school
children on a loan basis.[52]

The reaction of legal periodicals to *Cochran* generally favored
the Court's opinion, but they raised the question of the extent to
which the child-benefit theory could or would be applied in the
future.[53]

Cochran met varying interpretations in the decisions of three
state supreme courts. In Mississippi in 1941, the court upheld and
followed the *Cochran* child-benefit theory. It argued for the needs of
the pupils despite an incidental benefit to the religious institution.
It added that to deny a public school child his free textbook upon
his transfer to a parochial school would be "a denial of equal privi-

leges on sectarian grounds."[54] In South Dakota in 1943, the court denied such aid to children not enrolled in any part of the public school system of the state.[55] The 1961 *Dickman* case in Oregon outrightly attacked the child-benefit theory; for if it were to be accepted without qualification, then there would be no limit as to the spending of public funds for the education of nonpublic school children. The court argued that

> Where the aid is to pupils and schools the benefit is iden-
> tified with the function of education and if the educational
> institution is religious, the benefit accrues to religious in-
> stitutions in their function as religious institutions. And so
> it is the case at bar. Granting that pupils and not schools
> are intended to be the beneficiaries of the state's bounty,
> the aid is extended to the pupil only as a member of the
> school which he attends. Whoever else may share in its
> benefits such aid is an asset to the schools themselves.[56]

The U.S. Supreme Court denied *certiorari*, or review, of the state of Oregon's refusal to allow free textbooks to nonpublic school children in the *Dickman* case. This action raised some specu-lation that the Supreme Court might later reverse the *Cochran* deci-sion of 1930.[57]

Despite the Supreme Court's sanction of the practice of text-book loans to private school children, a memorandum issued by a cabinet officer in the Kennedy administration should be noted. Voicing a special concern for education, President Kennedy sent to Congress on February 20, 1961, a special message on federal aid to education, emphasizing "a new standard of excellence in education —and the availability of such excellence to *all* who are willing and able to pursue it."[58] Senator Wayne Morse, chairman of the Senate Subcommittee on Education, requested a memorandum from Sec-retary of Health, Education, and Welfare Abraham Ribicoff. Senator Morse desired information on the constitutionality of loans to sec-tarian schools and the benefits they receive under existing federal laws. In reference to the *Cochran* case, the memorandum argued that

> the Cochran case is dubious authority for the proposition
> that textbooks may be provided by a state to parochial
> school students. The crucial question of whether the estab-

lishment clause of the first amendment prohibits the expenditure of public funds for textbooks to be used by church school pupils was not presented to the Court in this case, and the Court therefore had no occasion to rule upon the question.[59]

Commenting on this memorandum, Joseph F. Costanzo criticized "this manner of reasoning" as it sought "to minimize the constitutional precedent of Cochran as a legitimate point of departure of the constitutionality of other forms of aid to all school children".[60] The *Cochran* case, when decided in 1930, was noted as involving only the Fourteenth and not the First Amendment.[61] But subsequent Court rulings, as in the *Everson* case, have argued that the establishment of the religion clause in the First Amendment binds the states by virtue of the due process clause of the Fourteenth Amendment.[62] This memorandum and the *Dickman* case paved the way more clearly for further challenging of the textbook issue.

In 1950, the state of New York enacted a law that permitted qualified voters of any school district to authorize a special tax for the purpose of making available free textbooks.[63] In 1965 the Education Law of 1950 was changed from "permitting" to "requiring" of free textbooks for public school students.[64] In 1966, the law was further amended so that local school boards were required to purchase textbooks and lend them without charge "to all children residing in such district who are enrolled in grades seven to twelve of a public or private school which complies with the compulsory education law."[65] Parochial schools were included in the 1966 amendment and their students could be loaned textbooks for a semester or more in the school they attended, approved by a board of education or similar body. The texts had to be considered "secular" and not "religious," but could be different from texts used in public schools.

The board of education of Central School District No. 1 in Rensselaer and Columbia counties brought suit against James E. Allen, Jr., commissioner of education for the state of New York, because it regarded the 1966 amendment in violation of both the state and federal constitutions. Appellants sought clarification from the courts as to the execution of the textbook law. A lower court held the law unconstitutional. But the Appellate Court dismissed the appellants' complaint on the ground that school boards had no standing to attack the validity of a state statute. The New York Court of Appeals upheld their right to attack the statute but declared the statute not in violation of either the state or the federal constitutions.[66] The appellants, therefore, brought the case to the U.S. Supreme Court.

Justice Byron White rendered the majority opinion in a six-to-three decision. He reaffirmed the Court's reasoning in the *Cochran* and *Everson* cases. No establishment of religion could be found in the textbook law, as it was not in the free bus transportation statute; such laws would be considered as having "a secular legislative purpose and a primary effect that neither advances nor inhibits religion."[67] Therefore, the child-benefit theory applied: The financial benefit is to parents and children, not to the parochial schools. As the books are lent at the pupil's request, ownership remained in the state. Appealing to *Cochran* specifically, Justice White regarded such cooperation between the state and students attending nonpublic schools a matter "properly of public concern," for the state's interest in the secular education provided by private schools not only aids individual interests, but safeguards the common interest of all in education. Justice White stressed that no evidence had been entered into the record that any of the textbooks were used by the parochial schools to teach religion, or that all teaching in a sectarian school is religious, or that secular and religious teaching are so intertwined that these secular textbooks aided in the teaching of religion.[68] Justice Harlan concurred with the majority as he saw the neutral attitude required by government toward religion safeguarded in the Education Law of New York State.[69]

Each of the three dissenting justices offered his own opinion. Black held the New York law as "a flat, flagrant, open violation of the First and Fourteenth Amendments." He referred to the *Everson* decision when he wrote, "No tax in any amount, large or small, can be levied to support any religious activities or institutions, whatever they may be called, or whatever form they may adopt to teach or practice religion." He envisioned the New York law as not yet formally establishing a religion but taking "a great stride in that direction," and if permitted, encourage further steps. He would not put bus fares in the same category as books, for books are "the most essential tool of education" and, therefore, can inevitably be utilized to propagate the religious views of a particular sect.[70]

In his dissent, Justice Douglas objected to the power given to the parochial school to request the books it wants. And he asked in this regard, "Can there be the slightest doubt that the head of the parochial school will select the book or books that best promote its sectarian creed?" In agreement with Black, he maintained that there is "nothing ideological about a bus . . . a school lunch, or a public nurse, or a scholarship." But a textbook is "the chief, although not solitary, instrumentality for propagating a particular creed or faith." As the *Engel* case was struck down because of the power of religious-political groups "to write their own prayers into law," so should the textbook law which gives parochial schools the initiative in selecting their own texts at public expense. Justice Douglas admitted the possibility of being wrong in judging that "a contest will be on to provide those books for religious schools which the dominant religious group concludes best reflect the theocentric or other philosophy of the particular church." But he felt that the judgment against the textbook loan arrangement should stand, because if school boards did not acquiesce to sectarian pressure or control of choice of books, and if the religious schools were to accept nonsectarian books, then "the long view would tend towards state domination of the church," which would violate the establishment clause of the First Amendment.[71]

The dissenting opinion of Justice Fortas concentrated on the argument that the choice of the textbooks resides in the hands of the sectarian schools, and that, therefore, it is not a matter of extending to children attending sectarian schools the same service or facility extended to children in public schools (the child-benefit theory), but "furnishing special, separate, and particular books, specially, separately, and particularly chosen by religious sects or their representatives for use in their sectarian schools."[72]

Commenting on the *Allen* case, Professor Paul A. Freund said that "the case is obviously the beginning, not the end, of constitutional litigation," because the "opinion is a narrow one . . . in its stress on the formal aspects of the arrangements, namely that the books were loaned, with title remaining in the state, and that the requests were made by and on behalf of the students, not the school."[73]

On the same date that the *Allen* decision was rendered on June 10, 1968, a group of taxpayers, members of the American Jewish Congress, the New York Civil Liberties Union, the United Federation of Teachers, and the United Parents Association, received a favorable decision to challenge provisions of the Elementary and Secondary Education Act (ESEA) passed by Congress in 1965.[74] Title I of ESEA established a program for financial assistance to local educational agencies for the education of low-income families and allowed private elementary and secondary schools to receive special educational services and arrangements, such as educational radio and television and mobile educational services and equipment. Title II also allowed private elementary and secondary schools to receive federal grants for the acquisition of school library resources, textbooks, and other printed and published instructional materials. In granting the right to challenge federal legislation involving spending, the U.S. Supreme Court reversed the 1923 *Frothingham* decision, which held that taxpayers lacked standing in court if their tax payments were considered too small.[75] But in 1968, the Court maintained that the challenged program involved a substantial expenditure of federal tax funds which could possibly violate the establishment and free exercise clauses of the First Amendment. The Court expressed no opinion on the specific claim of the unconstitutionality of Titles I and II of ESEA, but affirmed the right of the appellants to have them adjudicated in a federal court.[76]

BUS TRANSPORTATION

The provision of bus transportation to children in nonpublic schools has been a contested legal question since 1912, thirty-five years before the Supreme Court's *Everson* ruling. State courts handed down numerous, diverse decisions in this matter. In 1912, the state of Oklahoma permitted the extension of a regulation allowing reduced fares on public buses for public school children to children in a religious school.[77] In 1937, the Court of Appeals of New York State upheld a similar policy: "The Constitution no more forbids transportation to school children than it forbids supplying them with lunch."[78] Wisconsin and Delaware courts denied transportation to parochial schools on constitutional grounds.[79] Maryland and Kentucky viewed transportation for all children as connected with the state's requirement for compulsory education, while South Dakota rejected transportation to children who were not part of the public school system.[80] From 1938 to 1946, five state statutes requiring transportation for parochial school children were declared unconstitutional.[81] In 1946, the last case decided by a state supreme court before *Everson* permitted transportation.[82] Thus, at the time of the *Everson* ruling, nineteen states and one territory permitted the transportation of parochial school children at public expense, while seven denied it.[83]

The state of New Jersey had passed in 1941 a free bus transportation law which explicitly included the transportation of pupils in nonpublic schools.

> Whenever in any district there are children living remote from any schoolhouse, the board of education of the district may make rules and contracts for the transportation of such children to and from school, including the transportation of school children to and from school other than a public school as is operated for profit in whole or in part.
>
> When any school district provides any transportation for public school children to and from school, transportation from any point in such established school route shall be supplied to school children residing in such school district in going to and from school other than a public school, except such school as is operated for profit in whole or in part.[84]

A township school board established the policy of reimbursing parents for money spent for bus transportation to both public and parochial schools. A taxpayer brought suit against the school board for the "unconstitutional" reimbursement to parents sending their children to parochial schools. With the state courts upholding the statute, the taxpayer appealed to the Supreme Court. The Court's decision provided an expansion of the "child-benefit theory" as first stated in the *Cochran* textbook case and an exposition of the federal government's relation to religion and education.[85]

The Court sustained the right of school board authorities in New Jersey to provide free transportation for children attending private schools. As in *Cochran,* the Court distinguished between aid to the child and aid to a sectarian school: "The state contributes no money to the schools. It does not support them. Its legislation, as applied, does no more than provide a general program to help parents get their children, regardless of their religion, safely and expeditiously to and from accredited schools."[86] The Court did not question the possibility that some children would not attend sectarian schools if this aid of reimbursement of bus fares were not available. Yet in its reasoning the Court clearly implied indirect aid to sectarian schools when their children share some same benefit as children in public schools.

> Parents might be reluctant to permit their children to attend schools which the state had cut off from such general government services as ordinary police and fire protection, connections for sewage disposal, public highways and sidewalks. Of course, cutting off church schools from these services, so separate and so undisputably marked off from the religious function, would make it far more difficult for the schools to operate. But such is obviously not the purpose of the First Amendment. That Amendment requires the state to be a neutral in its relations with groups of religious believers and non-believers; it does not require the state to be their adversary. State power is no more to be used so as to handicap religions than it is to favor them.[87]

Thus neither the First nor the Fourteenth amendments were violated by the New Jersey law. However, the decision does not require, but merely permits, public transportation for parochial school children.

The implications of the *Everson* case for education, however, are much broader than the states' provision for free bus transportation to nonpublic school children under the "child-benefit" theory. The decision enunciated a philosophy of the relation between government and religion, a philosophy that has been challenged on the basis of both its legal and historical foundations.[88] Justice Hugo L. Black, speaking for the majority in a 5-to-4 decision, rendered the following interpretation of the First Amendment:

> The "establishment of religion" clause of the First Amendment means at least this: Neither a state nor the federal government can set up a church. Neither can pass laws which aid one religion, aid all religions, or prefer one religion over another. Neither can force nor influence a per-

son to go to or to remain away from church against his will
or force him to profess a belief or disbelief in any religion.
No person can be punished for entertaining or profes-
sing beliefs or disbeliefs, for church attendance or non-
attendance. No tax in any amount, large or small, can be
levied to support any religious activities or institutions,
whatever they may be called, or whatever form they may
adopt to teach or practice religion. Neither a state nor the
federal government can, openly or secretly, participate in
the affairs of any religious organizations and *vice versa.* In
the words of Jefferson, the clause against establishment of
religion by law was intended to erect "a wall of separation
between Church and State."[89]

Justice Black called for a policy and philosophy of strict neutrality between American government and religious schools. Jefferson's
metaphor of "a wall of separation" was to be the basic principle by
which to guide all relations between government and education
under the auspices of religious denominations. Subsequent court
decisions have demonstrated the acceptance of this philosophy, not
only for financial aid to denominational schools, but also as to the
matters of teaching religion, reading the Bible, and saying prayers
in public schools.[90]

The four dissenting justices in *Everson* may have disagreed with
Justice Black as to the constitutionality of the New Jersey statute, but
they were in accord with him as regards the interpretation of the
First Amendment. Justice Jackson's dissenting opinion, joined by
Justice Frankfurter's, stressed that "the New Jersey statute makes
the character of the school, not the needs of the children, determine
the eligibility of parents to reimbursement" and, therefore, contrary
to the First Amendment.[91] Justice Rutledge, in a dissenting opinion
with which Justice Burton concurred, also saw the statute as unconstitutional because "here parents pay money to send their children
to parochial schools and funds raised by taxation are used to reimburse them. This not only helps the children to get to school and
the parents to send them. It aids them in a substantial way to get
the very thing which they are sent to the particular school to secure,
namely, religious training and teaching."[92]

Both legal and educational experts have written critically of the
Everson decision. The child-benefit theory was labeled a "legal

fiction."[93] The extension of such aid to nonpublic schools was also feared, as expressed in the question: "How can it be proper for the public to pay for transport to religious instruction and worship from Monday through Friday if it could not provide free rides to Sunday or Saturday worship?"[94] Yet the child-benefit theory received support, with transportation to be placed on the same level as health services and school lunches as direct aids to the child with only incidental benefit to the school.[95] Some criticism was directed to the absolutist stand of Justice Black on the complete separation of church and state.[96] One critic of Black's analysis and interpretation of the establishment of religion clause distinguished between the state and religion and the state and "ecclesiastical" religion; the latter should not be confused with the former.[97]

As they were before the *Everson* decision, states are divided as to whether or not to permit free transportation to parochial school children; state courts have both approved and disapproved plans for transportation.[98] Legal scholars have attributed the difficulty of interpreting *Everson* to the "inherent contradiction . . . in the fact that judges and polemicists on both sides of the bus-ride struggle can find in all the opinions some strikingly probative sentences to support their thesis,"[99] to the questions it left unanswered as to the juridical status of religious schools, and to the extent that the child-benefit theory can be applied.[100]

SCHOOL AID DECISIONS OF 1971

On June 28, 1971, the U.S. Supreme Court handed down three decisions dealing with the constitutionality of financial aid to church-related colleges and schools. Two of the cases, *Lemon* v. *Kurtzman* and *Robinson* v. *DiCenso*, involved elementary and secondary schools; the third, *Tilton* v. *Richardson*, involved colleges.

In 1963, Congress passed the Higher Education Facilities Act. One of the act's provisions called for federal grants to be used for the construction of college and university facilities, excluding "any facility used or to be used for sectarian instruction or as place for religious worship, or . . . primarily in connection with any part of the program of a school or department of divinity." The federal government, moreover, retains an interest in the facilities constructed for twenty years, and if an educational institution violates any of the conditions under which it accepted the grant, the institution is bound to restore the amount of funds, equal in proportion to its present value, to the government.[101] An estimated thirty-two thousand construction grants, totaling $1.5 billion have been made since the law's enactment, and about 15 percent of this aid has gone to religious-related educational institutions.[102] The act entrusted the Office of Education with the task of enforcing its provisions primarily by on-site inspections.

The appellants in this higher education case were resident citizens and taxpayers of the state of Connecticut, who sought an injunction against the government officials who administer the act. The Office of Education functions within the jurisdiction of the secretary of health, education, and welfare; Elliott W. Richardson was secretary at the time the case was brought to court. The appellants charged that the act violated the establishment of religion clause of the First Amendment because four church-related colleges and universities in Connecticut received federal construction grants: (1) a library building for the Sacred Heart University in Bridgeport; (2) a music, drama, and arts building for Amhurst College in Woodstock; (3) a science building and a library building for Fairfield University in Fairfield; and (4) a language laboratory for Albertus Magnus College in New Haven. The U.S. District Court for Connecticut ruled that the Higher Education Facilities Act authorized grants to church-related colleges and universities and that the act had neither sought nor in effect promoted religion; it was, therefore, constitutional. The appellants appealed to the U.S. Supreme Court.[103]

Chief Justice Warren Burger wrote the Court's decision in *Tilton*. Only three other justices concurred so that, strictly speaking, there was no majority opinion; however, Justice White filed an opinion concurring in the result, thus the 5-to-4 vote upholding the 1963 act, with the exception of the twenty-year restriction on the use of the buildings constructed under the benefits of the act.[104] In his opinion, Chief Justice Burger cited the act as a response to the strong nationwide demand for expansion of college and university facilities as increasing numbers of young people sought higher education. Congress clearly intended the act to include all colleges and universities regardless of any affiliation or sponsorship by a religious body. Specifically excluded were buildings to be used for sectarian instruction or religious worship. Burger based his opinion on the answer to four questions. First, as to whether the act reflected a secular legislative purpose, the act's preamble set forth the need for expanded facilities, as required by "the security and welfare of the United States," to assure ample opportunity for the fullest development of our nation's intellectual talents. That religious educational institutions would acquire some benefits as a consequence of the legislative program was not the crucial question; rather the issue at hand was whether the principal or primary effect advanced religion. The act was so diligently designed to ensure that federally subsidized facilities would be directed to the secular rather than the religious function of the educational institutions, and the facilities constructed for the four Connecticut institutions comply with this requirement. Secondly, whether the primary effect of the act advances or inhibits religion, the enforcement provisions of the statute adequately ensure. If the institution violated any of the restrictions under which it accepted the federal funds, then the institution would be bound to make restitution to the government. The Court, however, objected to the twenty-year provision of the act, for at the end of this period the building could be used for any purpose, including a religious one: "It cannot be assumed that a substantial structure has no value after that period and hence the unrestricted use of a valuable property is in effect a contribution of some value to a religious body. . . . If, at the end of 20 years the building is, for example, converted into a chapel or otherwise used to promote religious interests, the original federal grant will in part have the effect of advancing religion. To this extent the Act therefore trespasses on the Religion Clauses." However, the unconstitutionality of a part of an act does not invalidate its other provisions and, therefore, the act remains constitutional except for the twenty-year limit on the use of the federally constructed buildings. Thirdly, as to whether excessive entanglement characterizes the relationship between government and church under the act, the Court decided that, unlike elementary and secondary education, higher education is less bound to religious indoctrination and influence, and more responsive to free and critical inquiry characterized by academic freedom. The Court utilized the judgment and findings of lawyers, educators, and sociologists in reading this distinction between church-related institutions of higher learning and parochial elementary and secondary schools. Furthermore, unlike the lower grades in religiously controlled schools, "the evidence shows institutions with admittedly religious functions but whose predominant higher education mission is to provide their students with a secular education." The government entanglements with religion in higher education, moreover, are minimal, limited to inspection and a one-time, single-purpose construction grant. In the lower grades, and specifically referring to the *Lemon* and *DiCenso* cases, the entanglement embraces direct and continuing payments and constant government surveillance to ensure religious neutrality. Fourthly, as to whether the implementation of the act did inhibit the free exercise of religion, as the appellants claimed because they were compelled to pay taxes from which the proceeds partially finance the grants, the Court found no coercion directed at the practice or exercise of the appellants' religious beliefs, nor deemed the share of their costs no more significant than the impact of tax exemptions to religious institutions or the provision of textbooks.[105]

The three dissenting justices, Douglas, Black, and Marshall, accepted the Court's classification of the twenty-year reversion aspect of the act as unconstitutional. They maintained that any financial grants to sectarian educational institutions violate the First Amendment. It did not matter whether the grant was a "one-time, single-purpose" form of aid; it was aid to support an institution where religious teaching and secular teaching were so enmeshed that only the strictest supervision and surveillance would insure compliance. Such kind of constant surveillance, as well as federal financing, is "obnoxious under the Establishment and Free Exercise Clauses" of the Constitution.[106]

Justice White accepted the Court's invalidation of the twenty-year restriction on the use of buildings constructed with federal funds; his observations on the *Tilton* case will be considered with the *Lemon* and *DiCenso* cases, with which White drew some comparative analyses and judgments.[107]

Two cases were decided on the same day as the *Tilton* higher education case involving financial aid from state governments to church-related elementary and secondary schools. The cases concerned statutes passed in the states of Rhode Island and Pennsylvania.

In 1969 Rhode Island's state legislature enacted the Salary Supplement Act, which considered the quality of education in the nonpublic elementary schools in jeopardy because of the rising salaries of teachers and the difficult financial strain imposed on these schools as a result. The act authorized payment by the state for the teachers of secular subjects in these schools, with payments to be made directly to the teacher in an amount not to exceed 15 percent of his current annual salary. The teacher's salary, plus the supplement, could not exceed the maximum salary paid to a public school teacher; in addition, the average per pupil expenditure in the nonpublic school for the teacher of secular education must be less than the average of that of the state's public schools. Teachers receiving salary supplements could not teach any course in religion, and could teach only those subjects taught in public schools, using the same educational materials.[108]

A group of citizens and taxpayers of Rhode Island challenged the Salary Supplement Act's constitutionality on the grounds that it violated the establishment and free exercise clauses of the First Amendment. Some 25 percent of pupils in the state attended non-public elementary schools and about 95 percent of these attended Roman Catholic schools. For the first semester of 1970–71 alone, the salary supplements to 219 nonpublic school teachers all of whom were employed in Roman Catholic schools amounted to $95,564.69.[109] After state and federal district court rulings, the case came before the U.S. Supreme Court in 1971.

In 1968, Pennsylvania adopted a law which resembled Rhode Island's law in some features. The Pennsylvania Nonpublic Elementary and Secondary Act also was passed in response to the rising costs plaguing the state's nonpublic schools and to aid them in "those purely secular educational objectives achieved through nonpublic education." The Pennsylvania statute authorized the state superintendent of public instruction to "purchase" specified "secular educational services" from nonpublic schools. These services included teachers' salaries, textbooks, and instructional materials. The act clearly delineated three restrictions for aid: (1) only courses in the "secular" subjects of mathematics, modern foreign languages, physical science, and physical education would be allowed; (2) the state superintendent of public instruction must approve the textbooks and instructional materials; and (3) any course dealing with religious teaching, morals, or forms of worship was excluded.[110] Pennsylvania citizens and taxpayers questioned the act's constitutionality for the same reasons as the Rhode Islanders. The annual cost under the Pennsylvania act approximated $5 million and recipients included some 1,181 nonpublic elementary and secondary schools totaling some 535,215 students, 96 percent of whom attended Roman Catholic schools.[111] Because of the lower court's upholding of the statute, the plaintiffs appealed to the U.S. Supreme Court.

Chief Justice Warren Burger rendered the decision in an 8-to-1 vote striking down the Rhode Island statute and an 8-to-0 vote for the Pennsylvania statute. The *Everson* decision again became the basis for the Court's opinion. It acknowledged the difficulty of perceiving "the lines of demarcation in this extraordinarily sensitive area of constitutional law"—interpretation of "establishment of religion"—because it is possible that a law does not necessarily "establish" a religion but can "end in the sense of being a step that could lead to such establishment." Statutes affecting aid to nonpublic schools must have a primarily secular legislative purpose, and their effect must neither advance nor inhibit religion, as *Allen* had declared regarding the loaning of textbooks to religious-controlled schools. But the statute must not foster "an excessive government entanglement with religion." Although the Rhode Island and Pennsylvania statutes were framed so as to guarantee the separation between the secular and religious functions of education, with the state supporting only the secular, the entire relationship involves excessive entanglement between government and religion. While some relationship is inevitable—such as inspections for fire, building and zoning regulations, and requirements for compulsory school attendance—it does not have to be excessive.

Roman Catholic elementary schools were the sole beneficiaries in Rhode Island. These schools, the Court pointed out, formed an integral part of the church. They are under the church's jurisdiction, run and staffed largely by religious nuns; a religious spirit permeates the school and person of the teacher, and even the laymen, all of whom, with few exceptions, are Roman Catholic. Furthermore, to ensure no intermingling of the secular and the religious, "a comprehensive, discriminating, and continuing state surveillance" must be had—and a teacher, unlike a book, renders such surveillance extremely difficult. Thus, the relationship is open to excessive government direction and supervision of church schools and, hence, of churches, also contrary to the First Amendment. The Pennsylvania statute, in addition to the same Rhode Island problem, provides state financial aid to the church-related school. The Court referred to the *Everson* and *Allen* cases as distinct in this matter, since the aid was intended primarily and directly to the students and their parents. It noted the *Walz* case which urged caution against direct payments to religious organizations: "Obviously a direct money subsidy would be a relationship pregnant with involvement and, as with most governmental grant programs, could encompass sustained and detailed administrative relationships for enforcement of statutory or administrative standards."[112] The Court saw in these two state programs a "divisive political potential" leading to candidates and voters involved in divisions along religious lines as additional monies are sought—an evil the First Amendment sought to avoid.[113]

Justices Douglas and Black, in their concurring opinions, stressed excessive entanglement because of the need for strict surveillance, especially because of the religious indoctrination that necessarily takes place in sectarian schools through the teachers, the curricula, and the program of religious activities and formation.[114] Justice Marshall took no part in the consideration of the *Lemon* case; he concurred with Douglas's opinion in the *DiCenso* case.[115] Justice Brennan, in addition to the arguments of the majority, reviewed state aid to private and sectarian schools, a practice which ceased with the advent of the common public school which, when firmly established, opposed the use of the state's taxing power to support sectarian schools. Furthermore, since 1840 the states have added provisions to their constitutions prohibiting the use of public school funds to aid sectarian schools. Many state constitutions include sectarian colleges and universities under the prohibition. The courts of the states have viewed public subsidies as impermissible. On the basis of this history, Justice Brennan concluded that the statutes involved in *Lemon*, *DiCenso*, and *Tilton* "require too close proximity" of government to the subsidized sectarian institutions; thus, an excessive entanglement between religion and government.[116]

Justice White, in dissenting from the majority's view in *Lemon* and *DiCenso*, noted contradictions in reasoning on the part of the Court. For in *Tilton*, the Court upholds the federal government's financing of the separate function of secular education conducted by church-related higher institutions; yet it rejects the aid programs of two states for elementary and secondary educational institutions. His interpretation of *Allen* was: "That religion may indirectly benefit from governmental aid to the secular activities of churches does not

convert that aid into an impermissible establishment of religion."
He would have sustained the state programs on the basis that the
state governments were financing a "separable secular function of
overriding importance." The Court, Justice White also noted, could
sanction the "separable secular functions" in higher Catholic education, of which the religious function is still an integral part, but
could not in elementary and secondary education, because of the
potential danger of the teachers unavoidably mixing the secular
with the religious, even though no evidence of entanglement difficulties was brought forth. He, therefore, would not, in both the
Rhode Island and Pennsylvania cases, "substitute presumption for
proof that religion is or would be taught in state financed secular
courses or assume that enforcement measures would be so extensive as to border on a free exercise violation."[117]

Reaction to *Lemon* and *DiCenso* was immediate. John Cardinal
Krol, archbishop of Philadelphia, viewed the Catholic parochial
school system as "now mortally threatened," but added that "we
remain staunchly committed to keeping the doors of our schools
open." In evaluating the impact of these decisions, Bishop Joseph
L. Bernardin, general secretary of the U.S. Catholic Conference,
said that financial problems of nonpublic schools have been made
more complicated by the decrease in the number of teaching nuns
which required higher salaries to hire lay teachers. Although the
Court rejected only the state plans of Rhode Island and Pennsylvania, fifteen other states had similar plans and would be, therefore,
affected by these decisions. The Rev. Albert J. Koob, of the National
Catholic Education Association, commented that "the decisions
outlined the parameters in which we've got to work, and sends us
back to the drawing boards to find some other means that avoids the
'entanglement with religion' which the Court found unconstitutional." Concerning one of these plans, the "semipublic school"
concept—whereby a city or town assigns publicly paid instructors to
teach secular subjects in a nonpublic school—would be questioned
as to its constitutionality.[118] Charles M. Whelan, of the Fordham
University Law School, in pointing out that opponents of aid to
nonpublic schools have received much encouragement from the
Lemon and *DiCenso* decisions, and that supporters will be redrafting
present and future programs to avoid the pitfalls of the decided
cases, concluded that

It is too early to assess all of these implications, but some are clear enough. The Supreme Court is finding it difficult to come to grips with religious pluralism at the institutional level in American life. It has accepted such pluralism at the individual level, but it is not all clear what it should do about the churches and especially about their growing collaboration with the state and federal governments in education, health services and welfare activities.[119]

Following the invalidation of the Pennsylvania program to reimburse nonpublic sectarian schools for secular educational services, the question of retroactivity arose. Upon remand by the Supreme Court to the federal district court, the district court permitted the state to reimburse nonpublic schools for services provided before the decision. But payment of any state funds was enjoined for services performed after June 28, 1971. The opponents of the Pennsylvania program challenged the district court's ruling that did not enjoin payment of some $24 million set aside by Pennsylvania to compensate nonpublic sectarian schools for educational services rendered during the 1970–71 school year.[120] Charging that the district court's injunction was of "limited scope," they appealed to the Supreme Court.

On April 2, 1973, five members of the Supreme Court, although not agreeing on an opinion, did agree on affirming the district court's judgment. They held that the district court had properly permitted the state to reimburse the schools for services rendered prior to the date (June 28, 1971) when the program was declared unconstitutional, particularly in view of "equitable principles and the totality of the circumstances."[121] A summary of the circumstances, as set forth in the judgment is:

> (1) such payments, which involved no further state oversight of the schools, other than the minimal contact of a final audit of school records, would not substantially undermine the constitutional interests at stake, (2) even assuming a cognizable constitutional interest in barring any state payments at all to sectarian schools, the final payments implicated such interest only once, under nonrecurring special circumstances, and the remote possibility of constitutional harm was offset by the schools' reliance

on the validity of the statutory program and the promised payments for expenses incurred before the Supreme Court's decision, (3) the plaintiffs had withdrawn their original motion in the District Court for a preliminary injunction against payments under the recently enacted program, and had not thereafter sought to suspend payments during the pendency of the litigation, until after the Supreme Court's decision, and (4) it could not be said that state officials and the schools had acted in bad faith in relying on the statutes, since the Supreme Court's decision that the program was unconstitutional involved an issue of first impression whose resolution could not have been clearly predicted.[122]

SCHOOL AID DECISIONS—1972

On April 17, 1972, the Supreme Court, in *Brusca* v. *Missouri*, affirmed the decision of a three-judge federal district court which denied the claim of parent-plaintiffs, as a matter of constitutional right, to be entitled to tax-raised funds for the purpose of affording a religious education to their children.[123] The district court had argued that there is nothing arbitrary or unreasonable in the determination of a state to deny public funds to sectarian schools or for religious instructions. A tax-paying parent who chooses to send his children to a religious-oriented school does not have a constitutional right to any credit for his taxes which support the public schools simply because he will not or cannot make use of them. The provisions of the Missouri constitution and implementing statutes, which provide for the funding of a free public school system and prohibit the use of public funds to aid religious schools directly or indirectly, do not violate either of the constitutional rights to free exercise of religion and equal protection.[124]

On October 10, 1972, the Supreme Court, in *Essex* v. *Wolman*, affirmed the decision of a three-judge federal district court in declaring state payments to parents of nonpublic school children unconstitutional.[125] During the fall of 1971 Ohio's general assembly incorporated in the state's first statewide income tax law a provision for parental reimbursement grants. The statute stated:

Programs of educational grants shall be established to reimburse parents of nonpublic school children for a portion of the financial burden experienced by them in providing to their children at reduced cost to taxpayers, educational opportunities equivalent to those available to public school pupils in the district. (Section 3317.062 O.R.C.)

For the school year 1971–72 it was estimated that $90 would be the reimbursement for each child. But the federal district court contended that although the amount may have been small, the issue was whether the statute fostered an excessive entanglement with religion. On the basis of the *Everson*, *Lemon*, and *DiCenso* cases especially, the district court considered it of no constitutional significance that state aid to nonpublic education goes indirectly to denominational schools through parental grants. Such a scheme, while it may express a valid secular purpose, fails to provide any mechanism to ensure that public monies provided to parents of parochial school children will not ultimately be used for religious purposes. "Payment to the parent for transmittal to the denominational school does not have a cleansing effect and somehow cause the funds to lose their identity as public funds . . . [for] one may not do by indirection what is forbidden directly; one may not by form alone contradict the substance of a transaction."[126]

On October 16, 1972, the U.S. Supreme Court declined to review a decision of the Nebraska Supreme Court which upheld the instruction of both public and parochial school children in a church-school building leased to public school authorities. The case arose when the Hartington School District requested the Nebraska State Board of Education to approve its application for a grant of federal funds to provide instructional activities and services to meet the special educational needs of educationally deprived children, in accordance with Title I of the Elementary and Secondary Education Act of 1965. However, because of shortage of space in buildings owned by the Hartington School District, instruction would take place in classrooms leased from the Hartington Cedar Catholic High School. The public school authorities would have full control of the educational program, and the classrooms would be stripped of all objects or pictures having a religious connotation. The Nebraska Board of Education denied the application. But the Nebraska Supreme Court saw no violation of the establishment clause of the

First Amendment, holding that it was not unconstitutional for parochial school children to participate in the educational program as it
was explicitly provided for by ESEA.[127] Justice Douglas, with whom
Justice Marshall concurred, favored the hearing of this case. Justice
Douglas saw the same reasons applying as those in *Lemon:* entanglement between government and religion and surveillance of the state
over a religious organization.[128]

SCHOOL AID DECISIONS—1973

On June 25, 1973, the U.S. Supreme Court again handed down
decisions concerning state aid to church-related schools and colleges. These decisions reaffirmed the Court's position and reasoning in 1971.

Hunt v. *McNair* concerned aid to a Baptist-controlled college.
In this case, the state of South Carolina's Educational Facilities Act,
which sought "to assist institutions for higher education in the
construction, financing and re-financing of projects," was challenged as unconstitutional.[129] The issuance of revenue bonds was
to be a prime means used by the state to aid colleges in improving
their facilities. The use of revenue "for sectarian instruction or as
a place of religious worship, or in connection with any part of the
program of a school or department of divinity of any religious
denomination" was explicitly forbidden.[130] The Baptist College at
Charleston, South Carolina, applied for the issuance of revenue
bonds for refinancing capital improvements and for completing the
dining hall. A South Carolina taxpayer, Richard W. Hunt, charged
that the proposed financial transaction violated the establishment
clause of the First Amendment of the federal Constitution, since it
would benefit a religious-controlled educational institution. The
South Carolina Supreme Court did not share the appellant's contention; thus, the appeal to the U.S. Supreme Court.[131]

Justice Powell delivered the Court's 6-to-3 opinion supporting
the South Carolina act and applied to it the three "tests" of purpose,
effect, and entanglement. He underscored the secular purpose of
the act: All institutions of higher education in the state were to
benefit, whether or not they had a religious affiliation. The state,
furthermore, benefited from a better trained and educated citizenry
as this particular college provided educational benefits to a student

body of which 95 percent were residents of the state. Powell reaffirmed the *Tilton* decision by declaring that aid given to a religious-affiliated college would not necessarily be a support of religion: "Aid normally may be thought to have a primary effect of advancing religion when it flows to an institution in which religion is so pervasive that a substantial portion of its functions are subsumed in the religious mission or when it funds a specifically religious activity in an otherwise substantially secular setting." Like the four Connecticut colleges in *Tilton,* the Baptist College was not "pervasively sectarian": no religious qualifications existed for faculty membership or student admission, with only 60 percent of the student body espousing the Baptist religion. The aid sought was primarily for the promotion of secular functions and not for any religious or sectarian use. The matter of entanglement was decided according to the degree and amount of inspection required for the facilities. Unlike the "substantial religious character" of church-related elementary and secondary schools and of religious indoctrination, "the entanglement problems with the proposed transaction would not be significant." Thus, aid to higher education under religious auspices was found, as in *Tilton,* to be not unconstitutional.[132]

The three dissenting justices, however, felt that the South Carolina arrangement failed to meet the "tests" for constitutionality: aid was directly to a sectarian institution, with the "substantive impact" of aid essentially the same as a direct subsidy from the state government, and a scheme existed that required "continuing financial relationships or dependencies," "annual audits," "government analysis," and "regulation and surveillance."[133]

As in 1971, the Court rejected plans of states—this time, in New York and Pennsylvania—for direct grants to religious elementary and secondary schools, as well as plans for tuition reimbursements and tax relief of parents. Such plans, on levels lower than higher education, were seen as advancing religion and so were deemed contrary to the establishment clause of the First Amendment. The *Nyquist* and *Levitt* cases originated in New York, while *Sloan* v. *Lemon* originated in Pennsylvania.

Nyquist resulted from a challenge to several amendments to New York State's Education and Tax Laws passed in May, 1972.[134] Three financial aid programs provided for direct money grants to "qualifying" nonpublic schools for "maintenance and repair" of facilities and equipment affecting the health, welfare, and safety of pupils. A school "qualified" if it was nonprofit and served a high concentration of students from low-income families. The grants amounted to $30 per pupil, or $40 if the facilities were more than twenty-five years old. The grants were to be paid on an annual basis and were not to exceed 50 percent of the average per pupil cost for similar services in the public schools. The Court rejected the argument that direct grants for maintenance and repairs were within the responsibility of the state, even if they were given directly to schools providing for the secular education of children. The issue at hand was the inevitable effect of these grants: to subsidize and advance the religious mission of sectarian schools. Although the Court admitted that some forms of aid may be channeled to the secular without providing direct aid to the sectarian, it characterized such channeling as "narrow," for "the provision of such neutral, nonideological aid, assisting only the secular functions of sectarian schools, [serves] indirectly and incidentally to promote the religious function by rendering it more likely that children would attend sectarian schools and by freeing the budgets of those schools for use in other nonsecular areas."[135]

New York State also established a tuition reimbursement plan for parents of children enrolled in nonpublic elementary and secondary schools. For parents whose annual taxable income amounted to less than $5,000, there would be a reimbursement of $50 for an elementary school child and $100 for a high school student. The amounts, however, could not exceed 50 percent of the actual tuition paid. The New York legislature had not only sought to alleviate the financial burden of parents whose children attended nonpublic schools, but had also sought to encourage "a healthy competitive and diverse alternative to public education" by granting the right to choose the school for the education of one's child as a sign of the "vitality of our pluralistic society."[136] Moreover, any massive increase in public school enrollment and costs would "aggravate an already serious fiscal crisis in public education" and would "seriously jeopardize the quality education of all children."[137] But the Court rejected any such type of reimbursement plan. *Everson* was cited as forbidding any amount of tax "to support any religious activities or institutions, whatever they may be called, or whatever form they may adopt to teach or practice religion." That the parents were made direct recipients of the reimbursements did not alter the result of providing aid to sectarian institutions. The Court further rejected any "statistical guarantee of neutrality" because of the small sums or percentage of costs involved solely for the secular aspects of education. The effect of the aid would be the same and "if accepted, this argument would provide the foundation for massive, direct subsidization of sectarian elementary and secondary schools," making it difficult "to sail between the Scylla and Charybdis of 'effect' and 'entanglement.' "[138]

New York State had further sought to provide tax relief to those parents who did not qualify for tuition reimbursements. Depending on the taxpayer's adjusted gross income, a designated amount for each pupil in a nonpublic school could be subtracted for state income purposes; the higher the income, however, the less the amount allowed for deduction.[139] The Court struck down this provision for tax relief because the Court could not assure that it would not have "the impermissible effect of advancing the sectarian activities of religious schools." The Court rejected the application of the *Walz* decision granting tax exemption for religious organization to the tax relief in question. While admitting that tax exemption confers an indirect and incidental benefit, its purpose is not to support or to subsidize; it is "a fiscal relationship designed to minimize involvement and entanglement between Church and State. . . . The granting of the tax benefits under the New York statute, unlike the extension of an exemption, would tend to increase rather than limit the involvement between Church and State. In reference to *Nyquist* as a whole, the Court, beyond declaring such aid programs passed by the New York legislature as contrary to the establishment clause, warned of the grave potential for entanglement in the broader sense of continuing and expanding political strife and divisiveness over aid to religion.[140]

The *Levitt* case was decided on the same day as *Nyquist*. *Levitt* originated from the challenge of an April, 1970, New York law. The law appropriated $28 million for the purpose of reimbursing nonpublic schools in the state "for expenses of services for examination and inspection in connection with administration grading and the compiling and reporting of the results of tests and examinations, maintenance of records of pupil enrollment and reporting thereon, maintenance of pupil health records, recording of personnel qualifications and characteristics and the preparation and submission to the state of various other reports as provided for or required by law or regulation."[141] By such "mandated services," the most common and expensive of which were tests and examinations, qualifying schools would receive $27 annually for each student in grades one through six and $45 for students in grades seven through twelve. The Supreme Court affirmed the judgment of the federal district court in declaring as unconstitutional the reimbursement to church-related schools for costs incurred in performing services "mandated" by state law. The New York statute was regarded as a means of impermissible aid to religion and thus was opposed to the establishment clause. The Court viewed internally prepared tests as "an integral part of the teaching process" and the statute provided no method of ascertaining that the tests are free of religious instruction and avoid inculcating pupils in the religious doctrine of the sect sponsoring the school. The basic issue for the Court lay not in whether the state should pay for "mandated" services, but "whether the challenged state aid has the primary purpose or effect of advancing religion or religious education or whether it leads to excessive entanglement by the State in the affairs of the religious institution. That inquiry would be irreversibly frustrated if the Establishment Clause were read as permitting a State to pay for whatever it requires a private school to do." Lump sum payments, whether for some secular or some potentially religious services violate the establishment clause, and the courts cannot "reduce the allotment to an amount corresponding to the actual costs incurred in performing reimbursable secular services."[142]

On June 28, 1971, the Supreme Court struck down the state of Pennsylvania's Nonpublic Elementary and Secondary Education Act as opposed to the establishment clause of the First Amendment. This was the case of Lemon v. Kurtzman, and the decision forbade the state from reimbursing nonpublic, sectarian schools for their expenditures on whatever teachers' salaries, textbooks, and instructional materials were employed in specified "secular" courses.[143] As a consequence of this decision, the Pennsylvania legislature enacted a new aid law on August 21, 1971. Known as the "Parent Reimbursement Act for Nonpublic Education," qualifying parents could receive $75 for each dependent in a nonpublic elementary school and $150 for a child in a nonpublic secondary school.[144] Although the Pennsylvania statute sought to stress its underlying purposes of reducing the costs of public education and of alleviating the burdens of parents who send their children to nonpublic schools, the

Court pointed out that 90 percent of private school children are enrolled in religious schools, most of them in Roman Catholic schools; thus, the "intended consequence is to preserve and support religious-oriented institutions." The reasoning in *Nyquist* was invoked as applicable to the Pennsylvania arrangement. Moreover, the Court rejected the argument that if tuition reimbursements could be granted to parents of children in nonsectarian private schools but not to those in sectarian private schools, then the latter would be denied by the state of equal protection by the laws. In the words of the Court: "The Equal Protection Clause has never been regarded as a bludgeon with which to compel a State to violate other provisions of the Constitution. Having held that tuition reimbursements for the benefit of sectarian schools violate the Establishment Clause, nothing in the Equal Protection Clause will suffice to revive that program."[145]

Dissenting opinions in the New York and Pennsylvania cases were all included in *Nyquist,* since the reasons favoring state aid to religious schools were substantially the same. The justices, with the exception of Justice White, dissented only in part. Among the major points brought out in dissent were a recognition of the secular function of religious schools which, because of serious financial difficulties today, could be compensated by state aid; the saving to the public treasury by religious schools, and the request of parents for reimbursement of some of their education taxes for use by their children in religious schools; and most importantly, emphasis on the right of "parents to follow the dictates of their conscience and seek a religious as well as secular education for their children."[146]

The *Allen* decision of 1968 approved the the state's lending of secular textbooks to nonpublic schools, including those that are church-related. As far back as 1940 the state of Mississippi enacted a program of providing free textbooks for all school children through the first eight grades. And in 1942 the program was extended to include high school students.[147] Both religious and non-religious private schools increased markedly in the last two decades, and many of these private and virtually all-white schools, for the purpose of avoiding integration. The Mississippi textbook lending statute was, therefore, challenged as to its constitutionality because some of the private schools excluded students on the basis of race. A federal district court upheld the statute.[148] But the U.S. Supreme Court, in a unanimous decision on June 25, 1973, declared the statute unconstitutional: "A State's constitutional obligation requires it to steer clear not only of operating the old dual system of racially segregated schools but also of giving significant aid to institutions that practice racial or other invidious discrimination." The Court reaffirmed the right of parents to establish private schools but denied that the equal protection clause can require aid to private schools equivalent to that received by the state's public schools without regard as to whether or not private schools practice racial discrimination. Thus, a private school, even if sectarian, can participate in a textbook lending program sponsored by the state, but not if the private school has a racially discriminatory admissions policy. In this sense, the Court argued, the establishment clause permits a greater degree of state assistance to sectarian schools than may be given to private schools which engage in discriminatory practices.[149]

Also on June 25, 1973, the Supreme Court, in *Grit* v. *Wolman*, affirmed a federal district court opinion that had declared unconstitutional an Ohio State statute providing tax credits to parents who incurred educational expenses in excess of those generally borne by parents in securing approved primary and secondary schooling for their children.[150] Following the district court's ruling in *Wolman* v. *Essex* on April 17, 1972 (and later upheld by the U.S. Supreme Court), denying state reimbursement to parents for parochial school tuition, the Ohio State legislature enacted tax credit provisions. But before the law could go into effect on June 21, 1972, the constitutionality of such provisions was challenged. Rather than conferring, in all instances, outright monetary grants, the new law allowed a tax "credit" which could not exceed the amount of $90. The court followed and employed all the reasons of Supreme Court decisions and its own decision in *Wolman* v. *Essex* which declared the tax credits provision as unconstitutional. "The only novel question raised . . . ," the court felt, "is whether consistent with the Establishment Clause the state, through the use of its taxing machinery, can confer benefits by way of tax credits upon a class of persons composed of parents of all nonpublic school students and a specialized segment of the public school population." It insisted that

> A tax credit . . . is a dollar for dollar forgiveness against the net payable tax as finally computed, after all exclusions and deductions have been taken. A credit, therefore, while perhaps less intensive than direct grants, tends to involve the

state more directly in assisting the benefited enterprise than do either exemptions or deductions . . . they are also more entanglement-intensive.[151]

AID TO NONPUBLIC SCHOOL POOR

On June 10, 1974, the U.S. Supreme Court ruled in favor of aid to nonpublic schools whose students come from educationally deprived areas. The case originated in 1970 from parents of children attending elementary and secondary parochial schools in the inner city area of Kansas City, Missouri. The parents brought suit in a federal district court against the state commissioner of education and members of the Missouri Board of Education who were accused of arbitrarily and illegally approving Title I programs under the Elementary and Secondary Education Act of 1965; these deprived eligible nonpublic school children of services comparable to those offered to eligible public school children. Title I of ESEA provides for federal funding of special programs for educationally deprived children in both public and nonpublic schools.[152] But Missouri's education officials argued that such aid contravened the state constitution and state law and public policy as well as the First Amendment's establishment clause. The district court dismissed the complaint of the parochial school children's parents. The Court of Appeals reversed this dismissal and remanded the case for trial.[153]

The district court found that most of the Title I funds allocated to public schools in Missouri were used to employ teachers to instruct in remedial subjects. Missouri officials refused to approve applications to allocate money to teachers in parochial schools during regular school hours. They did, however, in some instances use Title I funds to provide mobile educational services and equipment, visual aids, and educational radio and television in parochial schools; and teachers for after-school classes, all open to parochial school pupils, were all approved. Many parochial schools, however, would only accept services if Title I teachers would teach in their school during regular school hours. The parochial schools called for services "comparable" to the public schools. As a result of these findings, the district court concluded that there was no statutory obligation to provide on-the-premises nonpublic school instruction, and that Missouri school officials had fulfilled, by providing the services they did to nonpublic school children, their commitment under Title I.

The Court of Appeals, in considering the challenged ruling from the district court, reversed it. It argued that both the ESEA and the regulations concerning it require a program for educationally deprived nonpublic school children that is "comparable" in quality, scope, and opportunity, although it need not be equal in dollar expenditures to that provided in public schools. It also held that state constitutional provisions barring use of "public" school funds in private schools did not apply to Title I funds. It further declined to rule on whether the establishment clause of the First Amendment was violated since no plan for on-the-premises instruction in non-public schools had yet been implemented.[154]

On appeal to the Supreme Court by the Missouri commissioner of education and state Board of Education, an 8-to-1 ruling indicated areas of agreement and disagreement with the Court of Appeals decision.[155] The Court agreed with the failure of Missouri state school officials to comply with the ESEA's comparability requirement. Without considering the use of Title I teachers on private school premises during regular school hours, the Court characterized the services to the parochial school children as "plainly inferior, both qualitatively and quantitatively." The Court, however, asserted that "comparable" but not necessarily "identical" programs would have to be offered to parochial school children, but it left to Missouri officials the responsibility of determining which of "numerous" forms of comparable aid should be chosen: "If one form of service to parochial school children is rendered unavailable because of state constitutional proscriptions, the solution is to employ an acceptable alternative form." The Court of Appeals was considered in error in holding that federal law governed the question of whether on-the-premises private school instruction is permissible under Missouri law. For the Court felt that federal law under Title I provides that state law should not be disturbed: "Title I requires not that the law be preempted, but, rather that it be accommodated by the use of services not proscribed under state law."[156]

The Supreme Court instructed state school officials and local school agencies that they have the option to provide for on-the-premises instruction for nonpublic school children, but if they do not choose this method or if by state law such a method is prohibited, then three options remain: (1) they may approve a plan that does not utilize on-the-premises instruction in a nonpublic school, but which still complies with ESEA's requirement for comparability; (2) they may submit a plan that eliminates on-the-premises instruction in public schools and, instead, resorts to other means, such as neutral sites or summer programs, which are less likely to give rise to disparity of services charged in this case; or (3) they may choose not to participate at all in the Title I program. The Court warned that under the act, the U.S. commissioner of education, subject to judicial review, may refuse to provide funds if Missouri does not make a bona fide effort to formulate programs with comparable services.[157]

As to the issue of whether the establishment clause of the First Amendment prohibits Missouri from sending public school teachers paid with Title I funds into parochial schools to teach remedial courses, the Court agreed that since no order requiring on-the-premises nonpublic school instruction had been issued, "the matter was not ripe for review."[158]

The sole dissenter in this case, Justice Douglas, argued on the basis of his previous positions in cases involving federal aid to religious schools. He, therefore, concluded:

> The present case is plainly not moot; a case of controversy exists; and it is clear that if the traditional First Amendment barriers are to be maintained, no program serving students in parochial schools could be designed under this Act—whether regular school hours are used, or after-school hours, or weekend hours. The plain truth is that under the First Amendment, as construed to this day, the Act is unconstitutional to the extent it supports sectarian schools, whether directly or through its students.[159]

Although the following statement was written before the Court's opinion, it indicates the reception the decision would receive: "Americans United and several religious and educational organizations filed *amicus* briefs in the *Barrera* case pointing out that conducting tax supported educational programs in parochial schools is unconstitutional. The usual parochial lobby groups filed *amicus* briefs favoring federal aid to parochial schools."[160] After the Court's decision was handed down, constitutional lawyer Charles

M. Whelan offered this comment: "By the firmness of its mandate in *Barrera,* the Court has provided a solid basis for hope that the justices are now ready to sustain the constitutionality of many types of special educational programs for all disadvantaged children, regardless of the school they attend." And Whelan advised proponents of aid to nonpublic schools: "We have a solid chance now, if we sustain our efforts and pay attention to what the Supreme Court has told us, to expand the list of unquestionably constitutional auxiliary services. It is important for us to do so for the sake of the financial assistance such programs will provide to parents, for the enormous help such programs will provide to the children involved and for the step such programs represent towards full educational justice in this country."[161]

Religious Teaching and Activities in Public Schools

RELEASED TIME

The growth of the publicly supported common school in the nineteenth century led to the gradual elimination of all religious influence. The rivalry among the different religious denominations made necessary a nonsectarian public school in which the doctrines of a particular church would not be enunciated. Many parents were satisfied with Bible reading in the schools. Roman Catholics objected to the use of the Protestant version of the Bible, and either caused it to be eliminated on grounds of prejudice or, as in most cases, proceeded to establish their own schools. But the gradual secularization of the public schools leading to neutrality in religious matters caused many to brand them as "Godless" and "irreligious." One of the attempts to offset the neutral attitude of public schools towards religion was the adoption of released-time religious programs.[1] These programs permitted the religious instruction of children in a public school, for an allotted period each week, in the doctrines of their own religious faith, even by ordained clergymen. Such a practice is said to have begun in 1914 in the public schools of Gary, Indiana.[2] Many other states subsequently adopted this practice, and it has been estimated that where there were 619 pupils in one program for the 1914–1915 school year, there were some two million pupils in twenty-two hundred programs in 1947 in thirty-seven states.[3] State courts were divided on their approval of the practice.[4] It was the released-time program in Champaign, Illinois, that eventually came before the U.S. Supreme Court for decision.

197

In 1940 the school board of Champaign, Illinois, devised a program for religious instruction of public school children from grades four through nine. The Council on Religious Education, made up of members of the three major faiths, paid the religion teachers who taught the classes under the supervision of public school authorities in a regular thirty-minute period of a school day once a week. For students whose parents had signed "request cards" attendance was required as for any other school class. Students whose parents did not desire participation in the religious instruction program were not compelled to attend any religious class but were assigned for that period to some other activity within the school.

Objection to the Champaign program was raised by Mrs. Vashti McCollum, an avowed athiest. She maintained that her son, a student in the Champaign public school system, was subjected to embarrassment and was made conspicuous because of his particular belief. This program of a public system aiding religious instruction, she contended, violated the establishment of religion clause of the First Amendment and the due process clause of the Fourteenth Amendment. Upon dismissal of her objection by Illinois courts, Mrs. McCollum brought her case to the U.S. Supreme Court.

Justice Hugo Black, who a year earlier had spoken for the Court in the 5–4 *Everson* case which permitted free bus transportation for parochial school children under the "child-benefit" theory, now utilized the same arguments in the *McCollum* case, but for the purpose of outlawing the teaching of religion in public school buildings. Black reiterated that the interpretation of the First Amendment was that a wall had been erected between church and state.

> Here not only are the State's tax-supported public school buildings used for the dissemination of religious doctrines. The State also affords sectarian groups an invaluable aid in that it helps provide pupils for the religious classes through use of the State's compulsory public school machinery. This is not separation of Church and State.[5]

The declaring of released-time religious programs as unconstitutional, according to Justice Black, was not to be looked upon as governmental hostility to religion or religious teachings but rather that "both religion and the government can best work to achieve their lofty aims if each is left free from the other within its respective sphere."[6]

Three justices, Burton, Jackson, and Rutledge, joined Justice Frankfurter in a concurring opinion. The essence of their opinion is in these words: "The Champaign arrangement thus presents powerful elements of inherent pressure by the school system in the interest of religious sects. . . . Separation is a requirement to abstain from fusing functions of government and of religious sects, not merely to treat them all equally."[7] Justice Jackson, besides siding with the concurring decision, also offered a separate concurring opinion, which suggests hesitancy and perplexity in joining the majority opinion. For he alludes to the original request of the plaintiff, Mrs. McCollum, who asked the courts not only to ban released-time programs but every form of teaching which acknowledges God, including any reference to the Bible as the Word of God. Terming as a danger signal "the sweep and detail of these complaints," Jackson predicted accurately that "nothing but educational confusion and discrediting of the public school system can result from subjecting it to constant lawsuits." While agreeing with the Court that "we may and should end such formal and explicit instruction as the Champaign plan," he also expressed the fear that "to lay down a sweeping constitutional doctrine as demanded by complainant and apparently approved by the Court, applicable alike to all school boards of the nation . . . is to decree a uniform rigid, and, if we are consistent, an unchanging standard for countless school boards," amounting to the Court's assuming "the role of a super board of education for every school district in the nation."[8]

Justice Reed, in lone dissent, called the Court's interpretation of the First Amendment "erroneous," because "cooperation between the schools and a nonecclesiastical body (in this case, the Champaign Council of Religious Education) is not forbidden by the First Amendment." He argued on the basis of past practice, such as the long-standing tradition that all churches receive aid from the government in the form of freedom from taxation, the *Cochran* free textbook case, free transportation of children to church schools permitted by the *Everson* case, and the decision in *Bradfield* v. *Roberts* which held as constitutional the increased payments by the federal government to help build an addition to a hospital operated under religious auspices. He further maintained that the interpretation of the "establishment of religion" clause does "not bar every friendly gesture between church and state. It is not an absolute prohibition against every conceivable situation where the two may work together."[9]

As Justice Jackson predicted, the public school, envisioned by the Supreme Court as violating the Constitution's "establishment of religion" if it permitted religious denominations to teach their doctrines within its classrooms, would be the object of "discrediting." Many religious leaders of all faiths cried out that the Court had clearly made the public schools "Godless" and "atheistic." The need for private religious schools was urged all the more if parents wanted their children freed from the "corrupting" influence of schools which "bar God" from the classroom. The "confusion" predicted affected both educators and legal experts.[10] Educators were forced to examine the programs for religious instruction in their respective schools and districts, as such a wide variety of practices existed; questions were also raised as to Bible reading with or without comment.[11] An expert on school law commented: "For the specifics of the decision were so limited within a field of practice so complex that neither educators nor constitutional lawyers could derive much certainty therefrom."[12] A study on the Court's interpretation of the First Amendment in the *Everson* and *McCollum* cases concluded that "one can only say that . . . the *McCollum* case has not ended the controversy over separation of church and state. It is only the beginning."[13] Three noted scholars—Edwin Corwin, John Courtney Murray, and Alexander Meiklejohn—also disagreed with the Court's interpretation of the First Amendment in a symposium on "Religion and the State."[14]

The *McCollum* decision was not, however, without support. The Court had interpreted Madison and Jefferson correctly as to the true meaning of the First Amendment: "Separation means separation, not something else."[15] The decision was looked upon as maintaining the American historical tradition of religious freedom.[16]

In a 1964 report the American Association of School Administrators gave the following summary of how religious groups reacted to the decision:

> The McCollum decision received a highly mixed reaction
> from religious groups in the nation. Roman Catholics were
> especially disturbed over it. Protestant Evangelicals were
> disappointed. The decision was praised, however, by the

Christian Century, by Unitarians, Baptists, and most Jewish groups.[17]

The *McCollum* decision clearly prohibited the holding of religious classes in public school buildings. It did not, however, pass judgment upon another type of released-time program, more accurately called "dismissed-time," whereby children are permitted to leave public school buildings during regular school hours to attend religious classes in nonpublic school buildings, usually their own churches or neighboring church schools. A St. Louis court held such a plan unconstitutional under the *McCollum* decision, while New York courts regarded dismissed-time substantially different and, therefore, permissible, since no religious instruction was held in public buildings.[18] Two New York city residents, Tessim Zorach and Esta Gluck, having failed to render unconstitutional a dismissed-time program involving the cooperation of religious leaders and the public school system, appealed to the U.S. Supreme Court. They claimed that the New York plan was basically the same as the Champaign, Illinois, plan and therefore should be considered unconstitutional. They reasoned: "The school is a crutch on which the churches are leaning for support in their religious training; without the cooperation of the schools this . . . program, like the one in the *McCollum* case would be futile and ineffective."[19]

In a 6-to-3 decision the Supreme Court of the United States upheld the New York program. Speaking for the Court, Justice Douglas emphasized that the present case differed from the *McCollum* case in that the religious instruction was held outside the buildings and grounds of the public schools. The children were released at the request of their parents to allow them to attend religious classes. The students were not coerced in any way and school authorities remained neutral as to the student's decision to attend religious instruction. Thus, no case could be made for the New York program as being an "establishment of religion" within the meaning of the First Amendment. Although still accepting and following the reason given in the *McCollum* case, Douglas maintained that "We cannot expand it to cover the present released time program unless separation of Church and State means that public institutions can make no adjustments of their schedules to accommodate the religious needs of the people."[20]

Justice Douglas in the *Zorach* case not only distinguished, as

Justice Black did in the *McCollum* case, between church and state as distinct spheres divided by a high, impregnable wall, but he distinguished between religion and government. It is one thing to be speaking of the distinction between a religious institution and a public institution, each with its own rights and duties, separate and distinct, the cooperation between which has always historically posed problems but more so in a pluralistic society. It is another thing, however, to distinguish between religion and government, for the government, the promoter of the common good and the defender of the rights of all its citizens, minorities as well as those in the majority, guarantees freedom of worship. Douglas rendered examples of how students can apply for permission to leave school to attend religious services. Such permissions do require cooperation on the part of school authorities, but the state's cooperation with religious authorities "by adjusting the schedule of public events to sectarian needs" exemplifies a respect for "the religious nature of our people and accommodates the public service to their spiritual needs. To hold that it may not would be to find in the Constitution a requirement that the government show a callous indifference to religious groups. That would be preferring those who believe in no religion over those who do believe."[21] The New York City program was, therefore, one which safeguarded the separation of church and state, while permitting a friendly cooperation between the government and religion.

Three justices dissented from the majority decision and each offered a separate dissenting opinion. Justice Black, author of the *Everson* and *McCollum* decisions, saw in the strictest possible interpretation of the establishment clause "no significant difference between the invalid Illinois system and that of New York." "Except for the use of the school building in Illinois," he pointed out, "there is no difference between the systems I consider even worthy of mention." He regarded New York's plan as using "compulsory education laws to help religious sects get attendants presumably too unenthusiastic to go unless moved to do so by the pressure of this state machinery." He branded the idea of cooperation between government and religious authorities as a "soft euphemism." For him, "any use of such coercive power by the state to help or hinder some religious sects or to prefer all religious sects over nonbelievers or vice versa is just what I think the First Amendment forbids. . . . New York is manipulating its compulsory education laws to help religious sects get pupils. This is not separation but combination of Church and State."[22]

Justice Frankfurter's dissent also emphasized the employment of the coercive power of the state:

> The pith of the case is that formalized religious instruction is substituted for other school activity which those who do not participate in the released-time program are compelled to attend. The school system is very much in operation during this kind of released time. If its doors are closed, they are closed upon those students who do not attend the religious instruction in order to keep them within the school. That is the very thing which raises the constitutional issue. It is not met by disregarding it. Failure to discuss this issue does not take it out of the case.[23]

Frankfurter also called to task the religious denominations involved in the program for "a surprising want of confidence in [their] inherent power . . . to draw children to outside sectarian classes," since they must depend on the power of the public schools "as the instrument for security of attendance" at religious instruction.[24]

Justice Jackson also notes in his dissent the state's power of coercion and, therefore, the unconstitutionality of the New York program. But unlike his dissent in the *McCollum* case, he seems more ready to look upon the Court as "a super board of education" in striking down the released-time arrangement in New York. He attributes whatever effectiveness this voluntary attendance after school hours has to the public school truant officer who, in cooperation with the religious authorities, will refer back to the schoolroom any student absenting himself from religious class instruction for which he admittedly freely signed up. The public schoolroom, in his opinion, "serves as a temporary jail for a pupil who will not go to Church." Such an arrangement or cooperation becomes "governmental constraint in support of religion."[25]

As for the constitutionality of released-time programs, the *Zorach* decision has made permissible the cooperation of public school authorities with religious leaders to dismiss their students during regular school hours to attend religious instruction. More accurately, *Zorach* held as constitutional dismissed-time for attendance at religious instruction outside of public school buildings.

The reactions of legal experts and educators to *Zorach* were mixed. The element of coercion was noted.[26] The American Jewish Committee registered disapproval because it felt that the state was aiding religion in using school time for religious purposes and fostering a divisive spirit between those who did and those who did not participate in the plan.[27] Objection was raised to the shortening of the school day to provide religious instruction to denominational groups.[28] It was even argued that the "wall of separation" was being abandoned by the dismissed-time arrangement.[29]

Pleasure was expressed at what now could be regarded as a departure from Justice Black's principle of absolute separation of church and state.[30] Government schools' cooperation with religious leaders was considered more of "the natural norm of the church-state relationship in a nation which has a religious orientation."[31] One writer even called for an extension of the plan from one day to five days a week.[32]

PRAYERS IN PUBLIC SCHOOLS

It was not until 1962 that the issue of prayer in the public schools came for decision to the U.S. Supreme Court in the *Engel* case.[33] But recitation of prayers, often in conjunction with Bible reading, has had a long history in American education.[34] Of state courts deciding on the question, there were more who upheld them than those who declared such devotional exercises as unconstitutional.[35]

On November 30, 1951, the Board of Regents, which directs and supervises the public school system of the state of New York, issued a "Statement on Moral and Spiritual Training in the Schools." The opening words of the statement were: "Belief and dependence upon Almighty God was the very cornerstone upon which our founding fathers builded." As a means of stressing the moral and spiritual heritage of our country, the regents recommended that the public schools of the state begin each day with a brief prayer. In composing the prayer the regents felt that they had ensured its essential nonsectarian character, unoffensive to and acceptable by all religious denominations. The prayer stated: "Almighty God, we acknowledge our dependence upon Thee, and we beg Thy blessings upon us, our parents, our teachers, and our country."[36] Only 150 of the 900 school boards in the state adopted the use of this recommended prayer.[37] Furthermore, even if a student's local school board had adopted the prayer practice, the student, if opposed to saying it, was free to remain silent or to be excused from the classroom.

Opposition to the recitation of the prayer was initiated by Lawrence Roth, an unbeliever, who through newspaper advertisements urged other parents to join him in securing legislation against his local school board in the city of New Hyde Park, Long Island. Four families of the same city accepted his invitation, and together they challenged the legality of the prayer practice on the ground that it was coercive and, therefore, contrary to the First and Fourteenth amendments of the Constitution. Sixteen parents of Protestant, Jewish, and Roman Catholic faiths supported the local school board and the Board of Regents. The courts of the state of New York upheld the recitation of the prayer because no student was compelled to offer it against his own or his parents' objection.

The U.S. Supreme Court, after hearing the appeal from the plaintiffs, classified the recitation of the regents' prayer as "a practice wholly inconsistent with the Establishment Clause . . . [because it was] a religious activity." Justice Hugo Black, in presenting the majority decision, proceeded to enlarge upon the meaning of establishment of religion: "It is no part of the business of government to compose official prayers for any group of the American people to recite as part of a religious program carried on by government." Black offered as historical documentation for the statement the departure from England of early colonists who objected to the recitation of government-composed prayer for religious services. Black did not feel that the regents' prayer amounted to a "total establishment of one particular religious sect to the exclusion of all others—that, indeed, the governmental endorsement of that prayer seems relatively insignificant," but what is at issue, is government favoring a religious act.[38]

Justice Stewart alone dissented. He claimed that "the Court has misapplied a great constitutional principle." He saw no establishment of religion created when freedom was given to say or not to say the prayer. He regarded as irrelevant Justice Black's attempt to prove an analogy between the religious struggle over the Book of Common Prayer in sixteenth-century England and the history of the religious traditions of the American people. He cited, in addition to the prayer practice of the Court and both houses of Congress, the oath of office taken by every president to call upon God's help, the third stanza of the National Anthem which mentions God and the motto of the country "In God is Our Trust," the adding of the words "one Nation under God" to the pledge of allegiance to the flag by Congress in 1954, the National Day of Prayer called for by law in 1952, and the words "In God We Trust" imprinted on our coins since 1865. His conclusion after this enumeration is noteworthy: "I do not believe that this Court, or the Congress, or the President has by the actions and practices I have mentioned established an 'official religion' in violation of the Constitution. And I do not believe that the State of New York has done so in this case."[39]

The *Engel* decision received both praise and criticism on legal and historical grounds, with religious leaders divided among themselves.[40] Secularists and strict separationists strongly applauded the decision, but it was also looked upon as the Court's tendency "to institutionalize agnosticism as the official public religion."[41]

The American Civil Liberties Union has reported scores of complaints about school systems violating the ban on classroom prayers, and the hesitancy of school boards and the courts throughout the country in enforcing the *Engel* decision. Some school boards that did not have the practice before *Engel* have instituted it.[42] A survey of the practice of prayers in the public schools has concluded that

> It seems clear that prayer plays a very minor role in the public schools. Its importance is indicated by the fact that only one system in five even has a policy on the matter and less than one in ten has felt any public pressure with regard to it. Prayers offered over public address systems and at morning assemblies are found in less than 10% of the reporting schools although the South continues the practice in one quarter of its school systems.[43]

The protests against *Engel* crystallized in an effort to pass a constitutional amendment to permit prayer in public schools. After much discussion and delay in congressional committees, and opposition from religious leaders, the proposed amendment came to the House of Representatives on November 8, 1971. A majority of 240 to 162 voted in its favor, but the proposal fell twenty-eight votes short of the two-thirds majority required for a constitutional amendment. Representative William M. Colmer argued in the debate, "We exercise rights here denied our children." Noteworthy among the opponents was a Roman Catholic priest, Congressman Robert M. Drinan. Thus the proposed amendment, a persistent effort of the late Senator Everett M. Dirksen, was defeated. The arguments in the debate were essentially those of the justices in the *Engel* case.[44]

BIBLE READING IN PUBLIC SCHOOLS

The first case involving the reading of the Bible in public schools was heard by the U.S. Supreme Court in 1952. But the practice has long existed in American public education. Even in the common public school, free from the control of religious denominations, the Bible was read as an acceptable nonsectarian religious exercise. Such a practice was advocated by Horace Mann.[45] Many of the Protestant denominations looked upon the practice as an acceptable substitute in lieu of their own schools.[46] Opposition to reading the Bible in the King James version arose among Roman Catholics.[47] The Supreme Court of Maine in 1854 confirmed the right of a school board to expel children from school for refusal to read the Bible regardless of the religious convictions of the students and their parents.[48] The majority of other state courts at least maintained the practice in conforming to their constitutions.[49] It was not until 1890 that Wisconsin became the first state to hold the Bible as a sectarian book and its reading unconstitutional.[50] Five other state supreme courts made similar conclusions; most of the cases arose from Jews and Roman Catholics who objected to the use of the King James version.[51]

The first case to be appealed to the U.S. Supreme Court was a test of a New Jersey state law which required the reading of at least five verses from the Old Testament every day in the public schools. The courts of New Jersey ruled in 1950 that the law was constitutional since the Bible, although religious, was not sectarian, and it was read without comment. Furthermore, any student's participation in reading or hearing the Bible read was voluntary. Richard Doremus and Anna E. Klein appealed to the U.S. Supreme Court on the contention that the New Jersey practice conflicted with the

First Amendment. The Court rejected the appeal 6-to-3 on jurisdictional grounds. The daughter of one of the plaintiffs had already graduated from high school when the case was heard in 1952 and so the Court declared that "no decision we could render now would protect any rights she may once have had, and this Court does not sit to decide arguments after events have put them to rest." Besides, the child was in no way compelled to "any dogma or creed or even to listen when the Scriptures were read."[52] Thus, the right of the state to maintain the practice of Bible reading was sustained.

In 1954, the Court refused to review another New Jersey case involving the distribution of copies of the New Testament to students in public schools. The case arose when a Jewish parent, also supported by a Roman Catholic parent, sought to enjoin the Rutherford, New Jersey, Board of Education from carrying out an agreement with Gideon International to give copies of the New Testament to children whose parents would approve in a written request. The New Jersey Supreme Court in 1953 upheld a lower court's injunction against this cooperative effort, as the "distribution of the King James version in the public schools of this state would . . . cast aside all progress made in the United States and throughout New Jersey in the field of religious toleration and freedom."[53] The U.S. Supreme Court, not hearing the case, permitted the New Jersey court's decision to stand.

With the furor over the *Engel* case of 1952 still strong, the U.S. Supreme Court was confronted a year later with another major issue regarding the relation of religion and public education. The opinion in the *Doremus* case of 1952 had sustained a New Jersey statute permitting the reading of verses from the Bible without comment. The Court in 1963 was asked for a decision in two companion cases involving daily Bible reading and the recitation of the Lord's Prayer in public schools.

The first case had its history in the state of Pennsylvania, which had a law permitting Bible reading in the public schools since 1928.[54] The law was amended in 1959 to read: "At least ten verses from the Holy Bible shall be read, without comment, at the opening of each public school on each school day. Any child shall be excused from such Bible reading or attending such Bible reading, upon the written request of his parent or guardian."[55] Mr. and Mrs. Edward Lewis Schempp, Unitarians and parents of three children (by the time the case reached the U.S. Supreme Court one child had graduated and, therefore, could no longer be a party in the class) who attended Abington Senior High School, sought to enjoin their school district from continuing the practice of Bible reading and recitation of the Lord's Prayer on the grounds that the state statute violated the First and Fourteenth amendments of the federal Constitution. With the state courts issuing the injunction, officials of the Abington School District sought a reversal of the appeal through the U.S. Supreme Court.

The second case referred to a rule adopted in 1905 by the Board of School Commissioners of Baltimore, Maryland.[56] The rule provided for opening exercises of a public school day to consist of "reading, without comment, of a chapter in the Holy Bible and/or use of the Lord's Prayer." An atheist, Mrs. Madalyn Murray, whose son attended the Baltimore schools, sought the rescinding of the 1905 rule. Even though her son was excused from the religious exercise, she contended that the practice violated the First and Fourteenth amendments since it threatened "religious liberty by placing a premium on belief as against non-belief and subjects their freedom of conscience to the rule of the majority . . . renders sinister, alien and suspect beliefs and ideals . . . morality, good citizenship and good faith" of atheists. With the Maryland courts upholding the Baltimore rule, Mrs. Murray took the case to the U.S. Supreme Court.[57]

Justice Tom Clark rendered the majority decision of the Court. After reviewing previous cases decided by the Court on the relation of religion to public education, Clark concluded that "this wholesome 'neutrality' of which this Court's cases speak thus stems from a recognition of the teachings of history that powerful sects or groups might bring about a fusion of government and religious functions or a concert or dependency of one upon the other to the end that official support of the State or Federal Government would be placed behind the tenets of one or of all orthodoxies. This the Establishment Clause prohibits." And he added a further reason for neutrality as found in the free exercise clause, which he interpreted as guaranteeing "the right of every person to freely choose his own course with reference thereto, free of any compulsion from the state." Mindful of the objections that many religious leaders would have to his reasoning, especially that the denial of Bible reading and recitation of prayers would constitute establishment of the religion of secularism for the public schools, Justice Clark insisted that "the place of religion in our society is an exalted one" and that an individual's education should not be considered "complete without a study of comparative religion or the history of religion and its relationship to the advancement of civilization." He even recommended the study of the Bible, "worthy . . . for its literary and historic qualities," and of religion, when presented "objectively as part of a secular program of education," as not contrary to the First Amendment. Otherwise, the government must "maintain strict neutrality, neither aiding nor opposing religion."[58]

In a concurring opinion, Justice Douglas stressed that the state was conducting a religious exercise, thus violating neutrality in religion, and that the state made use of public facilities and funds to promote a religious exercise, thus violating what had been judged as unconstitutional: "Through the mechanism of the State, all of the people are being required to finance a religious exercise that only some of the people want and that violates the sensibilities of others."[59]

Justice Brennan, in a lengthy concurring opinion, considered "futile and misdirected" any attempt to interpret the mind of the founding fathers as to the issues of Bible reading and recitation of prayers, to draw analogies from the structure of American education in the latter part of the eighteenth and early part of the nineteenth centuries with the twentieth century, and to attempt to settle the problem of the relation of government to religion in the same manner as our forefathers—when largely only Protestant differences existed—when today's religious composition is of a far more heterogeneous and diversified nature. He proceeded to infer three principles from the Court's previous decisions on religious questions: (1) the First Amendment requires all branches of government, including the courts, to adopt a strict neutrality towards theological questions; (2) issues arising under the establishment clause may be isolated from problems implicating the free exercise clause; and (3) since the establishment and free exercise clauses may overlap, decisions under the free exercise clause bear considerable relevance to the present cases.[60]

In applying the three principles to Bible reading and the recitation of the Lord's Prayer, Justice Brennan came to the following conclusions: (1) since the state must be steadfastly neutral in all matters of religion and neither favor nor inhibit religion, the government cannot sponsor religious exercises in the public schools without jeopardizing that neutrality, but it would be hostility and not neutrality, for example, if the state should refuse to provide chaplains and places of worship for prisoners and soldiers who are severed from their accustomed way of life; (2) prayers said in, and the appointment of chaplains for, legislative chambers do not constitute similar situations in public schools; mature adults can absent themselves more easily and without incurring any penalty or embarrassment, directly or indirectly; (3) the Bible may be used in literature and history classes, but not for devotional use; (4) exemption from taxation available to religious institutions is "in spite of rather than because of their religious character"; all such organizations, regardless of size, popularity, belief in or rejection of God, qualify for exemption on a truly nondiscriminatory basis; (5) there is doubt that nondiscriminatory programs of governmental aid may include individuals who are eligible wholly or partially for religious reasons; and (6) activities or laws, such as reciting the pledge of allegiance to the flag with the words "under God" and laws traceable to some religious principle—although religious in origin—have now ceased to have a religious meaning. As to the cases at hand, Brennan concluded that they "leave no doubt that these practices . . . constitute an impermissible breach of the Establishment Clause." He would recommend patriotic or other nonreligious materials as adequate substitutes, but he would not permit the state to "employ religious means to reach a secular goal unless secular means are wholly unavailing."[61]

Justices Goldberg and Harlan joined in a concurring opinion which subscribed to the majority decision, but insisted on the distinction between "required and permissible accommodation" and "compelled or permitted accommodation" between church and state. The government, cognizant of the existence of religion and a nonhostile attitude toward it, provides military chaplains, and sanctions teaching *about* religion, but not the teaching *of* religion, in public schools. They classified the practices of *Schempp* and *Murray* as "compelled or permitted" because the state became "so significantly and directly involved in the realm of the sectarian as to give rise to those very divisive influences and inhibitions of freedom which both religion clauses of the First Amendment preclude."[62]

Justice Stewart was the sole dissenter in this case. He, like the other justices, appealed to interpretations of the Court in previous decisions. But his analysis of the meaning of the First Amendment differed from those of the other justices.

The First Amendment was adopted solely as a limitation upon the newly created National Government. The events leading to its adoption strongly suggest that the Establishment Clause was primarily an attempt to insure that Congress not only would be powerless to establish a national church, but would also be unable to interfere with existing state establishments. Each state was left free to go its own way and pursue its own policy with respect to religion. . . . So matters stood until the adoption of the Fourteenth Amendment. . . . I accept without question that the liberty guaranteed by the Fourteenth Amendment against impairment by the States embraces in full the right of free exercise of religion protected by the First Amendment, and I yield to no one in my conception of the breadth of that freedom.[63]

Justice Stewart, therefore, saw in *Murray* and *Schempp* "a substantial free exercise claim on the part of those who affirmatively desire to have their children's school day open with the reading of passages from the Bible." He granted that parents solicitous of religious influences in their children's education can have this provision met off school property and outside school time, but he added that such an "argument seriously misconceives the basic constitutional justification for permitting the exercises at issue in these cases."

> For a compulsory educational system so structures a child's life that if religious exercises are held to be an impermissible activity in schools, religion is placed at an artificial and state-created disadvantage. Viewed in this light, permission of such exercises for those who want them is necessary if the schools are truly to be neutral in the matter of religion. And a refusal to permit religious exercises thus is seen, not as the realization of state neutrality, but rather as the establishment of a religion of secularism, or at the least, as government support of the beliefs of those who think that religious exercises should be conducted only in private.[64]

As to the administrative problems connected with noncoercive religious exercises, Justice Stewart felt that this was the problem of a local community and its school board and not the Court's. Largely because of the voluntary and noncoercive guarantee in these cases, he saw no violation of the Constitution in the Pennsylvania and Maryland statutes.[65]

The criticism of the Court's 8-to-1 decision in *Schempp* and *Murray* became added fuel to a controversy already ignited by *Engel.* The expected charges of secularism and Godlessness appeared among the comments of religious leaders.[66] However, Arthur Lichtenberger, presiding bishop of the Episcopal Church, praised "the Court's sense of responsibility to assure freedom and equality to all groups of believers and non-believers as expressed in the First Amendment of the Constitution."[67] Executive officers of the United Presbyterian Church saw the decision as underscoring "our firm belief that religious instruction is the sacred responsibility of the family and the Churches."[68] The National Council of Churches issued this statement:

> The full treatment of some regular school subjects requires the use of the Bible as a source book. In such studies —including those related to character development—the use of the Bible has a valid educational purpose. But neither true religion nor good education is dependent upon the devotional use of the Bible in the public school program.[69]

Political leaders took issue with the decision. It has been estimated that over ninety congressmen have introduced constitutional amendments whereby Bible reading and prayers in the public schools would be allowed. Governor George C. Wallace of Alabama was quoted as saying that "I want the Supreme Court to know that we are not going to conform to any such decision. . . . If the courts rule that the Bible cannot be read in an Alabama school, I'm going to that school and read it myself."[70]

Bible reading statutes were invalidated by lower federal and state courts upon failure of some states to comply with the *Schempp* decision.[71] Through a 1961 statute passed by the Florida State legislature, the Dade County School District of Florida maintained the practice of devotional Bible reading. When asked to declare the state statute as unconstitutional, the Florida Supreme Court upheld the practice on the grounds that the neutrality required by *Schempp* was being preserved. It contended, moreover, that the practice was

grounded on secular rather than on religious foundations since the
U.S. Supreme Court had argued in *McGowan* v. *Maryland* that the
Sunday closing statute was enacted primarily as a day of rest and
recreation and not as an aid to religion.[72] The preamble to the
Florida statute was meant to ensure a secular aspect by the words
"good moral training," "good citizenship," and "a life of honorable
thought." However on June 6, 1964, the U.S. Supreme Court did
not accept the Florida court's reasoning and reversed its decision
to comply with *Schempp.*[73]

According to a 1965 survey, of the twenty-nine states in which
the practice of Bible reading existed before *Schempp,* only five states
withdrew the practice completely, fourteen states reported Bible
reading in a few school districts, and in six states the decision was
ignored.[74] A more recent survey has indicated that "devotional
Bible reading has increased somewhat from six years ago but still
takes place in less than one system in five. The sectional differences
are pronounced, with reading being done in nearly half of Southern
schools and almost completely eliminated in the East."[75]

Only a small number of legal periodicals discussed the *Schempp*
decision. Those favoring it pointed out its continuity with the *Everson* and *Engel* decisions, while the major argument of those opposing it stressed that it was the religious heritage of the American
people and that the government should recognize the importance
and value of that tradition in its public schools.[76] Justice Tom
Clark's espousing of the teaching of religion "objectively" was
praised by educators as both consistent with the Constitution and
the tradition of the country.[77] But the many practical difficulties of
teaching objectively *about* religion have been demonstrated.[78]

THE USE OF "ANTIRELIGIOUS" TEACHING MATERIALS

In 1952, the U.S. Supreme Court dealt with a New York case
involving the censorship of educational materials offensive to religious groups. The material under question was the film *The Miracle.*
Roman Catholics objected to it on the ground that it was "sacrilegious," and the film was denied a license to be shown. This action
by the censors had implications for schools because (1) censors over
movies in New York included certain school officials, and (2) films
used as a means of instruction have been noted as valuable and their

use has been increasing in schools. The Court's opinion was influenced by the matter of freedom and censorship, especially in regard to motion pictures. But as the case involved religion and education, the Court noted that if the New York courts' view that no religion "shall be treated with contempt, mockery, scorn and ridicule" were to be held up as a standard, then religious groups could pressure censors to reject any material considered offensive to their particular consciences. The Court argued that

> In seeking to apply the broad and all-inclusive definition of "sacrilegious" given by the New York Courts, the censor is set adrift upon a boundless sea amid a myriad of conflicting religious views with no charts but those provided by the most vocal and powerful orthodoxies. . . . Under such a standard the most careful and tolerant censor would find it virtually impossible to avoid favoring one religion over another, and he would be subject to an inevitable tendency to ban the expression of unpopular sentiments sacred to a religious minority. . . . The state has no legitimate interest in protecting any or all religious from views distasteful to them which is sufficient to justify prior restraints upon the expression of these views. It is not the business of government in our nation to suppress real or imagined attacks upon a religious doctrine, whether they appear in publications, speeches, or motion pictures.[79]

In a case more directly related to schools, but which did not appear before the Supreme Court, a New York court sustained a school board's selection of books for classroom use over the objection of a religious group. Jews maintained that the reading of *Oliver Twist* by Charles Dickens and *The Merchant of Venice* by William Shakespeare tended to produce hatred of Jews. The court's ruling noted the impossibility of selecting books for students that would be "free from derogatory reference to any religion, race, country, nation or personality." Rather, the court insisted on noting the intent and motive of the author to see whether "a book has been maliciously written for the apparent purpose of promoting and fermenting a bigoted and intolerant hatred against a particular racial or religious group."[80]

THE TEACHING OF EVOLUTION IN PUBLIC SCHOOLS

A more pressing issue decided by the Supreme Court relates to the teaching of certain scientific theories that offend the religious conscience of some students. The teaching of the Darwinian theory of evolution in public schools represents such an issue. It is questionable whether it should be regarded as a "difficult marginal issue," as Morgan does,[81] because it directly pertains to the rights of conscience of a society dedicated to respecting the beliefs of all its citizens. Although the Court did not strike down a state law forbidding the teaching of evolution until November, 1969, national notoriety was achieved on this issue in the famous "monkey trial," or the *Scopes* evolution case, of 1927.

Efforts to restore some religious influence in the public schools have included, besides released-time programs, Bible reading, and the saying of prayers, the passage of laws in some states forbidding the teaching of evolution. In the minds of religious fundamentalists, evolution conflicted with the story of the creation of the world and of man as told in the Bible. In 1925, Tennessee passed an Anti-Evolution Act, which forbade the teaching of "any theory that denies the story of divine creation of man as taught in the Bible, and to teach instead that man has descended from a lower order of animals" in any educational institution "supported in whole or in part by the public funds of the state."[82] John Scopes, a high school biology teacher, deliberately violated this law. Scopes was found guilty but escaped penalty through a technicality. The law itself was upheld by the Tennessee Supreme Court since it did not violate the state constitution's provision which prohibited giving of preference to any religious establishment or mode of worship, nor the due process clause of the Fourteenth Amendment of the federal Constitution. Furthermore, the court maintained that "there is no religious establishment or organized body that has in its creed or confession of faith any article denying or affirming such a theory . . . and the denial or affirmation of such a theory does not enter into any recognized mode of worship." Therefore, the court concluded, that "as the law thus stands, while the theory of evolution may not be taught in the schools of the state, nothing contrary to that theory is required to be taught."[83] The *Scopes* case was never appealed to the U.S. Supreme Court.

But in 1965, another biology teacher, Susan Epperson of Little

Rock Central High School, Arkansas, challenged the constitutionality of a 1928 Arkansas law which was similar to the Tennessee law.
A newly adopted textbook for the biology course contained Dar-
win's theory. Fearing dismissal if she taught the book's contents,
Mrs. Epperson sought to have the Arkansas statute declared void.
The Supreme Court of Arkansas sustained the statute as an exercise
of the state's power to specify the curriculum in public schools; thus
the appeal to the U.S. Supreme Court.

Justice Fortas, in rendering the Court's opinion, admitted the
vagueness of the Arkansas statute, but did not rest the decision
upon the problem of interpretation. Rather, he pointed out that
"the overriding fact is that Arkansas' law selects from the body of
knowledge a particular segment which it proscribes for the sole
reason that it is deemed to conflict with a particular religious doctrine; that is, with a particular interpretation of the Book of Genesis
by a particular religious group."[84] Reaffirming the neutrality of the
state in regard to religion—neither promoting nor being hostile to
one religion or religious theory against another—the Court asserted that "there is and can be no doubt that the First Amendment
does not permit the State to require that teaching and learning must
be tailored to the principles or prohibitions of any religious sect or
dogma."[85] The Court, therefore, concluded that

> The State's undoubted right to prescribe the curriculum
> for its public schools does not carry with it the right to
> prohibit on pain of criminal penalty, the teaching of a
> scientific theory or doctrine where that prohibition is
> based upon reasons that violate the First Amendment.
> . . . Arkansas' law cannot be defended as an act of religious
> neutrality. Arkansas did not seek to excise from the cur-
> ricula of its schools and universities all discussion of the
> origin of man. The law's effort was confined to an attempt
> to blot out a particular theory because of its supposed
> conflict with the Biblical account, literally read.[86]

The *Epperson* decision has not, however, extended the academic
freedom enjoyed by teachers in higher education to public school
teachers. Rather, it restricted itself solely to classifying a teaching
ban on evolution as an impermissible establishment of religion.
Morgan regards the reasoning in this decision as "a very neat twist":

"Fortas was able to underscore the teaching of the school prayer cases that the state may not favor religious doctrine; he got rid of an obnoxious, if archaic, statute; and he avoided diminishing the general power of states to prescribe public school curricula which would have resulted from launching a constitutional theory of academic freedom."[87]

CHAPEL ATTENDANCE AT SERVICE ACADEMIES

On December 18, 1972, the U.S. Supreme Court declined to hear an appeal by the Justice Department that would reinstate compulsory chapel attendance at the nation's armed service academies.[88] A U.S. court of appeals had declared in June of the same year that the founding fathers had written the establishment of religion clause into the First Amendment with the express purpose of prohibiting government-ordered church attendance. Although the regulations of the academies permitted exemptions for conscientious objectors, the court had found that only three midshipmen, and no one at West Point, had been exempted in the last forty years. Those who failed or refused to attend chapel services could be punished by demerits, extra marching tours, confinement to quarters, or even expulsion. The suit had been initiated by two West Point cadets, nine Annapolis midshipmen, and all the students at Colorado Springs.[89]

9

Teachers

A recent work dealing with the civil rights of teachers has observed that "until very recently teachers were certainly second-class citizens."[1] Regarded as public servants, many restrictions were placed on teachers so that there arose a tradition which too often refused to separate a teacher's private life from his professional life. Few other members of the community were subjected, as the teachers were, to restrictions from dancing, smoking, drinking, late hours, membership in certain organizations, participating in political campaigns, and becoming victims of unfounded rumors and bad publicity.[2]

The restrictions placed upon teachers stemmed from the days of colonial America, when teachers were commonly required to have religious orthodoxy, loyalty to the civil government, and an unquestionable moral character. A Massachusetts law passed in 1654 forbade the appointment of teachers who were "unsound in the faith or scandalous in their lives."[3] New Jersey had a similar requirement.[4] Loyalty oaths were required in several colonies at the time of the American Revolution.[5] Nor was the nineteenth century much different in its attitude toward teachers. In 1839 it was declared that "a practically Christian character may be regarded as the first and highest requisite" among the qualities of a teacher.[6] A Connecticut lawyer, observing the status of teachers in 1864, called attention to the fact that teachers were being employed "as passive tools, and every man became the teacher's censor."[7] A speaker at the American Institute of Instruction noted in 1851: "Boards of Trustees and School Committees on the one side, point out the path in which he is to walk, the books he is to use, and even the mode in which he is to use them; while, on the other hand, an unofficial, but by no means unimportant and very numerous board of fathers, uncles, aunts, grandmothers and cousins, claim for themselves authority to form and express opinions upon his qualifications and conduct."[8]

Progress towards removing many of the restrictions on teachers has been slow. Although professional organizations of teachers steadily grew between 1865 and 1918, efforts to secure more stable contracts free of political and social pressures were slow in being achieved.[9] Much state legislation has been passed regarding both the rights and duties of teachers. Both state and federal courts have dealt with them in their decisions. The U.S. Supreme Court has also issued decisions of great import to teachers; many of these decisions have not only clarified the constitutional rights of teachers as possessing the same inalienable rights enjoyed by other citizens, but have also stressed their positions of great responsibility as public employees involved in the education of the nation's youth.

The cases in this chapter on teachers are divided into three main areas: (1) contracts of employment and tenure, (2) loyalty oaths, and (3) freedom of expression and association.

CONTRACTS OF EMPLOYMENT AND TENURE

In *Meyer* v. *Nebraska* (1923), the Supreme Court rendered a legal interpretation of the meaning of "teacher": "Practically, education of the young is only possible in schools conducted by especially qualified persons who devote themselves thereto. The calling always has been regarded as useful and honorable,—essential, indeed to the public welfare." A teacher, furthermore, enjoyed the right to pursue his occupational calling, and the deprivation of this right involved a denial of due process of the law according to the Fourteenth Amendment, since the teacher's right to teach constituted a property right.[10]

Reduction of Salary

One of the effects of the depression of the 1930s was the reduction of teachers' salaries in practically all states; in some situations teachers went unpaid or were only partially paid.[11] In 1933 the state legislature of New Jersey, because of the state's depressed financial condition, enacted a law that enabled each school board "to fix and determine salaries to be paid officers and employees . . . notwithstanding any such person to be under tenure." The board of education of West New York, New Jersey, by virtue of this law, reduced the prevailing salaries of administrators and teachers on a proportionate percentage basis.

Teachers' and administrators' appeals to local and state school boards and courts were met by adverse decisions. A teacher named Phelps led an appeal to the U.S. Supreme Court, which rendered its affirmation of the New Jersey statute. The decision made some important distinctions.

The act of 1903 of the New Jersey legislature had empowered school boards to regulate the "terms and tenure of such employment, promotion, and dismissal, salaries and their time and mode of payment, and to change and repeal such rules and regulations from time to time." The act of 1909, in addition to sanctioning tenure status after three consecutive years of service in a school district, stated that "no principal or teacher shall be dismissed or subjected to reduction of salary in said school district except for inefficiency, incapacity, conduct unbecoming a teacher or other just cause, and after a written charge . . . shall have been preferred." On the basis of these laws the Court concluded that the tenure status of a teacher in New Jersey was statutory and not a contract. For the act of 1909 "established a legislative status" for teachers and not "a contractual one" that could not be modified by the legislature. Granted, the Court continued, that tenure of teachers is "in one sense perhaps contractual," in essence it depends on a statute which "the Legislature at will may abolish, or whose emoluments it may change." Since reductions in salary were on a proportionate basis and all of the same salaries were treated alike, the plan and formula of reduction was not deemed unreasonable and arbitrary, and thus within the concept of equality guaranteed by the Fourteenth Amendment.[12]

In an earlier case decided in 1874, *Head* v. *University of Missouri*, the Supreme Court had reasoned in a similar fashion. A professor-librarian, holding a six-year contract, had been dismissed after only four years of service. Since the contract contained the words "subject to law," the Court decided that the qualifying phrase empowered the authorities at the University of Missouri to terminate the contract without the consent of the professor-librarian.[13]

But before any conclusions can be drawn as to the interpretation of tenure under the federal Constitution, it is necessary to consider the *Brand* case decided only a year after *Phelps*.

Tenure as a Contract

The *Brand* case differs from the *Phelps* case because of the nature of the contract as stated in the tenure law of the state of Indiana. Furthermore, where *Phelps* dealt primarily with reduction of salary, *Brand* involved the validity of a contract to continue employment considered as permanent.

Brand arose from the dismissal of a public school teacher in Indiana.[14] Her service as a teacher began by a contract entered into in September, 1924; the contract was continuously renewed up to and including the academic year of 1932–33. Her contract for the years 1931–32 and 1932–33 contained the provision: "It is further agreed by the contracting parties that all of the provisions of the Teachers' Tenure Law, approved March 8, 1927, shall be in full force and effect in this contract." The teacher was notified of the termination of her service after the conclusion of the 1933–34 academic year. The teacher appealed to the terms of the Tenure Law of 1927, which established her as a permanent teacher after having served under contract for at least five consecutive years, and further provided that a contracting school board could dismiss a teacher only for incompetency, insubordination, neglect of duty, immorality, justifiable decrease in number of teaching positions, or other good or just cause. Her school board justified its action on the basis of an act passed in 1933, which exempted township school corporations from the Teachers' Tenure Act of 1927; the courts of Indiana concurred with the school board.

After hearing the appeal, the U.S. Supreme Court based its judgment upon the interpretation of the meaning of a contract in Indiana law: "The position of a teacher in the public schools is not a public office, but an employment by contract between the teacher and the school corporation. The relation remains contractual after the teacher has, under the provisions of the Teachers' Tenure Law, become a permanent teacher." With none of the reasons for dismissal as contained in the law of 1927 applicable to the teacher, the Court concluded: "We do not think that the asserted change of policy evidenced by the repeal of the statute is that school boards may be at liberty to cancel a teacher's contract for political reasons." The Court did not question the state legislature's action of placing contracts on an annual basis by the act of 1933, but maintained that this same act "left the system of permanent teachers and indefinite contracts untouched as respects school corporations in cities and towns of the State."[15] Thus, in comparison with the *Phelps* case concerning New Jersey law, the Court decided that the Indiana law had clearly established a legal contract and, therefore, under the guarantee of Article I, Section 10 of the federal Constitution: "No State shall . . . pass any bill of attainder, *ex post facto* law, or law impairing the obligation of contracts."

The legal recognition and protection of tenure for teachers has been the result of intense work by teachers' associations, which have argued that only through tenure would a genuine professional status be afforded the teacher, and at the same time spare the teacher from the practice of school boards to hire and fire without strong and reasonable grounds, and from the arbitrary decisions of administrators as to the discharge of teachers. Many school boards resisted the trend toward teacher tenure, as it would "tie their hands" in seeking to dismiss incompetent teachers.[16] Since 1918, when only seven states and the District of Columbia had some form of legislation on teacher tenure, tenure legislation has been adopted by all states.[17] On the college and university level, where the issue of academic freedom frequently arises, the efforts of the American Association of University Professors has helped secure tenure arrangements for teachers in higher education.[18]

Teacher Retirement Plan

The state of Illinois began a noncontributory plan for retired teachers in 1926 through the passage of the Miller Law. By an amendment to the law enacted in 1935, the annuities were reduced to as much as one-third of the previously stated annual amount of $1,500. The amendment applied not only to future teachers but also to those already retired. Illinois teachers contended that the amendment "impaired the obligation of contracts" according to Article I, Section 10, and deprived them of "due process" according to the Fourteenth Amendment of the federal Constitution. The Illinois Supreme Court classified the Miller Law and its amendment as statutory, and therefore subject to changes by the state's legislature, and not contractual; the teachers then brought the case before the U.S. Supreme Court.

The U.S. Supreme Court affirmed the judgment of the Supreme Court of Illinois. It declared that the "construction of the statute by language and circumstances implied no creation of a binding contract with the state's teachers. Since "the payments are gratuities, involving no agreement of the parties, the grant of them creates no vested right."[19] If the retirement plan had been a contribution on the part of both teachers and state, according to a legal expert's interpretation, then the members would have a "vested right which cannot be impaired by the legislature or by the retirement board in its by-laws, at least after a member has retired."[20] The Illinois plan at the time was supported wholly by public funds.

Equal Salaries for Black Teachers

A case involving equality, but not segregation, dealt with the salaries of black teachers. Melvin O. Alston, a black public school teacher, brought an injunction against the school board of Norfolk, Virginia. He claimed that the paying of lower salaries to blacks, who were equally situated and qualified with white teachers, was discrimination and thus in violation of the equal protection and due process clauses of the Fourteenth Amendment. The Supreme Court refused to grant a review of the case, thus affirming the decision of the Circuit Court of Appeals which acknowledged Alston's contention of discrimination on the ground of race.[21] The Supreme Court, therefore, maintained in effect that a disparate salary schedule for equally qualified and similarly assigned teachers would be in violation of the equality guaranteed by the Fourteenth Amendment.[22]

More Recent Tenure Cases

In 1966, the Supreme Court declined to hear an appeal from a nontenured teacher who claimed that he had been dismissed for teaching from a proscribed book.[23] The court of appeals did not deem the Fourteenth Amendment applicable in this case. Rather, it asserted: "Our decision rests entirely on the contract." By the terms of the contract, the teacher was only provisionally employed and wholly without academic tenure, express or implied. His contract could be terminated by either party at the end of the first or second year by giving thirty days' notice.[24]

In 1967, the Supreme Court declined to hear a case in which the court of appeals had upheld that minor infractions committed by a teacher were not sufficient to deny renewal of contract.[25] A North Carolina teacher with an excellent twelve-year record was charged with failure to stand at the door of her classroom and supervise pupils as classes changed, and with failure to see that cabinets in her home room were clean and free of fire hazards.

These infractions were neither individually nor collectively of such a nature as to justify the school board's failure to renew her contract.[26]

Tenure laws have varied considerably from state to state, and the state courts have arrived at different conclusions as to the rights of both tenured and untenured teachers. Even when appeals have been made to the federal courts, inconsistent rulings have been handed down.[27] Fischer and Schimmel have observed that the only rule that applies to all states is that all teachers, whether tenured or not, cannot be denied the right to procedural due process, if they are dismissed or refused renewal of contract on such constitutionally impermissible grounds as religion, sex, race, or the free exercise of speech, association, or assembly.[28] On June 29, 1972, in view of the many inconsistent lower-court rulings, especially in regard to probationary teachers, the Court clarified several basic issues involving tenure in two important cases: *Roth* and *Sinderman.* Although both cases dealt with college teachers, legal scholars feel that they will likely set precedents also for teachers in elementary and secondary schools.[29]

The *Roth* case involved a teacher's first teaching position as a university professor on a one-year contract. According to the laws of the state of Wisconsin—David Roth was an assistant professor of political science at Wisconsin State University—a state university teacher can acquire tenure as a permanent employee only after four years of year-to-year employment; when tenured, a teacher cannot be "discharged except for cause upon written charges and pursuant to certain procedures." A nontenured teacher has the opportunity for review, if dismissed before the end of the academic year. But the nontenured teacher need only be informed by February first "concerning retention or non-retention for the ensuing year." Furthermore, "no reason for nonretention need be given. No review or appeal is provided in such case."[30] Upon being informed that he would not be hired for the next year, Roth brought action against the university on two counts: first, for infringement of his right to freedom of speech, inasmuch as he felt that he was being punished for certain critical statements against the university; secondly, because no reason was given for his nonretention and no opportunity was afforded for a hearing, thus violating his right to procedural due process. With the federal courts ordering university officials to provide reasons for nonretention and in a hearing, the Board of Regents appealed the case to the U. S. Supreme Court.[31]

Justice Potter Stewart wrote the majority decision, with three justices dissenting and one justice not participating in the case. The main issue in the case was whether Roth had a constitutional right to a statement of reasons and a hearing on the university's decision not to rehire him. Justice Stewart saw no deprivation of procedural due process in this case, for no charge was made against Roth that would seriously damage his professional standing and reputation or would impede him in obtaining employment in other educational institutions. Moreover, Roth did not prove in lower court proceedings, and had not yet proven, that the decision not to rehire him was actually based on his free speech activities. Nor can Roth appeal to the Fourteenth Amendment in claiming that a "property" right was violated by not being rehired. The "property" interest in employment at Wisconsin State University "was created and defined by the terms of his appointment. . . . To have a property interest in a benefit," the Court explained, "a person clearly must have more than an abstract need or desire for it. He must have more than a unilateral expectation of it. He must, instead, have a legitimate entitlement to it." Thus, the untenured teacher did not have "a *property* interest sufficient to require the University authorities to give him a hearing when they declined to renew his contract of employment."[32] The three dissenting justices in the case argued that on the basis of the Fourteenth Amendment's due process clause a statement of reasons for his discharge and an opportunity to rebut those reasons should have been afforded.[33]

The *Sindermann* case dealt with a teacher employed in the state college system of Texas for ten years at three different institutions. He had taught for four years at the last institution under a series of one-year contracts. With the Board of Regents denying renewal of his contract without stating reasons and allowing a prior hearing, Robert Sindermann charged that such a decision resulted from his public criticism of the regents and the college administration, thus a violation of his free speech right and procedural due process right. The federal district court upheld the Board of Regents' decision, but the court of appeals reversed it and contended that, even without tenure, Sindermann's due process had been infringed upon if his contract was not being renewed for his protected free speech, and if in expectancy of reemployment no opportunity was granted for a hearing.[34]

Justice Stewart, speaking for a majority of five, with three justices dissenting and one justice not participating, rendered the Supreme Court's decision. The Court reiterated its position that lack of tenure alone does not foreclose the questioning of denial of rehirement, for "a teacher's public criticism of his superiors on matters of public concern may be constitutionally protected and may, therefore, be an impermissible basis for termination of his employment."[35] The Court, therefore, held that denying to Sindermann some kind of a hearing "without full exploration of this issue, was improper."[36] But even more of an issue in *Sindermann*, unlike *Roth*, was whether the "property" interest of tenure was actually secured. Sindermann contended that the college had a *de facto* tenure program under which he had already acquired permanent employment. He appealed the *Official Faculty Guide* that the college had in use for many years.

> *Teacher Tenure:* Odessa College has no tenure system. The Administration of the College wishes the faculty member to feel that he has permanent tenure as long as his teaching services are satisfactory and as long as he displays a cooperative attitude toward his co-workers and his superiors, and as long as he is happy in his work.[37]

Furthermore, Sindermann relied on guidelines promulgated by the Coordinating Board of the Texas College and University System that implied tenure for a teacher who had taught in the system for a period of seven or more years. The Court would not accept the subjective "expectancy" of reemployment as suggested by the court of appeals. Rather the Court argued as follows:

> A written contract with an explicit tenure provision clearly is evidence of a formal understanding that supports a teacher's claim of entitlement to continued employment unless sufficient "cause" is shown. Yet absence of such an explicit contractual provision may not always foreclose the possibility that a teacher has a "property" interest in re-employment. For example, the law of contracts in most, if not all jurisdictions long has employed a process by which agreements, though not formalized in writing, may be "implied" ... there may be an unwritten "common law" in a particu-

lar university that certain employees shall have the equivalent of tenure.[38]

And the Court concluded that Odessa College, although not having an explicit tenure system for even its senior faculty members, may have created one in practice. Sindermann, therefore, would be entitled to a hearing to question the grounds for his nonretention.

Age Discrimination

On January 15, 1973, the Court, by an 8-to-1 vote, declined to rule on the constitutionality of age discrimination in the hiring of a university professor.[39] The case involved Professor Paul Weiss, presently of the Catholic University of America. Having reached the mandatory retirement age of sixty-eight at Yale University, Weiss was offered a position at Fordham University, which later withdrew the offer because of Weiss's age. Weiss sued Fordham on the ground of age discrimination; but the federal district court upheld Fordham: "It cannot be said . . . that age ceilings upon eligibility for employment are inherently suspect, although their application will inevitably fall unjustly in the individual case."[40] The court of appeals upheld this ruling.[41]

Maternity Leaves

On January 21, 1974, the Supreme Court handed down a decision in two companion cases dealing with maternity leaves of teachers. Both cases examined the validity of school regulations governing such leaves under the due process clause of the Fourteenth Amendment. In the first case, Jo Carol La Fleur and other pregnant teachers instituted civil rights action challenging the constitutionality of a maternity leave rule of the Board of Education of Cleveland, Ohio. The rule required a pregnant teacher to take a maternity leave beginning five months before the expected birth of her child, to give notice of her pregnancy at least two weeks before the beginning of her maternity leave, and to become eligible for reemployment no earlier than the beginning of the next school semester after the child was three months old, on condition that a physician attest to health requisite for classroom teaching.[42] In the second case, a pregnant teacher, Susan Cohen, also instituted civil rights action challenging the constitutionality of the maternity leave rule of her school board in Chesterfield County, Virginia. The Chesterfield County rule required the teacher to leave work at least four months, and to give notice at least six months, before childbirth, with reemployment guaranteed no later than the first day of the school year after the date she is declared reeligible by a physician's certificate.[43]

Justice Stewart delivered the Court's opinion in a 7-to-2 decision. The basis for the decision is a series of cases that demonstrate the Court's recognition that freedom of personal choice in matters of marriage and family life is one of the liberties protected by the due process clause of the Fourteenth Amendment, and specifically the right "to be free from unwarranted governmental intrusion into matters so fundamentally affecting a person as the decision whether to bear or beget a child."[44] In regard to maternity leaves, the Court pointed out:

> By acting to penalize the pregnant teacher for deciding to bear a child, overly restrictive maternity leave regulations can constitute a heavy burden on the exercise of these protective freedoms. Because public school maternity leave rules directly affect "one of the basic civil rights of man" . . . the Due Process Clause of the Fourteenth Amendment requires that such rules must not needlessly, arbitrarily, or capriciously impinge upon this vital area of a teacher's constitutional liberty.[45]

Yet the Court took full cognizance of the problems brought on by maternity leaves to the educational process. It affirmed the importance of continuity of instruction and the problem of finding and hiring a qualified substitute teacher. It recognized that some teachers become physically incapable of adequate performance of certain duties during the latter part of pregnancy. So the Court accepted as sound and fair the requiring of advice notice as "wholly rational," but not the "absolute requirements of termination at the end of the fourth or fifth month of pregnancy." The Court further clarified: "Indeed, continuity would seem just as well attained if the teacher herself were allowed to choose the date upon which to commence her leave, at least so long as the decision were required to be made and notice given of it well in advance of the date selected."[46] As to the problem of potentially incapacitated pregnant teachers, the Court felt that the "rules sweep too broadly." For "there is no individualized determination by the teacher's doctor—or the school's board—as to any particular teacher's ability to continue at her job. The rules contain an irrebuttable presumption of physical incompetency, and that presumption applies even when the medical evidence as to an individual woman's physical status might be wholly to the contrary."[47] The unanimous agreement of medical experts was cited: The ability of any particular pregnant woman to continue work past any fixed time in her pregnancy is very much an individual matter. As to rules placing limitations upon a teacher's eligibility to return to work after giving birth, the Court regarded the Cleveland rule as lacking justification in requiring a mother to wait until her child reaches the age of three months before the return rules begin to operate. The requirement of a physician's certificate declaring adequate health for classroom duties fully protects the interests of the school. Chesterfield County had no return rule of fixed time, but Cleveland's rule of the three months age provision was seen as "wholly arbitrary and irrational," serving no legitimate state interest and unnecessarily penalizing the female teacher for asserting her right to bear children.

The Court, therefore, concluded in this matter of maternity leaves that

> neither the necessity for continuity of instruction nor the state interest in keeping physically unfit teachers out of the classroom can justify the sweeping mandatory leave regulations that the Cleveland and Chesterfield County School Boards have adopted. While the regulations no doubt represent a good-faith attempt to reach a laudable goal, they cannot pass muster under the Due Process Clause of the Fourteenth Amendment, because they employ irrebuttable presumptions that unduly penalize a female teacher for deciding to bear a child.[48]

LOYALTY OATHS

The state of Oklahoma required teachers, along with other employees of the state, to take a loyalty oath within thirty days of assuming a public office. This oath contained a disavowal of either direct or indirect affiliation with the Communist party or any foreign political organization determined as subversive. If there was a previous affiliation, there had to be a period of at least five years in which no affiliation was had. Additionally, the public employee or teacher had to swear to a willingness to bear arms in the defense of his country in time of war or of national emergency. When thirteen employees of the Oklahoma State Agricultural and Mechanical College refused to take this oath within the prescribed thirty days, a citizen sought to enjoin the payment of the thirteen employees, who thereupon brought suit in court.

Since the Oklahoma courts held the legislation constitutional, the employees appealed to the U.S. Supreme Court. Justice Tom Clark, in speaking for the Court, insisted on distinguishing between those whose membership in an organization are aware of its subversive purpose and activities and those whose "membership may be innocent, . . . unaware" of its true nature. Clark alluded to many loyal and innocent persons who had joined or allied themselves with such organizations, but later severed their ties with them when they became aware of their subversive tendencies. The oath required under the Oklahoma act was deemed unconstitutional as it offended the due process of law guaranteed by the Fourteenth Amendment.[49] Justice Clark also referred to the *Gerende* case in which the Supreme Court had upheld a Maryland law requiring a loyalty oath of all candidates for public office, because the law had been interpreted by the Maryland state court as disqualifying only those who "knowingly" belonged to any organization advocating violent overthrow of the government.[50] Justice Frankfurter offered in his concurring opinion a defense of academic freedom.

> To regard teachers— . . . from the primary grades to the university—as the priests of our democracy is . . . not to indulge in hyperbole. It is the special task of teachers to foster those habits of open-mindedness and critical inquiry which alone make for responsible citizens, who, in turn, make possible an enlightened and effective public opinion. Teachers must fulfill their function by precept and practice, by the very atmosphere which they generate; they must be exemplars of open-mindedness and free inquiry. They cannot carry out their great and noble task if the conditions for the practice of a responsible and critical mind are denied to them. They must have the freedom of responsible inquiry, by thought and action, into the mean-

ing of social and economic ideas, into the checkered history of social and economic dogma. They must be free to sift evanescent doctrine, qualified by time and circumstance, from that restless, enduring process of extending the bounds of understanding and wisdom, to assure which the freedoms of thought, of speech, of inquiry, of worship are guaranteed by the Constitution of the United States against infraction by national and state government.[51]

Also concurring was Justice Black. Aware of the witch-hunting spirit of McCarthyism, Black warned that "the present period of fear seems more ominously dangerous to speech and press than was that of the Alien and Sedition Laws. Suppressive laws and practices are the fashion. The Oklahoma oath statute is but one manifestation of a national network of laws aimed at coercing and controlling the minds of men."[52]

With its decision in *Wieman,* the position of the Court on loyalty oaths became clear. The Court would uphold only those oaths that affected teachers who "knowingly" affiliated themselves with subversive organizations, but it would reject innocent affiliation or guilt by association. Within a few years, a more liberal court found occasion to insist more on freedom and due process.

In 1961, the Court ruled on the loyalty oath required of teachers in the state of Florida. Failure to take the oath would result in perjury or immediate dismissal. Teachers of the state challenged the constitutionality of the oath as they felt it violated the due process clause of the Fourteenth Amendment. Upon appeal, the Supreme Court ruled that only one section of the oath should be eliminated: "That I have not (lent) or will lend my aid, support, counsel or influence to the Communist party." The remainder of the oath was considered valid and, therefore, remained in force and bound the teachers to it.[53]

In 1964, the Court was asked to rule on two loyalty oaths which sixty-four members of the faculty and student body of the State University of Washington charged as being unconstitutional. The first oath, enacted in 1931, required, under penalty of perjury, all teachers in the state of Washington to pledge support of the Constitution and the laws of their state and nation, including respect for the flag. The second oath, enacted in 1955, required teachers and state employees, also under penalty of perjury, to swear that they were not subversive persons or knowingly, members of the Communist party or other subversive organization. The Supreme Court supported the position of the plaintiffs and held the oaths as contrary to due process. As a result of the broad, uncertain, and unduly vague language employed in the oaths, academic freedom and guarantees of freedom of speech, association, and belief were jeopardized.[54]

In 1966, two teachers in the Tucson, Arizona, public school system, both Quakers, contested the loyalty oath of the state of Arizona. Their objection rested not on religious grounds but on the fact that the law did not provide for a hearing by which teachers could defend and explain their point of view. After five years of litigation in the lower courts, the case came before the U.S. Supreme Court. The Court struck down the Arizona statute as infringing upon the freedom of association guaranteed through the First Amendment, and subsequently made applicable to the states through the Fourteenth Amendment. The Court distinguished between an active member of an organization with the purpose of violent overthrow of the government and a member who does not share the unlawful purposes and activities of the organization; the latter type of member would not be considered a "threat, either as citizens or as public employees." The Court, therefore, concluded that "a law which applies to membership without specific intent to further the illegal aims of the organization infringes unnecessarily on protected freedoms. It rests on the doctrine of 'guilt by association,' which has no place here."[55]

In line with its decision in the *Baggett* case of 1964, the Supreme Court, in 1967, struck down a "negative" loyalty oath involving a University of Maryland professor in the *Whitehill* case. The oath required the signing of a statement that one was "not engaged in one way or another in the attempt to overthrow the Government . . . by force or violence." This Maryland law called for the dismissal of "subversive" persons and the charge of perjury against those who violated the oath. The Court defended the professor's refusal to sign the oath because it felt that one could not know, unless he risked a perjury prosecution, whether he was actually involved in an attempt to overthrow the government. The Court saw in such a situation the danger of a "continuing surveillance which this type of law places on teachers [as] hostile to academic freedom." Lacking preciseness and clarity, such an oath, the Court maintained, possessed an "overbreadth that makes possible oppressive or capricious application as regimes change . . ." and was, therefore, a violation of academic freedom. The dissent of Justice Harlan, who did not see academic freedom endangered by this Maryland oath, concluded that "the only thing that does shine through the opinion of the majority is that its members do not like loyalty oaths."[56]

On June 7, 1971, the Supreme Court affirmed the first part of a statutory loyalty oath required of all Florida public employees: "that I will support the Constitution of the United States and of the State of Florida." In regard to the second part of the oath, which stated "that I do not believe in the overthrow of the Government of the United States or of the State of Florida by force or violence," the Court held that the teacher involved could not be dismissed from public employment for refusing to take the oath without prior hearing or inquiry as required by due process.[57]

Writing in regard to loyalty oaths, Louis Fischer and David Schimmel have concluded (largely on the basis of the *Whitehill* and *Baggett* cases) that the Supreme Court has an apparent mistrust of loyalty oaths. As a result, they claim, "the Court's critical examination of such oaths—especially those that placed teachers under surveillance—has helped academic freedom and maintained a healthier climate in American schools during the past decade."[58] Chief Justice Burger in April, 1972, has even suggested that loyalty oaths are really "no more than an amenity." "The time may come," Burger has asserted, "when the value of oaths in routine public employment will be thought not 'worth the candle' for all the division of opinion they engender."[59]

FREEDOM OF EXPRESSION AND ASSOCIATION

In April, 1949, the New York State legislature passed the much disputed Feinberg Law in the hope of preventing subversive influences in schools. It was not New York's first attempt at such a legislation. In 1917, legislation was passed that provided for the removal of school personnel "for the utterance of any treasonable or seditious word or words or the doing of any treasonable or seditious act or acts while holding . . . positions" in schools. In 1929, the legislature clarified and extended the 1917 law by calling for dismissal from public employment anyone who would advise, advo-

cate, or teach the overthrow of the federal, state, or local governments by violent means, or is a member of an organization with such
a purpose. In the preamble to the Feinberg Law, doubt as to the
effectiveness of the previous legislation is expressed: "The legislature deplores the failure heretofore to prevent such infiltration,
which threatens to become a commonplace in our schools. . . . The
board of regents . . . should be admonished and directed to take
affirmative action to meet this grave menace and to report thereon
regularly to the state legislature." In ensuring that the law prevents
the infiltration of subversives into the public school system as stated
by the law, the Board of Regents was to draw up rules and regulations and a listing of the organizations clearly regarded as subversive, and to bar them from employment and to dismiss their members. The Board of Regents was required to report annually to the
state legislature on the carrying out of the law.[60]

Under the leadership of Irving Adler, legal action was taken to
declare the law invalid. After a series of legal battles in the courts
of New York State and the affirmation of the law by the New York
Court of Appeals, Adler brought the case to the U.S. Supreme
Court on the grounds that the Feinberg Law constituted "an
abridgement of the freedom of speech and assembly of persons
employed or seeking employment in the public schools of the State
of New York." Justice Minton, delivering the majority decision in a
6-to-3 division in the Court's vote, agreed with the plaintiffs that
persons have the right under our law to assemble, speak, think, and
believe as they will. However, he disagreed that they could "work
for the state in the school system on their own terms." Minton
insisted on such a legal clarification because of the "sensitive area"
of education. The state, he argued, has a vital concern in educational matters, especially in the influence of the teacher upon young
minds. Minton, furthermore, saw no denial of the due process of law
in the firing of a teacher knowingly associated with an organization
advocating the overthrow of the government by unlawful means.[61]

Three justices dissented from the majority opinion in *Adler.*
Justice Felix Frankfurter considered the case speculative, in as much
as no concrete case had been presented in behalf of a teacher dismissed by the Board of Regents for violating the Feinberg Law.
Justice Douglas dissented on the grounds that the New York law
"proceeds on a principle repugnant to our society—guilt by association." The teacher can be found guilty of subversion by mere mem-

bership in a stated organization, and can be dismissed or not hired as the result of a procedure "to which the teacher is not a party and in which it is not clear that she may even be heard." Teachers, more than other members of American society, need the constitutional guarantees of freedom of thought and expression. To create a situation which causes teachers "to shrink from any association that stirs controversy" leads to the stifling of freedom of expression. Justice Black's dissent pursued substantially the same reasoning as that of Justice Douglas in sustaining a "law which effectively penalizes school teachers for their thoughts and their associates." The freedoms of thought and expression are guaranteed by the First Amendment and, as made applicable to the states by the Fourteenth, encourage a governmental policy of varied intellectual outlooks.[62] The dissenting views of Justices Douglas and Black in *Adler* in 1952 were to become, however, the majority opinion in later cases.

In 1956 the Supreme Court declared Section 903 of the Charter of the City of New York as unconstitutional. That section called for the termination of the employment of a public official who uses the privilege against self-incrimination to avoid answering a question relating to his official conduct. A Brooklyn College professor invoked the privilege against self-incrimination under the Fifth Amendment before an investigating committee of the United States Senate, and was thereby dismissed from his teaching position at an educational institution supported by New York City. Slochower, the professor involved, stated that he was not a member of the Communist party, and was willing to answer all questions about his political beliefs and memberships since 1941. He refused, however, to answer questions about his membership in 1940 and 1941 on the ground that his answers could incriminate him. He was suspended from his teaching position, but he appealed the decisions of the New York courts to the U.S. Supreme Court, which upheld his suspension.

The Supreme Court justified Slochower's invoking of his constitutional right under the Fifth Amendment, and insisted on condemning the practice of placing a sinister meaning to a person's exercise of his rights. The state courts, in upholding Slochower's dismissal on the basis of the New York City Charter, produced a situation where "in practical effect the questions asked are taken as confessed and made the basis of the discharge." No inference, therefore, can be made from claiming privilege against self-incrimination.[63]

In a 1957 case, the Supreme Court struck down the dismissal of a university professor for declining to answer questions before a subversive activities committee of the New Hampshire legislature. A 1951 law of the state legislature had set up a comprehensive scheme for the regulation of subversive activities. It dissolved "subversive organizations," made "subversive persons" ineligible for government employment, and instituted a loyalty program whereby all government employees were required to make sworn statements declaring that they were not "subversive." When summoned to answer questions regarding his activities in support of the Progressive party in 1948, and opinions and ideas expressed in his classroom lectures, the university professor declined. The New Hampshire courts concurred in his dismissal. But the U. S. Supreme Court maintained that the legislative committee's activities did not constitute restraint supported by a reasonable governmental interest, thus endangering the constitutional liberties guaranteed by the due process clause.[64] Of more importance was the Court's opinion, written by Chief Justice Warren, which commented on the desirability and necessity of a free flow of ideas in a university; it stands as strong legal support for academic freedom.

> We believe that there unquestionably was an invasion of petitioner's liberties in the areas of academic freedom and political expression—areas in which government should be extremely reticent to tread.
>
> The essentiality of freedom in the community of American universities is almost self evident. No one should underestimate the vital role in a democracy that is played by those who guide and train our youth. To impose any strait jacket upon the intellectual leaders in our colleges and universities would imperil the future of our Nation. No field of education is so thoroughly comprehended by man that new discoveries cannot yet be made. Particularly is that true in the social sciences, where few, if any, principles are accepted as absolutes. Scholarship cannot flourish in an atmosphere of suspicion and distrust. Teachers and students must always remain free to inquire, to study and to evaluate, to gain new maturity and understanding; oth-

erwise our civilization will stagnate and die.

Equally manifest as a fundamental principle of a democratic society is political freedom of the individual. Our form of government is built on the premise that every citizen shall have the right to engage in political expression and association. This right was enshrined in the First Amendment of the Bill of Rights. Exercise of these basic freedoms in America has traditionally been through the media of political associations. Any interference with the freedom of a party is simultaneously an interference with the freedom of its adherents. All political ideas cannot and should not be channeled into the programs of our two major parties. History has amply proved the virtue of political activity by minority, dissident groups, who innumerable times have been in the vanguard of democratic thought and whose programs were ultimately accepted. Mere unorthodoxy or dissent from the prevailing mores is not to be condemned. The absence of such voices would be a symptom of grave illness in our society.[65]

In tune with the *Adler* decision, the Supreme Court in 1958 affirmed the dismissal of a Philadelphia public school teacher. Herman A. Beilan, a teacher for twenty-two years, refused to answer questions from his superintendent regarding past activities in the Communist party and was judged "incompetent," in accordance with the Pennsylvania Public School Code of 1949. Pennsylvania also had a Loyalty Act under which public employees could be discharged for disloyal or subversive conduct. Beilan argued that his dismissal resulted from suspected disloyalty. Both the Pennsylvania Board of Education and courts sustained the superintendent on the charge of "incompetency" without referring to violation of the Loyalty Act.

The Supreme Court proceeded to hear the case on only the question of "incompetency," and affirmed Beilan's dismissal in as much as the Pennsylvania Supreme Court "merely equated refusal to answer the employing Board's relevant questions with statutory 'incompetency.' " The Supreme Court thereby accepted a broad interpretation of "incompetency." It reasoned:

By engaging in teaching in the public schools, petitioner did not give up his right to freedom of belief, speech or association. He did, however, undertake obligations of frankness, candor and cooperation in answering inquiries made of him by his employing Board examining into his fitness to serve it as a public school teacher.[66]

And the Court referred to *Adler:*

A teacher works in a sensitive area in a schoolroom. There he shapes the attitude of young minds toward the society in which they live. In this, the state has a vital concern. It must preserve the integrity of the schools. That the school authorities have the right and the duty to screen the officials, teachers, and employees as to their fitness to maintain the integrity of the schools as a part of ordered society, cannot be doubted.[67]

In a companion case decided in conjunction with *Beilan,* a New York City subway conductor's discharge was sustained. He had refused to answer questions regarding membership in the Communist party and was thereby considered of doubtful trust and reliability under the New York Security Risk Law.[68]

The dissenting justices in *Beilan* pointed out that the invoking of the Fifth Amendment is an invalid basis for discharge from public employment since the theory of our legal system is that every person is innocent until he is proven guilty in accordance with the due process of law required by the Fourteenth Amendment.[69]

In 1959 the Supreme Court heard the case of a college teacher who refused to answer questions regarding past or present membership in the Communist party before a U.S. House of Representatives Subcommittee on Un-American Activities. The committee at the time was concerned about alleged Communist infiltration into the field of education. The teacher preferred to invoke the guarantees of freedom of speech, religion, and association under the First Amendment rather than the Fifth Amendment.

The Court affirmed the authority of a congressional committee to investigate educational matters as they pertain to the "nationwide, indeed worldwide problem" of communism. Academic freedom, the Court maintained, does not preclude the questioning of a witness merely because he is a teacher: "An educational institution is not a constitutional sanctuary from inquiry into matters that may otherwise be within the constitutional legislative domain merely for the reason that inquiry is made of someone within its walls."[70] The dissenting justices affirmed Barenblatt's stand based on the interpretation of the First Amendment as an abridgment of his rights.[71]

In 1960, the Court, in dealing with membership in organizations of questionable subversive purpose, held as unconstitutional a statute of the state of Arkansas. The statute required teachers to file annually a list of organizations in which they held membership. The Court declared that "there can be no doubt of the right of a State to investigate the competence and fitness of those whom it hires to teach in its schools." But, the Court continued, "to compel a teacher to disclose his every associational tie is to impair that teacher's right of free association, a right closely allied to freedom of speech and a right which, like free speech, lies at the foundation of a free society." The Court further expressed fear that membership in unpopular or minority organizations could bring pressures upon school boards to discharge teachers, a situation which "would simply operate to widen and aggravate the impairment of constitutional liberty."[72]

In 1962, the Supreme Court dismissed the appeal of a teacher who had been discharged by his school board for flagrant discussion of sexual matters in his high school classes.[73] The Court thereby affirmed a decision handed down by the Supreme Court of Wisconsin, which held that the evidence sustained the findings of the school board that the teacher's discussion of sex matters in class was such as to constitute bad behavior warranting his discharge. The teacher had acquired tenure status. Following hearings at which the teacher was allowed to defend himself, the board found that "the charges of inefficiency and lack of good behavior under the evidence adduced are proved." The Wisconsin court regarded the suspension of the teacher as invalid only insofar as it deprived the teacher of his salary prior to his discharge by the board.[74]

The *Adler* decision of 1952 upheld New York State's Feinberg Law. Although the law went through some modification in its application, it still upheld the disqualification of any teacher or administrator in the public educational institutions of New York if he advocated overthrow of the government by unlawful means or was a member of any organization, such as the Communist party, which so advocated. In 1962, a teacher at the Buffalo campus of the State University of New York, Harry Keyishian, refused to comply with the Feinberg Law by testifying in writing that he was not a Communist. His contract was, therefore, not renewed. Joined by several other university professors, Keyishian challenged the constitutionality of the law responsible for the nonrenewal of his contract. The *Keyishian* case reached the Supreme Court for decision in 1967 when, in a 5-to-4 vote, the Feinberg Law was declared unconstitutional and the *Adler* decision was reversed.[75]

The Court in 1967 concluded that "mere knowing membership without a specific intent to further the unlawful aims of an organization is not a constitutionally adequate basis for exclusion from such positions as those held by appellants." The Court staunchly rejected guilt by association.

> Under our traditions, beliefs are personal and not a matter of mere association, and men in adhering to a political party or other organization do not subscribe unqualifiedly to all of its platforms or asserted principles. A law which applies to membership, without the specific intent to further the illegal aims of the organization, infringes unnecessarily on protected freedoms. It rests on the doctrine of guilt by association which has no place here.[76]

Also in the minds of the majority justices was academic freedom. Another strong advocacy of this cherished right of the academic profession was made by the Court.

> Our nation is deeply committed to safeguarding academic freedom, which is of transcendent value to all of us and not merely to the teachers concerned. That freedom is therefore a special concern of the First Amendment, which does not tolerate laws that cast a pall of orthodoxy over the classroom. . . . The nation's future depends upon leaders trained through wide exposure to that robust exchange of ideas which discovers truth out of a multitude of tongues rather than through any kind of authoritative selection. . . . Scholarship cannot flourish in an atmosphere of suspicion and distrust. Teachers and students must always remain free to inquire, to study, and to evaluate, to gain new maturity and understanding; otherwise our civilization will stagnate and die.[77]

Justice Tom Clark wrote a strong dissent stating "that the majority has by its broadside swept away one of our most precious rights, namely, the right of self-preservation."[78] But the Court clearly affirmed, as Justice Clark sadly noted, its rejection of the *Adler* doctrine that Communist party membership as such constituted *prima-facie* evidence for disqualification. Furthermore, the Court declared that *Adler* must be overruled as inconsistent with decisions made since it was decided in 1952.

Legal scholars, although of the opinion that the Burger Court will be more conservative than the Warren Court and thus more likely to give greater weight to the rights of the community, believe that the law concerning teacher membership in controversial or revolutionary organizations will continue to be guided by the *Keyishian* decision. Thus, school boards or state legislatures could not disqualify teachers for membership in controversial or extremist organizations, unless it could be clearly shown that the teacher intended to pursue the illegal aims and activities of such an organization.[79]

The *Pickering* case of 1968 deals with the matter of a teacher dismissed because of his remarks critical of school authorities. Marvin L. Pickering, a teacher in Township High School District 205, Will County, Illinois, was dismissed from his position because of a letter he sent to a local newspaper. The letter criticized the Board of Education and the district superintendent of schools in their handling of proposals to raise new revenue for the schools and the allocation of funds to be used for education. The board dismissed Pickering on the grounds that his published letter was "detrimental to the efficient operation and administration of the schools of the district" and therefore, under state law, the interest of the school made his dismissal necessary. The courts of Illinois rejected Pickering's claim to protection by the First Amendment on the ground that his teaching position placed an obligation upon him to refrain from making statements about the operation of schools "which in the absence of such position he would have an undoubted right to engage in."[80]

The Supreme Court affirmed "the public interest in having free and unhindered debate on matters of public importance—the core value of the Free Speech Clause of the First Amendment." Upon examination of the statements of Pickering and finding "absent proof of false statements knowingly or recklessly made by him, a teacher's exercise of his right to speak on issues of public importance may not furnish the basis for his dismissal from public employment."[81] The Court did examine Pickering's statements, some of which were found to be erroneous, but which could have been rebutted by the board's disclosure of accurate information. The Court, recognizing free and open debate as vital to informed decision-making by the electorate, singled out the important contributions that teachers can make: "Teachers are, as a class, the members of a community most likely to have informed and definite opinions as to how funds allotted to the operation of the schools should be spent. Accordingly, it is essential that they be able to speak out freely on such questions without fear of retaliatory dismissal."[82] As to this case the Court concluded:

> What we do have before us is a case in which a teacher has made erroneous public statements upon issues then currently the subject of public attention, which are critical of his ultimate employer but which are neither shown nor can be presumed to have in any way either impeded the teacher's proper performance of his daily activities in the classroom or to have interfered with the regular operation of the schools generally. In these circumstances we conclude that the interest of the school administration in limiting teachers' opportunities to contribute to public debate is not significantly greater than its interest in limiting a similar contribution by any member of the general public.[83]

Both in 1972 and 1973 the U.S. Supreme Court upheld a court of appeals' ruling that a high school teacher who did no more than wear a black armband in class as a symbolic protest against the Vietnam War could not be discharged.[84] The appeals court had reasoned that since the wearing of the armband did not disrupt classroom activities, had no influence on the students, and did not engender protests from students, teachers, or parents, the courts cannot countenance the arbitrary censoring by school authorities of a teacher's freedom of expression just because they may not agree with his political philosophy, especially when no interference is found with the teacher's obligation to teach and no coercion is used by the teacher to inculcate arbitrarily doctrinaire views in the minds of students.[85] The Supreme Court had in 1969 dealt with a similar case of the wearing of armbands by students.[86]

10

Students

All court decisions in education affect the student. It is the student for whom education exists and any area of education about which a judgment is made must ultimately affect the student. This chapter records only those cases in which a student or a group of students were directly involved in court proceedings that led to action by the U.S. Supreme Court. Many cases covering numerous issues involving rights of students have been argued in state and federal courts.[1] Although not an education case, the 1965 decision *In re Gault* noted that children too have the protection of constitutional safeguards.[2] Both educators and lawyers have addressed themselves to what has been referred to as the "developing civil rights of students."[3] And the student protests of the past decade have convinced many in and out of education of the fact of student power.

COMPULSORY VACCINATION OF SCHOOL CHILDREN

In two cases, *Jacobson* v. *Massachusetts*[4] in 1905 and *Zucht* v. *King*[5] in 1922, the Supreme Court maintained the judgments of lower courts in sustaining compulsory vaccination laws enacted either by states or local municipalities. It regarded such laws as "within the police power of a state" and "that a state may, consistently with the Federal Constitution, delegate to a municipality authority to determine under what conditions health regulations shall become operative."[6]

More recently, on June 4, 1973, the U.S. Supreme Court, in an appeal from the Supreme Court of Texas, dismissed a case involving compulsory immunization for want of a federal question.[7] The Texas court had upheld a state statute that required immunizations against a variety of diseases as a prerequisite to admission to elementary or secondary school or institution of higher learning. The arguments that it was unconstitutional interference with the right of parents to require compulsory immunization and thus a denial of due process, equal protection of the law, and "invidious discrimination" against attendance at state-supported schools were rejected.[8]

SECRET SOCIETIES IN SCHOOLS

In applying for admission to study law at Mississippi University, student J. P. Waugh refused to sign a pledge forswearing allegiance to a secret Greek letter fraternity, to which he had belonged in a previously attended college. Denied admission, Waugh sued the university on the grounds that his rights under the Fourteenth Amendment were infringed upon. Not satisfied with an adverse decesion of the Supreme Court of Mississippi, Waugh appealed to the U.S. Supreme Court.

The Supreme Court's decision upheld the university regulation and contended that there was no discrimination against the individual or his fraternity since such organizations were not permitted to anyone or any group at the university. As an institution established by, and under the control of, the state, the Court concurred with the state legislature's contention "that membership in prohibited societies divided the attention of the students, and distracted from the singleness of purpose which the state desired to exist in its public institutions."[9] Most states prohibit such societies in public institutions.[10]

CONSCIENCE—MILITARY TRAINING

Two cases involving compulsory military training in a state university were decided in favor of the institution imposing participation in the Reserve Officers Training Corps program of all physically able males.

The first case, *Pearson* v. *Coale*, arose when Ennis Coale, a member of the Epworth League of the Methodist Episcopal Church, was suspended in 1932 from the University of Maryland for refusal, on the basis of conscientious objection, to comply with the university's regulatory participation in its ROTC program. As a land grant college under the Morrill Act of 1862, the university required training and instruction in military science. Upon his suspension from the university, Coale's father appealed the action of the university to the superior court in Baltimore, which ordered a reinstatement of the student. University authorities took the case to Maryland's highest state court and were granted a reversal of the lower court's decision. When an appeal was brought to the U.S. Supreme Court, the case was dismissed "for want of a substantial Federal question." The University of Maryland could, therefore, continue its requirement of compulsory military training.[11]

The second case, *Hamilton* v. *Regents of the University of California,* involved two young men who had enrolled at the University of California in the fall of 1933. Both students were sons of ordained ministers of the Methodist Episcopal Church, and like Ennis Coale of Maryland, were members of the Epworth League and conscientious objectors to military training. Their petition, as well as the petition of the bishop of their church in California for exemption from the ROTC requirement, was denied by university authorities. Since the California Supreme Court also upheld the university, an appeal was made to the U.S. Supreme Court on the grounds that their rights and privileges under the Fourteenth Amendment were violated, their religious convictions were not respected, and the California law requiring military training at state educational institutions opposed the spirit of the Kellogg-Briand Peace Pact, which the U.S. Senate had ratified in 1929.

The Supreme Court upheld the university's regulation of compulsory military training under the Morrill Act of 1862 and reasoned that "California has not drafted or called them to attend the University. They are seeking education offered by the state" and, therefore, must meet the requirements that a state institution imposes upon its students. The military obligation was considered a legitimate state power not contrary to the federal Constitution.[12]

Whatever may have been the original intent of the Morrill Acts as to military training in state-sponsored colleges and universities, the policy in practice of these institutions has been largely to make military training optional for the students.[13] Furthermore, the Supreme Court has been progressively adopting a more liberal policy towards conscientious objectors.[14]

CONSCIENCE—COMPULSORY FLAG SALUTING

Refusal to salute the national flag as part of a daily school exercise led to another case before the Supreme Court on the issue of religious conscience. The Gobitis children, twelve-year-old Lillian and ten-year-old William, were expelled from the public school they attended in Minersville, Pennsylvania, for the infraction of this school regulation. As members of the Jehovah's Witnesses religious sect, their parents maintained that to salute the flag would be contrary to their religious conviction based on the literal interpretation of the Old Testament Book of Exodus: "Thou shalt not make unto thee any graven image, or any likeness of anything that is in heaven above, or that is in the earth beneath, or that is in the water under the earth; thou shalt not bow down thyself to them nor serve them" (20:4–5). Although Jehovah's Witnesses respect the flag, they may not salute it as that would imply the bowing down before a "graven image."

The courts of Pennsylvania accepted the argument of religious conscience as explained by Witness Walter Gobitis on behalf of his children and called for their reinstatement to school. The school district appealed to the U.S. Supreme Court, which had previously refused to hear cases involving the saluting of the flag.[15] The Court, in the words of Justice Felix Frankfurter, now felt "a grave responsibility" for "situations like the present are phases of the profoundest problem confronting a democracy." The Court's "judicial conscience" was placed "to its severest test" in seeking to "reconcile the conflicting claims of liberty and authority." The Court decided in favor of the authority of the school district and its right to insist on saluting the flag as a means to achieve national unity and feeling, thus approving an educational policy for the promotion of patriotism. Exemption of students from such a school policy "might introduce elements of difficulty into school discipline, might cast doubts in the minds of the other children which would themselves weaken the effect of the exercise."[16] Thus the Court viewed the common good as superior to the alleged violation of individual rights.

In analyzing some of the consequences of the *Gobitis* decision, Victor Rotnem and F. G. Folsom, Jr., members of the Department of Justice, found that there were many attempts to persecute Jehovah's Witnesses' children and their parents, that arrests were made of Witnesses who distributed literature explaining their position in regard to the flag salute, that the children had been termed incorrigible delinquents. They concluded that "the placing of symbolic exercises on a higher plane than freedom of conscience has made this symbol an instrument of oppression of a religious minority. The flag has been violated by its misuse to deny the very freedoms it is intended to represent."[17]

The Court, however, reversed itself in the next case involving compulsory flag saluting, *West Virginia State Board of Education* v. *Barnette.* Leading to the Court's reversal was the notoriety given to the adverse effects of the *Gobitis* case and the enactment by Congress in 1942 of a law which, although reiterating the words of the pledge and prescribing the salute, added that "however, civilians will always show full respect to the flag when the pledge is given by merely standing at attention, men removing the headdress."[18]

On the strength of the *Gobitis* decision, the West Virginia legislature on June 30, 1940, imposed a requirement upon all schools, public, private, and denominational, to teach courses in history, civics, and in the constitutions of the United States and West Virginia, "for the purpose of teaching, fostering, and perpetuating the ideals, principles, and spirit of Americanism, and increasing the knowledge of the organization and machinery of the government." On January 9, 1942, the West Virginia Board of Education, also in consideration of the *Gobitis* decision, ordered the salute to the flag to become "a regular part of the program of activities in the public schools," and refusal to do so would "be regarded as an act of insubordination, and shall be dealt with accordingly," which in practice resulted in expulsion, the declaration of such children as unlawfully absent and to be regarded as delinquents, with their parents subject to the payment of fines and incarceration.

The appeal of the school board's regulation by the Jehovah's Witnesses to a U.S. district court was decided in restraining the enforcement of the compulsory saluting of the flag. But the board of education sought a reversal by the U.S. Supreme Court. With the Court's membership having changed since 1940, the majority ruled in favor of the religious conscience of the Witnesses. The Court emphasized that it was not within the province of school boards and state legislatures to define the meaning and implications of a religious ceremony, but within the purpose and the scope of the First Amendment, it was the province of the individual and his conscience. Furthermore, the Court argued in favor of rectifying what it deemed a misapplication of constitutional justice in the *Gobitis* decision, that

> the Fourteenth Amendment, as now applied to the States, protects the citizen against the State itself and all of its creatures—Boards of Education not excepted. These have, of course, important, delicate, and highly discretionary functions, but none that they may not perform within the limits of the Bill of Rights. That they are educating the young for citizenship is reason for scrupulous protection of Constitutional freedoms of the individual, if we are not to strangle the free mind at its source and teach youth to discount important principles of our government as mere platitutdes.[19]

The three dissenting justices, with Justice Felix Frankfurter expressing their views, remained steadfast in their upholding of the right of the state to exercise power, for in the case "we all recognize as a legitimate legislative end, namely the promotion of good citizenship, by employment of the means here chosen."[20] However, the *Gobitis* decision was reversed and the supremacy of religious conscience was clearly asserted, even in educational policy and practice.

Where legal experts and educators overwhelmingly denounced the *Gobitis* decision, they endorsed *Barnette* as a more accurate expression of the rights of individual conscience in a democracy.[21] Three state courts had directly repudiated *Gobitis* before the *Barnette* decision and four state courts ruled in favor of the Jehovah's Witnesses, while only two state courts followed *Gobitis*.[22]

DUE PROCESS FOR STUDENTS

In 1961, the U.S. Supreme Court declined to hear an appeal on a court of appeal's ruling that due process requires notice and an opportunity for a hearing before students at a tax-supported university can be expelled for misconduct.[23] Considered "the landmark case concerning constitutional due process rights of students,"[24] the Court's reasoning is worthy of note:

Admittedly, there must be some reasonable and constitutional ground for expulsion or the court would have a duty
to require reinstatement. The possibility of arbitrary action
is not excluded by the existence of reasonable regulations.
There may be arbitrary application of the rule to the facts
of a particular case. Indeed, that result is well nigh inevitable when the Board hears only one side of the issue. In the
disciplining of college students there are no considerations
. . . which should prevent the Board from exercising at least
the fundamental principles of fairness by giving the accused students notice of the charges and an opportunity to
be heard in their own defense. Indeed, the example set by
the Board in failing to do so, if not corrected by the courts,
can well break the spirits of the expelled students and of
others familiar with the injustice, and do inestimable harm
to their education.[25]

THE RIGHT OF STUDENT PROTEST

In February, 1969, the Supreme Court rendered a decision
affecting the right of public school students to protest symbolically.
Although the case involved high school students, the decision is
considered to have relevance to higher education as well.[26] The case
originated with the determination of a group of adults and students
in Des Moines, Iowa, to express their objections to the Vietnam War
and to ask for support of a truce by wearing black armbands. Upon
hearing of the plan, the principals of Des Moines schools met and
adopted a policy forbidding a student from wearing an armband,
and if he refused to remove it, he would face suspension until he
returned without the armband. Despite this policy, several students
wore black armbands to school; they were suspended and their
parents filed complaints in federal district courts, which upheld the
constitutionality of the action of the school authorities as a reasonable measure to prevent disturbance of school discipline.[27] An
equally divided court of appeals affirmed the lower court's decision,
but the parents pressed for action by the U.S. Supreme Court.[28]

The Supreme Court, in an opinion written by Justice Abe Fortas, pinpointed the problem in the case as involving the "direct,
primary First Amendment rights akin to 'pure speech.' "[29] Such

rights, even in light of the special characteristics of the school environment, are available to teachers and students, who are not expected to forego their constitutional rights to freedom of speech or expression in the school setting. For, the Court elaborated:

> The principal use to which the schools are dedicated is to accommodate students during prescribed hours for the purpose of certain types of activities. Among those activities is personal intercommunication among the students. This is not only an inevitable part of the process of attending school. It is also an important part of the educational process. A student's rights therefore, do not embrace merely the classroom hours. When he is in the cafeteria, or on the playing field, or on the campus during the authorized hours, he may express his opinions, even on controversial subjects like the conflict in Vietnam, . . . Under our Constitution, free speech is not a right that is given only to be so circumscribed that it exists in principle but not in fact.[30]

But while upholding the right of students to express themselves freely anywhere on school property, the Court did establish an important condition upon any protest or exercise of such freedom of expression. That condition was "any facts which might reasonably have led school authorities to forecast substantial disruption of or material interference with school activities." Since there was disruption of the work and discipline of the school by the students' wearing of armbands, the Court concluded that "in the circumstances, our Constitution does not permit officials of the State to deny their form of expression."[31]

Justice Hugo Black dissented strongly: "The Court's holding in this case ushers in what I deem to be an entirely new era in which the power to control pupils by the elected 'officials of state supported schools . . .' in the United States is in ultimate effect transferred to the Supreme Court. . . ." While maintaining a firm belief in the exercise of free speech, he would deny that "any person has a right to give speeches or engage in demonstrations where he pleases and when he pleases." He emphasized that "school discipline . . . is an integral and important part of training our children to be good citizens—to be better citizens. Here a very small number of students have crisply and summarily refused to obey a school order designed to give pupils who want to learn the opportunity to do so." And the majority holding in this case would lead some students already "ready, able, and willing to defy their teachers on practically all orders," as is evidenced by so many groups of students "already running loose, conducting break-ins, sit-ins, lie-ins, and smash-ins." Justice Black concluded his dissent: "I wish, therefore, wholly to disclaim any purpose on my part, to hold that the Federal Constitution compels the teachers, parents, and elected school officials to surrender control of the American public school system to public school students."[32]

A legal scholar has concluded from the *Tinker* decision as follows:

> The Court more importantly established a "balancing test" which was to guide school authorities when seeking to regulate student behavior in constitutionally protected interests. The interests which are in conflict are the right of the students to be protected in constitutionally assured areas of behavior and the necessity of the state to maintain an efficient system of public schools. When the student meets the burden of showing the state it is intruding into an area of constitutionally protected activity, the burden of proof shifts to the state to show some compelling reason for establishing rules and regulations in this area. The courts have insisted that these rules be based on something more than vague fears or unpopular positions or attitudes being expressed.[33]

In 1970, the U.S. Supreme Court upheld a court of appeals' ruling that reinstated two high school students expelled for writing and distributing remarks critical of school policies and authorities.[34] The appeals court had claimed that the expulsion of the students was an unjustified invasion of their First and Fourteenth amendment rights on the ground that the distribution of the critical remarks did not constitute a direct and substantial threat to the effective operation of the high school. It was maintained that the school must make "affirmative showing" that there could be reasonably forecasted "substantial disruption" of school affairs. The opinion contained an interesting observation on the expected role of the school to promote critical and independent thinking of students.

While recognizing the need for effective discipline in operating schools, the law requires that the school rules be related to the state interest in the production of well-trained intellects with constructive critical stances, lest students' imaginations, intellects and wills be unduly stifled or chilled. Schools are increasingly accepting student criticism as a worthwhile influence in school administration.[35]

While strongly supporting the right of student protest and free expression, the courts have also been careful to place restrictions on actions of students which may infringe upon the rights of others by violent and disruptive behavior. In June, 1970, the U.S. Supreme Court declined to hear an appeal of a decision handed down by a court of appeals that suspended students of Central Missouri State College in Warrensburg, Missouri.[36] The appeals court had held that the conduct of college students who participated in a mass gathering that engaged in potentially disruptive conduct, aggressive action, disorder and disturbance, acts of violence, and destructive interference with the rights of others, did not constitute protected free speech and assembly. It further stated that the college regulation calling for students to adhere to standards of conduct befitting a college student was not so vague or broad as to deny substantive due process to the students involved. The suspension of students under such conditions was deemed proper.[37] The court of appeals' opinion presented valuable clarification as to the school regulations regarding protest and dissent.

Let there be no misunderstanding as to our precise holding. We do not hold that any college regulation, however loosely framed, is necessarily valid. We do not hold that a school has the authority to require a student to discard any constitutional right when he matriculates. We do hold that a college has the inherent power to promulgate rules and regulations; that it has the inherent power properly to discipline; that it has power appropriately to protect itself and its property; that it may expect that its students adhere to generally accepted standards of conduct; that, as to these, flexibility and elbow room are to be preferred over specificity; that procedural due process must be . . . afforded by way of adequate notice, definite charge, and a hearing with opportunity to present one's own side of the case and with all necessary protective measures; that school regulations are not to be measured by the standards which prevail for the criminal law and for criminal procedure; and that the courts should interfere only where there is a clear case of constitutional infringement.[38]

In 1973, the U.S. Supreme Court declined to hear a case involving students at San Francisco State College, California.[39] The court of appeals had held that the police report, which consisted of the general account of a rally and protest held at the college but which contained no statement as to the students' particular conduct, furnished no basis for the college's taking of disciplinary action against students for academically related misconduct.[40]

OFFICIAL RECOGNITION OF CAMPUS ORGANIZATIONS

In September, 1969, a group of students at Central Connecticut State College, a state-supported institution, requested official recognition for their newly organized local chapter of Students for a Democratic Society (SDS). Official recognition permitted use of campus facilities for meetings and of college news channels for announcements and publicity. The interested students, in their formal application for recognition, argued for a forum of discussion and stated that they would not affiliate with, but would remain completely independent of, the national SDS. Despite approval from the Students Affairs Committee, the president of the college, Dr. F. Don James, rejected the application because he felt that the organization's philosophy was antithetical to the college's policies, and because he doubted the group's independence from the national SDS. The students challenged the president's decision in federal district court on the ground that their First Amendment rights of expression and association had been denied. The district court ordered the college to grant another hearing on the application. Although reaffirming their independence from the national SDS, the students equivocated, when asked whether they would respond to "issues of violence" as other SDS chapters had done, and whether they would advocate interruption of classes. The president again rejected the application, expressing fear that such a group would be a disruptive influence on the college campus. The federal district court, upon receiving the case again after its second hearing, dismissed the case,[41] and the students failed in their request for a hearing by a U.S. court of appeals.[42]

The students brought their case to the U.S. Supreme Court, and on June 26, 1972, Justice Powell spoke in behalf of eight members of the Court. Powell's opinion began by presenting a brief but succinct synopsis of the climate of unrest on American college campuses in the 1960s. He noted that many SDS chapters had been intimately involved in "widespread civil disobedience," seizing, burning, and vandalizing buildings, looting files, and destroying valuable manuscripts. "SDS chapters on some of those campuses had been a catalytic force during this period," he affirmed on the basis of reports on campus unrest. These activities by a few, he further maintained, led to the denial of the lawful exercise of First Amendment rights to the majority of students.[43]

But despite the situation of the 1960s, Powell asserted that denial of official recognition, without justification, to college organizations violates the right of free association. This right is further limited by denying access to the customary media for communicating with administration, faculty, and other students; the organization cannot fully participate in the intellectual give and take of campus debate. Powell dealt with four reasons that college president James offered for nonrecognition; three of these reasons he rejected, but saw merit in the fourth reason: (1) While appreciative of the fear that some SDS chapters have been associated with campus disruption, it ought not be concluded that all chapters do or will call for unlawful action. The students claimed complete independence from the national organization; thus, the relationship was not sufficient ground for denying recognition. (2) The philosophy of violence and disruption characteristic of SDS goals could be considered "abhorrent" and contrary to the official policy of the college. But the Court held that mere disagreement with an organization's philosophy affords no reason for nonrecognition, for speech or association cannot be restricted just because they appear repugnant to other people's views. (3) That this group could be a disruptive influence at the college could not be assumed. The Court insisted that if nonrecognition resulted from fear or apprehension, then such a kind of fear or apprehension of disturbance is not enough to overcome, as was declared in *Tinker*, the right to freedom of expression. There is a constitutional difference between "permissible speech" and "impermissible conduct." (4) A college administration, just as a community at large, may impose the requirement that a group seeking official recognition affirm in advance its willingness to adhere to reasonable campus law; thus the rights to free speech and assembly or to petition for changes in school rules are not infringed upon, but reasonable standards of conduct are respected. The equivocation of the students as to possible use of violence and possible disruption of the orderly conduct of classes has merit for denying recognition. On the basis of this last point, the Court would grant recognition if the students would affirm their willingness to abide by reasonable campus rules and regulations.[44]

Justice Rehnquist concurred in the result only, and with Chief Justice Burger's concurring opinion, felt that it were better for the academic community to resolve its own problems and have the courts become only the last resort.[45] But Justice Douglas, although joining in the Court's opinion, added that the fact that the case had come to the Supreme Court for ultimate resolution indicated "the sickness of the academic world." He explained:

> Students as well as faculty are entitled to credentials in their search for truth. If we are to become an integrated, adult society, rather than a stubborn status quo opposed to change, students and faculties should have communal interests in which each age learns from the other. Without ferment of one kind or another, a college or university . . . becomes a useless appendage to a society which traditionally has reflected the spirit of rebellion.[46]

HAIR STYLES OF MALE STUDENTS

In 1970, the U.S. Supreme Court declined to reexamine a court of appeals ruling regarding a Wisconsin school's regulation concerning hair styles of male students.[47] The appeals court had affirmed the reinstatement by a federal district court judge of male students who had been suspended for refusing to comply with a school regulation regarding length of male students' hair.[48] The judge wrote: "It is hereby adjudged that the regulation of the Williams Bay Board of Education limiting the length of male students' hair, requiring male students to be clean shaven, and prohibiting long sideburns, violates the due process clause of the Fourteenth Amendment to the Constitution of the United States, and is null and void."[49]

TUITION AND FEES FOR RESIDENT AND NONRESIDENT STUDENTS

On February 2, 1970, the U.S. Supreme Court dismissed, for want of a substantial federal question, a case involving the payment of higher tuition and fees for nonresident students in California.[50] A California law was challenged because of the one-year waiting period requirement for resident tuition purposes. The Supreme Court thus gave approval to the decision and main argument of the court of appeals of California.

> This state has a valid interest in providing tuition-free education to those who have demonstrated by a year's residence a bona fide intention of remaining here and who, by reason of that education will be prepared to make a greater contribution to the state's economy and future. Accordingly, we hold that the regulation classifying students as residents or nonresidents for tuition purposes is not arbitrary or unreasonable and bears a rational limitation to California's objective and purpose of financing, operating and maintaining its many publicly financed educational institutions of higher learning.[51]

On March 29, 1971, the U.S. Supreme Court affirmed the decision of the U.S. District Court in Minnesota on the same issue.[52] Two students at the University of Minnesota challenged a regulation made by the university's Board of Regents: "No student is eligible for residence classification in the University . . . unless he has been a bona fide domiciliary of the state for at least a year immediately prior thereto." The students claimed that the residency requirement for tuition purposes created two classes of residents: those who have resided within Minnesota for over one year and those who resided for less than one year. This classification, being unreasonable and discriminatory, it violated the equal protection clause according to the students. The three-judge district court's ruling quoted *Kirk* to uphold the university regulation, and added:

> We believe that once the law affords recognition to the right of a State to discriminate in tuition charges between a resident and nonresident, that right to discriminate may be applied reasonably to the end that a person retains a non-resident classification for tuition purposes until he has completed a twelve-month period of domicile within the State. We believe that the State of Minnesota has the right to say that those new residents of the State shall make some contribution, tangible or intangible, towards the State's welfare for a period of twelve months before becoming entitled to enjoy the same privileges as long-term residents possess to attend the University at a reduced resident's fee.[53]

In June, 1973, the Supreme Court dealt more fully with the determination of residence and nonresidence for the purpose of fixing tuition and fees in public colleges. The case arose from a state of Connecticut law—similar in many other states—which requires nonresidents of the state who are enrolled in the state university system to pay tuition and other fees at rates higher than for the state's own residents. The Connecticut law, however, provided an irreversible and irrebuttable statutory presumption that because the legal address of a student, if married, was outside the state at the time of application for admission or, if single, was outside the state at some point during the preceding year, he remains a nonresident as long as he is a student in Connecticut. Two students challenged the Connecticut law.[54] One student was Margaret Marsh Kline, married to a life-long Connecticut resident in California, from where she made her application to attend the University of Connecticut, and thereafter established a permanent residence in Connecticut. But at the time of her application she had been classified as a nonresident student. The other student, Patricia Catapano, applied for admission from Ohio and then moved her residence to Connecticut before beginning the academic year. The Connecticut statute, as interpreted by university officials, required both students to pay higher tuition and other fees as nonresident students. A three-judge federal court concluded that both students were bona fide Connecticut residents, held the Connecticut statute unconstitutional, and ordered refunds of tuition and fees paid by the students in excess of those ordinarily charged to resident students.[55]

University officials appealed the decision to the U.S. Supreme Court which, in a 5-to-4 vote, upheld the lower court's decision. Justice Stewart's majority opinion centered on the interpretation and application of the due process clause that it is forbidden

> to deny an individual the resident rates on the basis of a permanent and irrebuttable presumption of nonresidence, when that presumption is not necessarily or universally true in fact, and when the State has reasonable alternative means of making the crucial determination. Rather, standards of due process require that the State allow such an individual the opportunity to present evidence showing that he is a bona fide resident entitled to the in-state rates.[56]

Since both students had Connecticut driving licenses and car registrations, and were registered to vote in Connecticut, they had become bona fide Connecticut residents and, therefore, could not be held by a "permanent irrebuttable presumption of nonresidence."

But Justice Stewart, mindful of the special problems involved in determining bona fide residence of college students, affirmed previous Court action in *Kirk* and *Starns*.

> Our holding today should in no wise be taken to mean that Connecticut must classify its students in its university system as residents, for purposes of tuition and fees, just because they go to school there. Nor should our decision be construed to deny a State the right to impose on a student, as one element in demonstrating a bona fide residence, a reasonable durational residency requirement, which can be met while in student status. We fully recognize that a State has a legitimate interest in protecting and preserving the quality of its colleges and universities and the right of its own bona fide residents to attend such institutions on a preferential tuition basis.[57]

CORPORAL PUNISHMENT

In 1972, the U.S. Supreme Court declined to review a court of appeals ruling regarding corporal punishment in a Dallas, Texas, school district.[58] The appeals court had affirmed a federal district court judge's opinion on the practice.

> It is not within this Court's function, or individual competence, to pass judgment upon the merits of corporal punishment as an educational tool or means of discipline. The wisdom of the policy is not the Court's concern. The only judgment is that the evidence has not shown this policy to be arbitrary, capricious, unreasonable or wholly unrelated to the competency of the state of determining its educational policy. . . . The Court does not find that corporal punishment as authorized by the state law and the rules of the Dallas Independent School District amounts to cruel and unusual punishment. It must be pointed out in this context that if the corporal punishment is unreasonable or excessive, it is no longer lawful and the perpetrator of it may be criminally and civilly liable. The law and policy do not sanction child abuse.[59]

CHARGE FOR TEXTBOOKS TO INDIGENT CHILDREN IN PUBLIC SCHOOLS

According to New York State law, local school districts are required to loan textbooks for free to students in grades seven through twelve. No such provision is made for children in grades one through six; free textbooks can be made available to children in those grades only upon a vote of the majority of the district's eligible voters to levy a tax to provide funds for the purchase of the textbooks.[60] A New York school district did not have a law to furnish free textbooks and so indigent parents, who were recipients of public assistance, challenged the constitutionality of the New York statute. They claimed that it created a wealth classification in violation of the equal protection clause of the Fourteenth Amendment. They documented their case with specific instances which demonstrated unequal treatment because of not having the required textbooks, and which resulted in a widespread feeling of inferiority and unfitness in poor children, leading to a condition psychologically, emotionally, and educationally disastrous to their well-being. Both a federal district court and court of appeals dismissed their complaint and upheld the constitutionality of the New York law.[61]

The appeal to the U.S. Supreme Court led to the case's being remanded to the federal district court to determine whether the case had become moot, for on May 3, 1972, the qualified voters of the school district involved had voted to assess a tax for the purchase of all textbooks for grades one through six in the schools of the district. Justice Marshall, however, while concurring with the unanimous decision, set forth a number of questions for the district court to consider one of which was "this case [is] in fact moot." Mindful of the wealth classification violation, Marshall's questions are summarized in his last: "Is it possible that litigation would again have to proceed for an entire school year or more, while indigent children are deprived of books, before the constitutionality is finally determined?"[62]

RIGHT TO SPECIAL CLASSES FOR NON-ENGLISH SPEAKING CHILDREN

On January 21, 1974, the Supreme Court dealt with a class suit brought by non-English speaking Chinese students. These students charged the public school system of San Francisco, California, of violating the Fourteenth Amendment by not providing supplemental courses in the English language. Of the 2,856 students of Chinese ancestry who do not speak English, about 1,000 were being given special courses in the English language; about 1,800, however, were not. The lower federal courts had decided against the suit.[63]

The U.S. Supreme Court took special consideration of California educational laws, provisions against discrimination in the 1964 Civil Rights Act, and regulations of the Department of Health, Education, and Welfare. Granting that English is the basic language of instruction and its mastery should be rightfully asked of all pupils, as the California education laws state, the Court pointed out that these same laws can authorize bilingual instruction. With students subject to compulsory full-time education from ages six to sixteen and mastery of English a requirement for the grade twelve diploma, the Court concluded:

> Under these state-imposed standards there is no equality of treatment merely by providing students with the same facilities, text books, teachers, and curriculum; for students who do not understand English are effectively foreclosed from any meaningful education.
>
> Basic English skills are at the very core of what these public schools teach. Imposition of a requirement that, before a child can effectively participate in the educational program, he must already have acquired those basic skills is to make a mockery of public education. We know that those who do not understand English are certain to find their classroom experiences wholly incomprehensible and in no way meaningful.[64]

The Court did not base its decision on a direct violation of the equal protection clause argument but relied on Section 601 of the 1964 Civil Rights Act that bans discrimination "on the ground of race, color, or national origin," in "any program or activity receiving federal assistance." HEW, authorized by the 1964 act, has issued regulations to school systems receiving such assistance. A 1968 guideline stated that "school systems are responsible for assuring that students of a particular race, color, or national origin are not denied the opportunity to obtain the education generally obtained by other students in the system."[65] A 1970 guideline ordered specifically "to rectify the language deficiency" for students:

> Where inability to speak and understand the English language excludes national origin-minority group children from effective participation in the educational program offered by a school district, the district must take affirmative steps to rectify the language deficiency in order to open its instructional program to these students.
>
> Any ability grouping or tracking system employed by the school system to deal with the special language skill needs of national origin-minority group children must be designed to meet such language skill needs as soon as possible and must not operate as an educational deadend or permanent track.[66]

Justice Blackman's concurring opinion, however, stressed that "numbers are at the heart of this case," and that if few youngsters, or only a single child were involved, he would not regard the decision to apply "conclusively."[67]

But the importance of the Court's decision in this case extends beyond the immediate issue of Chinese-speaking pupils. The coming of many Spanish-speaking people to the United States has caused similar problems. A study of the U.S. Commission on Civil Rights in 1971 noted that the educational disadvantages of the non-English speaking Chinese children are "dramatically similar" to those of the approximately 1.4 million Mexican-American children who attend school in the Southwest.[68] A 1970 study on the need for bilingual schooling demonstrated the intensity of the problem and the wisdom of the Court's decision.

> Seventy-five percent of all Mexican-American children of school age are enrolled in school, but the number in high school is only one-third what it should be on the basis of population. In New Mexican schools, of 60,000 Spanish speakers enrolled, over one-third are in the first grade. (One wonders how many years they spend there). . . . In Texas, among Mexican-American children entering the first grade, about 80 percent are not promoted.[69]

REVERSE DISCRIMINATION IN STUDENTS' ADMISSIONS

On April 23, 1974, the U.S. Supreme Court, in a 5-to-4 vote, refused to review a case dealing with reverse discrimination alleged by a student seeking admission to law school. Marco De Funis, a magna cum laude college graduate and white, was refused admission to the University of Washington Law School in 1971, although black applicants with lower test scores were admitted, in line with the school's policy of separate screening for admission applicants of minority groups. De Funis sued, and a state court upheld his charge of racial discrimination; he was admitted. The state of Washington Supreme Court upheld the university's admission policy for it was seen as justified for seeking to correct the effects of past racial discrimination against blacks. De Funis was allowed to remain in law school, however.

In an appeal to the U.S. Supreme Court, a majority of five

opinions held that no civil rights issue existed any longer, since De Funis had been admitted and was completing his law studies, and that the law student's suit was moot. But the majority did feel that the Court would eventually have to decide this same issue in other cases, thus justifying its present mootness.[70]

Justices of the minority were strong in their dissent. Justice Brennan questioned the mootness of the case, should De Funis, because of illness, economic necessity, or even academic failure, be forced to withdraw and then reapply for admission. Brennan also charged the majority for disserving the public interest: "The constitutional issues which are avoided today concern vast numbers of people, organizations and colleges and universities, as evidenced by the filing of 26 *amici curiae* [friends-of-the-court] briefs. Few constitutional questions in recent history have stirred as much debate, and they will not disappear."[71] Justice Douglas's separate opinion examined the merits of the case. He noted that the admissions committee of the law school admitted thirty-seven students from the minority groups of blacks, Mexican-Americans, American Indians, and Filipinos. All of these students except one had scores and grade averages lower than those of De Funis. Furthermore, thirty of them would not have met the normal admission requirements of the law school. Douglas suggested that the case be remanded to the state court to ascertain whether the admissions procedures were in violation of the equal protection clause of the Fourteenth Amendment as being racially discriminatory. "The key to the problem," insisted Douglas, "is the consideration of each applicant in a racially neutral way." He maintained that preferences for students from deprived backgrounds could be valid if these were granted without regard to race: "A De Funis who is white is entitled to no advantage by reason of that fact; nor is he subject to any disability. . . . Whatever his race, he had a constitutional right to have his application considered on his individual merits in a racially neutral manner."[72]

Thus, as of April 23, 1974, the Supreme Court left unanswered the question of whether it is constitutional to discriminate against a white person to help make up for the effects of past discrimination against blacks or other minorities. The Court's action allows continuation of programs that give preference to blacks in school admissions and employment. The *American Bar Association Journal* has noted the significance of this case for admissions policies in law schools and other educational programs. When the Court decides on a similar case, the journal suggested that its outcome will have effect on admissions policies and compensatory and affirmative-action employment programs that take into consideration the race factor.[73]

11

Integration

BLACKS AND EQUALITY OF EDUCATIONAL OPPORTUNITY

A "nation dedicated to the principle that all men are created equal" did not fully apply this principle to the black segment of its population. As a matter of fact, it excluded blacks from the rights of citizenship for approximately one hundred years after the enunciation of the principle of equality for all men regardless of race, color, or creed. Even after Lincoln's emancipation proclamation in 1863 and the passage of constitutional amendments and acts of Congress, the matter of equal educational opportunity was delayed. Many Americans would argue today that, despite the Supreme Court's 1954 decision disavowing segregation of the races in education and a series of vast improvements in educational opportunities, blacks are still not treated as equal to whites in many areas of the country. The educational philosophy of American government in reference to blacks has certainly not kept pace with the nation's political philosophy.

The policy of the federal government in dealing with educational opportunity for the black may be said to have been marked by three stages: (1) unequal and separate; (2) equal but separate, and (3) equal and unseparate.

Regarded as slaves, blacks were forbidden by the laws of many states to be taught how to write and to read.[1] However, some states permitted the religious instruction of blacks.[2] Education for whites in the South was not comparable to the efforts made in the North. The movement for a common public school system in the South did not begin to parallel the North's until after the Civil War.[3] With blacks ineligible for citizenship—as declared by the decision of the

Dred Scott case in 1857[4]—one of the strongest reasons for educating them was lacking.[5]

President Abraham Lincoln's emancipation proclamation in 1863 and the defeat of the North over the South in the Civil War began a new phase for the rights of blacks, including the right to be educated. Congress enacted a series of amendments to the Constitution: the Thirteenth (1865) abolished slavery; the Fourteenth (1868) granted citizenship to all persons born or naturalized in the United States, and forbade the states from abridging the privileges or immunities of citizens, and denying equal protection of the laws; and the Fifteenth (1870) granted to citizens the right to vote regardless of race, color, or former state of servitude. Congress, furthermore, passed legislation that would enforce both the letter and the spirit of those amendments, the most important of which was the Civil Rights Act of 1875, which guaranteed to all persons "the full and equal enjoyment of the accommodations, advantages, facilities, and privileges of inns, public conveyances on land or water, theaters, and other places of public amusement; subject only to the conditions and limitations established by law, and applicable alike to citizens of every race and color, regardless of any previous condition of servitude."[6]

While Northern military governors ruled the Southern states during the period of Reconstruction, the blacks enjoyed a social, political, and economic progress previously unknown to them. Upon the withdrawal of the northern troops in 1877, however, there began a continuous enactment of "Jim Crow" laws throughout the Southern states, including provisions against mixed schools. Appeal was made to the Supreme Court against these laws as opposing both the 1875 act and the Fourteenth Amendment, but the Court, while maintaining in theory that all individuals had certain basic rights, forbade Congress to regulate by law the social associations of persons, as this was clearly a state right.[7]

In 1865 Congress established the Freedmen's Bureau to aid and help educate former slaves.[8] Hundreds of schools enrolling several hundred thousand students were made possible by this act. It has been estimated that by 1877 there were some 600,000 blacks in elementary and secondary schools, several normal and industrial schools and three institutions of higher learning.[9] Furthermore, the reconstructed states provided in their new constitutions for full public education for both blacks and whites.[10] The report of the

U.S. commissioner of education for 1892–93 gives the impression that the South had placed blacks on a par with whites: "The enfranchisement of the blacks called loudly for their education. Nothing more strongly reveals Southern appreciation of the change that the war accomplished than the promptness with which those States have established schools . . . under . . . their constitutions.[11] But schools for blacks were usually inferior, in both the physical plants and the quality of instruction available. Many private philanthropic and religious groups aided educational efforts for blacks.[12]

Public and private schools remained segregated for many decades after the Civil War. Provisions in some state constitutions and laws especially enacted ensured segregated educational facilities.[13] In 1849, the Northern state of Massachusetts enunciated a doctrine which was reiterated by the U.S. Supreme Court in 1896: the provision of substantially equal but separate schools did not constitute segregation by race.[14] A black in the city of Boston sought to enroll his five-year-old daughter in a public white primary school since it was closer to home than the "colored" school. The case was argued on the basis that having to walk a greater distance because of one's color denied the equality of citizens as guaranteed by the state's constitution. The state court, in a unanimous decision, ruled that separate schools for black children did not violate equality of rights. Although the city of Boston abolished segregated schools in 1855, the Supreme Court in *Plessy* v. *Ferguson* cited the Massachusetts case as a major precedent for segregation and established the "separate but equal" doctrine, not only for segregation in public conveyances, but also for hotel accommodations, restaurants, places of amusements, and schools.[15]

CASES BEFORE THE 1954 BROWN DECISION

It was not until 1899 that the first case directly involving race and public schools was decided by the Supreme Court. Blacks of Richmond County, Georgia, were forced to appeal a school board's closing of a high school for their children while the "white" high school was continued. The Court sustained the school board's judgment of suspending the black high school on the basis of economic necessity. The board had contended that maintaining the high school for sixty black children would jeopardize the efficiency of the "white" high school and even the primary schools for three hundred black children. The Court saw no infringement of the rights of the blacks according to the Fourteenth Amendment and claimed that

> While all admit that the benefits and burdens of taxation must be shared by citizens without discrimination against any class on account of their race, the education of the people in schools maintained by state taxation is a matter belonging to the respective states, and any interference on the part of federal authority with the management of such schools cannot be justified, except in the case of a clear and unmistakable disregard of rights secured by the supreme law of the land. We have here no such case to be determined.[16]

The *Berea College* case has been treated along with cases involving the rights of nonpublic educational institutions. In the history of racial segregation, however, it must be pointed out that the Court in 1908 imposed segregated instruction on a privately chartered school. The Court upheld the state of Kentucky's law prohibiting mixed schools on the ground that an educational institution is a corporation created by the state and "has no natural right to teach at all. Its right to teach is such as the State sees fit to give to it. The State may withhold it altogether, or qualify it."[17]

In 1927 the Supreme Court heard the case of Martha Lum, a native-born citizen of Chinese descent, who was refused admittance into a "white" school of Bolivar County, Mississippi, because "colored" schools were readily available to her. In the Mississippi supreme court's interpretation of the state constitution of 1890 provision that "separate schools shall be maintained for children of the white and colored races," Martha Lum as a member of the yellow race was to be considered "colored" and not "white."[18] The U.S. Supreme Court referred to the *Cumming* decision in upholding the Mississippi court, since the federal government has no right to interfere with a state's management of its schools, and to the *Plessy* decision, since there was no conflict with the Fourteenth Amendment in violating anyone's equal rights.

Upon his graduation from Lincoln University, a state black educational institution in Missouri, Lloyd L. Gaines sought admission to the law school of the University of Missouri. He was denied admission on the basis of Section 9622 of the Revised Statutes of Missouri (1929), which prohibited black students from attending "white" educational institutions but which provided for the payment of reasonable tuition fees to a university of any adjacent state for courses taught at the State University of Missouri but not taught at Lincoln University. Gaines challenged the constitutionality of the Missouri statute by arguing that admission was denied to him solely because he was a black. Unsuccessful in the state courts of Missouri, Gaines appealed to the U.S. Supreme Court.

Chief Justice Charles Evans Hughes wrote the Court's decision. "The pivot upon which this case turns," he claimed, depended upon whether providing for a legal education in other states for blacks of Missouri satisfies the constitutional requirement of equal protection under the law. He found the arrangement for the legal education of a black as "a privilege . . . created for white law students which is denied to Negroes by reason of their race." Justice Hughes did not challenge the "separate" part of the *Plessey* v. *Ferguson's* "separate but equal" doctrine but the "equal" part since, under the constitutional right to equal protection of the laws, "the state was bound to furnish . . . within its borders facilities for legal education substantially equal to those which the state there afforded for persons of the white race, whether or not other Negroes sought the same opportunity."[19] The matter of inequality in educational opportunity was now recognized by the Supreme Court and the *Gaines* decision has been considered the "real forerunner" of the decisions of the 1940s in making available to the blacks graduate study in the South.[20]

The Supreme Court's decision in *Gaines* led to the establishment of many state-supported black professional and graduate schools in the South; the reason for their creation was to ensure educational segregation. With their own educational facilities, it was felt that blacks would not request admission to white state-supported colleges and universities. Larger expenditures for public schools begun to be made throughout the South.[21] But such "advances" did not satisfy the blacks, who saw themselves being treated like "second-rate" American citizens. They wanted an educational philosophy to correspond with the stated political philosophy of their country. They, therefore, chose to challenge the validity of segregation in higher education in three cases: *Sipuel, Sweatt,* and *McLaurin.*

In 1946, the University of Oklahoma Law School, the only publicly supported institution for training lawyers in the state, refused admittance to Ada Louis Sipuel, solely because she was black. The Oklahoma courts upheld the university's ruling, but on appeal to the U.S. Supreme Court, the *Gaines* decision was affirmed and stated that Ada Louis Sipuel was

> entitled to secure legal education afforded by a state institution. To this time it has been denied her although during the same period many white applicants have been afforded legal education by the State. The State must provide it for her in conformity with the equal protection clause of the Fourteenth Amendment and provide it as soon as it does for applicants of any other group.[22]

The Oklahoma Board of Regents took advantage of the Supreme Court's decision in *Sipuel,* which did not render a specific ruling on segregation, by providing equal facilities. The board hired three professors to conduct a law school in space designated for that purpose in the state capitol for Ada Sipuel and "all others similarly situated." Ada Sipuel, who had now become Mrs. Fisher, again appealed to the Supreme Court, which upheld the Oklahoma Board of Regents in its compliance with the Court's earlier decision for equal facilities.[23]

Hemon Sweatt, a black, applied for admission to the University of Texas Law School for the February, 1946, term. Denied admission solely because he was black, and there being no law school in Texas that admitted blacks, Sweatt commenced legal proceedings. The state court, recognizing that a black had been denied equal opportunity to obtain a legal education, deferred judgment on the case for six months to allow the state of Texas to provide substantially equal facilities. But despite the fact that a law school for blacks was established, Sweatt appealed to the Supreme Court on the contention that the new law school would not offer him a legal education equal to the one afforded to white citizens of his state. The Court, after noting the educational inequalities between the white and the black law schools (such as number of faculty and students, library facilities, variety of courses), granted Sweatt the right to be admitted to the white law school. The Court maintained:

The law school, the proving ground for legal training and practice, cannot be effective in isolation from the individuals and institutions with which the law interacts. Few students and no one who has practiced law would choose to study in an academic vacuum, removed from the interplay of ideas and the exchange of views with which the law is concerned. The law school to which Texas is willing to admit petitioner excludes from its student body members of the racial groups which number 85% of the population of the State and include most of the lawyers, witnesses, jurors, judges and other officials with whom petitioner will inevitably be dealing when he becomes a member of the Texas Bar. With such a substantial and significant segment of society excluded, we cannot conclude that the education offered petitioner is substantially equal to that which he would receive if admitted to the University of Texas Law School.[24]

The Court did not abandon the *Plessey* doctrine in *Sweatt*, but it did give more attention to the meaning of "equal" than it previously had.

In 1948, G. W. McLaurin was denied admission to the University of Oklahoma Graduate School on the basis of an Oklahoma statute which insisted upon segregated education. McLaurin appealed to the U.S. district court which declared, in line with the *Sipuel* case, that the state must enroll him in the University of Oklahoma, since Langston University, the black college, did not offer a doctorate in education, the program for which McLaurin had applied. The Oklahoma legislature thereby amended the state statutes to permit blacks to study in "white" schools for those programs not available in black schools, but it required that instruction to blacks be afforded "upon a segregated basis." Thus, while enrolled in a "white" university and entitled to all its facilities, McLaurin was assigned spaces in the classroom, dining hall, and library but in a manner apart from white students. McLaurin appealed to the Supreme Court, which found that these "restrictions impair and inhibit his ability to study, to engage in discussions and exchange views with other students, and, in general, to learn his profession." Thus, he "is handicapped in his pursuit of effective graduate instruction." The Court noted, furthermore, that those who would be educated by McLaurin as a "leader and trainer of others" would be "directly affected by the education he receives. Their own education and development will necessarily suffer to the extent that his training is unequal to that of his classmates. State-imposed restrictions which produce such inequalities cannot be sustained."[25]

The *McLaurin* decision is of significance because, in the words of Spurlock, "The Court went about as far as it could go in assuring equality for Negro graduate students without abolishing segregation itself."[26] The previous cases of *Gaines, Sipuel,* and *Sweatt* upheld the *Plessy* decision of "separate, but equal," making progress in the improvement of educational opportunities for blacks by their insistence upon equality of facilities. Although *McLaurin* did not reject *Plessy,* it at least attacked the matter of segregation and acknowledged the *de facto* situation that segregation did not promote substantially equal educational opportunities. The Court, furthermore, in cases not dealing with education, had demonstrated the beginning of a trend away from segregation. In *Shelley* v. *Kramer* (1948) the Court maintained that state enforcement of private agreements which prohibit the transfer of real estate to persons of a certain color or race amounts to a denial of equal protection under law.[27] In *Henderson* v. *United States* (1950) the Court, upon request of a federal attorney to overrule the *Plessy* doctrine, held that segregation in an interstate railroad dining car was contrary to the federal Constitution.[28]

But the progress, as evidenced in these cases, toward eliminating inequality was only a part of the total American social context. President Franklin D. Roosevelt had called attention to discrimination in employment. President Harry S Truman's Committee on Civil Rights issued an important report in 1947, "To Secure These Rights," which became the basis for a civil rights program and an issue in the political campaigns of 1948 and 1952. The statement emphasized the right to equality of opportunity for all Americans regardless of race, color, creed, or national origin, and maintained that this equality would be strengthened if segregation in housing, employment, the armed services, health services, public services, and education could be eliminated.[29] Moreover, blacks themselves sought, through such organizations as the National Association for the Advancement of Colored People, the Southern Regional Council, and other groups, a more concerted action for their demands for equal rights in all areas. Successes in the Supreme Court with regard to cases in higher education spurred them not only to challenge inequalities on the elementary and secondary school levels but also to meet head-on the basic issue of segregation.[30]

THE INTEGRATION CASES OF 1954

In 1952, five separate cases were brought before the Supreme Court and each directly challenged the *Plessy* doctrine of "separate but equal." Four of these cases were from states: *Briggs* v. *Elliott,* Clarendon, South Carolina; *Gebhart* v. *Belton,* Wilmington, Delaware; *Davis* v. *County School Board,* Prince Edward County, Virginia; and *Brown* v. *Board of Education,* Topeka, Kansas. *Bolling* v. *Sharpe* was from the District of Columbia. The state cases were argued on the basis of the Fourteenth Amendment, while the District case was argued under the Fifth Amendment. But all of the cases were aimed at segregation as the constitutional issue at stake. They were argued together before the Supreme Court in December, 1952; in June, 1953, the Court ordered a reargument for December and the decision was not announced until May 17, 1954.

Although the state cases, with the exception of Kansas, involved different aspects of substantial equality of educational opportunity and differences in specifics and local conditions, the judgment in the cases was rendered in a consolidated opinion because of a common legal question. The Kansas case conceded the substantial equality of the separate schools provided by the local board on the basis of the distinction of races, but contended that segregation resulted in social and psychological damages to black children and thereby denied them "equal protection of the laws." With segregation itself as *the* issue and substantial equality considered as secondary to it, the state cases were grouped together under *Brown.*

The unanimous opinion of the Court, written by Chief Justice Earl Warren, stated its preference for approaching the problem of segregated facilities in education by considering "public education in light of its full development and its present place in American life throughout the Nation" rather than in the light of the year 1868 when the Fourteenth Amendment was adopted or in the light of the year 1896 when the *Plessy* case was decided. Describing education's role and importance as a requisite for good citizenship and personal success, the Court affirmed that education as an opportunity is "a right which must be made available to all on equal terms." Even though physical and all other facilities for education are equal, segregation on the basis of race deprives children of a minority group equal educational opportunities, for feelings of social and psychological inferiority may be generated to a degree that they can never be undone. In strong, unequivocal language the Court rejected the doctrine of "separate but equal" in public education because it produced a sense of inferiority of the black race: "Whatever may have been the extent of psychological knowledge at the time of *Plessy* v. *Ferguson,* this finding is amply supported by modern authority. Any language in *Plessy* v. *Ferguson* contrary to this finding is rejected." The Court, in view of its social and psychological argument, deemed any discussion as to whether segregation also violates the Fourteenth Amendment's due process clause unnecessary.[31]

The decision in the District of Columbia case, which originated from the refusal to admit black children to a "white" public school, centered around the Fifth rather than the Fourteenth Amendment. Even though the Fifth Amendment, applicable to the District, does not contain an equal protection clause as the Fourteenth, which is applicable only to the states, the Court affirmed that "the concepts of equal protection and due process, both stemming from an American ideal of fairness, are not mutually exclusive." Arguing from the *Brown* decision, the Court, on the basis that the Constitution forbids the states from maintaining racially segregated schools, concluded that due process of law guaranteed by the Fifth Amendment *a fortiori* would forbid the same in the nation's capital.[32]

The Supreme Court in both the *Brown* and *Bolling* decisions ordered reargument by interested parties on whether the principle of desegregation it enunciated was to be implemented immediately or allow for "an effective gradual adjustment." The hearings did not take place until April 11, 1955; the ruling has also been referred to as *Brown II.* On May 31, 1955, Chief Justice Warren rendered a unanimous ruling that desegregation must take place at "all deliberate speed"; no deadline, however, was mentioned. The federal district courts were assigned the task of supervising the process of desegregation "because of their proximity to local conditions." While requiring "a prompt and reasonable start toward full compliance," administrative problems, brought on by physical facilities, transportation, personnel, and redistricting, could warrant "additional time."[33]

The "adjustment" and the "speed" which the Court asked for

in desegregation met with varying degrees of compliance. Not all states and school districts moved their machinery with equal speed; some, in fact, engaged in delaying tactics. By 1958, the process of desegregation was advancing in ten out of the seventeen states which had once required compulsory school segregation; 764 out of 2,889 southern school districts had made some progress, with about 40 of them having been compelled to do so by specific orders from federal district courts.[34]

Members of both the legal and educational professions have written voluminously as to the theoretical and practical aspects of the *Brown* decisions. Noteworthy are the remarks of legal scholars Kern Alexander and Edwin S. Solomon:

> Without exaggeration, the decision has had more impact on public education in the United States than any other development in American history. . . . The Court did, in fact, forge ahead and assume the responsibility for establishing desirable social as well as judicial precedent, the Court relied on sociology, psychology and what it intuitively considered to be the appropriate standard of moral human behavior to justify its conclusion.[35]

Constitutional lawyer and historian Louis H. Pollak assessed the impact of *Brown* in this fashion:

> Except for waging and winning the Civil War and World Wars I and II, the decision in the School Segregation Cases was probably the most important American governmental act of any kind since the Emancipation Proclamation. . . . The Court was simply making a judgment about the dominant moral values of the American community, values which have altered in substantial measure since *Plessey* was decided in 1896.[36]

On August 25, 1971, Justice Douglas of the Supreme Court made it clear that *"Brown* v. *Board of Education* was not written for blacks alone." Americans of Chinese ancestry sought a stay of a federal district court order reassigning pupils of Chinese ancestry to elementary public schools in San Francisco. Until 1947 the California education code provided for the establishment of separate schools for children of Chinese ancestry. Despite repeal of the provision, the San Francisco school board drew up school attendance lines in a manner that maintained racial imbalance. A district court, furthermore, had found no evidence that even since *Brown I* "San Francisco school authorities had ever changed any school attendance line for the purpose of reducing or eliminating racial imbalance."[37] Justice Douglas saw the school desegregation plan offered by the San Francisco school board, and approved by the district court, as being within established legal bounds, for "the theme of our school desegregation cases extends to all racial minorities treated insidiously by a State or any of its agencies."[38]

On the twentieth anniversary of the *Brown I* decision, on May 17, 1974, HEW secretary Caspar Weinberger issued a statement depicting the progress of integration in the public schools. Weinberger commented: "The full achievement of equal educational opportunity for all Americans is still before us and it will be difficult to achieve."[39] Weinberger substantiated his statement with statistical data. Some 11.2 percent of the nation's black children still attend schools where there are no white students. In twenty large cities, both in the North and the South, one black child in every four attends an all-black school.[40] Those same twenty cities have more than 31 percent of all the black children in the nation, and more than 71 percent of all those who attend all-black schools. Of the public schools in the North, 71 percent have enrollments which are more than half black, while in the border states it is 68 percent, and in the public schools of the Deep South it is almost 51 percent.[41]

A study of the Supreme Court cases involving segregation after the 1954 decisions leads to an appreciation of the many and varied difficulties encountered in seeking to achieve whatever integration exists today.

DESEGREGATION CASES IN HIGHER EDUCATION

Both appeal and resistance to the *Brown* cases became the concern of subsequent legal and educational history in a series of court cases.

A young black woman, Autherine J. Lucy, having been refused admission to the University of Alabama in 1952, sought a court order for admission in 1955. Granted admission by the federal courts on the basis of *Brown*, she began her studies on February 1, 1956.[42] Her admission, however, led to protests and disturbances on the campus. Fear for her welfare, as well as that of other students, led the board of trustees to require her withdrawal only a few days after her admission. She filed suit in federal district court with the charge that her suspension was a "cunning stratagem for denying her right to attend and pursue courses of study at the University of Alabama." But her legal appeal for reinstatement was denied because "the action which the Trustees and officials took to protect her and others from bodily harm was not taken in defiance of the court's injunction, but was taken in good faith."[43] The Supreme Court refused to review the lower court's judgment.[44]

In 1955 three black youths were denied admission to undergraduate programs at the University of North Carolina. The university's policy did accept qualified blacks to graduate and professional programs, however. The students' appeal led to a federal district court order that the university admit the students.[45] The university's trustees appealed the district court's decision to the Supreme Court. The trustees rested their case on the contention that *Brown* was not applicable to higher education. Desegregation was required only for black children whose educational progress was retarded by segregation; adults were not so affected. The Court rejected this argumentation and upheld the district court's ruling requiring admission of the black youths.[46]

Before and after *Brown*, the law school at the University of Florida in Gainesville denied admission to blacks. The Florida Supreme Court, in 1949, rejected the appeal for admission of Virgil D. Hawkins, a black, as a "separate but equal" law school was in the process of being established at the Florida Agricultural and Mechanical University in Tallahassee.[47] The U.S. Supreme Court, in 1951, denied review of the case pending the judgment of the Florida Supreme Court on the equality of the law school to be established at Tallahassee.[48] Another appeal for admission by Hawkins to the Gainesville law school in 1952 was denied by the Florida court, but on the basis of *Brown*, Hawkins appealed to the Supreme Court which remanded the case to the Florida court "for consideration in the light of the segregation cases and the conditions that now prevail."[49] Procrastination by both the Florida court and university officials led to another appeal in 1956, to the U.S. Supreme Court, which now ordered prompt admission. Following its earlier decisions in *Sweatt, Sipuel,* and *McLaurin,* the Court saw no reason for delay: "In doing so, we did not [i.e., on May 24, 1954] imply that decrees involving graduate study present the problems of public and elementary schools."[50] Integration in higher education, therefore, would not be subjected to delays made possible by the benign interpretation of "all deliberate speed" afforded to elementary and secondary schools. Using the *Lucy* case however, the Florida Supreme Court persisted in its denial of admission to Hawkins on the grounds that his presence in the Gainesville law school would cause "great public mischief" by endangering his safety and that of others at the university; and the U.S. Supreme Court, on the other hand, refused to review the federal district court's position.[51] In 1958, however, as the pressure of public opinion and events mounted, the federal court in Florida maintained that no black could be arbitrarily denied admission as long as he furnished evidence of eligibility.[52]

In 1958 the Supreme Court refused to review a federal court's nullifying of a Louisiana law regarded as a segregation device.[53] The law, passed in 1956, provided for admission to college only after a certificate acknowledging eligibility and good moral character had been attested to by the applicant's local school superintendent and high school principal. Segregation was ensured by giving to black high school principals certificates for black colleges only.[54]

Where in Arkansas in 1957 the struggle for desegregation by the use of federal troops involved a high school, in Mississippi and Alabama admission to state universities was the issue. The Mississippi case concerned James Meredith, a black Air Force veteran, whose previous collegiate scholastic attainments had been clearly above average, but who was denied admission to the University of Mississippi at Oxford. Meredith's first appeal to the courts was not successful; sufficient evidence was not produced to prove that denial of admission was obviously on the basis of racial discrimination.[55] But a subsequent hearing of the case led to a favorable decision for Meredith; the arguments forwarded by the university—such as alumni certificates, possible false registration as a voter, and the charge that Meredith would cause trouble—were looked upon as without foundation.[56] The university's appeal resulted in a delay in carrying out the court order, pending final judgment by the U.S. Supreme Court. On September 10, 1962, the Court vacated the stay and later denied a review of the case; thus, Meredith was allowed to enroll in the University of Mississippi.[57] The governor of Mississippi, Ross Barnett, personally refused, however, to enroll Meredith and issued a proclamation calling for the arrest of any federal official who would obstruct a state official carrying out the orders of the governor. Whereupon, the president of the United States proclaimed the supremacy of federal law, took command of the Mississippi National Guard, and despite the rioting and opposition on the campus, assured the admittance of Meredith to classes.[58] Commenting on the Meredith case, Alexander and Solomon have stated: "The federal government had prevailed in its enforcement of desegregation, but probably just as important a new chapter had been written in the book of federal-state legal relations. It was clearly established that a state could not interpose itself between the individual's rights and the federal government's enforcement of those rights."[59]

A similar attempt to bar the enrollment of black students in a state university took place in Alabama. The *Lucy* case of 1955 had permanently enjoined the denial of admission to qualified black students to the University of Alabama. This injunction was declared to be in effect on May 16, 1963, by a federal district court judge, when two qualified black students sought admission. The request for a delay in the order by the board of trustees of the university was denied on May 21, 1963. Alabama's governor, George C. Wallace, announced that he would personally stand at the door of the university to prevent the enrollment of the black students. The federal district court, however, issued an injunction restraining the governor, its order to be supported by federal legal officials.[60] The federal court's words affirmed the action in the *Meredith* case: "Thoughtful people, if they can free themselves from tensions produced by established principles with which they violently disagree must concede that the governor of a sovereign state has no authority to obstruct or prevent the execution of the lawful orders of a court of the United States."[61]

DESEGREGATION CASES IN ELEMENTARY AND SECONDARY EDUCATION

Despite progress in higher education, there was still strong feeling among southern white political leaders against the *Brown* decision as "the usurpation and encroachment" on the reserved powers of the states. On March 12, 1956, southern congressmen, seventeen senators and seventy-seven representatives, issued a statement condemning federal interference with state school systems of elementary and secondary education.

> Without regard to the consent of the governed, outside agitators are threatening immediate and revolutionary changes in our public school systems. If done, this is certain to destroy the system of public education in some of the States.[62]

The events that led to the case of *Cooper* v. *Aaron* demonstrated both the unwillingness of some southerners to accept *Brown* and the tactics used to implement its mandate for integrated school systems. In May, 1954, the Little Rock District school board of Arkansas announced its intention to comply with the Supreme Court's decision outlawing segregation and its suggestions as to its practical implementation. Even before *Brown II*, the board had instructed and approved the school superintendent's plan for desegregating the district's high school as the initial phase of the integrating process so that, beginning in 1957 with the high school, complete integration would be achieved by 1963. A group of blacks challenged the plan by calling for a more rapid completion of the desegregation process. The federal district court, however, upheld the board's plan and the court of appeals affirmed.[63]

During the school board's preparations for desegregation, however, state authorities were taking measures to prevent integration. In November, 1956, an amendment to the state constitution was voted to authorize the Arkansas State legislature to oppose the *Brown* decision "in every Constitutional manner" possible. In February, 1957, the state legislature passed a law to relieve school children from compulsory attendance at racially mixed schools. School authorities, notwithstanding these efforts, initiated the first step in the desegregation process with the admission of nine black children to enter Central High School in Little Rock in September, 1957. But before the school's opening day Governor Orville Faubus, acting independently of the school board, sent Arkansas national guardsmen to the high school, which he officially placed as "off limits" to black students. Upon orders from the federal district court, the guardsmen were removed and the black children were admitted to the school under the protection of the Little Rock and state police officers, who deemed it necessary to remove the students due to the uncontrollable large crowd that had assembled at the school. President Eisenhower then acted by dispatching federal troops to the school where they, later replaced by federalized national guardsmen, remained for the remainder of the year to protect the black students in attendance.

As a result of the above events, the school board petitioned the district court for a postponement of its desegregation plan, transferring the black students at the school to "black" schools, in view of what it termed "extreme public hostility" making it impossible to conduct a sound educational program at an integrated school. While the district court complied with the board's request, the court of appeals denied it and the case was brought to the Supreme Court.

The Supreme Court sympathized with the frustrating conditions that confronted the board and even praised its "good faith" in seeking to comply with *Brown*, but would not accept it as a "legal excuse for delay in implementing the constitutional rights" of the black children "when vindication of those rights was rendered difficult or impossible by the actions of other state officials . . . [for] law and order are not here to be preserved by depriving the Negro children of their constitutional rights."[64] Citing not only the Fourteenth Amendment's principle of equal justice under law and the Fifth Amendment's concept of due process of law, but also Article VI of the Constitution which denotes the Constitution as the "supreme Law of the Land," the Court denied the Little Rock school board's request for delay of desegregation:

> The constitutional rights of children not to be discriminated against in school admission on grounds of race or color declared by this Court in the *Brown* case can neither be nullified openly and directly by state legislators or state executive or judicial officers, nor nullified indirectly by them through evasive schemes for segregation whether attempted "ingeniously or ingenuosly".[65]

Another mode of circumventing *Brown* took place in St. Clair County, Illinois. Black students alleged that the Chenot School in St. Clair County, Illinois, was built in 1957 with its attendance area boundaries so drawn up that it was a school exclusively without blacks. Overcrowded conditions in the adjacent school of Centre-ville, in the same school district, led to the transferring to Chenot of all the fifth and sixth grade classes, 97 percent of whose students were white and, therefore, kept segregated. The addition of the transferred students gave Chenot an enrollment of 251 blacks and 254 whites. Since black students, with the exception of eight who transferred from Centreville, attended classes in one part of the school building, used entrances and exits of their own, and were kept separate and apart from the white students, a suit was brought against the school board.

The federal district court, subsequently affirmed by the court of appeals, dismissed the complaint for failure to exhaust the ad-ministrative remedies that were provided under Illinois law forbid-ding racial segregation in public schools.[66] But the U.S. Supreme Court declared that since rights protected by the Fourteenth Amendment had been denied, the case "is as plainly federal in origin and nature as those indicated in *Brown.*"[67]

The public school boards of the city of Knoxville and of David-son County in Tennessee, adopted substantially the same kind of desegregation plans by re-zoning school districts without regard to race. Each plan, however, provided for the possibility of transfer by any student who, because of his own race and the racial composition of the school assigned to him in the re-zoning process, could re-quest a transfer from a school where he would be in the racial minority back to his former segregated school where his race would form a majority. Appeals from parents of black students that the plans were unconstitutional were denied by district courts and the court of appeals.[68] The U.S. Supreme Court, however, reversed the rulings of the lower courts on the grounds that "transfer programs are invalid because they are based solely on race and tend to per-petuate the pre-existing racially segregated school system, . . . While transfers are available to those who choose to attend school where their race is in the majority, there is no provision whereby a student might transfer upon request to a school in which his race is in a minority." Thus the Court saw in the transfer plans "racial segrega-tion . . . [as] the inevitable consequence," and a violation of the equal protection clause of the Fourteenth Amendment.[69]

On March 31, 1964, the Court heard a pupil assignment and transfer policy as devised in Atlanta, Georgia.[70] Subsequent to argu-ment of the case, the Atlanta Board of Education adopted additional provisions authorizing free transfers. Although black petitioners denied that the board's actions would meet constitutional standards and that desegregation for the elementary schools would not be achieved until the 1970s, the Court commended Atlanta's efforts to effect desegregation and remanded the entire Atlanta plan to the federal district court for compliance with the *Griffin* and *Goss* decisions on school desegregation and the *Watson* decision on desegregation of parks and other recreational areas.[71]

The *Griffin* case deals with another kind of tactic to avoid compliance with the *Brown* decision. It began in 1951 with a group of black children in Prince Edward County, Virginia, contending that they had been denied admission to public schools attended by white children. Despite the Supreme Court's rulings of 1954 and 1955 declaring segregation laws as denying equal protection and ordering integration at "all deliberate speed," school officials of Prince Edward County engaged in a series of legislative and judicial efforts to resist desegregation. Among these efforts was included the adoption of a constitutional amendment in 1956 by the state of Virginia to appropriate funds for students to attend any public or nonsectarian private school. The general assembly enacted a law that could close any public school attended by both white and black children and deny it state funds. When the Supreme Court of Appeals of Virginia held such a law unconstitutional in 1959, the general assembly went on to repeal Virginia's compulsory attendance laws, making school attendance a matter of local option, and granting tuition grants to attend schools of one's choice. With all of these efforts declared unconstitutional by federal courts,[72] the supervisors of Prince Edward County did not levy taxes for the 1959–60 school year and did not likewise open the county's public schools. Instead, white citizens formed the Prince Edward School Foundation as an independent private corporation with the purpose of operating private schools for white children of the county. Blacks objected to a similar private undertaking for schools of their children and preferred to wage legal battles for integrated schools. Private contributions supported the foundation's schools for the 1959–60 school year, but in 1960 the general assembly enacted a new tuition grant program whereby all children, regardless of race, were entitled to a $125 grant toward an elementary and a $150 grant toward a secondary nonsectarian private school or public schools outside of their locality. Since the new program permitted localities to supplement the state's grants, children attending the Prince Edward School Foundation's schools received an additional $100. The Prince Edward County board of supervisors allowed property tax credits of up to 25 percent for contributions to the nonprofit, nonsectarian schools of the county.

In 1961 black parents, through federal district court action, were able to enjoin the county from paying tuition grants and allowing tax credits but the court deferred judgment on whether the public schools of the county could be closed until 1962, when it declared that

> The public schools of Prince Edward County may not be closed to avoid the effect of the law of the land as interpreted by the Supreme Court, while the Commonwealth of Virginia permits other public schools to remain open at the expense of the taxpayers.[73]

The state of Virginia's Supreme Court of Appeals, in the meantime, held that the state constitution and statutes did not impose upon the county board of supervisors any mandatory duty to levy taxes and appropriate money to support free public schools,[74] and later held that the state constitution did not require the state to reopen public schools in Prince Edward County.[75] But the district court, notwithstanding the court of appeals judgments, repeated its order that the county's public schools may not be closed while other public schools in the state remained open.

Upon appeal, the U.S. Supreme Court affirmed the district court's judgment that the Prince Edward County's actions denied black students equal protection of the laws as guaranteed by the Fourteenth Amendment. The Court recognized the state's discretionary power of deciding whether laws should operate statewide or only in certain counties, depending on needs and desires of the component divisions of the state.

> But the record in the present case could not be clearer that Prince Edward's public schools were closed and private schools operated in their place with state and county assistance, for one reason, and one reason only: to ensure, through measures taken by the county and the State, that white and colored children in Prince Edward County

would not, under any circumstances, go to the same school. Whatever nonracial grounds might support a State's allowing a county to abandon public schools, the object must be a constitutional one, and grounds of race and opposition to desegregation do not qualify as constitutional.[76]

Thus, Prince Edward County's tactic of circumventing the *Brown* decisions by establishing private, but state-supported, segregated schools was declared unconstitutional and county officials were directed "to levy taxes to raise funds adequate to reopen, operate, and maintain without racial discrimination a public school system . . . like that operated in other counties in Virginia."[77]

The *Griffin* case demonstrates the tenacity of some southerners in regard to segregation. A three-judge federal district court had declared unconstitutional a similar "evasive scheme" in the state of Louisiana. The St. Helena Parish school board was restrained and enjoined by the federal district court from continuing the practice of racial segregation on February 9, 1961.[78] But on the same day the state's governor called the legislature into session for the purpose of enacting laws to prevent school integration. A plan was adopted by which public schools under desegregation orders would be changed into "private schools" operated in the same buildings and manner with the same public money as the other public schools. Included in the plan where the public schools would have been "closed" would be provision for free lunches, transportation, and grants-in-aid to children attending the "private schools." The statute was invalidated as "a transparent artifice" to deny black children from attending desegregated schools in one part of the state, while the state was providing public schools in other parts of the state irrespective of race.[79] Although the *Hall* case did not appear before it, the Court, while noting differences in the operation of the public schools converted into private schools, declared both the Virginia and Louisiana plans as having the same purpose: "the perpetuation of racial segregation by closing public schools and operating only segregated schools supported directly or indirectly by state or county funds."[80]

In accord with *Griffin,* the U.S. Supreme Court in 1968 affirmed a federal district court's invalidating of a Louisiana program giving tuition grants to students in racially segregated private schools.[81]

The district court had argued in the *Poindexter* case that "any affirmative and purposeful state aid promoting private discrimination violates the equal protection clause." It further "has the effect of encouraging discrimination," because the privately operated schools were for white children and intended to be racially segregated.[82]

In 1971, in tune with *Griffin* and *Poindexter,* a federal district court in *Green* v. *Connally* upheld class action by black parents of school children attending public schools in Mississippi to enjoin officials of the U.S. Treasury from according tax-exempt status and deductibility of contributions to private schools in Mississippi discriminating against black students. The Supreme Court had upheld in the *Walz* decision the granting of tax exemptions for real property owned by churches and used for religious worship.[83] But racially discriminatory private schools are not entitled to federal tax exemptions provided for charitable educational institutions, and persons making gifts to such schools are not entitled to the deductions allowed for gifts to charitable, educational institutions. The district court was emphatic in its ruling: "Governmental and constitutional interest of avoiding racial discrimination in educational institutions embraces the interest of avoiding even the 'indirect economic benefit' of a tax exemption."[84] *Griffin, Poindexter,* and *Green* clearly enjoin discriminatory state action.

In June, 1973, the U.S. Supreme Court in *Norwood* v. *Harrison* declared unconstitutional the granting of free textbooks to segregated private schools. The Court reasoned that free textbooks, like tuition grants directed to students in private schools, are a form of tangible financial assistance benefiting the schools themselves, and the state's constitutional obligation requires it to avoid not only operating the old dual system of racially segregated schools but also providing tangible aid to schools that practice racial discrimination.[85]

A "freedom-of-choice" plan devised, according to *Brown II,* by "revision of school districts and attendance areas to achieve a system of determining admission to the public school on a nonracial basis"[86] was questioned as unconstitutional. The plan in operation in New Kent County, a rural county in eastern Virginia, was challenged in March, 1965, as a means of maintaining a racially segregated school system. The county's population was four thousand five hundred; approximately one-half were blacks living throughout the area. So although the entire county was served by only two schools, there was no residential segregation. New Kent School was attended by white elementary and high school students, while the George W. Watkins School served as the combined elementary and high school for blacks. School buses transported the students to these schools by traveling overlapping routes.

Through the Pupil Placement Act, a state pupil placement board, instead of local boards, took over the assigning of children to particular schools.[87] As a result of this act, students were automatically reassigned to the school attended the previous year unless they requested another school, and students enrolling for the first time were assigned by the state board. White pupils continued to attend New Kent and black pupils, Watkins. On August 2, 1965, the New Kent County school board initiated a "freedom-of-choice" plan. Eligibility for federal financial aid depended on compliance with the Civil Rights Act of 1964 and petitioners had brought suit in March.[88] The plan provided for each pupil, except those entering the first and eighth grades, to choose anually between New Kent and Watkins; otherwise, the pupil would be assigned to the school he previously was attending. First and eighth grade pupils must affirmatively choose a school. Petitioners sought an injunction against this plan; while it was denied, the federal district court permitted an amendment which they sought to add to the plan to require the employment and assignment of teachers and staff on a racially non-discriminatory basis. The district court approved the plan and its amendment. The court of appeals also approved the "freedom-of-choice" provisions but remanded the case to the district court on the teacher issue.

When appealed to the Supreme Court, however, the plan was declared unconstitutional. The Court's opinion reaffirmed its previous rulings in other cases involving desegregation and the methods and speed required to achieve it. It noted that the New Kent County school board adopted the "freedom-of-choice" plan some eleven years after *Brown I* was decided and ten years after *Brown II* directed a "prompt and reasonable start" in desegregation. The Court did not reject "freedom-of-choice" as a constitutionally acceptable plan, because there may be instances where it can serve as an effective device for desegregating.[89] But as for this particular plan, the Court concluded:

> The New Kent School Board's "freedom-of-choice" plan cannot be accepted as a sufficient step to "effectuate a

transition" to a unitary system. In three years of operation not a single white child has chosen to attend Watkins school and although 115 Negro children enrolled in New Kent school in 1967 (up from 35 in 1965 and 111 in 1966) 85% of the Negro children in the system still attend the all-Negro Watkins school. In other words, the school system remains a dual system. Rather than further the dismantling of the dual system, the plan has operated simply to burden children and their parents with a responsibility which *Brown II* placed squarely on the School Board. The Board must be required to formulate a new plan and, in light of other courses which appear open to the Board, such as zoning, fashion steps which promise realistically to convert promptly to a system without a "white" school and a "Negro" school, but just schools.[90]

On the same day that the Court handed down its decision in the *Green* freedom-of-choice plan of desegregation, the Court dealt with a similar case involving the Gould school district of the state of Arkansas. With the facts of the case substantially the same as in *Green*, the Court imposed the same charges on the district school board.[91]

Also on May 27, 1968, the Supreme Court decided on a plan for segregation referred to as "free transfer," considered as a variant of "freedom-of-choice." The *Monroe* case involves the board of commissioners of the city of Jackson in midwestern Tennessee. After *Brown*, only token efforts were made to integrate the public schools, since a pupil placement law empowered school boards to approve assignment and transfer requests of children to public schools. As a result no white children requested transfers and only a few black children applied for transfer to "white schools." Upon petition to the federal district court in January, 1963, the Court acknowledged the operation of a compulsory racially segregated school system and ordered school officials to formulate a plan for desegregation. This was duly filed and became effective immediately in the elementary schools and was to be gradually extended over a four-year period to the junior high and senior high schools.[92] The plan provided for automatic assignment of pupils living within attendance zones drawn up along geographic or "natural" boundaries and depending on the adequacy of the physical facilities of the schools within the zones. Moreover, the plan contained a provision for "free transfer," whereby a child, after having registered annually in his assigned school, may choose to transfer freely to another school if space is available. After one year of operation, black petitioners brought suit in district court alleging that the plan was being administered with racial discrimination. The Court found that the board had systematically denied black children the right to transfer from their all-black zone schools to schools where white children formed the majority, while white students were granted transfers from black schools to white schools. Furthermore, the Court found that the board had gerrymandered school zones to exclude black residential areas from white school zones.[93] In conjunction with the court proceeding, the board filed proposed zones for three junior high schools. Despite petitioners' charge that the proposed zones were so gerrymandered that black children would be assigned to one school and white children to the two other schools, the district court felt that "it does not appear that Negro pupils will be discriminated against,"[94] and the circuit court of appeals affirmed the lower court.[95]

In reviewing the case in 1968, the Supreme Court noted that the three school years after the district court's approval of the attendance zones for the junior high schools had resulted in producing only meaningless desegregation of all three schools. One school enrolled over 80 percent of the system's black students. White students assigned to black schools exercised options to transfer to white schools, and most black students chose to transfer out of white schools. Only one school had as many as one-third of its student body comprised of blacks. The Court found a similar situation in the district's elementary schools. The Court, therefore, held as unconstitutional the district's essentially dual school system and its plan of "free transfer" as inadequate to achieve integration of educational facilities.

> We do not hold that "free transfer" can have no place in a desegregation plan. But like "freedom of choice", if it cannot be shown that such a plan will further rather than delay conversion to a unitary, nonracial, nondiscriminatory school system, it must be held unacceptable.[96]

The Supreme Court denied a request for delay of a school desegregation plan prepared by School District No. 1, Denver,

Colorado, in order to attain public support. It repeated previously enunciated principles that in the case of *de jure* segregation the time for "deliberate speed" has run out *(Griffin)*, that school boards today must come forward with plans that realistically work *now* *(Green)*, and that the desirability of developing public support for plans designed to redress *de jure* segregation cannot be justification for delay in implementation.[97]

Another case dealing with delay of desegregation involved thirty-three school districts in the state of Mississippi. On July 3, 1969, the court of appeals for the Fifth Circuit ordered submission of plans for desegregation to be put into effect for the school year beginning in September. But upon motion of the Department of Justice and the recommendation of the secretary of health, education, and welfare, the Court suspended the July 3 order and postponed the date of submission of new plans until December 1, 1969.[98] On appeal of this order, the U.S. Supreme Court reiterated its stand that the continued operation of racially segregated schools under the standard of "all deliberate speed" was no longer constitutionally permissible. The Court declared:

> Each of the school districts here involved may no longer operate a dual school system based on race or color, and . . . that they begin immediately to operate as unitary school systems within which no person is to be effectively excluded from any school because of race or color.[99]

The Court further ordered the court of appeals to direct the Mississippi schools to put into effect "all or any part of the August 11, 1969, recommendations of the Department of Health, Education, and Welfare, with any modifications" the Court deems proper to terminate dual school systems based on race and operate only unitary school systems.[100] Justice Black urged desegregation "not only promptly but at once—*now,*" since he concluded that "all deliberate speed has turned out to be only a soft euphemism for delay."[101]

The *Alexander* decision had immediate application to two other cases. In *Carter* v. *West Feliciana School Board,* plans for desegregation in three Louisiana school districts were ordered to begin on or before February 1, 1970, in accordance with guidelines submitted by the Department of Health, Education, and Welfare and to be in effect by September, 1970.[102] In *Dowell* v. *Board of Education,* the

Supreme Court upheld a district court's approval of the Oklahoma City school board's proposal for furthering desegregation of its schools by revising school attendance boundaries and a comprehensive plan for the complete desegregation of the entire school system, despite a court of appeals ruling that granted a stay on proposed boundary changes.[103]

Also on the basis of *Alexander* v. *Holmes*, the U.S. Supreme Court let stand a court of appeals ruling in *Singleton* v. *Jackson Municipal Separate School District*.[104] This case was decided with fifteen other cases and involved school districts in Jackson, Mississippi; Marshall County and Holly Springs, Mississippi; Longview, Texas; Jefferson County and Bessemer, Alabama; Mobile County, Alabama; East and West Feliciana Parishes, Louisiana; Concordia Parish, Louisiana; St. John the Baptist Parish, Louisiana; Burke County, Georgia; Bibb County, Georgia; Houston County, Georgia; and Alachua County, Florida. The court of appeals had remanded all of the cases to the federal district courts for compliance with desegregation. Pursuant to *Alexander* v. *Holmes* the school districts were directed to "begin immediately to operate as unitary school systems within which no person is to be effectively excluded from any school because of race or color." The order specifically called for the merging of faculties and staff, transportation, services, athletics, and other extracurricular activities during the present school term (1969–70), or by a two-step merger by February 1, 1970, and by the fall term of 1970.[105]

BUSING AS A MEANS OF DESEGREGATION

On April 20, 1971, the U.S. Supreme Court decided five cases dealing with desegregation. The first and most important of these cases is *Swann* v. *Charlotte-Mecklenburg Board of Education*. The issue of *de facto* segregation came before the Court as the desegregation plans of Charlotte-Mecklenburg County school board of the state of North Carolina were reviewed.[106] The school board had taken steps toward desegregation, but in the 1968–1969 school year approximately 29 percent of the black students and 71 percent of the white students still remained substantially segregated. Moreover, two-thirds of the black students in the city of Charlotte attended twenty-one schools that were either totally or more than 99 percent black.[107] On the basis of the *Green, Rainey,* and *Monroe* decisions of the Supreme Court in 1968, proceedings were initiated against the school board to require further efforts of desegregation. Hearings and evidence in the federal district court attributed *de facto* segregation due largely to residential patterns in the city and county served by the school district; new plans for both faculty and student desegregation were, therefore, ordered. After the required revisions by the court were drawn up in consultation with an appointed expert in educational administration, the court ordered the reassigning of faculty members in each school according to the ratio of black and white faculty members throughout the school system and the creation and re-zoning of attendance zones for the elementary and junior and senior high schools, thus providing a better racial balance on all levels. Of significant importance was the court's order that the amount of busing be substantially increased.[108] The court of appeals approved the lower court's faculty desegregation plan and the re-zoning and busing of secondary school students but did not affirm additional busing for elementary school students as it would be "unnecessarily extensive."[109]

The Supreme Court, in a unanimous opinion written by Chief Justice Burger, affirmed the district court's judgment on the basis of other desegregation cases the Court had decided regarding reassigning of teachers to achieve faculty desegregation, the use of racial ratios, the altering of attendance zones, including the pairing or grouping of schools for these zones, and the use of busing as a means of school desegregation both for secondary and elementary school students.

Regarding "the central issue in this case . . . [as] that of student assignment," the Court sanctioned the use of racial ratios as a starting point in the process of shaping a remedy to segregation, although it is not constitutionally required that the number of students in every school in every community always must reflect the racial composition of the school system as a whole.[110] Realizing the existence of *de facto* segregation because of residential patterns, the Court did acknowledge that "the existence of some small number of one-race, or virtually one-race, schools within a district is not in and of itself the mark of a system that still practices segregation by law." However, the Court urged the district courts or school authorities to make every effort "to achieve the greatest possible degree of actual desegregation" to eliminate one-race schools. Where school districts continue some schools that are all or predominately of one race, they must demonstrate that school assignments are "genuinely nondiscriminatory" and that their racial composition is not due to present and past discriminatory actions. Optional majority-to-minority transfers can be useful for desegregation, and "in order to be effective," the Court pointed out, "such a transfer arrangement must grant the transferring student free transportation and space must be made available in the school to which he desires to move."[111] Although the Court refrained from imposing a "judicially ordered assignment of students on a racial basis," and stated that "no fixed or even substantially fixed guidelines can be established as to how far a court can go," school authorities must always keep in mind that "the objective is to dismantle the dual school system," and, therefore, permitted the remedial altering of attendance zones.

In the matter of the problem of busing, the Court set forth the following interpretation:

> The scope of permissible transportation of students as an implement of a remedial decree has never been defined by this Court and by the very nature of the problem it cannot be defined with precision. No rigid guidelines as to student transportation can be given for application to the infinite variety of problems presented in the thousands of situations. Bus transportation has been an integral part of the public education system for years, and was perhaps the single most important factor in the transition from the one-room schoolhouse to the consolidated school. Eighteen million of the Nation's public school children, approximately 39%, were transported to their schools by bus in 1969–1970 in all parts of the country. The importance of bus transportation as a normal and accepted tool of educational policy is readily discernible in this . . . case.[112]

The Court in this opinion clearly held that local school authorities may employ bus transportation as one tool of desegregation: "Desegregation plans cannot be limited to the walk-in school." But the Court proceeded to uphold as a valid objection to busing "when the time or distance of travel is so great as to either risk the health of the children or significantly impinge on the educational process."

As a guide to the soundness of any transportation plan, the Court asked district courts to consider the issues of racial balances and quotas, one-race schools, and the remedial altering of attendance zones as discussed in this case. The Court also concluded that the Civil Rights Act of 1964 did not restrict the use of busing for achieving racial desegregation and that federal district courts had broad power to fashion a remedy, busing included, to insure unitary school systems.[113]

On the same day of *Swann*, the U.S. Supreme Court dealt with an inadequate school desegregation plan for Mobile County, Alabama. The metropolitan area is divided by a major north-south highway, with 94 percent of the black students living on the east side and 88 percent of white students living on the west side of the highway. Previous plans adopted by federal district and appeals' courts were deemed inadequate, "treating the western section in isolation from the eastern."[114] Stressing that "the measure of any desegregation plan is its effectiveness," the Supreme Court ordered the use of "all available techniques including restructuring of attendance zones and both contiguous and noncontiguous attendance zones." The Court also stated that "inadequate consideration was given to the possible use of bus transportation and split zoning."[115]

Also on April 20, 1971, the U.S. Supreme Court upheld the student-assignment plan of the Clarke County Board of Education, Georgia. Parents had objected to the plan, which had received the approval of the U.S. Department of Health, Education, and Welfare, and sought to enjoin it, which was done by the Georgia Supreme Court.[116] But the U.S. Supreme Court saw the plan achieving greater racial balance. One of the plan's features provided for pupils in five heavily black areas to either walk or be transported by bus to schools located in other attendance zones.[117]

The Supreme Court also upheld on the same day a federal district court's declaration of the North Carolina Anti-Busing Law as unconstitutional. The law stated: "No student shall be assigned or compelled to attend any school on account of race, creed, color or national origin, or for the purpose of creating a balance or ratio of race, religion or national origins. Involuntary bussing of students in contravention of this article is prohibited, and public funds shall not be used for any such bussing."[118] The Court's opinion stated "that an absolute prohibition against transportation of students assigned on the basis of race . . . will . . . hamper the ability of local authorities to effectively remedy constitutional violations . . . bus transportation has long been an integral part of all public educational systems, and it is unlikely that a truly effective remedy could be devised without continued reliance upon it."[119]

The fifth case decided together with *Swann* resulted in a dismissal by the Court. Both parties challenged a school desegregation plan and sought the same result: to hold North Carolina's Anti-Busing constitutional. The Court felt it had no jurisdiction since no injunction was sought to restrain the enforcement of an unconstitutional state statute. The Court, moreover, had clearly spoken of the constitutionality of busing to achieve desegregation in cases decided on the same day, most particularly of the North Carolina Anti-Busing Law.[120]

The *Swann* decision approved of busing as "one tool of desegregation," but a furor exists as to the use of busing to accomplish this purpose. The 1964 Civil Rights Act passed by Congress says of busing: "Nothing herein shall empower any official or court of the United States to issue any order seeking to achieve a racial balance in any school by requiring the transportation of pupils from one school to another or one school district to another in order to achieve such racial balance."[121]

The Supreme Court has ruled that this congressional provision sought to prohibit the Civil Rights Act from "granting new powers . . . [and] to foreclose any interpretation of the Act as expanding the *existing* powers of federal courts to enforce the Equal Protection Clause." The intent of Congress, then, was not to use the Civil Rights Act itself as authority for busing to attain racial balance and so that "the Act might be read as creating a right of action under the Fourteenth Amendment in the situation of so-called 'de facto segregation' when all it sought was to limit *de jure* segregation."[122]

But busing has been ordered by state courts and agencies as well as federal courts. Officials of HEW do not specifically order busing and have even sought to refrain from large-scale busing, but they do contend that busing in certain cases is the only way to achieve desegregation—a policy upheld by the Supreme Court.[123] On October 26, 1971, the Supreme Court refused to review a federal district court's ruling which ordered the busing of about ten thousand students to help achieve racial balance in Pontiac, Michigan.[124] The Pontiac school board argued that the imbalance in some of its schools resulted from residential patterns, thus it was *de facto* segregation and could not be ruled illegal by the Supreme Court. District Court Judge Damon J. Keith, a black, declared the school board "guilty of *de jure* segregation" because it had not taken steps necessary to improve a situation which leads to "perpetuate the pattern of segregation within the city." He also maintained that "when the power to act is available, failure to take the necessary steps so as to negate or alleviate a situation which is harmful is as wrong as is the taking of affirmative steps to advance that situation. Sins of omission can be as serious as sins of commission."[125] The U.S. Court of Appeals for the Sixth Circuit upheld Judge Keith's ruling.[126] The Supreme Court's unanimous decision not to review the Pontiac ruling—neither giving reason nor comment, besides— gives the effect of letting the district court's position stand.

Even before the Pontiac decision, President Nixon, on August 3, 1971, repeated his opposition to busing as a means of attaining racial balance in public schools, urged the attorney general and the secretary of health, education, and welfare to collaborate with local school officials to hold busing to the minimum required by law, and asked Congress to amend a pending $1.5 billion appropriation for aid to desegregate school districts so that it would "expressly prohibit the expenditure of any of those funds for busing." The president, however, in referring to the Court's ruling in *Swann* as applicable to a case in Austin, Texas, maintained that "The executive branch will continue to enforce the orders of the Court, including court-ordered busing."[127] On March 17, 1972, Nixon, in a special message on busing, advocated only as a "last resort" the busing of students to achieve desegregation. He further urged that no increased busing be imposed for students up to the sixth grade, with busing orders for students in the higher grades to be regarded as temporary and subject to stays pending appeal. Addressing Congress, he called for legislation placing a moratorium on pupil-busing orders by federal courts, to remain effective until July 1, 1973, unless broader legislation would be passed earlier.[128]

Both houses of Congress, meanwhile—the House on November 5, 1971, and the Senate on February 29, 1972—had adopted restrictions on busing. Both branches agreed to bar the use of federal funds for busing to overcome racial imbalance or carry out a plan of school racial desegregation and agreed to forbid any federal employee, including the courts, to order local officials to undertake a busing program until all legal appeals have been exhausted. The House proposal did not include the Senate's exception for cases in which busing is constitutionally required by court order.[129] The differences between the two branches were eventually resolved and became included in the education amendments of 1972 enacted on June 23. The act provided that:

(1.) there be no transportation or assignment of students or teachers to overcome racial imbalance.

(2.) there be no federal funds used to bus students to overcome racial imbalance without "the express written voluntary request" of local school officials.

(3.) there be no use of federal funds for busing if "the time or distance of travel is so great as to risk the health of children or significantly impinge on the educational process."

(4.) there be no use of federal funds to bus a student to a school where educational opportunities would be "substantially inferior" to those in the school which he would ordinarily attend under a nondiscriminatory system of assignment based on geographic zones.

(5.) no federal official or employee could compel the use of state or local funds for busing "unless constitutionally required," i.e., as under a federal court order.

(6.) no federal court order requiring busing to overcome racial imbalance could become effective until the exhaustion of all appeals or until January 1, 1974.[130]

President Nixon, although he signed the 1972 act, said that he would have vetoed the antibusing provisions if they had come to him as separate legislation. For he claimed that "Congress has not given us the answer we requested. . . . It has not provided a solution to the problem of court-ordered busing. It has provided a clever political evasion. The moratorium it offers is temporary. The relief it provides is illusory."[131] A spokesman for the president suggested that if Congress would not later pass a follow-up bill that would make busing a limited, last-resort method of school desegregation, Mr. Nixon may have "to go to the country on the question of a constitutional amendment."[132]

Despite antibusing sentiment and steps by Congress to curb busing, the federal courts have continued to require new or increased transportation to achieve greater racial balance in the public schools. In a case before him as circuit justice, Chief Justice Burger, on August 31, 1971, denied stay of a plan to achieve racial balance in a school system, as a court of appeals had ordered the plan to be in accord with *Swann*.[133] Burger declined to pass judgment as to whether the "average" travel time in the transportation of pupils in the plan "trespasses the limits . . . indicated in *Swann* . . . [because it] cannot be determined from a recital of a 'one hour average' travel time."[134] But he did supply this significant footnote as to possible limits on school bus transportation:

> By way of illustration, if the record showed—to take an extreme example of a patent violation of *Swann*—that the average time was *three* hours daily or that some were compelled to travel three hours daily when school facilities were available at a lesser distance, I would not hesitate to stay such an order forthwith until the Court could act, at least as to the students so imposed on. The burdens and hardships of travel do not relate to race; excessive travel is as much a hardship on one race as another. The feasibility of a transfer program to give relief from such a patently offensive transportation order as the one hypothesized, would also be relevant.[135]

On October 10, 1972, the Supreme Court declined to hear a court of appeals' ruling that upheld busing.[136] The appeals court had maintained that the Norfolk, Virginia, school district, as part of a desegregation plan, must provide a practical method of affording free busing for students assigned to schools beyond the normal walking distance of their homes. It also claimed that where "bus trips required of pupils under the plan generally fall within a range of thirty minutes each way," the plan would not be objectionable on the ground that pupils would be subjected to unreasonable risks to their health and safety.[137] On November 6, 1972, the Supreme Court also declined to hear a court of appeals' ruling that upheld a desegregation plan involving the busing of three thousand students over an average round trip of approximately seven miles.[138] The Supreme Court, on January 26, 1973, refused to delay a plan for school desegregation for Prince Georges County, Maryland.[139] Only four days earlier the Fourth U.S. Circuit Court of Appeals had unanimously denied a delay of the plan which a federal district judge on December 29, 1972, had ordered because the county had failed to meet constitutional requirements for elimination of the last remnants of its once legally segregated school system. Some thirty-three thousand students, about twelve thousand of whom formerly walked to school, would have to be bused.[140]

On January 15, 1973, the Supreme Court agreed to rule on the consolidation of mostly black urban schools with adjoining white suburban schools.[141] A federal district judge had proposed a merger that would have required the busing of 78,000 of the 101,000 students of the city of Richmond, of which 70 percent of the public schools are "black," with the neighboring Virginia counties of Henrico and Chesterfield, which are predominantly "white." This would have resulted in a single school system that would be 66 percent white and 34 percent black. The court argued that the perpetuation of suburban "white islands" unconstitutionally denied urban black children the equal protection guarantee of the Fourteenth Amendment.[142] In June of the same year, however, the Fourth U.S. Circuit Court of Appeals overturned the district court judge's order because he exceeded his authority by ordering a merger of the city and the county school systems to improve racial balance throughout the area.[143]

Other city-suburban busing plans under consideration in both southern and northern cities were expected to be affected by the Supreme Court's ruling in the Richmond case. But on May 21, 1973, the Supreme Court found itself deadlocked in a 4-to-4 vote, thus effectively blocking a merger of predominantly black public schools of the city of Richmond with the mostly white schools of two neighboring suburban counties. Justice Powell of Virginia had disqualified himself from the case because he had served on both the city and state boards of education while plans for desegregation were at issue. Although the tie vote upheld the decision of the Fourth Circuit Court, the decision would not extend beyond the jurisdiction of the circuit court; thus only the states of Virginia, West Virginia, Maryland, and the Carolinas were affected.[144] Clarification as to the constitutionality of the merging of city and suburban school districts would depend on the Supreme Court's actions in the Detroit case.

On October 12, 1972, the Supreme Court heard arguments in a Denver, Colorado, school case. The decision in this case can set a precedent in how cities are to deal with *de facto* segregation caused by patterns of housing, especially those found in northern cities. The Denver case began in 1969 when the school board voluntarily agreed to use busing to create a better racial balance in its public schools. Later that year voters elected opponents to busing as members of the board, which then rejected plans for busing. Eight black families subsequently appealed to the federal court for full integration of the schools. Although only about 14 percent of the public school students are black and about 20 percent are Mexican Americans, these minority groups, because of residential patterns, are concentrated heavily in two of the city's sections. The district court judge concluded that some of the policies of the school board had resulted in racial segregation in some of the schools in one area while not in the other area; but he maintained that educational opportunities in these two areas were inferior because of disproportionate allocation of resources. He, therefore, ordered busing, rezoning, and compensatory education as means of providing these two areas with equal educational opportunities.[145] On appeal, the Tenth U.S. Circuit Court of Appeals agreed to the finding of racial discrimination in one area for which it approved the use of busing; as to the other area, the court considered it a matter of *de facto* segregation, which required no action by the school board.[146] U.S. Justice Department attorneys, in their memorandum submitted to the Supreme Court on October 6, 1972, stressed President Nixon's antibusing stand as an argument: "We share the view of the district court that significant disparities in educational opportunities in a group of schools defined by racial and ethnic concentrations would constitute violations of the equal protection clause. We do not concur with the district court's assumption that the only effective remedy for such a violation is to eliminate the racial concentration —and therefore the long-standing neighborhood-school policy— by transferring the affected students. It would be equally effective to eliminate the disparities rather than disperse the students."[147]

The Supreme Court handed down its decision in the Denver case on June 21, 1973. In a 7-to-1 vote, the Court ruled that public school systems in the North can be found guilty of unconstitutional racial segregation and so be required to effectuate a racially nondiscriminatory school system. Justice William Brennan, Jr., in writing the majority opinion, declared that once a school system has been found guilty of significant acts of discrimination, then the burden is shifted to the school authorities to prove that other segregated schools in the system have not resulted from intentionally segregated actions. Since the Denver school board had been found to have practiced deliberate racial segregation in schools attended by over one-third of the black school population, a *prima facie* case of intentional segregation had already been established in the core city schools, an area known as Park Hill. The Court did not reverse the court of appeals' judgment; rather the judgment was vacated and the case was remanded to the district court to allow the school board the opportunity to prove that the Park Hill area should be treated as isolated from the rest of the school district. If the school board could not prove that a dual school system exists because of the Park Hill segregation, then there must take place the desegregation of the entire school system, "root and branch." And Justice Brennan emphatically added that if discriminatory acts are clearly proven, without sufficient rebuttal of an already existing *prima facie* case of intentional segregation, then no school board protests about "neighborhood-school" policies will suffice by themselves to prevent a sweeping, system-wide reassignment of pupils. Thus, except for the rare cases in which geography divides a school district into separate units, "proof of state-imposed segregation in a substantial portion of the district will suffice to support a finding by the trial court of the existence of a dual system."[148]

While concurring in the majority opinion, Justice Douglas declared that there is no constitutional difference between *de jure* and *de facto* school segregation[149]—a judgment with which Justice Powell not only agreed but went on to say further that the distinction should be abolished in favor of a constitutional rule requiring genuinely integrated school systems. Powell also called for no separate rules for the North and the South and cautioned against the extent of busing that the courts may order, for he saw in the widespread use of compulsory busing, especially in the elementary grades, "the single most disruptive element in education today."[150]

The lone dissenter, Justice Rehnquist, asserted that unconstitutional segregation in the Park Hill area did not prove that the entire district was unconstitutionally segregated. He believed that "the Court has taken a long leap in this area of constitutional law in equating the district-wide consequences of gerrymandering individual attendance zones in a district where separation of the races was never required by law, with statutes or ordinances in other jurisdictions which did so require."[151]

On December 8, 1972, the Sixth District Court of Appeals upheld a ruling by a federal district court judge that public schools in Detroit, Michigan, must be desegregated through a plan that would bus students between predominantly white suburban districts and the city of Detroit, whose school system is almost two-thirds black. The circuit court reasoned that since school districts and school boards are instruments of the state, their boundaries can be altered to achieve integration. Not to cross school boundaries for desegregation would open the way to nullify the *Brown* decision. If a desegregation plan were limited only to Detroit, the Court argued that it would then "lead directly to a single desegregated Detroit school district overwhelmingly black in all of its schools, surrounded by a ring of suburbs and suburban school districts overwhelmingly white in composition. . . . Big city school systems where blacks surrounded by suburban school systems for whites cannot represent equal protection of the law."[152] However, the circuit court later stayed this ruling until the full court of nine members could convene on February 8, 1973, to hear reargument on whether federal judges have the power to remedy inner-city segregation by merging city and suburban school districts. The December 8 ruling, although unanimous, was composed of a three-judge panel.[153]

On June 12, 1973, the full court set forth its ruling by a 6-to-3 vote, and it declared that the racial segregation that exists in Detroit's public schools can be remedied only by a merger of the city's schools with those of the neighboring suburbs. The majority opinion stated that "the discriminatory practices on the part of the Detroit School Board and the State of Michigan revealed by this record are significant, pervasive and causally related to the substantial amount of segregation found in the Detroit school system."[154] The plan of the federal district court to combine the Detroit and fifty-three suburban districts was, however, set aside until each of the suburbs could have the opportunity to present objections in hearings to a merger. But forty-three of these suburban districts decided to appeal to the U.S. Supreme Court on the ground that the circuit court's ruling denied due process of law to their school children and parents. On November 19, 1973, the Supreme Court agreed to hear the case.[155]

On July 25, 1974, the Supreme Court rendered its decision in the Detroit case. By a 5-to-4 vote the Court rejected cross-district busing between Detroit and its suburbs.[156] Speaking for the majority, Chief Justice Burger reiterated the long-standing principle of local control of education, reaffirmed as recently as in *Rodriguez* on March 21, 1973. Where the lower courts had conceived school district lines as "arbitrary" lines drawn up for political convenience, the Supreme Court insisted on respecting these districts already legally established. The inter-district remedy would disrupt and change the structure of public education in Michigan. For the consolidation of the fifty-four independent school districts would require a vast new super school district, which the Court viewed as contrary to local autonomy in education and, additionally, as raising innumerable problems in financing and operating a new school system.[157] The Court would, however, impose the inter-district remedy only in the case of proven deliberate acts of racial integration by which a suburban district keeps black children out of its schools. Burger reasoned: Before the boundaries of separate and autonomous school districts may be set aside by consolidating the separate units for remedial purposes or by imposing a cross-district remedy, it must first be shown that there has been a constitutional violation within one district that produces a significant segregative effect in another district. Specifically it must be shown that racially discriminatory acts of the state or local school districts, or of a single school district have been a substantial cause of inter-district segregation. Thus an inter-district remedy might be in order where the racially discriminatory acts of one or more school districts caused racial segregation in an adjacent district, or where district lines have been deliberately drawn on the basis of race. In such circumstances an inter-district remedy would be appropriate to eliminate the inter-district segregation caused by the constitutional violation. Conversely, without an inter-district violation and inter-district effect, there is no constitutional wrong calling for an inter-district remedy.[158]

Justice Thurgood Marshall's dissent called the decision "a giant step backwards." In support of the district court's ruling, Marshall claimed that it was the state of Michigan, and not simply the Detroit Board of Education, which bore the obligation of curing the condition of segregation within the Detroit city schools. And under the Fourteenth Amendment, the state is ultimately responsible for the actions of its local agencies.[159] Justice William Douglas, in his dissenting opinion, said that the ruling placed us in "a dramatic retreat" from the discredited *Plessey* (1896) decision, since it would create schools that would be both inferior and racially separate.[160]

REDISTRICTING OF SCHOOL DISTRICTS

On January 17, 1972, the Supreme Court affirmed a federal district court's ruling in a New Jersey case. Black students had initiated civil rights action, alleging that failure to achieve racial balance among several districts in the state system of public schools violated the Fourteenth Amendment. The district court dismissed the complaint largely on the basis of the *Swann* decision. It found that the laws of New Jersey intended to maintain a nonsegregated unity school system. The racial imbalance that exists is no discriminatory action of state authorities.[161] Justice Douglas wrote a dissent in which he maintained that by establishing school district lines to coincide with the boundaries of the state's political subdivisions, the state imposed upon the public schools patterns of racial imbalance. For Douglas, "the remedy is redistricting."[162] And he cited Senator Jacob Javits on the problem brought on by so many whites leaving the cities for the suburbs and thus causing highly concentrated residential areas of blacks in the cities: "Whatever you call it, '*de facto* segregation,' 'racial unbalance,' or 'the absence of intergroup activity,' it is a serious block to effective education of children of minority groups anywhere in the country, especially in the north and central part of the country where you don't have the established social order of segregation."[163]

On June 22, 1972, the U.S. Supreme Court dealt with two similar cases involving the redistricting of school districts. Federal district courts enjoined the creation of new school districts but their decisions were reversed by appeals courts.

One of the cases concerned the city of Emporia near the center of Greensville County, Virginia.[164] Until 1967, Emporia was a "town" under Virginia law and thus a part of the surrounding county for the purpose of providing free public education for the children of the county. Becoming a "city" in 1967, Emporia became politically independent from the surrounding county and thereby undertook the obligation of providing free public schooling for its children. Since 1965 complaints had been filed on behalf of black children seeking an end to state-enforced racial segregation in the Greensville County school system. Prior to 1965, the elementary and high schools located in Emporia served all-white children in the county, while black children throughout the county were assigned to a single high school or one of four elementary schools, all but one of which were located outside the Emporia town boundary. The federal district court, from 1966 on, considered several plans in the hope of further desegregating the county's school system.[165] None of these plans proved effective until 1969, at which time Emporia took its children out of the county schools and set up its own independent school district. The district court found that the effect of Emporia's withdrawal from the county school district would be a "substantial increase in the proportion of whites in the schools attended by city residents, and a concomitant decrease in county schools."[166] The Supreme Court concurred with the district court in enjoining Emporia's creation of a separate school system "because of the effect it would have had at the time upon the effectiveness of the remedy ordered to dismantle the dual system that had long existed in the area." But it also ruled that once the county and city of Emporia had begun to work for neither "white" nor "black" schools but just schools, then Emporia, if it still desired to do so, could establish an independent system. For the Court stressed: "We hold only that a new school district may not be created where its effect would be to impede the process of dismantling a dual system."[167] Thus, the federal courts may enjoin state or local officials from carving out a new school district from an existing district that has not yet completed the process of dismantling a system of enforced racial segregation.

The second case concerned the creation of a new school district for Scotland Neck, North Carolina, a city that was part of the larger Halifax County school district, engaged in the process of dismantling a dual school system.[168] Until 1965, the schools of Halifax County were completely segregated by race. Efforts made by the county since 1965 to desegregate were so inadequate that, in 1968, the U.S. Department of Justice ordered the Halifax County school board to bring the county's school system into compliance with federal law, and the county board began efforts to comply. But in 1969 citizens of Scotland Neck, through a bill passed in the state legislature and a special referendum, created a new school district. With this newly carved-out district and a transfer plan devised by the newly appointed Scotland Neck City Board of Education, the disparity in the racial composition of the Scotland Neck schools and the schools adjoining the city in Halifax County was considered "substantial" by the federal district court.[169] The court of appeals reversed the district court's enjoinment of the new district,[170] but the Supreme Court upheld the district court's action on the same grounds as the city of Emporia case decided on the same day.

DESEGREGATION OF TEACHING STAFFS

After plans for desegregating the public school systems of two cities in Virginia—Richmond and Hopewell—were approved by federal district courts, the plans were challenged as inadequate because they did not provide for faculty allocation on a racial basis.[171] The Supreme Court, in 1965, held that it is improper for a court to approve school desegregation plans without considering, through prior hearings, the impact on those plans of faculty allocation on an alleged racial basis.[172] And again in the same year, in a case involving the public high schools of Fort Smith, Arkansas, the Supreme Court contended that the right to challenge an alleged policy of allocating a public school teaching faculty on a racial basis is not limited to students who are already in desegregated grades, but is also available to black students who are in grades that have not yet been desegregated, and who are entitled to be immediately transferred to a high school that has previously had only white students. Furthermore, the Court maintained that racial allocation of a public school faculty may constitute a denial of equality of educational opportunity without regard to segregation of pupils, and it may render inadequate an otherwise constitutional pupil desegregation plan that was soon to be put into use.[173]

In 1969, the Supreme Court again affirmed that faculty and staff desegregation are to be recognized "as an important aspect of the basic task of achieving a public school system wholly free from racial discrimination."[174] The case involved efforts to obtain integration in the Montgomery County, Alabama, public schools. In a 1966 federal court order, the school board had been asked to begin the process of faculty desegregation in the 1966–67 school year.[175] But a federal judge noted in 1968 that, because of insufficient progress, he would order "the substantial desegregation of the faculties of all schools in the system commencing with the school year of 1968–69," and even proposed that boards move toward a goal under which "in each school the percent ratio of white to Negro faculty members is substantially the same as it is throughout the system."[176] A court of appeals, while affirming the need for faculty desegregation, struck down the order requiring "fixed mathematical" ratios and called for a ratio that would be only *"substantially* or *approximately"* feasible.[177] The Supreme Court upheld the order of the federal district court judge "as written," because it felt that the modifications set forth by the court of appeals would take from the district court's order some of its capacity to expedite, by means of specific commands, the day when a nondiscriminatory school system would become a reality.[178]

On January 14, 1970, in refusing to hear a Jackson, Mississippi, case, the U.S. Supreme Court let stand a court of appeals ruling on the desegregation of faculty and staff.[179] The appeals court called for the hiring, assigning, promoting, paying, demoting, and dismissing of faculty and staff to be "treated without regard to race, color, or national origin."[180] The formation of unitary, desegregated school districts brought forth staff reductions. In an attempt to protect black teachers and administrators against displacement in such situations, the *Singleton* decision stated that where staff reduction results in a dismissal or demotion, "no staff vacancy may be filled through recruitment of a person of a race, color, or national origin different from that of the individual dismissed or demoted until each displaced staff member who is qualified has had an opportunity to fill the vacancy and has failed to accept an offer to do so."[181]

In 1971, the U.S. Supreme Court declined to hear a case of reverse discrimination in the promotion of teachers.[182] A court of appeals had approved the suspension of an ordinary promotion system, in existence since 1953, for the selection of principals and vice-principals. A group of white teachers alleged that the school board had bypassed them in abolishing the regular promotion schedule and procedure for administrative posts, and had given priority to black candidates.[183] The court's reason was: "State action based partly on considerations of color, when color is not used per se, and in furtherance of a proper governmental objective, is not necessarily a violation of the Fourteenth Amendment."[184]

PAYMENT OF DESEGREGATION LITIGATION FEES

Section 718 of the Emergency School Aid Act of 1972, a part of the education amendments of 1972, provides that upon the entry of a federal court's final order against school officials in an action seeking to redress unconstitutional discrimination in elementary and secondary education, the court may, upon finding that the proceedings were necessary to bring about compliance, allow the prevailing party, other than the United States, a reasonable attorney's fee as part of the costs. Plaintiffs in a litigation suit aimed at desegregating the public schools of Memphis, Tennessee, were denied a motion for such payment by a U.S. court of appeals. But the U.S. Supreme Court, in an unsigned opinion on June 4, 1973, ruled that school boards and other agencies which lose school desegregation cases must, in most circumstances, pay the court costs of lawyers representing black parents and children. For "the plaintiffs in school cases are 'private attorneys general' vindicating national policy." The NAACP Legal Defense Fund, which handles most major school discrimination suits, argued that school boards opposing integration can finance their lawsuits with tax moneys, including some paid by black parents. Where the 1972 educational act said trial courts may allow reasonable fees in school court cases, the Court made it a requirement "unless special circumstances would render such an award unjust."[185]

Notes

INTRODUCTION

1. Herbert Johnston, *A Philosophy of Education* (New York, 1963), pp. 87–121.
2. Jacques Maritain, *Man and the State* (Chicago, 1951), p. 12.
3. Harold Laski, *A Grammar of Politics* (London, 1935), p. 69.
4. Thomas E. Dubay, *The Philosophy of the State as Educator* (Milwaukee, 1959), pp. 63–66.
5. *Journal of the Continental Congress,* II, 339.
6. B. A. Hinsdale, "Documents Illustrative of American Educational History," *Report of the Commissioner of Education, 1892–93* (Washington, 1895), II: 1312–18.
7. See section on land grants in Chapter 2.
8. Helen A. Miller and Andrew J. Shea, *Federal Assistance for Educational Purposes* (Washington, 1963), pp. 83–107.
9. George N. Rainsford, *Congress and Higher Education in the Nineteenth Century* (Knoxville, 1972), p. 132.
10. Henry Barnard, "Education—A National Interest," *Report of the Commissioner of Education* (Washington, 1868), p. 42.
11. Sidney W. Tiedt, *The Role of the Federal Government in Education* (New York, 1966), pp. 33–104. See also Sidney C. Suffrin, *Issues in Federal Aid to Education* (Syracuse, 1962).
12. Justice Robert Jackson in McCollum v. Board of Education, 333 U.S. 237 (1948).
13. Cooper v. Aaron, 358 U.S. 19 (1958).
14. Epperson v. Arkansas, 393 U.S. 104 (1968).
15. Hollis P. Allen, *The Federal Government and Education* (New York, 1950).
16. Truman M. Pierce, *Federal, State, and Local Government in Education* (New York, 1964).

17. Hsien Lu, *Federal Role in Education* (New York, 1965).
18. Tiedt, *Role of Federal Government.*
19. Homer D. Babbidge, Jr. and Robert M. Rosenzweig, *The Federal Interest in Higher Education* (New York, 1962).
20. Clark Spurlock, *Education and the Supreme Court* (Urbana, Ill., 1955).

CHAPTER 1. OFFICE OF EDUCATION

1. William Torrey Harris, "Establishment of the Office of the Commissioner of Education of the United States and Henry Barnard's Relation to It," *Proceedings of the National Educational Association* (1901): 407–437.
2. *Ibid.*
3. *The American Journal of Education*, XV (1970): 180, 806, 810; XVI (1971): 229, 299.
4. *Ibid.*, XVI: 177. A copy of the statement can be found in B. A. Hinsdale, "Documents Illustrative of American Educational History," *Report of the Commissioner of Education, 1892–93* (Washington, 1895), II: 1290–1291.
5. 14 Stat. 434 (1867).
6. 15 Stat. 92 (1869).
7. 45 Stat. 1021 (1929).
8. 53 Stat. 1424 (1939).
9. 67 Stat. 631 (1953).
10. Anne Gibson Buis, "An Historical Study of the Role of the Federal Government in the Financial Support of Education, with Special Reference to Legislative Proposals and Action" (Ph.D. diss., Ohio State University, 1953), pp. 52–59.
11. Arguments both for and against these bills have been conveniently summarized from the *Congressional Record* by *ibid.*, pp. 59–114.
12. 12 Stat. 503 (1862), sec. 2; 26 Stat. 418 (1890), sec. 2.
13. 23 Stat. 24, 27 (1884).
14. 33 Stat. 616, 619 (1905).
15. 29 Stat. 140, 171 (1896). The commissioners of education had, however, already begun the publishing of such valuable studies in their annual reports. This aspect of the of-

fice's function was praised in 1883 by Charles Warren: "The amount of information . . . with respect to educational systems, school laws, and important institutions is such as has never previously been made generally accessible in the United States, such as no agency belonging merely to a single State could possibly have gathered, and such as private persons could not have obtained, even with vast labor and at great expense." *Answers to Inquiries about the U.S. Bureau of Education: Its Work and History* (Washington, 1883), pp. 18–19.

16. 45 Stat. 1021 (1928). See section on Howard University in Chapter 3.
17. 27 Stat. 395 (1892).
18. 31 Stat. 1010, 1039 (1901).
19. 46 Stat. 1156 (1931).
20. For an in-depth analysis of the varied and complex activities of the Office of Education, see U.S. Congress, House, Special Subcommittee on Education, *Study of the United States Office of Education*, 90th Cong., 1st sess., 1967, Doc. 193. For purposes of comparison of the work of the office in 1923, see Darrel Hevenor Smith, *The Bureau of Education: Its History, Activities, and Organization* (Baltimore, 1923).
21. P.L. 90–247 (1968); P.L. 90–576 (1968); P.L. 91–230 (1970). Some further minor clarifications were made in the 1972 education amendments. See P.L. 92–318, sec. 501–503.
22. P.L. 91–230 (1970), sec. 402–406.
23. *Ibid.*, sec. 411–417, 431–438.
24. *Ibid.*, sec. 422.
25. P.L. 92–318 (1972), sec. 405(a)(1).
26. *Ibid.*, sec. 405 (b)(1).
27. *Ibid.*, sec. 405 (c)(1).
28. *Ibid.*, sec. 405 (h).

CHAPTER 2. ELEMENTARY AND SECONDARY EDUCATION

1. *Journals of the American Congress*, IV, 521.
2. *Federal and State Constitutions*, ed. F. N. Thorpe, 2: 958.

3. Howard Cromwell Taylor, *The Educational Significance of the Early Federal Land Grant Ordinances* (New York, 1922), pp. 9–14.

4. *Ibid.,* pp. 38–53. In his definitive study, Taylor has concluded: "The full influence of the Ordinance of 1787 upon public education can never be exactly measured and evaluated. The facts remain that this ordinance was the organic law of the great Northwest Territory, in which the value of land grants for education was first demonstrated; that its main provisions were later extended to other territories, and that the policy of land grants for education, as well as other means for the encouragement of education, were inspired by the language of this ordinance." (P. 122.)

5. U.S., *Land Laws,* vol. 1, 85; U.S., *Statutes at Large,* vol. 2, 173.

6. Taylor, *Educational Significance,* pp. 82–113.

7. F. H. Swift, *Federal Aid to Public Schools* (Washington, 1922), p. 10.

8. G. W. Knight, "History and Management of Land Grants for Education," *Papers of the American Historical Association,* 1 (1885): 79–247.

9. Taylor, *Educational Significance,* pp. 124–125.

10. It can be argued that the devisers of these plans would not have presented them if they believed that the Constitution forbade a national system of education.

11. Allen Oscar Hansen, *Liberalism and American Education in the Eighteenth Century* (New York, 1926), pp. 44–48.

12. Benjamin Rush, *Thoughts upon the Mode of Education in a Republic* (Philadelphia, 1786), p. 14.

13. Robert Coram, *Plan for the General Establishment of Schools throughout the United States* (Wilmington, Del., 1791), pp. 93–94, 99–101.

14. James Sullivan, *Observations upon the Government of the United States of America* (Boston, 1791), p. 29. His plan for a national system of education is delineated in *Thoughts upon the Political Situation of the United States of America* (Worcester, Mass., 1788).

15. Daniel Chipman, *The Life of the Honorable Nathaniel Chipman* (Boston, 1846), pp. 87–88. Nathaniel Chipman's national education plan is found in his *Sketches of the Principles of Government* (Rutland, Vt., 1793).

16. Noah Webster, *On Education of Youth in America* (Boston, 1788).
17. Samuel H. Smith, *Remarks on Education* (Philadelphia, 1798).
18. Samuel Knox, *Essay on Education* (Baltimore, 1799), pp. 31–32.
19. R. Freeman Butts and Lawrence A. Cremin, *A History of Education in American Culture* (New York, 1953), p. 190.
20. Edward H. Reisner, *Nationalism and Education since 1789* (New York, 1922), p. 325.
21. Butts and Cremin, *History of Education*, p. 244.
22. Bernard Bailyn, *Education in the Forming of American Society* (New York, 1960), p. 113.
23. *Messages and Papers of the President*, IX, pp. 4288–4289.
24. Allan P. Stauffer, *Anti-Catholicism in American Politics* (Cambridge, Mass., 1933).
25. Francis X. Curran, *The Churches and the Schools* (Chicago, 1954), pp. 118–130.
26. M. Laurina Kaiser, *The Development of the Concept and Function of the Catholic Elementary School in the American Parish* (Washington, 1955), pp. 71–108.
27. Richard J. Gabel, *Public Funds for Church and Private Schools* (Washington, 1937); and Sr. Raymond McLaughlin, *A History of State Legislation Affecting Private Elementary and Secondary Schools in the United States, 1870–1945* (Washington, 1946).
28. McLaughlin, *History of State Legislation*, p. 200.
29. Daniel F. Reilly, *The School Controversy, 1891–1893* (Washington, 1943), p. 29.
30. *Congressional Record*, December 14, 1875, 4, pt. 6: 5189.
31. *Congressional Record*, 4, pt. 6: 5595.
32. Laurence R. Gardner, "The Blaine Amendment of 1876 (M.A. thesis, The Catholic University of America, 1947), pp. 29–37, 57.
33. 55 Stat. 361 (1941).
34. Hollis P. Allen, The *Federal Government and Education*, (New York, 1950), p. 105.
35. P.L. 81–815 (1950) and P.L. 81–874 (1950).
36. P.L. 815 and 874 (1959), p. 33.
37. P.L. 89–10 (1965).
38. P.L. 90–576 (1968), sec. 305.
39. P.L. 91–230 (1970), sec. 241.

40. Sidney W. Tiedt, *The Role of the Federal Government in Education* (New York, 1966), pp. 192–193.
41. Allen, *Federal*, p. 83.
42. 49 Stat. 774 (1935).
43. 49 Stat. 151 (1936).
44. Allen, *Federal*, pp. 83–84.
45. 60 Stat. 230 (1946).
46. 74 Stat. 899 (1960) and 75 Stat. 411 (1961).
47. 63 Stat. 1052 (1949).
48. Helen A. Miller and Andrew J. Shea, *Federal Assistance for Educational Purposes*, (Washington, 1963), p. 60.
49. 84 Stat. 210 (1970). The Department of Agriculture's regulations have been issued in the *Federal Register*. See 7 C.F.R., sec. 245 (1971). For discussion of the implications of the 1970 amendments, see Comment, "The National School Lunch Act and the 1970 Amendments: Rennaissance or Rhetoric?" 17 WAYNE L. REV. 955 (1971); and Note, "The National School Lunch Program, 1970: Mandate to Feed the Children," 60 GEORGETOWN L. JOUR. 711 (1972).
50. Davis v. Robinson, 346 F. Supp. 847 (1972).
51. P.L. 93–13 (1973).
52. "Shaping Up: A 'Grave Threat' to School Lunches," *U.S. News and World Report*, 15 April 1974, p. 43.
53. 60 Stat. 839 (1946). See also 2 U.S.C., sec. 88a.
54. Harry G. Good and James D. Teller, *A History of American Education* (New York, 1973), p. 430.
55. P.L. 84–597 (1956). The law was updated on December 30, 1970, with increased appropriations and special concern for the needs of the handicapped. See P.L. 91–600 (1970).
56. *Ibid.*, sec. 101.
57. *Ibid.*, sec. 201.
58. *Ibid.*, sec. 401.
59. P.L. 91–345 (1970).
60. *Ibid.*, sec. 2.
61. *Ibid.*, sec. 5.
62. P.L. 85–864 (1954), sec. 301–305, 311–315, 601–603.
63. *Ibid.*, sec. 501–505.
64. Harry Kursh, *The United States Office of Education* (Philadelphia, 1965), p. 91.

65. U.S. Office of Education, *Education 65, A Report to the Profession* (Washington, 1966), p. 34.

66. *Ibid.*, p. 43.

67. Francis Keppel, *The Necessary Revolution in American Education* (New York, 1966), p. 128.

68. Robert J. Havighurst, "Social-Class Influences on American Education," *NSSE Yearbook* (1960), p. 135.

69. Kursh, *United*, pp. 66–67.

70. "Five Years of NDEA," *School Life*, October, 1963, p. 12. Other studies evaluating NDEA in whole or in part may be found in Sidney C. Sufrin, *Administering the National Defense Education Act* (New York, 1963), pp. 40–65.

71. Kursh, *United*, p. 49.

72. P.L. 85–875 (1958).

73. Some of these studies are: Frank Riesman, *The Culturally Deprived Child* (New York, 1962); Martin Deutsch, *Minority Group and Class Status as Related to Social and Personality Factors in Scholastic Achievement* (New York, 1960); Basil Bernstein, "Social Structure, Language and Learning," *Educational Research* 3 (1961): 163–176; and C. W. Hunnicutt, ed., *Urban Education and Cultural Deprivation* (Syracuse, New York, 1964).

74. P.L. 88–452 (1964), sec. 222 (a)(1).

75. *U.S. Code Congressional and Administrative News* (1973), II, 3228.

76. U.S. Office of Education, Bureau of Elementary and Secondary Education, Division of Compensatory Education, "Preliminary Report of the Advisory Committee on Follow-Through," July, 1967.

77. P.L. 90–222 (1967), sec. 222 (a)(2).

78. P.L. 90–177 (1969).

79. For precise data on these eligibility requirements, see *U.S. Code Congressional and Administrative News* (1973), II, 3239–3240.

80. "Special Message to Congress on Civil Rights," *Public Papers, 1963*, pp. 221–230.

81. "Special Message to Congress on Civil Rights and Job Opportunities," *ibid.*, pp. 487, 494.

82. *Public Papers of the President, Lyndon B. Johnson* (1963–64), 1:8.

83. *Ibid.*, 112–118.

84. P.L. 88–352 (1964), sec. 401.

85. *Ibid.*, sec. 402–410.
86. *Ibid.*, sec. 601–605.
87. *Ibid.*, sec. 407 (a).
88. Swann v. Charlotte-Mecklenburg Board of Education, 402 U.S. 15–18 (1971).
89. *Ibid.*, 17.
90. P.L. 92–318 (1972), sec. 802(A).
91. See section on busing in Chapter 11.
92. Oscar T. Jarvis and Marion J. Rice, *An Introduction to Teaching in the Elementary School* (Dubuque, Ia., 1972), pp. 462–463.
93. United States v. Jefferson County Board of Education, 380 F. 2d 385 (1967).
94. *Federal Register* 33 (1968):4956. "Compliance with the law requires integration of facilities, faculties, and activities, as well as students, so that there are no Negro or minority group schools and no white schools—just schools."
95. Alexander v. Holmes County Board of Education, 396 U.S. 19 (1969). See Chapter 11 for further details on the course of integration as a result of Supreme Court decisions.
96. Adams v. Richardson, 351 F. Supp. 636 (1972), 356 F. Supp. 92 (1973), and 480 F. 2d 1159 (1973).
97. For the text of the education plank of the Democratic party platform adopted at the Democratic National Convention in Los Angeles, July 12, 1960, see William T. O'Hara, *John F. Kennedy on Education* (New York, 1966), p. 14.
98. "Special Labor Day Message from Democratic Presidential Candidate John F. Kennedy, September 5, 1960," *Freedom of Communications: Final Report of the Committee on Commerce, United States Senate, Prepared by Its Subcommittee on Communications* (Washington, 1961), I, 109–110.
99. *Public Papers*, 1971, p. 22.
100. *Ibid.*, pp. 107–111.
101. 107 *Congressional Record* (1961), 2338, 2918.
102. *Public Papers, 1961*, pp. 142–143.
103. *Constitutionality of Federal Aid to Education in its Various Aspects. S. Doc. 29*, 87th Cong., 1st sess., pp. 21, 22. The legal brief pointed out, however, that a less restrictive approach existed in regard to higher education. There was no question as to scholarships and cost-of-education allowances, and loans for constructing college academic facilities were "less

constitutionally vulnerable than grants." *Ibid.*, p. 26.

104. 107 *Congressional Record* (1961), 6133.

105. 108 *Congressional Record* (1961), 9054.

106. 107 *Congressional Record* (1961), 12941.

107. *Public Papers, 1962*, pp. 112–113.

108. *Public Papers, 1963*, pp. 105–116.

109. O'Hara, *Kennedy*, pp. 26–27.

110. P.L. 80–10 (1965). For in-depth studies of this act, see Stephen K. Bailey and Edith K. Mosher, *ESEA: The Office of Education Administers a Law* (Syracuse, N.Y., 1968); Philip Meranto, *The Politics of Federal Aid to Education in 1965* (Syracuse, N.Y., 1967); James W. Guthrie, "The 1965 ESEA: The National Politics of Educational Reform" (Ph.D. diss., Stanford University, 1967); Richard Henry Bucher, "The Elementary and Secondary Act of 1965: A Study in Policy Change" (Ph.D. diss., Duke University, 1971).

111. Bailey and Mosher, *ESEA.*

112. Jerome T. Murphy, "Title I of ESEA: The Politics of Implementing Federal Education Reform," *Education and the Legal Structure* (Cambridge, Mass., 1971), p. 68.

113. *Ibid.*, p. 69.

114. P.L. 89–750 (1966). Education for the handicapped is treated in the chapter on "Vocational Education and Rehabilitation."

115. P.L. 90–247 (1968).

116. *Ibid.*, sec. 702.

117. *Ibid.*, sec. 404(c).

118. Dean M. Kelley and George R. LaNoue, "The Church-State Settlement in the Federal Aid to Education Act," in Donald A. Giannella, *Religion and the Public Order* (Chicago, 1966), p. 110.

119. Murphy, "Title I," p. 65.

120. Good and Teller, *History of Education*, p. 531.

121. Kelley and LaNoue, "Church-State," p. 111.

122. Gilbert R. Austin and Stephen P. Holowenzak, "Catholic Schools and Public Aid: The Elementary and Secondary Education Act and the Principle of Accommodation," *Notre Dame Journal of Education* 3 (1973): 373.

123. Kelley and LaNoue, "Church-State," p. 160.

124. For legal discussion of Title I's aid to religious schools, see

Comment, "The Elementary and Secondary Education Act
—The Implications of the Trust-Fund Theory for the
Church-State Questions Raised by Title I," 65 MICHIGAN L.
REV. 1184 (1967); and George R. LaNoue, "Church-State
Problems in New Jersey: The Implementation of Title I
(ESEA) in Sixty Cities," 22 RUTGERS L. REV. 219 (1968).

125. Wheeler v. Barrera, 42 LW 4877 (1974). For a discussion of
this case, see section on aid to nonpublic school poor in
chapter on "Private and Religious Schools."

126. U.S., Congress, House Committee on Education and Labor,
H. Rept. 91–1362; Senate Committee on Labor and Public
Welfare, 1970, S. Rept. 91–1164.

127. P.L. 91–516 (1970), sec. 2(b).

128. *Ibid.*, sec. 3(a)(2).

129. *Ibid.*, sec. 3 (2)(b)(1), sec. 7.

130. P.L. 91–527 (1970).

131. *Ibid.*, sec. 2.

132. *Ibid.*, sec. 3–4.

133. P.L. 92–318 (1972), sec. 702.

134. Adams v. Richardson, 351 F. Supp. 636 (1972), 356 F.
Supp. 92 (1973), and 480 F. 2d 1159 (1973).

135. P.L. 92–318 (1972), sec. 703 (b).

136. *Ibid.*, sec. 704–706.

137. *Ibid.*, sec. 707.

138. *Ibid.*, sec. 716.

139. Among the many studies that deal with the problems of
immigration and acculturation in American history, the
reader is directed to Marcus L. Hansen, *The Immigrant in
American History* (Cambridge, Mass., 1940); I. B. Berkson,
Theories of Americanization (New York, 1920); and Horace
Kallen, *Culture and Democracy in the United States* (New York,
1924).

140. P.L. 92–318 (1972), sec. 901.

141. *Ibid.*, sec. 902–907.

142. Felix S. Cohen, *Handbook of Federal Indian Law* (Albuquerque, N.M., 1972), pp. 9–12; Elwood P. Cubberly,
State School Administration (Boston, 1927), pp. 109–110.

143. Cohen, *Handbook*, p. 240; Cubberly, *State*, p. 110.

144. Cubberly, *State*, p. 110.

145. Quick Bear v. Leupp, 210 U.S. 50 (1908). This case has also

been discussed under the section dealing with public funds for church schools.

146. Cubberly, *State,* pp. 110–111.
147. 48 Stat. 596 (1934).
148. Cohen, *Handbook,* pp. 238–242.
149. P.L. 92–318 (1972), sec. 302 (f), 303–307.
150. *Ibid.,* sec. 421 (b).
151. *Ibid.,* sec. 421, 431.
152. *Ibid.,* sec. 441–442.
153. Daniel M. Rosenfelt, "Indian Schools and Community Control," 25 STANFORD L. REV. 489–550 (1973).
154. U.S. Congress, Senate, Special Subcommittee on Indian Education, Committee on Labor and Public Welfare, *Indian Education: A National Tragedy—A National Challenge,* 91st Cong., 1st sess., 1969, S. Rept. 501, p. 106.
155. *Message from the President of the United States,* H.R. 363, 91st Cong., 2d sess., 1970, p. 6.
156. Daniel M. Rosenfelt, "The Renaissance of Indian Education," *Inequality in Education,* November, 1973, pp. 19–20.

CHAPTER 3. HIGHER EDUCATION

1. Jonathan Elliot, *Debates on the Adoption of the Federal Constitution* (New York, 1888), 5:130.
2. *Ibid.,* 439–40.
3. *Ibid.,* 440.
4. *Ibid.,* 544.
5. Hinsdale, "Documents," pp. 1293–1294.
6. Max Farrand, *The Framing of the Constitution* (New York, 1913), p. 196.
7. Adrienne Koch, *Notes on Debates in the Federal Convention of 1787 Reported by James Madison* (Athens, Ohio, 1966), p. xxiii.
8. Samuel Blodget, *Economica: A Statistical Manual for the United States* (Washington, 1806), pp. 22–23; G. Brown Goode, "The Origins of the National Scientific and Educational Associations of the United States," *Papers of the American Historical Association* 4 (1890):19.
9. Hinsdale, "Documents," p. 1296.
10. *Ibid.,* pp. 1297–1300.

11. *Ibid.,* p. 1306.
12. Roy J. Honeywell, *The Educational Work of Thomas Jefferson* (Cambridge, Mass., 1933); *The Papers of Thomas Jefferson,* ed. Julian P. Boyd, (Princeton, N.J., 1950), 2:526–543.
13. Hinsdale, "Documents," pp. 1307–1308.
14. Allen Oscar Hansen, *Liberalism and American Education in the Eighteenth Century,* (New York, 1926), p. 180.
15. Goode, "Origins," pp. 132–146.
16. *Compilation of the Messages and Papers of the Presidents,* ed. J. D. Richardson, (Washington, 1907), 1:740.
17. *Ibid.,* 2:553.
18. *Ibid.,* 561.
19. *Exec. Doc.,* 11th Cong., 3rd sess., 1811.
20. *Exec. Doc.,* 14th Cong., 2d sess., 1816.
21. Richardson, *Messages,* 2:587.
22. *Ibid.,* 879–880.
23. *The Smithsonian Institution: Documents Relative to Its Origin and History, 1835–1899,* William Jones Rhees, ed. (Washington, 1901), 1:125. For a copy of the bequest, see pp. 5–6, and for the correspondence between officials of the United States government with Smith's lawyers (Smith, an Englishman, had died in 1829), see pp. 7–110.
24. *Ibid.,* 142–143.
25. *Ibid.,* 145–146.
26. *Ibid.,* 173–174.
27. *Ibid.,* 429–434.
28. Richardson, *Messages,* 9:4208.
29. *Proceedings of the National Educational Association* (1901): 457–467.
30. Edgar B. Wesley, *Proposed: The University of the United States* (Minneapolis, 1936), pp. 16–24.
31. *American Archives,* ser. 5, 2:1373, 1387.
32. *Ibid.,* 1383.
33. Hinsdale, "Documents," p. 1303.
34. 2 Stat. 132 (1802).
35. James R. Soley, *History of the Naval Academy* (Washington, 1876), p. 39.
36. The establishment was the personal decision of Navy secretary George Bancroft; he later received congressional approval. See William D. Puleston, *Annapolis* (New York,

1942), pp. 2–3; and John Crane and James Kiely, *U.S. Naval Academy* (New York, 1945), p. 42.

37. 19 Stat. 107 (1876).

38. *U.S. Coast Guard Academy* (Washington, 1939), p. 18.

39. *Ibid.*, pp. 16–17. See also Stephen H. Evans, *The United States Coast Guard* (Annapolis, Md., 1949), pp. 95–96, 157.

40. 32 Stat. 854, 859 (1903).

41. *U.S. Coast Guard Academy*, p. 19.

42. 49 Stat. 1985 (1936).

43. *The U.S. Merchant Marine Cadet Corps and Academy* (Kings Point, N.Y., 1972), p. 10.

44. Charles A. Quattlebaum, *Federal Educational Policies, Programs and Proposals* (Washington, 1968), pt. I, p. 29.

45. 61 Stat. 503 (1947), sec. 208.

46. 68 Stat. 47 (1954).

47. 12 Stat. 503 (1862), sec. 4.

48. Gene M. Lyons and John W. Masland, *Education and Military Leadership: A Study of the R.O.T.C.* (Princeton, N.J., 1959), pp. 31–33.

49. 39 Stat. 191 (1916).

50. Lyons and Masland, *Education,* pp. 35–37.

51. 41 Stat. 775–781 (1920).

52. 43 Stat. 1276 (1925).

53. Lyons and Masland, *Education,* p. 88.

54. Hsien Lu, *Federal Role in Government* (New York, 1965), pp. 233–235.

55. Wesley, *Proposed,* p. 27.

56. Rayford W. Logan, *Howard University: The First Hundred Years* (New York, 1969), pp. 3, 12–14. Most of the persons connected with this plan belonged to the Congregational church. *Ibid.,* p. 12.

57. U.S. Department of Education, *Special Report of the Commissioner of Education on the Condition and Improvement of Public Schools in the District of Columbia* (Washington, 1871), p. 245.

58. Logan, *Howard,* pp. 17–18; and 14 Stat. 438 (1867).

59. Charles E. Williams, *The Howard University Charter Annotated: Upon the Centenary of Howard University* (Washington, 1967), pp. 29–33.

60. 30 Stat. 1101 (1899).

61. 26 Stat. 973 (1891).

62. P.L. 70–634 (1928).

63. P.L. 87–262 (1961).

64. 14 Stat. 174 (1865).

65. H. G. Good, *A History of American Education* (New York, 1956), p. 289.

66. A. C. True, *History of Agricultural Education in the United States, 1785–1925* (Washington, 1928), pp. 35–36.

67. *Ibid.*, p. 37.

68. Palmer C. Ricketts, ed., *Centennial Celebration of Rensselaer Polytechnic Institute* (Troy, N.Y., 1925), pp. 39, 63–64, 104–108.

69. Walter Stemmons, *Connecticut Agricultural College—A History* (Storrs, Conn., 1931), pp. 20–21, 42; C. W. Burkett, *History of Ohio Agriculture* (Concord, N.H., 1900), pp. 199–200; C. R. Woodward, *The Development of Agriculture in New Jersey, 1640–1880, a Monograph Study in Agricultural History* (New Brunswick, N.J., 1927), p. 133.

70. Good, *History of Education*, pp. 289–290; Earl D. Ross, *Democracy's College: The Land-Grant Movement in the Formative State* (New York, 1969), pp. 20–24.

71. Rhees, *Smithsonian*, 1:238–239.

72. Ross, *Democracy's College*, pp. 40–43. This combination was urged by the U.S. Agricultural Society established in 1852 with headquarters at the Smithsonian Institution. See Lyman Carrier, "The U.S. Agricultural Society, 1852–1860," *Agricultural History* 11 (1937): 278–288. See also I. L. Kandel, *Federal Aid for Vocational Education* (New York, 1917), pp. 73–79.

73. *Congressional Globe*, 35 Cong., 1st sess., 1857, 36.

74. *Ibid.*, 2d sess., 1859, 1412.

75. *House Journal*, 36 Cong., 1st sess., 1861, p. 467.

76. 12 Stat. 503 (1862).

77. 14 Stat. 208 (1866).

78. For details as to how each state applied the benefits of the Morrill Act, see Frank W. Blackman, *The History of Federal and State Aid to Higher Education in the United States* (Washington, 1890), pp. 83–327.

79. Good, *History of Education*, pp. 295–297; Ross, *Democracy's College*, pp. 68–85. Ross has commented: "The lack of . . . stabilizing influence opened the way for rivalries in which

the real interest of the classes for whom the act was specially designed was little regarded. The consequent scrambling, maneuvering, and intriguing for the federal largess reflected the financial desperation of the majority of colleges and the misconception among educational promoters of the peculiar field and special requirements of the new institutions." (P. 69.)

80. Good, *History of Education*, pp. 297–299; Ross, *Democracy's College*, pp. 113–125.

81. Elwood F. Cubberly, *State School Administration* (Boston, 1927), pp. 44–45; Good, *History of Education*, pp. 296–299.

82. True, *History of Agricultural Education*, p. 195; U.S. Department of Agriculture, *National Agricultural Convention held at Washington, D.C., February 15, 16, and 17, 1872* (Washington, 1872).

83. *Congressional Globe*, 42 Cong., 2d sess., 1872, 275.

84. For a convenient summary of the legislative actions on Morrill's bill, see Kandel, *Federal Aid*, pp. 19–54.

85. George Rainsford, *Congress and Higher Education in the Nineteenth Century* (Knoxville, Tenn., 1972), pp. 106–108.

86. 26 Stat. 418 (1890).

87. 34 Stat. 1281 (1907).

88. 49 Stat. 439 (1935).

89. Kandel, *Federal Aid*, p. 59.

90. *Ibid.*, pp. 59–60.

91. *Ibid.*, pp. 60–65.

92. A. C. True and V. A. Clark, *The Agricultural Experiment Stations in the United States* (Washington, 1900), pp. 68–75.

93. Ross, *Democracy's College*, pp. 141–142.

94. 34 Stat. 63 (1906).

95. 43 Stat. 970 (1925).

96. 49 Stat. 439 (1935).

97. 60 Stat. 1082 (1946).

98. 48 Stat. 115 (1935).

99. 84 *Congressional Record* (1939), 4710.

100. Hollis P. Allen, *The Federal Government and Education* (New York, 1950), p. 97.

101. John S. Brubacher and Willis Rudy, *Higher Education in Transition* (New York, 1958), p. 236.

102. Hollis, *Federal*, p. 103.

103. *Ibid.*, p. 104.
104. P.L. 78–346 (1944).
105. P.L. 82–550 (1952).
106. Quattlebaum, *Federal Educational Policies* (1960 ed.), p. 221.
107. Allen, *Federal*, p. 165.
108. P.L. 81–610 (1948).
109. P.L. 82–550 (1952).
110. Quattlebaum, *Federal Educational Policies* (1960 ed.), p. 221.
111. P.L. 89–358 (1966).
112. P.L. 93–208 (1973).
113. *U.S. Code Congressional and Administrative News* (1973), II, 3011–3013.
114. R. Freeman Butts and Lawrence A. Cremin, *A History of Education in American Culture* (New York, 1953), pp. 582–583.
115. P.L. 84–634 (1956). Some minor changes were made by P.L. 89–358 (1966), P.L. 90–77 (1967), and P.L. 90–631 (1968).
116. P.L. 83–531 (1954).
117. P.L. 89–10 (1965), sec. 401, 403; P.L. 89–750 (1966), sec. 141–143; P.L. 91–247 (1968), sec. 401 (g), 402, 423, 706; P.L. 91–230 (1970), sec. 401–402, 808–810, P.L. 92–318 (1972), sec. 303.
118. U.S. Congress, Senate, Subcommittee on War Mobilization, "The Government's Wartime Research and Development, Findings and Recommendations, from Report of Subcommittee on War Mobilization, Part II," *Legislative Proposals for the Promotion of Science* (Washington, 1945), pp. 19–47.
119. Vannevar Bush, *Science, The Endless Frontier* (Washington, 1945).
120. U.S. Congress, Senate, Subcommittee of the Committee on Military Affairs, *Science Legislation, Analytical Summary of Testimony* (Washington, 1945).
121. U.S. Congress, Senate, *Science and Technology Act of 1947, Analysis and Summary* (Washington, 1947), p. 24.
122. P.L. 81–247 (1950).
123. P.L. 86–232 (1959).
124. P.L. 81–247 (1950). For a detailed description of the many activities under the direction of the National Science Foundation, see *Listing of Operating Federal Assistance Programs Compiled During the Roth Study* (Washington, 1969), pp. 883–941.
125. P.L. 85–864 (1958), sec. 901.

126. P.L. 89–688 (1966).

127. P.L. 93–73 (1973).

128. P.L. 89–209 (1965), sec. 2.

129. *Ibid.*, sec. 3–11.

130. P.L. 90–348 (1968) and P.L. 90–575 (1968).

131. Sidney C. Sufrin, *Administering the National Defense Education Act* (New York, 1963), pp. 1–2, 73. Americo D. Lapati, *A High School Curriculum for Leadership* (New York, 1961), pp. 22–23.

132. Sufrin, *Administering*, pp. 55–60.

133. Committee for the White House Conference on Education, *A Report to the President* (Washington, 1956), p. 5.

134. P.L. 85–864 (1958).

135. For a more detailed analysis of the various titles of NDEA, their practical implementation, and implications for educational improvement, see Sufrin, *Administering*, pp. 16–27.

136. Tom Kaser, "The Loyalty Oath, 1964–65," *Saturday Review*, 21 November 1964, p. 60.

137. 104 *Congressional Record* (1959), 1330.

138. 105 *Congressional Record* (1960), 1378–1379.

139. P.L. 87–835 (1962).

140. U.S. Office of Education, *Report on the National Defense Education Act: Fiscal Year Ending June 30, 1959* (Washington, 1960), p. 3.

141. U.S. Office of Education, *Report on the National Defense Education Act: Fiscal Year Ending June 30, 1960* (Washington, 1961), p. 1.

142. P.L. 85–934 (1958).

143. P.L. 88–665 (1964).

144. P.L. 89–329 (1965); P.L. 89–752 (1966); and P.L. 90–575 (1968).

145. P.L. 89–698 (1966), sec. 102.

146. "John F. Kennedy's Campaign Declarations," *The Congressional Quarterly*, 13 January 1961, p. 35.

147. "The President's State of the Union Message," *The Congressional Quarterly*, 3 January 1961, p. 192. American educators expressed views similar to Kennedy's. See Francis H. Horn, Jonathan King, James J. Morisseau, "Facilities and Learnings: An Overview of Developments," Samuel Baskin, ed., *Higher Education: Some New Developments* (New York, 1965),

pp. 153–173; John Dale Russell, "Dollars and Cents: Some Hard Facts," *ibid.*, pp. 273–303; Seymour E. Harris, *Financing Higher Education: 1960–1970* (New York, 1959); *Higher Education: Resources and Finance* (New York, 1962); Selma J. Mushkin, editor, *Economics of Higher Education* (Washington, 1962); John Millet, "Financing Higher Education: Ten Years Later," *The Educational Record*, January, 1963, pp. 44–53; and Sidney G. Tickton, *Needed: A Ten Year College Budget* (New York, 1961).

148. "Special Message to the Congress on Education," *Public Papers of the Presidents: John F. Kennedy* (Washington, 1962), pp. 109–110.

149. "Letter from President John F. Kennedy," *The Congressional Quarterly*, 17 March 1961, p. 451.

150. American Council on Education, *A Proposed Program to Strengthen Higher Education* (Washington, 1961).

151. 109 *Congressional Record* (1963), 19859–19892.

152. "President Kennedy's Second State of the Union Message," *The Congressional Quarterly*, 11 January 1962, p. 55.

153. "Special Message to the Congress on Education," *Public Papers, 1962*, pp. 111–112.

154. "Special Message to the Congress on Education," *Public Papers, 1963*, pp. 109–110.

155. 109 *Congressional Record* (1963), 14941–14999.

156. P.L. 88–204 (1963).

157. Tilton v. Richardson, 403 U.S. 672 (1971).

158. "Higher Education Facilities Act of 1963," *Higher Education and National Affairs*, 22 December 1964, p. 3; *ibid.*, 25 November 1965, pp. 1–3; "The Higher Education Facilities Act of 1963," *School Life*, May, 1964, p. 13.

159. American Library Association, *Federal Library Legislation, Programs and Services* (Chicago, 1965), p. 30.

160. "The Passage of the Higher Education Facilities Act of 1963," *Christian Century*, January, 1964, p. 43.

161. "President Johnson's State of the Union Message," *Public Papers, 1965*, p. 7.

162. "Special Message to the Congress on Education," *ibid.*, pp. 25–33.

163. 111 *Congressional Record* (1965), 21876–21948.

164. "Presidential Remarks on House Passage of H.R. 9567,"

Congressional Quarterly, 3 September 1965, p. 1815; and "Presidential Remarks on Senate Passage of H.R. 9567," *Congressional Quarterly,* 10 September 1965, p. 1857.

165. "Signing of the Higher Education Act of 1965," *Congressional Quarterly,* 12 November 1965, p. 2336.

166. P.L. 89–329 (1965).

167. "Two Focal Points for 1966," *Journal of Higher Education,* April, 1966, p. 187.

168. "The Higher Education Act of 1965," *American Association of University Professors Bulletin,* Winter, 1965, p. 431.

169. P.L. 89–752 (1966).

170. P.L. 90–35 (1967).

171. *Ibid.,* sec. 501.

172. *Ibid.,* sec. 502.

173. *Ibid.,* sec. 511, 513. Appropriations were increased by P.L. 91–230 (1970).

174. P.L. 90–35 (1967), sec. 518 (a)(b). Appropriations were increased by P.L. 90–575 (1968), sec. 233.

175. P.L. 90–35 (1967), sec. 521–522.

176. *Ibid.,* sec. 531.

177. *Ibid.,* sec. 541.

178. P.L. 90–575 (1968).

179. *Ibid.,* sec. 101–102.

180. *Ibid.,* sec. 105.

181. *Ibid.,* sec. 111–120.

182. *Ibid.,* sec. 131–139, 141.

183. *Ibid.,* sec. 171–176.

184. *Ibid.,* sec. 201–203, 211–218, 221–223, 231–239, 241–243.

185. *Ibid.,* sec. 251.

186. *Ibid.,* sec. 261, 271, 281.

187. *Ibid.,* sec. 301–304.

188. *Ibid.,* sec. 311–314, 321–322, 331.

189. *Ibid.,* sec. 401–406.

190. *Ibid.,* sec. 503–504.

191. P.L. 91–95 (1969).

192. P.L. 92–318 (1972), sec. 134.

193. *Ibid.,* sec. 101.

194. *Ibid.,* sec. 106, 201.

195. *Ibid.,* sec. 301–306.

196. *Ibid.,* sec. 401, 411–413D, 417A and B, 461–466.

197. *Ibid.,* sec. 439.

198. *Ibid.,* sec. 521, 531.
199. *Ibid.,* sec. 701 seq.
200. *Ibid.,* sec. 901 seq.
201. *Ibid.,* sec. 1001–1017.
202. *Ibid.,* sec. 1018.
203. *Ibid.,* sec. 1060.
204. *Ibid.,* sec. 1056 (6)(1).
205. *Ibid.,* sec. 1071, 1072.
206. *Ibid.,* sec. 1202–1206.
207. *Ibid.,* sec. 140.
208. P.L. 93–35 (1973). See also *U.S. Code Congressional and Administrative News* (1973), I, 1392–1393.
209. P.L. 92–318 (1972), sec. 901 (a).
210. *Ibid.,* sec. 902, 903, 907.
211. K. Patricia Cross, *The Undergraduate Woman* (Washington, 1971); American Council on Education, *Discrimination Against Women: A Special Report* (Washington, 1970); Malcom G. Scully, "Women In Higher Education," *The Chronicle of Higher Education,* 9 February 1970, pp. 2–4; Carnegie Commission on Higher Education, *New Students and New Places: Policies for the Future Growth and Development of American Higher Education* (New York, 1971), p. 30.
212. Task Force to the Secretary of Health, Education, and Welfare, *Report on Higher Education* (Washington, 1971), p. 52.
213. Interdepartmental Committee on the Status of Women, *American Women, 1963–68* (Washington, 1968), pp. 27–28.
214. Jo Freeman, "The Revolution Is Happening In Our Mind," *College and University Business* 48 (1970): 67.
215. Equal Pay Act, 29 U.S.C., sec. 206 (1963). Amended thereby was the 1938 Fair Labor Standards Act, 29 U.S.C., sec. 213 (1938).
216. Civil Rights Act, 42 U.S.C., sec. 2000 (e)(1964).
217. Fair Labor Standards Act, 29 U.S.C., sec. 213 (1938), and Civil Rights Act, 42 U.S.C., sec. 2000 (e)(1)(1964).
218. U.S. President, "Executive Order 11375, Amending Executive Order 11246, Relating to Equal Employment Opportunity," *Federal Register* 32 (1967): 14303–14304.
219. U.S. Department of HEW, Office of Civil Rights, "Sex Discrimination Guidelines," *Federal Register* 36 (1970): 8888–8889.
220. U.S. Department of HEW, Office of Civil Rights, "Revised

Order No. 4, Affirmative Action Programs," *Federal Register* 36 (1971): 23152–23164. See also Carol H. Shulman, *Affirmative Action: Women's Rights on Campus* (Washington, 1972).

221. Bernice Sandler, "Equity for Women in Higher Education," in Dyckman W. Vermilye, *The Expanded Campus: Current Issues in Higher Education* (San Francisco, 1972), pp. 78–79.

222. *H.R. 16098*, 91st Cong., 2d sess., 1970, and *H.R. 18849*, 91st Cong., 2d sess., 1970.

223. U.S. Congress, House, Subcommittee on Education and Labor, *Hearings on H.R. 16098*, 91st Cong., 2d sess., 1970, 2 vols.

224. U.S. Congress, House, Subcommittee on Education, *Hearings on H.R. 5191*, 92nd Cong., 1st sess., 1971; and U.S., Congress, Senate, Subcommittee on Education, *Hearings on S. 1123*, 92d Cong., 1st sess., 1971. Other bills introduced were: *H.R. 5191*, Higher Education Opportunity Act of 1971 (March 1, 1971), and its companion bill *S. 1123* (March 4, 1971); *H.R. 7248*, Higher Education Act of 1971 (April 6, 1971).

225. For a summary of the legislative history and analysis of the arguments on Title IX, see Majorie J. Corrigan, "Prohibition of Sex Discrimination in Admissions: The Development of a Federal Policy for Higher Education" (Ph.D. diss., Catholic University of America, 1974), pp. 188–229.

226. U.S. Department of HEW, *Higher Education Guidelines: Executive Order 11246* (Washington, 1972); U.S. Department of HEW, Office of Civil Rights, *Proposed Regulation of Title IX of the Education Amendments of 1972*, issued October 1, 1972. On May 4, 1973, Department of HEW, Office of Civil Rights and Office of Education jointly distributed memorandum describing intention and procedures under which certain former single sex institutions may operate pursuant to a plan for transition to nondiscriminatory admissions.

CHAPTER 4. VOCATIONAL EDUCATION, REHABILITATION, AND THE HANDICAPPED

1. Earl D. Ross, *Democracy's College: The Land-Grant Movement in the Formative State* (New York, 1969), pp. 164–165.

2. A. C. True, *History of Agricultural Education in the United States* (Washington, 1928), pp. 14–25.

3. I. L. Kandel, *Federal Aid for Vocational Education* (New York, 1917), p. 93.

4. *Ibid.;* and "Legislation Leading to the Federal Vocational Act," *School and Society* 6 (1917): 144–146.

5. P.L. 64–347 (1914).

6. H.G. Good, *A History of American Education* (New York, 1956), pp. 303–304.

7. *Ibid.*, p. 304.

8. Senate Joint Resolution, No. 5 (April 7, 1913).

9. U.S. Congress, House, *Report of the Commission on National Aid to Vocational Education*, 63rd Cong., 2d sess., 1914, H. Doc. 1004.

10. The bill is named after Senator Hoke Smith and Representative Dudley M. Hughes who introduced the bill in their respective branches of Congress.

11. P.L. 64–347 (1917). The bill is officially known as the Vocational Education Act of 1917.

12. National Resources Committee, *Public Works Planning* (Washington, 1936), pp. 197–198.

13. P.L. 70–702 (1929).

14. P.L. 72–245 (1934).

15. P.L. 74–673 (1936).

16. P.L. 79–586 (1946). This bill is officially known as the Vocational Education Act of 1946.

17. Hollis Allen, *The Federal Government and Education* (New York, 1950), pp. 77–79.

18. Edward C. Roeber, Garry R. Walz, and Glenn E. Smith, *A Strategy for Guidance* (New York, 1969), pp. 25–26.

19. *Ibid.*, pp. 22–23.

20. U.S. Office of Education, *Circular Letter 2107: Inauguration of a Program of Occupational Information and Guidance* (Washington, 1938).

21. Roeber, Walz, and Smith, *Strategy*, p. 26.

22. James Michael Lee and Nathaniel J. Pallone, *Guidance and Counseling in Schools: Foundations and Processes* (New York, 1966), p. 24.

23. P.L. 85–864 (1958), sec. 800.

24. 45 Stat. 711 (1928).

25. 49 Stat. 436 (1935).
26. 59 Stat. 231 (1945).
27. P.L. 81–740 (1950).
28. P.L. 85–875 (1958).
29. William T. O'Hara, *John F. Kennedy on Education* (New York, 1966), p. 45.
30. "Special Message to the Congress on Education," *Public Papers, 1962*, pp. 114–115; "Speech of Senator John F. Kennedy, October 10, 1960," *Freedom of Communications*, I: 545–546.
31. P.L. 88–129 (1963).
32. *Ibid.*, sec. 720–728.
33. *Ibid.*, sec. 740–746; 770–774.
34. *Ibid.*, sec. 780–793.
35. *Ibid.*, sec. 801–808, 821–829, 841, 860–868. Subsequent amendments to this act have not materially changed the essential features. See P.L. 88–581 (1964); P.L. 88–654 (1965), and P.L. 90–174 (1967).
36. "Special Message to the Congress on Education," *Public Papers, 1961*, pp. 107–111.
37. "Special Message to the Congress on Education," *Public Papers, 1963*, p. 120.
38. *Ibid.*, p. 121. Kennedy also stressed better vocational education in his civil rights message of June, 1963. See *ibid.*, pp. 468–471, 483–494.
39. O'Hara, *Kennedy*, pp. 25–26.
40. U.S. Congress, House, *Vocational Education Act of 1963, H.R. 469, Congressional Record*, 88th Cong., 1st sess., August 6, 1963, CIX: 14297.
41. U.S. Congress, Senate, *Vocational Education Opportunities Act of 1963, H.R. 4955, Congressional Record*, 88th Cong., 1st sess., August 6, 1963, CIX: 18999.
42. P.L. 88–210 (1963), sec. 101.
43. U.S. Department of Health, Education, and Welfare, Office of Education, *Education 65, A Report to the Profession* (Washington, 1966), p. 5.
44. P.L. 88–210 (1963), sec. 100.
45. Roy W. Roberts, *Vocational and Practical Arts Education* (New York, 1971), pp. 343–344.
46. John C. Donovan, "Implications of Manpower Training," *Phi Delta Kappan* 46 (1965): 366–367.

47. P.L. 87–27 (1961).
48. P.L. 87–415 (1962).
49. P.L. 88–214 (1963); P.L. 89–15 (1965); P.L. 89–792 (1966); P.L. 89–794 (1966); P.L. 90–636 (1968).
50. P.L. 89–15 (1965).
51. P.L. 90–636 (1968).
52. U.S. Department of Labor, Manpower Administration, *Manpower Report of the President for 1969* (Washington, 1969), p. 81.
53. HEW, *Education 65*, p. 11.
54. P.L. 93–203 (1973).
55. *Public Papers of the President, Lyndon B. Johnson* (1963–64), 1: 375, 376.
56. *Ibid.*, p. 376.
57. P.L. 88–452 (1964), sec. 101–171.
58. *Ibid.*, sec. 202–245.
59. *Ibid.*, sec. 801–835.
60. P.L. 89–794 (1966).
61. P.L. 90–222 (1967).
62. P.L. 91–177 (1969); P.L. 91–222 (1969); P.L. 92–424 (1972).
63. P.L. 93–203 (1973).
64. P.L. 89–84 (1965). The act was amended in 1967 (P.L. 90–103) and in 1971 (P.L. 92–65); the educational provisions are substantially the same, but with increased appropriations.
65. P.L. 89–287 (1965).
66. P.L. 90–575 (1968), sec. 116 (c)(1).
67. P.L. 89–329 (1965), sec. 421–437.
68. Benjamin B. Warfield, "The 90th Congress and Vocational Education," *National Association of Secondary Schools Bulletin*, February, 1969, p. 58.
69. "The Vocational Education Amendments of 1968, Public Law 90–576," *Exceptional Children*, May, 1969, pp. 751–752.
70. Warfield, "90th Congress," p. 58.
71. *Ibid.*
72. *Congressional Record*, CXIV, 2031 (1968).
73. U.S. Congress, House, "Partnership for Learning and Earning Act of 1968," Hearings before the Subcommittee on Education of the Committee on Education and Labor, 90th Cong., 2d sess., 1968.

74. 109 *Congressional Record* (1968), 29483.
75. P.L. 90–576 (1968), sec. 101.
76. *Ibid.*, sec. 122.
77. *Ibid.*, sec. 108.
78. *Ibid.*, sec. 141.
79. *Ibid.*, sec. 161.
80. *Ibid.*, sec. 171.
81. *Ibid.*, sec. 191.
82. *Ibid.*, sec. 181–184.
83. *Ibid.*, sec. 151.
84. *Ibid.*, sec. 308.
85. *Ibid.*, sec. 104(a). According to Warfield, "If the Council's annual reports maintain the high caliber of the 1968 report, they may well become the greatest single influence on the course of future Federal legislation in this field." See "90th Congress," p. 60.
86. *Ibid.*, sec. 104(b).
87. *Ibid.*, sec. 123.
88. Roberts, *Vocational*, p. 122.
89. *Ibid.*, p. 121.
90. P.L. 92–318 (1972), sec. 201–209.
91. *Ibid.*, sec. 1001 et seq. For an evaluation of vocational education in the junior college from an historical perspective, see W. Norton Grubb and Marvin Lazerson, "Vocational Education in American Schooling: Historical Perspectives," *Inequality in Education*, March, 1974, pp. 15–17.
92. For a summary of the legislative history of this act, see *U.S. Code Congressional and Administrative News*, II (1973), pp. 2935–2937.
93. P.L. 93–203 (1973). For a discussion of possible legislative changes for vocational education, see Leonard A. Lecht, "Legislative Priorities for Vocational Education," *Inequality in Education*, March, 1974, pp. 19–27.
94. P.L. 66–236 (1918).
95. Allen, *Federal*, p. 80.
96. Elwood F. Cubberly, *State School Administration* (Boston, 1927), p. 65. Cubberly has also pointed out, however, that "this was a most important educational service, worthy of a great Nation, and but a slight expression of the national gratitude for the help these men rendered in the saving of civilization from destruction."

97. 41 Stat. 735 (1920).
98. Federal Security Agency, Order no. 3, Supp. 1, September 4, 1943.
99. 53 Stat. 1381 (1939).
100. P.L. 78–113 (1943).
101. P.L. 83–565 (1954).
102. P.L. 89–333 (1965).
103. P.L. 90–99 (1961).
104. P.L. 90–391 (1968).
105. P.L. 93–112 (1973).
106. For a study of Edward Miner Gallaudet's life and work, see Maxine Tull Boatner, *Voice of the Deaf: A Biography of Edward Miner Gallaudet* (Washington, 1859).
107. P.L. 830420 (1954), sec. 1.
108. *Ibid.*, sec. 2–8.
109. P.L. 89–694 (1966).
110. P.L. 91–587 (1970).
111. P.L. 89–36 (1965).
112. P.L. 88–164 (1963), sec. 302.
113. *Ibid.*, sec. 501–503.
114. P.L. 85–926 (1958).
115. P.L. 85–905 (1958). See also subsequent amendments: P.L. 89–258 (1965) and P.L. 90–247 (1968).
116. P.L. 90–538 (1968).
117. P.L. 89–750 (1966), sec. 601.
118. *Ibid.*, sec. 609.
119. *Ibid.*, sec. 610.
120. *Ibid.*, sec. 611, 612.
121. P.L. 91–230 (1970).
122. 20 Stat. 467.
123. P.L. 59–288 (1906); P.L. 62–427 (1913); P.L. 66–73 (1919); P.L. 84–922 (1956); P.I. 87–294 (1961), sec. 1–4, P.L. 91–230 (1970), sec. 811 (a)(b).

CHAPTER 5. INTERNATIONAL EDUCATION

1. William W. Brickman, "Historical Development of Governmental Interest in International Higher Education," in Stewart Fraser, ed., *Governmental Policy and International Education* (New York, 1965), pp. 17–46.

2. For examples, see Letter of Benjamin Waterhouse to Benjamin Franklin in 1780 in Brook Hindle, *The Pursuit of Science in Revolutionary America, 1735–1789* (Chapel Hill, N.C., 1956), p. 289; Letter of Thomas Jefferson to J. B. Bannister in 1785 in Sauk K. Padover, ed., *The Complete Jefferson* (New York, 1943), p. 1056; Letter of Jefferson to his nephew in 1787 in *ibid.*, p. 1060; Letter of George Washington to John Adams in 1795 in Edgar W. Knight, ed., *A Documentary History of Education in the South before 1860* (Chapel Hill, N.C., 1950), 2: 86.

3. Horace Mann, *Seventh Annual Report of the Secretary of the Board* (Boston, 1844); Henry Barnard, *National Education in Europe* (Hartford, Conn., 1854); and Calvin E. Stowe, *Report on Elementary Public Instruction in Europe* (Boston, 1837).

4. For example, see *Report of the Commissioner of Education* (1889–1890), I: 1185–1243; (1892–1893), I: 157–356; (1896–1897), I: 3–348; (1899–1900), I: 721–894, 1167–1244.

5. Walter Johnson and Francis J. Colligan looked upon the growing trend of international exchange after World War I as a sort of compensation for America's not joining the League of Nations. *The Fulbright Program: A History* (Chicago, 1965), p. 15.

6. See Ruth W. Tyron, *Investment in Creative Scholarship* (Washington, 1957); Raymond B. Fosdick, *The Story of the Rockefeller Foundation* (New York, 1952), pp. 279–284; William Peters, *Passport to Friendship* (New York, 1957); Stephen Duggan, *Professor at Large* (New York, 1943); Institute of International Education, *The Institute of International Education—Its Aims and Achievements during Twenty-five Years: 1919–1944* (New York, 1945); Institute of International Education, *Blueprint for Understanding: A Thirty-Year Review* (New York, 1949); Edward R. Morrow, *Cultural Cooperation with Latin America: Institute of International Education Program Analysis No. 2* (New York, 1933); and I. L. Kandel, *United States Activities in International Cultural Relations* (Washington, 1945).

7. Johnson and Colligan, *Fulbright Program*, pp. 13–14.

8. U.S. Congress, Senate, Committee on Military Affairs, *S. Report 1039 to accompany S. 1636*, 79th Cong., 2d sess., 1946.

9. *New York Times*, September 14, 1946.*

10. P.L. 79–584 (1944).

11. Johnson and Colligan, *Fulbright Program,* p. 110. For some of the financial complexities in administering the Fulbright Act, see *ibid.,* pp. 107–118.

12. *Foreign Buildings Act of 1946,* 22 U.S.C. 295b (1973).

13. *Mutual Security Act of 1952,* 50 U.S.C. 1641 (1973).

14. *Supplemental Appropriation Act of 1953,* 31 U.S.C. 724 (1973). For an explanation of the complexity of the arrangement between the United States and foreign governments in regard to proceeds arising from sale of American goods, see Robert E. Asher, *Grants, Loans, and Local Currencies: Their Role in Foreign Aid* (Washington, 1961).

15. Johnson and Colligan, *Fulbright Program,* p. 92.

16. *Mutual Security Act of 1954,* 22 U.S.C. 1766 (1973).

17. *Agricultural Trade Development and Assistance Act of 1954,* P.L. 83–480, sec. 104h.

18. U.S. Congress, Senate, Committee on Appropriations, *Hearings on the Supplemental Appropriation Bill of 1954,* 83rd Cong., 1st sess., 1953, pp. 566–642. See also Charles A. Thomson and Walter Loves, *Cultural Relations and U.S. Foreign Policy* (Bloomington, Ind., 1962), pp. 99–105.

19. Johnson and Colligan, *Fulbright Program,* pp. 96–104.

20. *United States Informational and Educational Exchange Act of 1948,* 22 U.S.C. 1431–1479 (1973).

21. *Finnish Exchange Act of 1949,* 20 U.S.C. 222–224 (1973).

22. *India Emergency Food Aid Act of 1951,* 50 U.S.C. 2311–2316 (1973).

23. *International Cultural Exchange and Trade Fair Participation Act of 1956,* 22 U.S.C. 1991–20001.

24. *An Act Providing for Membership and Participation by the United States in the United Nations Educational, Scientific and Cultural Organization and Authorizing an Appropriation,* 22 U.S.C. 287 m t.

25. U.S. Congress, Senate, *Hearings before a Subcommittee of Committee on Foreign Relations on Overseas Information Programs of the United States,* 83rd Cong., 1st sess., 1953, pt. 2: 863–864, 895, 1046.

26. J. L. Morrill, *A Proposal for the Coordination of the Exchange of Persons and Programs of the International Educational Exchange Service and of the International Cooperation Administration* (Washington, 1956).

27. *The Committee on the University and World Affairs Report* (New York, 1960), p. 52.

28. *Congressional Record,* March 2, 1961, 3028–3029. Efforts were made periodically, however, to avoid unnecessary duplication and to coordinate activities in international and exchange areas. See U.S. Department of State, *Guide to Policy Statements of the Board of Foreign Scholarships* (Washington, 1950).

29. U.S. Congress, Senate, Committee of Foreign Relations, *Hearings on S. 1154,* 87th Cong., 1st sess., 1961; and U.S., Congress, House, Committee on Foreign Affairs, *Hearings on H.R. 5203 and 5204,* 87th Cong., 1st sess., 1961.

30. Senate, *Hearings on 1154,* p. 95.

31. *Ibid.,* p. 104.

32. U.S. Congress, House, *Conference Report to Accompany H.R. 8666,* September 15, 1961, H. Rept. 1197.

33. *Mutual Education and Cultural Exchange Act of 1961,* P.L. 87–256.

34. Johnson and Colligan, *Fulbright Program,* p. 312.

35. J. William Fulbright, *Old Myths and New Realities* (New York, 1964), p. 59.

36. *Freedom of Communications: The Speeches, Remarks, Press Conferences, and Statements of Senator John F. Kennedy, August 1 through November 7, 1960* (Washington, 1961), I: 1084.

37. *Ibid.,* p. 1260.

38. "Annual Message to the Congress on the State of the Union," *Public Papers,* 1961, p. 25.

39. William T. O'Hara, John F. *Kennedy on Education* (New York, 1966), p. 204.

40. *Exec. Ord. 10924,* March 1, 1961.

41. *Public Papers, 1961,* pp. 143–146.

42. *Ibid.,* p. 144.

43. *Ibid.,* p. 145.

44. *Ibid.,* pp. 143–144.

45. See appropriate pages in 107 *Congressional Record* (1961).

46. *Public Papers, 1961,* pp. 415–416.

47. *Peace Corps Act of 1961,* P.L. 87–293. See also 20 U.S.C. 425; 22 U.S.C. 2501–2523; 26 U.S.C. 912, 1303, 1321, 3122, 3401, 6051; 42 U.S.C. 405, 409–410 (1973).

48. *Congressional Quarterly Almanac, 1962,* p. 341.

49. O'Hara, *Kennedy*, pp. 206–207. See sections in *U.S. Code*, fn. 47 *supra*.

50. *Exec. Ord. 11603*, June 30, 1971.

51. "Reverse Peace Corps Soon To Be Underway," *NEA Journal* 56 (May, 1967): 3.

52. *Public Papers of the Presidents of the United States* (Washington, 1965), p. 1005.

53. *Public Papers of the Presidents of the United States* (Washington, 1966), pp. 128–136.

54. 112 *Congressional Record*, 12241–12257. *U.S. Code, Congressional and Administrative News*, III: 3565–3574.

55. Task Force on International Education, *International Education: Past, Present, Problems and Prospects: Selected Readings to Supplement H.R. 14643* (Washington, 1966), p. xi.

56. *Ibid.*, p. xii.

57. *International Education Act of 1966*, P.L. 89–698. See also 20 U.S.C. 511, 592, 601–602, 1085, 1171–1172; 22 U.S.C. 2452, 2454–2455 (1973).

58. P.L. 90–575 (1968), sec. 502.

59. P.L. 92–318 (1972), sec. 183.

CHAPTER 6. THE FINANCING AND CONTROL OF PUBLIC EDUCATION

1. Olan Kenneth Campbell, "An Analysis of Provisions of State Constitutions Affecting Support of Public Schools" (Ed.D. diss., Duke University, 1954), pp. 23–31; Edward C. Bolmeier, *The School in the Legal Structure* (Cincinnati, 1968), pp. 66–75.

2. Bolmeier, *School*, p. 63.

3. Council of State Governments, *The Forty-Eight State School Systems* (Chicago, 1948), and Legislative Reference Service, Library of Congress, *Federal Educational Activities and Educational Issues Before Congress* (Washington, 1951).

4. John Kaplan, "Segregation Litigation and the Schools— Part II: The General Northern Problem," 58 NORTHWEST-ERN UNIVERSITY L. REV. (1963) 162. For further discussion of the problem, see David K. Cohen, Thomas F. Pettigrew, and Robert T. Riley, "Race and the Outcomes of School-

ing," in Frederick Mosteller and Daniel P. Moynihan, eds., *On Equality of Educational Opportunity* (New York, 1972), pp. 343–366.

5. See, for example, Sweatt v. Painter, 339 U.S. 629 (1950); McLaurin v. Oklahoma State Regents, 339 U.S. 637 (1950); *Griffin* v. *Prince Edward County*, 377 U.S. 218 (1964).

6. Hobson v. Hansen, 269 F. Supp. 401 (1967).

7. J. Coleman, *et al.*, *Equality of Educational Opportunity* (Washington, 1966). See also P. Sexton, *Education and Income* (New York, 1961); D. Hunter, *The Slums* (New York, 1964); A. Wise, *Rich Schools, Poor Schools: The Promises of Equal Educational Opportunity* (Chicago, 1968); C. Benson, *The Economics of Public Education* (Boston, 1961); and David L. Kirp, "The Poor, the Schools, and Equal Protection," in *Education and the Legal Structure* (Cambridge, Mass., 1971), pp. 1–34.

8. John E. Coons, *et al.*, *Private Wealth and Public Education* (Cambridge, Mass., 1970). For the financing policies in other states, see J. Thomas Dunn, "The Double Standard in Public Education, Part II—Wealth Discrimination," 10 AMERICAN BUSINESS L. JOUR. (1973) 231–265.

9. William Greider, " 'Novel Theory' of School Spending Cashiered by Court," *The Washington Post*, 22 March 1973, p. A 16.

10. Serrano v. Priest, 5 Cal. 3d 584 (1971); 96 Cal. Reptr. 601 (1971). For an interesting article discussing the implications of this decision, see James Warren Beebe, "School Financing—*Serrano v. Priest:* The Death Knell to Ad Valorem School Financing?" 44 PENNSYLVANIA BAR ASSOCIATION QUARTERLY (1973) 474–492.

11. Van Dusartz v. Hatfield, 334 F. Supp. 870 (1972); Robinson v. Cahill, 118 N.J. 223 (1972); Milliken v. Green, 54, 809, Mich. (1973); Hollins v. Shofstall, Civil No. C–253652, Ariz. (1972); Sweetwater County Planning Commission for the Organization of School Districts v. Hinkle, 491 P 2d 1234, Wyo. (1971), 493 P 2d 1050, Wyo. (1972).

12. Rodriguez v. San Antonio Independent School District, 337 F. Supp. 280 (1971).

13. San Antonio Independent School District v. Rodriguez, 36 L.Ed 2d 16 (1973).

14. *Ibid.*, p. 37.
15. *Ibid.*, pp. 37–40.
16. *Ibid.*, pp. 43–46.
17. *Ibid.*, p. 57.
18. *Ibid.*, p. 52.
19. *Ibid.*, pp. 64–101.
20. *Ibid.*, pp. 60–64.
21. John E. Coons, "Financing Public Schools After 'Rodriguez,'" *Saturday Review-World*, 9 October 1973, pp. 44–47.
22. "San Antonio Independent School District v. Rodriguez— Commentary," 2 JOURNAL OF L. AND EDUC. (1973) 461–484; Paul D. Carrington, "Financing the American Dream: Equality and School Taxes," 73 COLUMBIA L. REV. (1973) 1226–1260; "Disparity in Financing Public Education: Is There an Alternative to Rodriguez?" 8 UNIVERSITY OF RICHMOND L. REV. (1973) 88–97; and Pat Goss, "Equal Protection and School Finance," 26 ARKANSAS L. REV. (1973) 508– 533.
23. "Court Backs Property Tax for Schools, But—," *U.S. News and World Report*, 2 April 1973, p. 91.
24. McInnis v. Shapiro, 293 F. Supp 327 (1968), affirmed *sub nomine* McInnis v. Ogilvie, 394 U.S. 322 (1969).
25. Askew v. Hargrave, 401 U.S. 476 (1971).
26. Florida Laws, sec. 23, chap. 68–18 (F.S.A., sec. 236.251, 1968).
27. Hargrave v. Kirk, 313 F. Supp. 944 (1970).
28. S. Bowles, "Toward Educational Opportunity," *Harvard Educational Review* 38 (1968): 90.
29. David L. Kirp, "The Poor," p. 140.
30. Christopher Jenks, *Inequality, a Reassessment of the Effect of Family and Schooling in America* (New York, 1972). A similar thesis has been espoused by Everett Reimer, *School is Dead: Alternatives in Education* (New York, 1972).
31. Coleman, *Equality*, p. 325.
32. Michael S. Sorgen, Patrick S. Duffy, William A. Kaplin, Ephraim Margolin, *State, School, and Family* (New York, 1973), pp. K 13–49, 50.
33. Economic Opportunity Act, 42 U.S.C., sec. 2781–2791; Elementary and Secondary Education Act, 20 U.S.C., sec. 241a–411.

34. Philip B. Kurland, "Equal Educational Opportunity: The Limits of Constitutional Jurisprudence Undefined," 35 UNIVERSITY OF CHICAGO L. REV. (1969) 591.
35. Rodriguez, pp. 48–49. Sources referred to in the decision on this question are in fn. 85 and 86, pp. 48–49.
36. Sailors v. Board of Education, 387 U.S. 105 (1967).
37. Kramer v. Union Free School District, 395 U.S. 621 (1969).
38. Hadley v. Junior College District, 397 U.S. 50 (1970).
39. Among these cases are: Wesberry v. Sanders, 376 U.S. 1 (1964); Reynolds v. Sims, 377 U.S. 533 (1964); WMCA, Inc. v. Lomenzo, 377 U.S. 633 (1964); Maryland Committee v. Tawes, 377 U.S. 656 (1964); Davis v. Mann, 377 U.S. 678 (1964); Roman v. Sincock, 377 U.S. 695 (1964); Lucas v. Colorado General Assembly, 377 U.S. 713 (1964).
40. Hadley, p. 52.
41. Ibid., p. 55.
42. Turner v. Fouche, 396 U.S. 346 (1970).
43. Ibid., pp. 362–363.
44. Ibid., pp. 363–364.

CHAPTER 7. PRIVATE AND RELIGIOUS SCHOOLS

1. Clark Spurlock, *Education and the Supreme Court* (Urbana, Ill., 1955), p. 18.
2. Trustees of Dartmouth College v. Woodward, 4 Wheat. 518 (U.S. 1819).
3. Donald G. Tewksbury, *The Founding of American Colleges and Universities before the Civil War* (New York, 1932), p. 14; Newton Edwards and Herman G. Richey, *The School in the American Social Order* (Boston, 1947), pp. 251–253.
4. Elwood Cubberly, *Public Education in the United States* (Boston, 1934), p. 272.
5. Tewksbury, *Founding*, pp. 55–129; 133–183.
6. H. G. Good, *A History of American Education* (New York, 1956), p. 99. Cubberly concluded that "since the states could not change charters and transform old establishments, they began to turn to the creation of state universities of their own." In *Public Education*, p. 272.
7. R. Freeman Butts and Lawrence Cremin, *A History of Educa-*

tion in American Culture (New York, 1953), pp. 210–211; 264–265.

8. F. A. P. Barnard, "On Improvements Practicable in American Colleges," *American Journal of Education and College Review* 1 (1856): 176.

9. For a comprehensive biographical study of Girard, see Harry Emerson Wildes, *Lonely Midas: The Story of Stephen Girard* (New York, 1943).

10. Edgar W. Knight and Clifton L. Hall, *Readings in American Educational History* (Chapel Hill, N.C., 1951), pp. 252, 254.

11. Vidal v. Girard's Executors, 2 How. 127 (U.S. 1844).

12. Spurlock, *Education*, p. 71.

13. *Ibid.*, pp. 184–185.

14. Berea College v. Commonwealth of Kentucky, 211 U.S. 45 (1908).

15. *Ibid.*

16. Spurlock, *Education*, p. 186.

17. *International Text-Book Co.* v. *Pigg*, 277 U.S. 91 (1910).

18. See Newton Edwards, *The Courts and the Public Schools* (Chicago, 1958); p. 29. The number of states that had all instruction being given in English in the private schools totaled thirty-one. Butts and Cremin, *History*, p. 525. For a discussion of the legal problems involved in teaching foreign languages immediately after World War I, see I. N. Edwards, "The Legal Status of Foreign Languages in the Schools," *Elementary School Journal* 24 (1923): 270.

19. Meyer v. Nebraska, 262 U.S. 390 (1923)

20. *Ibid.*

21. Farrington v. Tokushige, 273 U.S. 284 (1927).

22. Stainback v. Mo Hock Ke Lok Po, 336 U.S. 368 (1949).

23. Meyer v. Nebraska, 262 U.S. 390 (1923).

24. Pierce v. Society of Sisters, 268 U.S. 535 (1925).

25. Donald E. Boles, *The Two Swords* (Ames, Iowa, 1967), p. 307.

26. John L. Childs, *Education and Morals: An Experimentalist Philosophy of Education* (New York, 1950), p. 242.

27. *The Saturday Review of Literature*, 3 May 1952, p. 11.

28. Hollis L. Caswell, "The Great Reappraisal of Public Education," *Teachers College Record* 54 (1952) 12–22.

29. Theodore Brameld, *Patterns of Educational Philosophy: A Democratic Interpretation* (New York, 1950), pp. 39, 665.

30. Americo D. Lapati, " 'Not the Mere Creature of the State': The Supreme Court and Parental Rights in Education," *Notre Dame Journal of Education* 4 (1973): 363.

31. Wisc. Stat. Ann., sec. 118.15.

32. Wisconsin v. Yoder, 406 U.S. 205 (1972).

33. *Ibid.*, pp. 213–214.

34. *Ibid.*, pp. 218–219.

35. *Ibid.*, p. 222.

36. *Ibid.*, p. 245. Justice Douglas, in matters of the rights of children, was referring to Haley v. Ohio, 332 U.S. 596 (1948); In re Gault, 387 U.S. 1 (1967); In re Winship, 397 U.S. 358 (1972); Tinkner v. Des Moines School District, 393 U.S. 503; Board of Education v. Barnette, 319 U.S. 624 (1943).

37. "Amish Education," *Church and State* 26 (1973): 75.

38. Wisconsin v. Yoder, pp. 207–210. See also J. Hostetler, *Amish Society* (Baltimore, 1968); and J. Hostetler and G. Huntington, *Children in Amish Society* (New York, 1971).

39. Joseph F. Costanzo, *This Nation Under God* (New York, 1964), p. 178. Costanzo has argued that "ordinances are highly meaningful because they were incorporated into the constitutions of the several states which arose from these territories."

40. *American State Papers,* IV, Class 2 Indian Affairs 54 (Cong. 1832).

41. *Ibid.*, I Class 2 Indian Affairs 687 (Cong. 1803). In reference to "this historic instance," Costanzo has written that "the President and Congress supported the sulvention of one religion and one church without any intent or effect of conferring upon it a preferential status in law or discriminating advantages by benefit of law." Costanzo, *This Nation*, p. 179.

42. See Felix S. Cohen, *Handbook of Federal Indian Law* (Albuquerque, 1972), pp. 238–242.

43. 30 Stat. 62, 79 (1897). Included in the same law was a provision that stated that appropriations could continue in diminishing sums until 1900.

44. Quick Bear v. Leupp, 210 U.S. 50 (1908).

45. *Ibid.*

46. Spurlock, *Education*, p. 75.

47. Mooney v. Bell, 8 Ohio 658 (1901).

48. Smith v. Donahue, 195 N.Y.S. 715 (1922).

49. Boles, *Two Swords,* p. 118.

50. Cochran v. Louisiana State Board of Education, 281 U.S. 370 (1930).

51. Spurlock, *Education,* p. 78.

52. "Should Taxpayers Support Non-public Schools," *U.S. News and World Report,* 2 December 1955, p. 35. This article listed six states for the year 1955. Rhode Island passed a textbook law in 1963 and New York in 1966.

53. "Cases of Interest—Statute Providing for Free School Books Held Unconstitutional," 34 L. Notes (1931) 233; "Notes—The Furnishing of Free Textbooks to Private Schools," 25 Illinois L. Rev. (1931) 547. A comment in a Roman Catholic periodical is interesting concerning the possible implications of the decision: "May it not be deduced . . . that state educational authorities might justifiably claim other forms of control (besides textbooks) in the interest of education." See "Free Textbooks Constitutional," *Commonweal* 12 (1930): 35. It is to be noted that at this time in American history Roman Catholics were opposing state aid to schools because they feared state control.

54. Chance v. Mississippi State Textbook Rating and Purchasing Board, 190 Miss. 453 (1941).

55. Haas v. Independent School District, 69 S.D. 303 (1943).

56. Dickman v. School District, 232 Ore. 238 (1961).

57. The *Dickman* decision received severe criticism for its rejection of the child-benefit theory and for espousing such a complete separation of church and state called for by neither the federal nor the Oregon State constitutions: "If the court intends the term 'benefit' to include all indirect and incidental benefits, however remote, it imperils all state support of hospitals, child-care agencies, and other charitable institutions if maintained by a religious group." See "Recent Cases—Oregon Textbook Statute Unconstitutional as a Benefit to a Religious Institution," 31 Univ. of Cincinnati L. Rev. (1962) 335.

58. *Public Papers of the Presidents, John F. Kennedy* (Washington, 1961), p. 108.

59. "Memorandum on Aid to Education," Costanzo, *This Nation,* p. 229.

60. *Ibid.*
61. Cochran, p. 370. Spurlock also makes this point in *Education,* p. 77.
62. Everson, p. 1.
63. N.Y. Sess. Laws 1950, c. 239.
64. N.Y. Sess. Laws 1965, c. 320.
65. N.Y. Sess. Laws 1966, c. 795.
66. Board of Education v. Allen, 392 U.S. 240 (1968).
67. *Ibid.,* p. 243.
68. *Ibid.,* pp. 246–248.
69. *Ibid.,* pp. 249–250.
70. *Ibid.,* pp. 250–254.
71. *Ibid.,* pp. 254–269.
72. *Ibid.,* pp. 269–272.
73. Paul A. Freund, "Public Aid to Parochial Schools," 82 HARVARD L. REV. (1969) 1680.
74. Flast v. Cohen, 392 U.S. 83 (1968).
75. Frothingham v. Mellon, 262 U.S. 447 (1923).
76. Flast, p. 103. Almost $1 billion was appropriated to implement the Elementary and Secondary Education Act in 1965. See P. L. 89–10 (1965).
77. Oklahoma Railway v. St. Joseph's Parochial School, 33 Okl. 755 (1912).
78. Lewis v. Board of Education, 275 N. Y. 480, 544 (1937).
79. State ex rel. Van Straten v. Milquet, 180 Wis. 190 (1923); State ex rel. Traub v. Brown, 36 Del. 181 (1934).
80. Board of Education v. Wheat, 174 Md. 314 (1938); Adams v. County Commissioners, 180 Md. 550 (1942); Nichols v. Henry, 301 Ky. 434 (1946); Hlebanja v. Brewe, 58 S.D. 351 (1931); Schlitz v. Piston, 66 S.D. 301 (1938).
81. Sheffard v. Jefferson County Board of Education, 294 Ky. 469 (1943); Mitchell v. Consolidated School, 17 Wash. 2d 61 (1943); Costigan v. Hall, 249 Wis. 94 (1946); Gurney v. Ferguson, 190 Okl. 254 (1942); Judd v. Board of Education, 278 N.Y. 200 (1938). Subsequently the 1938 constitutional convention proposed an amendment to the New York State constitution (art. 11, sec. 4) to permit the state legislature to provide for the expenditure of public funds for the transportation of children to and from any school; the constitutionality of the amendment was later affirmed in Board of

Education v. Allen, 192 N. Y. 2d 186 (1959).

82. Bowker v. Baker, 73 C. A. 2d 653, 167 P. 2d 256 (1946).

83. Boles, *Two Swords*, pp. 5, 26.

84. Knight and Hall, *Readings*, pp. 767–768.

85. Everson v. Board of Education, 330 U.S. 1 (1947).

86. *Ibid.*, p. 18.

87. *Ibid.*, pp. 17–18.

88. See, for example, Wilfrid Parsons, *The First Freedom* (New York, 1948); Chester James Antieau, Arthur T. Downey, and Edward C. Roberts, *Freedom from Federal Establishment: Formation and Early History of the First Amendment Religion Clauses* (Milwaukee, Wisc., 1964); Anson Phelps Stokes, *Church and State in the United States*, 3 vols. (New York, 1950); Edward S. Corwin, *The Constitution and What It Means Today* (Princeton, N.J., 1954); Loren P. Beth, *The American Theory of Church and State* (Miami, Fla., 1958); Evarts B. Greene, *Religion and the State: The Making and Testing of an American Tradition* (New York, 1941).

89. Everson, pp. 15–16.

90. Lapati, " 'Not the Mere Creature of the State,' " pp. 364–371.

91. Everson, p. 20.

92. Everson, p. 45.

93. Leo Pfeffer, "Religion, Education and the Constitution," 8 LAWYERS GUILD REV. (1948) 387. Writing in 1953, Pfeffer expressed the fear that "when the *Everson* decision is coupled with the *Cochran* decision, they lead logically to the conclusion that the state may, notwithstanding the First Amendment, finance practically every aspect of parochial education, with the exception of such comparatively minor items as the proportionate salaries of teachers while they teach the catechism." *Church, State, and Freedom* (Boston, 1953), p. 476.

94. Thomas Reed Powell, "Public Rides to Private Schools," *Harvard Educational Review* 17 (1947): 73. A similar view was expressed by B. H. Jarman, "Religious Education and the Public Schools," *School and Society* 67 (1948): 44.

95. J. L. Toner, "Does A. F. T. Support 'Zeal for Democracy' Program?" *The American Teacher* 32 (1948): 2.; Kenneth R. and Daniel E. O'Brien, "Separation of Church and State in

Restatement of Inter-Church-and-State Common Law," *The Jurist* 7 (1947): 259.

96. John C. Murray, "Law or Prepossessions?" *Law and Contemporary Problems* 14 (1949): 23.; E. H. Dana, "Mounting Church-State Issues: Time for a Showdown," *Education* 69 (1948): 124.

97. W. A. Wetzel, "Religious Education, A Layman's Analysis," *National Association of Secondary School Principals Bulletin* 33 (1949): 66.

98. Connell v. Board of School Directors, 356 Pa. 585 (1947); Silver Lake Consolidated School District v. Parker, 238 Ia. 984 (1947); State ex rel. Church of Nazarene v. Fogo, 150 Ohio 45 (1948); McVey v. Hawkins, 346 Mo. 44 (1953); Snyder v. Town of Newton, 147 Conn. 374 (1960); Board of Education v. Antone, Okl., 384 P. 2d 911 (1963); Rawlings v. Butler, Ky., 209 S.W. 2d 801 (1956); Squires v. Inhabitants, 155 Me. 151 (1959); Wooley v. Spalding, Ky., 293 S.W. 2d 563 (1956); School District v. Houghton, 387 Pa. 236 (1956).

99. Robert C. Drinan, *Religion, the Courts, and Public Policy* (New York, 1963), pp. 140–141.

100. Robert E. Cushman, *Leading Constitutional Decisions* (New York, 1950), p. 145.

101. 20 U.S.C. 751.

102. Douglas C. Wilson, "Church School Aid Question Is Argued Before High Court," *Providence Journal*, 3 March 1971, p. 3.

103. Tilton v. Finch, 312 F. Supp. 1191 (1970).

104. Lemon v. Kurtzman, 403 U.S. 783–789 (1971).

105. Tilton v. Richardson, 403 U.S. 674–689 (1971).

106. *Ibid.*, pp. 689–697.

107. See fn. 104 *supra.*

108. R.I. Gen Laws Ann., sec. 16–51–1 et seq. (Supp. 1970).

109. *Providence Journal*, 29 June 1971, p. 24.

110. Pa. Stat. Ann., Tit: 24, sec. 5601–5609 (Supp. 1971).

111. *Providence Journal*, 29 June 1971, p. 24.

112. Walz v. Tax Commission, 397 U.S. 664 (1970).

113. Lemon v. Kurtzman, 403 U.S. 606–625 (1971).

114. *Ibid.*, pp. 625–642.

115. *Ibid.*, p. 642.

116. *Ibid.*, pp. 642–661.
117. *Ibid.*, pp. 661–671.
118. *Providence Journal,* 29 June 1971, p. 6.
119. Charles M. Whelan, "The School Aid Decisions," *America* (July 10, 1971), p. 11.
120. Lemon v. Kurtzman, 348 F. Supp. 300 (1972).
121. *Ibid.*, 411 U.S. 192 (1973).
122. *Ibid.*, in 36 L. Ed. 2d No. 1 (April 23, 1973), pp. 151–152.
123. Brusca v. Missouri, 409 U.S. 1050 (1972).
124. *Ibid.*, 332 F. Supp. 275 (1971).
125. Essex v. Wolman, 409 U.S. 808 (1972).
126. Wolman v. Essex, 342 F. Supp. 399 (1972).
127. State ex rel. the School District of Hartington v. Nebraska State Board of Education, 188 Neb. 1, 195 N.W. 2d 161 (1972).
128. Nebraska State Board of Education v. School District of Hartington, 409 U.S. 921 (1972).
129. S.C. Code Ann., sec. 22–41.4 (1971).
130. *Ibid.*, 22–41.2(b)
131. Hunt v. McNair, 255 S.C. 71 (1970); 258 S.C. 97 (1972).
132. *Ibid.*, 93 S. Ct. 2868 (1973).
133. *Ibid.*, pp. 2877–2880.
134. N.Y. Laws 1972, c. 414, amending N.Y. Educ. Law, art. 12, sec. 549–553 (McKinney Supp. 1972).
135. Committee for Public Education and Religious Liberty v. Nyquist, 93 S. Ct. 2955 (1973).
136. N.Y. Laws 1972, c. 414, amending N.Y. Educ. Law, art. 12, sec. 559 (1).
137. *Ibid.*, 559 (3).
138. Nyquist, pp. 2960–2968.
139. N. Y. Laws 1972, c. 414, amending N. Y. Educ Law, sec. 612(c), 612(j).
140. Nyquist, pp. 2968–2971.
141. N.Y. Laws 1970, c. 138, sec. 2.
142. Levitt v. Committee for Public Education and Liberty, 93 S. Ct. 2814 (1973).
143. Lemon v. Kurtzman, 403 U.S. 602 (1971).
144. Law of Pa. 1971, Act 92, Pa. Stat. Ann., sec. 5701–5709 (Supp. 1972).

145. Sloan v. Lemon, 93 S. Ct. 2982 (1973). The Court had held similarly in Brusca v. State Board of Education, 405 U.S. 1050 (1972) in affirming 332 F. Supp. 275 (1971).
146. Nyquist, pp. 2971–2982.
147. Miss. Code of 1942, sec. 6634.
148. Norwood v. Harrison, 340 F. Supp. 1003 (1972).
149. Norwood v. Harrison, 93 S. Ct. 2804 (1973).
150. Grit v. Wolman, 413 U.S. 901 (1973).
151. Kosydar v. Wolman, 353 F. Supp. 744 (1972).
152. P.L. 89–10 (1965), sec. 101.
153. Barrera v. Wheeler, 441 F. 2d 795 (1971).
154. *Ibid.*, 475 F. 2d 1338 (1973).
155. Wheeler v. Barrera, 42 LW 4877 (1974).
156. *Ibid.*, pp. 4881–4882.
157. *Ibid.*, pp. 4883–4884.
158. *Ibid.*, pp. 4884–4885.
159. *Ibid.*, p. 4886.
160. *Church and State* 27 (1974): 12.
161. Charles M. Whelan, " 'Barrera': Hope for the Children," *America,* June 29, 1974, p. 514.

CHAPTER 8. RELIGIOUS TEACHING AND ACTIVITIES IN PUBLIC SCHOOLS

1. R. Freeman Butts and Lawrence A. Cremin, *A History of Education in American Culture* (New York, 1953), p. 547; William R. Hazard, *Education and the Law* (New York, 1971), p. 49.
2. Robert R. Hamilton and Paul R. Mort, *The Law and Public Education* (Chicago, 1941), p. 29.
3. Hazard, *Education,* p. 49.
4. Donald E. Boles, *The Two Swords* (Ames, Iowa, 1957), pp. 28–34.
5. McCollum v. Board of Education, 333 U.S. 212 (1948).
6. *Ibid.*, p. 212.
7. *Ibid.*, p. 227.
8. *Ibid.*, pp. 232–238.
9. *Ibid.*, pp. 238–256. See also Bradford v. Roberts, 175 U.S. 291 (1899).

10. F. E. Johnson, "Church, State and School," *Education* 71 (1951): 353.; S. P. Franklin, "Religious Education, A Layman's Analysis," *National Association of Secondary School Principals Bulletin* 33 (1949): 66; G. P. Schmidt, "Religious Liberty and the Supreme Court of the United States," 17 FORDHAM L. REV. (1948): 173; F. E. Johnson, "Religion and the Schools—What Can We Hope For," *Religious Education* 43 (1948): 201. Possibly the MARQUETTE L. REV. rendered the most scathing criticism as it declared that "the Founding Fathers believed in freedom *of* religion and not freedom *from* religion." It also stated: "Take away the 'Everson Amendment,' reinstate the First Amendment, and the *McCollum* decision is clearly wrong." "Result of the 'Everson Amendment'—The McCollum Case," (1948) 32:145; 138.

11. M. K. Remmlein, "The Legal Situation Resulting From the Recent Supreme Court Decision," *Religious Education* 43 (1948): 211.; "Supreme Court Bans Released-Time Classes," *Education Digest* 13 (1948): 4.

12. Clark Spurlock, *Education and the Supreme Court* (Urbana, Ill., 1955), p. 123.

13. Wilfrid Parsons, *The First Freedom* (New York, 1948), p. 178.

14. E. S. Corwin, "The Supreme Court as a National School Board," *Law and Contemporary Problems* 14 (1949): 1; John C. Murray, "Law or Presuppositions?" in *ibid.*, p. 23; A. Meiklejohn, "Education Cooperation Between Church and State," in *ibid.*, p. 61.

15. Milton R. Konvitz in Boles, *Two Swords*, p. 45.

16. Leo Pfeffer, "Religion, Education and the Constitution," *Lawyers Guild Review* 8 (1948): 387.

17. Boles, *Two Swords*, p. 46.

18. Boles, *Two Swords*, p. 47; Butts and Cremin, *History*, p. 548.

19. Zorach v. Clauson, 343 U.S. 309 (1952).

20. *Ibid.*, p. 315.

21. *Ibid.*, p. 314.

22. *Ibid.*, p. 318.

23. *Ibid.*, p. 321.

24. *Ibid.*, p. 323.

25. *Ibid.*, p. 324.

26. "Comments—Released Time," 26 SOUTHERN CALIFORNIA

L. Rev. (1953) 186; "Constitutionality of the New York Released Time Program," 49 Columbia L. Rev. (1949) 826.

27. American Jewish Committee, "Religion in Public Education," *Religious Education* 50 (1955): 232.

28. R. B. Tapp, "Released Time for Religious Education?" *National Education Association Journal* 47 (1958): 573.

29. "Current Decisions—'Released Time' Held Valid if School Buildings Not Used," 25 Rocky Mountain L. Rev. (1952) 104.

30. E. L. Shaver, "Weekday Religious Education Secures Its Charter and Faces a Challenge," *Religious Education* 48 (1953): 38; L. A. Weigle, "Crisis of Religion in Education," *Religious Education* 49 (1954): 73.

31. G. E. Reed, "Church and the Zorach Case," *Notre Dame Lawyer* 27 (1952): 529. J. Larson also regarded the dismissed-time plan's approval by the Court as consistent with America's tradition of separation of church and state and saw no merit in the divisiveness argument. See "Released Time for Religious Education," *National Education Association Journal* 47 (1958): 572.

32. J. Lookstein, "Strategies for Making Adequate Provision of Religious Education for All Our Young," *Religious Education* 49 (1954): 95.

33. Engel v. Vitale, 370 U.S. 424 (1962).

34. "Comment," 20 Vanderbilt L. Rev. (1966–67) 1083–1113.

35. State courts upholding the Lord's Prayer, usually combined with Bible reading were: Moore v. Monroe, 64 Iowa 367 (1884); Billiard v. Board of Education, 69 Kan. 53 (1904); Church v. Bullock, 104 Tex. 1 (1908); Knowlton v. Baumhover, 182 Iowa 691 (1918); State ex rel. Finger v. Weedman, 55 S. D. 343 (1929); Doremus v. Board of Education, 5 N.J. 435 (1950); and Murray v. Curlett, 228 Md. 239 (1962). State courts holding such exercises as unconstitutional were: People ex rel. Ring v. Board of Education, 245 Ill. 335 (1910), and Herold v. Parish Board of Education, 136 La. 1034 (1915).

36. New York Board of Regents, *Statement on Moral and Spiritual Training in the Schools* (Albany, N. Y., 1951).

37. "Teaching Is Urged on Moral Values," *New York Times*, 29 March 1955.

38. Engel, pp. 424–425.
39. *Ibid.,* pp. 445–450.
40. Boles, *Two Swords,* pp. 74–77, 80–82.
41. Charles E. Rice in the *American Bar Association,* quoted from *ibid.,* p. 75.
42. News service report, *New York Times,* November 8, 1971.
43. R. B. Dierenfield, "Religion in Public Schools," *Religious Education* 68 (1973): 99.
44. *Washington Post,* 9 November 1971, pp. A1, 6.
45. *Twelfth Annual Report of the Board of Education, Together With The Twelfth Annual Report of the Secretary of the Board* (Boston, 1849), pp. 116–117.
46. Francis X. Curran, *The Churches and the Schools* (Chicago, 1954), pp. 34, 55, 94, 130.
47. *Ibid.,* pp. 8–9; Butts and Cremin, *History,* pp. 215–216; *New York Freeman's Journal,* vol. I, no. 2 (July 11, 1840), p. 12; Ray A. Billington, *The Protestant Crusade* (New York, 1938), pp. 142 ff.; George H. Martin, *Evolution of the Massachusetts Public School System* (New York, 1894), p. 230; Arthur J. Hall, *Religious Education in Public Schools* (Chicago, 1914), p. 55.
48. Donahue v. Richards, 38 Maine 376 (1854).
49. Carter v. Bland, 199 Tenn. 665 (1956); Kaplan v. Independent School District, 171 Minn. 142 (1927); Wilkerson v. Rome, 152 Ga. 762 (1922); Church v. Bullock, 104 Tex. 1 (1908); Hackett v. Brooksville Graded School District, 120 Ky. 608 (1905); Billiard v. Board of Education, 69 Kan. 53 (1904); Pfeiffer v. Board of Education, 118 Mich. 560 (1898); Moore v. Monroe, 64 Iowa 367 (1884).
50. Weiss v. District Board, City of Edgerton, 76 Wisc. 177 (1890).
51. State ex rel. Finger v. Weedman, 55 S. D. 343 (1929); State ex rel. Dearle v. Frazier, 102 Wash. 369 (1918); Herold v. Parish Board of School Directors, 136 La. 1034 (1915); People ex rel. Ring v. Board of Education, 245 Ill. 334 (1910); State ex rel. Freeman v. Scheve, 65 Neb. 853 (1902).
52. Doremus v. Board of Education, 342 U.S. 429 (1952).
53. Gideons International v. Tudor, 348 U.S. 816 (1954).
54. Abington School District v. Schempp, 374 U.S. 203 (1963).
55. 24 Pa. Stat., sec. 15–1516, as amended, P.L. 1928 (Supp. 1960) Dec. 17, 1959.

56. Murray v. Curlett, 374 U.S. 203 (1963).

57. Murray v. Curlett, 228 Md. 239 (1962).

58. Schemmp, pp. 222–226.

59. *Ibid.*, p. 229.

60. *Ibid.*, pp. 232–265.

61. *Ibid.*, pp. 266–304.

62. *Ibid.*, pp. 305–308.

63. *Ibid.*, pp. 309–310.

64. *Ibid.*, p. 313.

65. *Ibid.*, pp. 315–316.

66. Hazard, *Education,* p. 60.

67. Donald E. Boles, *The Bible, Religion and the Public Schools* (Ames, Iowa, 1965), p. 60.

68. *Ibid.*

69. Leo Pfeffer, *Church, State and Freedom* (Boston, 1967), p. 474.

70. Hazard, *Education,* p. 64.

71. Johns v. Allen, 231 F. Supp. 852 (1964); Adams v. Engelking, 232 F. Supp. 666 (1964); Attorney General v. School Committee, 347 Mass. 775 (1964); Sills v. Board of Education, 42 N.J. 351 (1965).

72. McGowan v. Maryland, 366 U.S. 420 (1961).

73. Chamberlain v. Dade County Board of Public Instruction, 377 U.S. 402 (1964).

74. Hazard, *Education,* p. 64.

75. R. B. Dierenfield, "Religion in the Public Schools: Its Current Status," *Religious Education* 68 (1973): 101.

76. Boles, *Two Swords,* pp. 111–112.

77. "Supreme Court Decision on Bible Reading and Prayer Recitation," *National Education Association Journal* 52 (1963): 55.; American Jewish Committee, "Religion in Public Education," *Religious Education* 50 (1955): 232., and entire issue of *Religious Education* 59, (Nov.–Dec., 1964).

78. Boles, *Two Swords,* pp. 112–113; Frederick A. Olafson, "Teaching About Religion: Some Reservations," *Harvard Educational Review* 37 (1967): 238; Niels C. Nielsen, Jr., *God in Education* (New York, 1966), pp. 153–163.

79. Burstyn v. Wilson, 343 U.S. 495 (1952).

80. Rosenberg v. Board of Education of the City of New York, 196 N. Y. Misc. 542 (1949).

81. Richard E. Morgan, *The Supreme Court and Religion* (New York, 1972), p. 156.

82. Tenn., Acts of 1925, chap. 27.
83. Scopes v. State, 154 Tenn. 105 (1927).
84. Epperson v. Arkansas, 393 U.S. 97 (1968).
85. *Ibid.*, p. 106.
86. *Ibid.*, pp. 107, 109.
87. Morgan, *Supreme Court*, p. 157.
88. Anderson v. Laird, 409 U.S. 1076 (1972).
89. Anderson v. Laird, 466 F. 2d 283 (1972).

CHAPTER 9. TEACHERS

1. Louis Fischer and David Schimmel, *The Civil Rights of Teachers* (New York, 1973), p. 1.
2. *Ibid.*, pp. 3–4.
3. R. Freeman Butts and Lawrence Cremin, *A History of Education in American Culture* (New York, 1953), p. 131.
4. Edgar W. Knight and Clifton Hall, *Readings in American Educational History* (Chapel Hill, N.C., 1951), pp. 35–36.
5. *Ibid.*, pp. 36–38.
6. David Mack, "The Claims of Our Age and Country Upon Teachers," *The Introductory Discourse, and the Lectures Delivered Before the American Institute of Instruction, August, 1839* (Boston, 1840), p. 138.
7. J. W. Allen, "The Teacher Is An Agent, Not a Servant," *The Lectures Delivered Before the American Institute of Instruction, August, 1864* (Boston, 1865), p. 43.
8. Thomas Cushing, Jr., "The Teacher in the Nineteenth Century," *The Lectures Delivered Before the American Institute of Instruction, August, 1951* (Boston, 1951), p. 76.
9. For extensive, in-depth studies of the status of teachers in American history, see Howard K. Beale, *Are American Teachers Free?* (New York, 1936), and Willard S. Elsbree, *The American Teacher* (New York, 1939). For the role of teachers' organizations in improving the standards and in securing the rights of teachers, see Myron Liebermann and Michael H. Moskow, *Collective Negotiations for Teachers: An Approach to School Administration* (Chicago, 1966), and Timothy M. Stinnet, *Turmoil in Teaching: A History of the Organizational Struggle for America's Teachers* (New York, 1968).

10. Meyer v. Nebraska, 262 U.S. 390 (1923).

11. H. G. Good, *A History of American Education* (New York, 1956), pp. 513–514.

12. Phelps v. Board of Education, 300 U.S. 319 (1937). The Court judged the reduction of salaries as "a regulation of the conduct of the board and not a term of a continuing contract of indefinite duration with the individual teachers."

13. Head v. University of Missouri, 19 Wall 526 (U.S. 1874).

14. Indiana ex rel. Anderson v. Brand, 303 U.S. 95 (1938).

15. *Ibid.*

16. For a review of the many cases and problems involving teacher employment and dismissal decided in cases before state courts, see Robert R. Hamilton and Paul R. Mort, *The Law and Public Education* (Brooklyn, N. Y., 1959), pp. 357–462; Newton Edwards, *The Court and the Public Schools* (Chicago, 1946), pp. 402–468; and William R. Hazard, *Education and the Law* (New York, 1971), pp. 293–301; 358–375.

17. Butts and Cremin, *History,* pp. 455–456; and Hazard, *Education,* pp. 277–279; 281–288.

18. The AAUP has issued the following statements on the issues of tenure and academic freedom: 1940 Statement on Principles on Academic Freedom and Tenure, 1958 Statement on Procedural Standards in Faculty Dismissal Proceedings, 1961 Statement on Recruitment and Resignation of Faculty Members, 1964 Statement on Standards for Notice of Non-reappointment, 1966 Statement on Governance of Colleges and Universities, 1968 Recommended Institutional Regulations on Academic Freedom and Tenure. Report of Committee A on Academic Freedom and Tenure, "Procedural Standards in the Renewal or Nonrenewal of Faculty Appointments," *AAUP Bulletin* 56 (1970): 21. A policy of the *AAUP Bulletin* is to report on all cases involving academic freedom and tenure to its members and to the nation's academic community.

19. Dodge v. Board of Education of Chicago, 302 U.S. 74 (1937).

20. Madaline Kinter Remmlein, *School Law* (New York, 1950), p. 204.

21. Alston v. School Board of City of Norfolk, 112 F. 2d 995 (1940).

22. *Ibid.*, 311 U.S. 693 (1940). Although legal clarification exists against discrimination in salary schedules, the application of administrators of the principle in particular situations remains ambiguous. See the following cases decided by federal district courts: Reynolds v. Board of Education for Dade County, Florida, 148 F. 2d 754 (1945); Morris v. Williams, 149 F. 2d 703 (1945); Freeman v. County School Board, 82 F. Supp. 167 (1948).
23. Parker v. Board of Education, 382 U.S. 1030 (1966).
24. *Ibid.*, 348 F. 2d 464 (1965).
25. Johnson v. Branch, 385 U.S. 1003 (1967).
26. *Ibid.*, 364 F. 2d 177 (1966). Under North Carolina law all teachers' contracts are for one year only, renewable at the discretion of school authorities, which includes recommendation of the principal of the school where the teacher is employed.
27. Hazard, *Education,* pp. 307–326.
28. Fischer and Schimmel, *Civil,* p. 142.
29. *Ibid.*
30. Wisc. Stat., sec. 37.31(1), (1967).
31. Roth v. Board of Regents of State Colleges, 310 F. Supp. 972 (1970) and 446 F. 2d 806 (1971).
32. Board of Regents of State Colleges v. Roth, 408 U.S. 564 (1972).
33. *Ibid.*, pp. 580–92.
34. Sindermann v. Perry, 430 F. 2d 939 (1970).
35. Perry v. Sindermann, 408 U. S. 593 (1972). The Court similarly ruled in Pickering v. Board of Education, 391 U.S. 568 (1963).
36. *Ibid.*, p. 599.
37. *Ibid.*, p. 600.
38. *Ibid.*, pp. 601–602.
39. Weiss v. Walsh, 35 L. Ed. 2d 262 (1973).
40. *Ibid.*, 324 F. Supp. 75 (1971).
41. *Ibid.*, 461 F. 2d 846 (1972).
42. Cleveland Board of Education v. La Fleur, 39 L. Ed. 2d 52 (1974). The complete regulations for maternity leaves of the school boards in both cases are found in the fn., pp. 57–59, of the case.

43. Cohen v. Chesterfield County School Board, 39 L. Ed. 2d 52 (1974).
44. Eisenstadt v. Baird, 405 U.S. 438 (1972).
45. La Fleur, p. 60.
46. *Ibid.*, p. 61.
47. *Ibid.*, p. 62.
48. *Ibid.*, p. 64.
49. Wieman v. Updegraf, 344 U.S. 183 (1952).
50. Gerende v. Board of Supervisors, 341 U.S. 56 (1951).
51. Wieman, p. 196.
52. Wieman, p. 193.
53. Cramp v. Board of Public Instruction, 368 U.S. 278 (1961).
54. Baggett v. Bullitt, 377 U.S. 360 (1964).
55. Elfbrandt v. Russell, 381 U.S. 11 (1966).
56. Whitehill v. Elkins, 389 U.S. 54 (1967).
57. Connell v. Higginbotham, 403 U.S. 207 (1971).
58. Fischer and Schimmel, *Civil Rights*, p. 84.
59. *Ibid.*, pp. 84–85.
60. Clark Spurlock, *Education and the Supreme Court* (Urbana, Ill., 1955), pp. 137–138.
61. Adler v. Board of Education, 342 U.S. 485 (1952).
62. *Ibid.*, pp. 496–511.
63. Slochower v. Board of Education, 350 U.S. 551 (1956).
64. Sweezy v. New Hampshire, 354 U.S. 234 (1957).
65. *Ibid.*, pp. 249–250.
66. Beilan v. Board of Education of Philadelphia, 357 U.S. 399 (1958).
67. Adler, p. 493.
68. Lerner v. Casey, 357 U.S. 468 (1958).
69. Beilan, pp. 411–25.
70. Barenblatt v. United States, 360 U.S. 109 (1959).
71. *Ibid.*, pp. 134–66.
72. Shelton v. Tucker, 364 U.S. 479 (1960).
73. State ex rel. Wasilewski v. Board of School Directors, 370 U.S. 720 (1962).
74. *Ibid.*, 14 Wis. 2d 243, 111 N.W. 2d 198 (1961).
75. Keyishian v. Board of Regents of New York, 385 U.S. 589 (1967).
76. *Ibid.*, p. 607.
77. *Ibid.*, p. 603.

78. *Ibid.*, p. 614.
79. Fischer and Schimmel, *Civil Rights*, p. 94.
80. Pickering v. Board of Education of Township High School, 36 Ill. 2d 568, 225 N.E. 2d 1 (1967).
81. *Ibid.*, 391 U.S. 563 (1968).
82. *Ibid.*, p. 572.
83. *Ibid.*, pp. 572–73.
84. Board of Education v. James, 409 U.S. 1042 (1972) and 410 U.S. 947 (1973).
85. James v. Board of Education, 461 F. 2d 566 (1972).
86. Tinker v. Des Moines Independent School District, 393 U.S. 511 (1969).

CHAPTER 10. STUDENTS

1. For a convenient summary of state and federal court cases involving the rights of students, see William R. Hazard, *Education and the Law* (New York, 1971), pp. 205–276; and Edward C. Bolmeier, *Legal Limits of Authority over the Pupil* (Charlottesville, Va., 1970).
2. In re Gault, 387 U.S. 1 (1965).
3. For valuable studies and analyses of the issue of rights of students as to both educational and legal ramifications, see the following: Strahan, *The Courts and the Schools* (Lincoln, Nebraska, 1973), pp. 92–111; Grace W. Holmes, ed., *Student Protest and the Law* (Ann Arbor, Mich., 1969); Thomas A. Shannon, *The Developing Civil Rights of Students in the Public and Elementary Schools in 1970's* (San Diego, Cal., 1971); Anne Flowers and Edward C. Bolmeier, *Law and Pupil Control* (Cincinnati, 1964); American Council on Education, *A Judicial Document on Student Discipline* (Washington, 1969); Clarence J. Bakken, "Student Rights as Seen by a Lawyer-Educator," *Journal of College Student Personnel* 6 (1965): 136.; Joseph Katz and Nevitt Sanford, "The New Student Power and Needed Educational Reform," *Phi Delta Kappan* 47 (1966): 397.; and National School Public Relations Association, *Student Rights and Responsibilities, Courts Force Schools to Change* (Washington, 1972).
4. Jacobsen v. Massachusetts, 197 U.S. 11 (1905).

5. Zucht v. King, 260 U.S. 174 (1922).

6. *Ibid.* For a review of the many cases involving compulsory vaccination for all persons and school children, even those argued on the basis of religious reasons, in the various state courts, see Newton Edwards, *The Courts and the Public Schools* (Chicago, 1946), pp. 536–549. For a more recent state case, see Dalli v. Board of Education, 358 Mass. 753 (1971).

7. Itz v. Penick, 37 L. Ed. 152 (1973).

8. Itz v. Penick, 493 S.W. 2d 506 (1973).

9. Waugh v. Mississippi University, 273 U.S. 589 (1915).

10. See Hazard, *Education,* p. 160; Edward C. Bolmeier, "The Authority of School Boards to Limit the Attendance of Students Because of Marriage or Fraternity Membership," in Lee O. Garber, ed., *Current Legal Concepts in Education* (Philadelphia, 1966), pp. 148–162.

11. Pearson v. Cole, 290 U.S. 597 (1933).

12. Hamilton v. Regents of the University of California, 293 U.S. 245 (1934).

13. Harry G. Good and James D. Teller, *A History of American Education* (New York, 1973), p. 276. See also section on ROTC in chapter on "Higher Education."

14. For example, see Seeger v. United States, 380 U.S. 163 (1965); Welsh v. United States, 398 U.S. 333 (1970). For a more extensive discussion of this issue, see Richard E. Morgan, *The Supreme Court and Religion* (New York, 1972), pp. 164–182; and Mulfred Q. Sibley and Philip E. Jacob, *Conscription of Conscience: The American State and the Conscientious Objector* (Ithaca, New York, 1952).

15. These cases were Leoles v. Landers, 302 U.S. 656 (1937); Herring v. State Board of Education, 303 U.S. 624 (1938); Gabrielli v. Knickerbocker, 306 U.S. 621 (1939); and Johnson v. Deerfield, 306 U.S. 621 (1939).

16. Minersville School District v. Gobitis, 310 U.S. 586 (1940).

17. Victor W. Rotnem and F. G. Folsom, Jr., "Recent Restrictions upon Religious Liberty," *American Political Science Review* 36 (1942): 1053–1068.

18. West Virginia State Board of Education v. Barnette, 319 U.S. 624 (1943).

19. *Ibid.,* p. 637.

20. *Ibid.,* p. 647.

21. Donald E. Boles, *Two Swords* (Ames, Ia., 1957), pp. 148–149; 162–163; 168–170.
22. *Ibid.*, pp. 150–151; 169.
23. Alabama State Board of Education v. Dixon, 368 U.S. 930 (1961).
24. Hazard, *Education*, p. 228.
25. Dixon v. Alabama State Board of Education, 294 F. 2d 150 (1961).
26. D. Parker Young, *The Legal Aspects of Student Dissent and Discipline in Higher Education* (Athens, Ga., 1970), p. 36.
27. Tinker v. Des Moines Independent School District, 258 F. Supp. 971 (1966).
28. *Ibid.*, 383 F. 2d 988 (1967).
29. *Ibid.*, 393 U.S. 511 (1969).
30. *Ibid.*, pp. 512–513.
31. *Ibid.*, p. 514.
32. *Ibid.*, pp. 515–526.
33. Strahan, *The Courts*, p. 96.
34. Board of Education v. Scoville, 400 U.S. 826 (1970).
35. Scoville v. Board of Education, 425 F. 2d 10 (1970).
36. Esteban v. Central Missouri State College, 398 U.S. 965 (1970).
37. *Ibid.*, 415 F. 2d 1077 (1969).
38. *Ibid.*, p. 1089. In regard to regulation of student conduct, Stephen R. Goldstein has concluded: "Both in the *in loco parentis* doctrine and the doctrine of legislative delegation of authority lead to the same result: a state board has that power, and only that power, over student conduct and status which is properly related to its function of educating the pupils in its charge." In "The Scope and Source of School Board Authority to Regulate Student Conduct and Status: A Nonconstitutional Analysis," *University of Pennsylvania Law Review* 117 (1969): 373.
39. Wong v. Hayakawa, 409 U.S. 1130 (1973).
40. *Ibid.*, 464 F. 2d 1282 (1972).
41. Healy v. James, 319 F. Supp. 113 (1970).
42. *Ibid.*, 445 F. 2d 1122 (1971).
43. *Ibid.*, 408 U. S. 169 (1972).
44. *Ibid.*, pp. 171–194.
45. *Ibid.*, pp. 195–196, 201–203.

46. *Ibid.*, p. 197.
47. Breen v. Kahl, 398 U.S. 937 (1970).
48. *Ibid.*, 419 F. 2d 1034 (1969).
49. *Ibid.*, 296 F. Supp. 702 (1969). For an interesting case involving student dress, see Cordova v. Chonko, 315 F. Supp. 953 (1970).
50. Kirk v. Board of Regents of the University of California, 396 U.S. 554 (1970).
51. *Ibid.*, 273 Cal. App. 2d 430, 78 Cal. Rptr. 260 (1969).
52. Starns v. Malkerson, 401 U.S. 985 (1971).
53. *Ibid.*, 326 F. Supp 234 (1970). The plaintiffs sought to invoke the Supreme Court's decision in *Shapiro* as applicable to their case, for the Court had found that the one-year waiting period for welfare assistance had the effect of denying the basic necessities of life to needy residents; thus, the deterring effects on interstate movement by the use of the residency requirement was readily apparent. See Shapiro v. Thompson, 394 U.S. 618 (1969).
54. Conn. Gen. Stat., sec. 10–329 (b), as amended by Pub. Act No. 5, sec. 122 and sec. 126 a, 2, 3 (1971).
55. Kline v. Vlandis, 346 F. Supp. 526 (1972).
56. Vlandis v. Kline, 93 S. Ct. 2230 (1973).
57. *Ibid.*, p. 2236.
58. Ware v. Estes, 409 U.S. 1027 (1972).
59. *Ibid.*, 458 2d 1360 (1972); 328 F. Supp. 657 (1971).
60. NY Educ. Law, sec. 701, 703 (1971).
61. Johnson v. New York State Education Department, 319 F. Supp. 271 (1970) and 449 F. 2d 871 (1971).
62. *Ibid.*, 409 U.S. 75 (1973).
63. Lau v. Nichols, 483 F. 2d 791 (1973).
64. *Ibid.*, 94 S. Ct. 786 (1974).
65. 33 CFR, sec. 4955 (1968).
66. 35 CFR, sec. 11595 (1970).
67. Lau v. Nichols, p. 791.
68. U.S. Commission on Civil Rights, *Mexican-American Education Study* (Washington, 1971), p. 16.
69. T. Anderson and M. Boyer, *Bilingual Schooling in the United States* (Washington, 1970), p. 108.
70. De Funis v. Odegard, 42 LW 4578 (1974).
71. *Ibid.*, pp. 4588–4589.

72. *Ibid.*, pp. 4584–4585.
73. "Race as a Factor in Law School Admissions," *American Bar Association Journal,* April, 1974, p. 429.

CHAPTER 11. INTEGRATION

1. These laws of the various states can be found in Edgar W. Knight and Clifton L. Hall, *Readings in American Educational History* (Chapel Hill, N.C., 1951), pp. 661, 664–665, 666–667, 669–670.
2. *Ibid.*, pp. 666–667, 669.
3. R. Freeman Butts and Lawrence Cremin, *A History of Education in American Culture* (New York, 1953), pp. 250–251.
4. Dred Scott v. Sandford, 19 How. 393 (U.S. 1857).
5. For an in-depth study of education in the South, see Edgar W. Knight, *Public Education in the South* (Boston, 1922).
6. *Civil Rights Act of 1875,* 42 U.S. Code, sec. 1984 (1973).
7. Carl Brent Swisher, *Historic Decisions of the Supreme Court* (Princeton, N. J., 1958), pp. 91–94. Commenting on these cases, constitutional lawyer Swisher has pointed out that "by the time when cases involving the act reached the Supreme Court, in 1883, much of the country had grown weary of the perennial difficulties of giving protection to Negroes against discrimination. In this atmosphere of disillusionment, the Supreme Court held that the Fourteenth Amendment had not given Congress substantive power to correct abuses by the states. By this decision Congress was relieved of its basic obligation for the protection of the civil rights of Negroes. Again the Court showed itself more concerned with the federal balance of power than with substantive rights." In *ibid.*, pp. 91–92. See also *Civil Rights Cases,* 109 U.S. 3 (1883).
8. 13 Stat. 507 (1865).
9. Samuel Eliot Morrison and Henry Steele Commager, *The Growth of the American Republic* (New York, 1942), 2: 21.
10. *Report of the Commissioner of Education, 1892–93* (Washington, 1895), II: 1341–1414.
11. *Ibid.*, p. 1341.
12. *Ibid.*, pp. 1552–1553. See also Knight, *Public Education.*

13.   Knight and Hall, *Readings,* p. 685, 691; and *Report of the Commissioner of Education, 1892–93,* II: 1349, 1378, 1385, 1387, 1411.

14.   Roberts v. City of Boston, 59 Mass. 198 (1849).

15.   Plessy v. Ferguson, 163 U.S. 537 (1896)

16.   Cumming v. County Board of Education, 175 U.S. 528 (1899).

17.   Berea College v. Commonwealth of Kentucky, 211 U.S. 45 (1908).

18.   Gong Lum v. Rice, 275 U.S. 78 (1927).

19.   Missouri ex rel. Gaines v. Canada, 305 U.S. 337 (1938).

20.   Virgil A. Clift, "The History of Racial Segregation in American Education," *School and Society* 88 (1960): 223.

21.   *Ibid.,* p. 225.

22.   Sipuel v. Oklahoma, 332 U.S. 631 (1948).

23.   Fisher v. Hurst, 333 U.S. 147 (1948).

24.   Sweatt v. Painter, 339 U.S. 629 (1950).

25.   McLaurin v. Oklahoma State Regents, 339 U.S. 637 (1950).

26.   Clark Spurlock, *Education and the Supreme Court* (Urbana, Ill., 1955), p. 205.

27.   Sheeley v. Kramer, 334 U.S. 1 (1948).

28.   Henderson v. United States, 339 U.S. 816 (1950).

29.   President's Commission on Civil Rights, *To Secure These Rights* (New York, 1948).

30.   S. Robinson and T. Marshall, "An Evaluation of Recent Efforts to Achieve Racial Integration in Education Through Resort to the Courts," *Journal of Negro Education* 21 (1952): 332–336.

31.   Brown v. Board of Education, 347 U.S. 483 (1954). The Court cited authorities in sociology and psychology to substantiate its conclusion.

32.   Bolling v. Sharpe, 347 U.S. 497 (1954).

33.   Brown v. Board of Education, 349 U.S. 294 (1955).

34.   Clift, "History," pp. 228–229.

35.   Kern Alexander and Edwin S. Solomon, *College and University Law* (Charlottesville, Va., 1972), p. 529.

36.   Louis H. Pollak, *The Constitution and the Supreme Court, A Documentary History* (New York, 1966), 2: 266–267. For an in-depth discussion of the impact of *Brown* in the history of segregation, as well as its meaning and immediate impact, see Albert P. Bloustein and Clarence Clyde Ferguson, Jr.,

Desegregation and the Law: The Meaning and Effect of the School Segregation Cases (New Brunswick, N.J., 1957). Many excellent articles and studies may be found by the use of the *Education Index* and *Index to Legal Periodicals.*

37. Johnson v. San Francisco Unified School District, 339 F. Supp. 1315 (1971).

38. Guey Heung Lee v. Johnson, 404 U.S. 1215 (1971). It is to be noted that for purposes of segregation, all nonwhites had been previously placed into the same class. See Gong Lum v. Rice, 275 U.S. 78 (1927).

39. Austin Scott, "20 Years After School Ruling Institutions Still Segregated," *Washington Post,* 18 May 1974, p. A 2.

40. The twenty cities are New York, Chicago, Los Angeles, Philadelphia, Detroit, Miami, Baltimore, Dallas, Cleveland, Washington, D.C., St. Louis, New Orleans, Atlanta, Newark, East Baton Rouge, Kansas City, Birmingham, Charleston, S.C., and Gary.

41. Scott, "20 Years," p. A 2.

42. Lucy v. Adams, 134 F. Supp. 235 (1955).

43. *Ibid.,* 228 F. 2d 619 (1955).

44. *Ibid.,* 351 U.S. 931 (1956).

45. Frasier v. Board of Trustees, 134 F. Supp. 589 (1955).

46. Board of Trustees v. Frasier, 350 U.S. 979 (1956).

47. State ex rel. Hawkins v. Board of Control of Florida, 47 So. 2d 608 (1950).

48. *Ibid.,* 342 U.S. 877 (1951).

49. *Ibid.,* 347 U.S. 971 (1954).

50. *Ibid.,* 350 U.S. 413 (1956).

51. *Ibid.,* 355 U.S. 839 (1957).

52. *Ibid.,* 162 F. Supp. 851 (1958). It has been reported that Hawkins was never admitted to the University of Florida law school for reasons other than race; yet in 1958 another black was admitted as a law student. See Kern Alexander and Erwin Solomon, *College and University Law* (Charlottesville, Va., 1972), p. 533.

53. Ludley v. Board of Supervisors of Louisiana State University and Lark v. Louisiana State Board of Education, 358 U.S. 819 (1958).

54. M. M. Chambers, *The Colleges and the Courts since 1950* (Danville, Ill., 1964), pp. 43–44.

55. Meredith v. Fair, 298 F. 2d 696 (1962).

56. *Ibid.*, 305 F. 2d 343 (1962).
57. Fair v. Meredith, 371 U.S. 828 (1962).
58. Pollak, *Constitution*, p. 282.
59. Alexander and Solomon, *College*, p. 537.
60. Chambers, *Colleges*, pp. 43–44.
61. United States v. Wallace, Governor, 218 F. Supp. 290 (1963).
62. Gerald Lee Gutek, *An Historical Introduction to American Education* (New York, 1970), p. 207.
63. Aaron v. Cooper, 143 F. Supp. 855 (1956) and 243 F. 2d 361 (1957).
64. Cooper v. Aaron, 358 U.S. 1 (1958).
65. *Ibid.*, p. 17.
66. McNeese v. Board of Education, 199 F. Supp. 403 (1961).
67. *Ibid.*, 373 U.S. 688 (1963). Justice Harlan dissented from the Court's opinion because in his judgment the state of Illinois had provided adequate administrative remedy through appeal to the superintendent of public instruction; and since Illinois had outlawed racial discrimination long before the *Brown* decision, "we should be slow to hold unavailing an administrative remedy afforded by a State." (PP. 672–682.)
68. Goss v. Board of Education, 301 F. 2d 164 (1962) and 301 F. 2d 828 (1962).
69. *Ibid.*, 377 U.S. 683 (1963).
70. Calhoun v. Latimer, 377 U.S. 263 (1964).
71. Watson v. Memphis, 373 U.S. 526 (1963).
72. Allen v. County School Board of Prince Edward County, 266 F. 2d 507 (1959).
73. Allen v. County School Board of Prince Edward County, 207 F. Supp. 349 (1962).
74. Griffin v. Board of Supervisors of Prince Edward County, 203 Va. 321 (1962).
75. County School Board of Prince Edward County v. Griffin, 204 Va. 650 (1963).
76. Griffin v. School Board, 377 U.S. 218 (1964). This is in conformity with the Court's decision in Salsbury v. Maryland, which enunciated that there is no rule that counties, as counties, must be treated alike, for the Fourteenth Amendment is directed to equal protection of the laws "between persons as such rather than between areas." 346 U.S. 545 (1954).

77. Griffin, p. 233.
78. St. Helena Parish School Board v. Hall, 287 F. 2d 376 (1961).
79. Hall v. St. Helena Parish School Board, 197 F. Supp. 651 (1961).
80. Griffin, p. 232.
81. Louisiana Financial Assistance Committee v. Poindexter, 389 U.S. 571 (1968).
82. Poindexter v. Louisiana Financial Assistance Committee, 275 F. Supp. 833 (1967).
83. Walz v. Tax Commission, 397 U.S. 664 (1970).
84. Green v. Connally, 330 F. Supp. 1150 (1971).
85. Norwood v. Harrison, 413 U.S. 825 (1973).
86. Brown II, p. 294.
87. Va. Code, sec. 22–232.1 (1964).
88. Green v. County School Board, 391 U.S. 430 (1968).
89. *Ibid.*, p. 439, fn. 5. The Court included in a footnote the views of the U.S. Commission on Civil Rights in regard to freedom-of-choice plans, which the Court claimed neither to adopt nor refused to accept.
90. *Ibid.*, pp. 441–442.
91. Rainey v. Board of Education, 391 U.S. 443 (1968).
92. Monroe v. Board of Commissioners, 221 F. Supp. 968 (1963).
93. *Ibid.*, 244 F. Supp. 353 (1965).
94. *Ibid.*, p. 362.
95. *Ibid.*, 380 F. 2d 955 (1967).
96. *Ibid.*, 391 U.S. 1215 (1968).
97. Keyes v. Denver School District, 396 U.S. 1215 (1969).
98. Alexander v. Holmes County Board of Education, 417 F. 2d 852 (1969).
99. Alexander v. Holmes County Board of Education, 396 U.S. 19 (1969).
100. *Ibid.*, p. 21.
101. *Ibid.*, pp. 1219, 1220.
102. Carter v. West Feliciana Parish School Board, 396 U.S. 226 (1969). Certiorari denied on January 14, 1970, West Feliciana Parish School Board v. Carter, 396 U.S. 1032 (1970).
103. Dowell v. Board of Education, 396 U.S. 269 (1969).

104. Jackson Municipal Separate School District v. Singleton, 396 U.S. 1032 (1970).

105. Singleton v. Jackson Municipal Separate School District, 419 2d 1211 (1969).

106. The Court, however, did not rule on the matter of *de facto* segregation in itself: "We do not reach in this case the question whether a showing that school segregation is a consequence of other types of state action, without any discriminatory action by the school authorities is a constitutional violation requiring remedial action by a school desegregation decree. This case does not present that question and we therefore do not decide it. Our objective in dealing with the issues presented by these cases is to see that school authorities exclude no pupil of a racial minority from any school, directly or indirectly, on account of race; it does not and cannot embrace all the problems of racial prejudice, even when those problems contribute to disproportionate racial concentrations in some schools." Swann v. Charlotte-Mecklenburg Board of Education, 402 U.S. 23 (1971).

107. For events and court action prior to 1968, see 243 F. Supp. 667 (1965) and 369 F. 2d 29 (1966).

108. 306 F. Supp. 1299 (1969) and 311 F. Supp. 265 (1970).

109. 431 F. 2d 138 (1970).

110. Swann v. Charlotte-Mecklenburg Board of Education, 402 U.S. 22–25 (1971).

111. *Ibid.*, pp. 25–27.

112. *Ibid.*, p. 29.

113. *Ibid.*, pp. 16–18. For studies on the implications and importance of the *Swann* case, see "School Desegregation After Swann: A Theory of Government Responsibility," 39 UNIVERSITY OF CHICAGO L. REV. (1971) 421, and Owen M. Fiss, "The Charlotte-Mecklenburg Case—Its Significance for Northern School Desegregation," 38 UNIVERSITY OF CHICAGO L. REV. (1971) 697.

114. Davis v. School Commissioners of Mobile County, 414 F. 2d 609 (1969) and 430 F. 2d 883 (1970).

115. *Ibid.*, 402 U.S. 33 (1971).

116. Barresi v. McDaniel, Superintendent of Schools, 226 Ga. 456 (1970).

117. McDaniel, Superintendent of Schools v. Barresi, 402 U.S. 39 (1971).

118. N. C. Gen. Stat., sec. 115–176.1 (Supp. 1969).
119. North Carolina State Board of Education v. Swann, 402 U.S. 43 (1971).
120. Moore v. Charlotte-Mecklenburg Board of Education, 402 U.S. 47 (1971).
121. P. L. 88–352 (1964), sec. 407(a).
122. Swann, pp. 17–18.
123. *Ibid.*, p. 11.
124. School District of the City of Pontiac, Inc. v. Davis, 404 U.S. 913 (1971).
125. *Ibid.*, 309 F. Supp. 734 (1970).
126. Davis v. School District of the City of Pontiac, 443 F. 2d 573 (1971).
127. "Raging Again: Battle Over School Busing," *U.S. News and World Report*, 15 August 1971, p. 38.
128. "Nixon Message on Busing," in *ibid.*, 27 March 1972, pp. 70–79.
129. "Educational Amendments of 1972," *United States Code, Congressional and Administrative News*, 92nd Cong., 2nd sess., II, 2669–2671.
130. P.L. 92–318 (1972), sec. 801–806.
131. *Washington Post*, 24 June 1972, p. A 4.
132. *Ibid.*, p. A 1. Nixon himself had so suggested on April 30, 1972. See "Nixon Answers Questions," *U.S. News and World Report*, 15 May 1972, p. 104.
133. Winston-Salem/Forsyth Board of Education v. Scott, 404 U.S. 1221 (1971).
134. *Ibid.*, p. 1227.
135. *Ibid.*, fn. 1.
136. Allgood v. Brewer, 409 U.S. 892 (1972).
137. Brewer v. School Board of City of Norfolk, Virginia, 456 F. 2d 943 (1972).
138. Jefferson Parish School Board v. Dandridge, 409 U.S. (1972); and Dandridge v. Jefferson Parish School Board, 456 F. 2d 552 (1972).
139. Vaughns v. Board of Education of Prince Georges County, Maryland, 93 S. Ct. 1350 (1973).
140. *Ibid.*, 4th Circuit, no. 73–1023 (1973); and 355 F. Supp. 1051 (1972).
141. Bradley v. State Board of Education of the Commonwealth of Virginia, 93 S. Ct., 936 (1973).

142. Bradley v. School Board of the City of Richmond, Va., 338 F. Supp. 67 (1972).

143. Bradley v. School Board of the City of Richmond, Virginia, 462 F. 2d 1058 (1972).

144. Bradley v. State Board of Education of Commonwealth of Virginia, et al., 41 LW 4685 (1973). As is the custom in deadlocked decisions, the Court issued no opinion; its brief stated: "The judgment [of the appellate court] is affirmed by an equally divided Court."

145. Keyes v. School District No. 1, Denver, 303 F. Supp. 279, 289 (1969).

146. *Ibid.*, 445 F. 2d 990 (1971).

147. "Segregation, Northern Style—How Nixon Would Deal With It," *U.S. News and World Report*, 23 October 1972, pp. 39–40.

148. Keyes v. School District No. 1, Denver, U. S. Supreme Court Reports (August 8, 1973), pp. 553–566.

149. *Ibid.*, pp. 567–568.

150. *Ibid.*, pp. 568–589.

151. *Ibid.*, pp. 589–595.

152. Bradley v. Milliken, Detroit, Eastern Dist. of Mich. Civil Action No. 35257 (1972).

153. Bradley v. Milliken, 6th Circuit, No. 72–1801–10 (1973).

154. 42 LW 2022 (1973).

155. 42 LW 3306 (1973).

156. Milliken v. Bradley, 94 S. Ct. 3112 (1974).

157. *Supreme Court Reporter*, 94 (August 15, 1974), pp. 3125–3126.

158. *Ibid.*, p. 3127. See also the following section in this chapter on the redistricting of school districts.

159. *Ibid.*, pp. 3145, 3147.

160. *Ibid.*, p. 3135.

161. Spencer v. Kugler, 326 F. Supp. 1235 (1971).

162. *Ibid.*, 404 U.S. 1027 (1972).

163. *Ibid.*, pp. 1031–1032. Senator Javits's remarks were made in the Hearings on Emergency School Aid Act of 1970 before the Subcommittee on Education of the Senate. 91st Cong., 2d sess. (1970), p. 21.

164. Wright v. Council of City of Emporia, 407 U.S. 451 (1972). For the opinion of the reversed decision of the court of

appeals, see Wright v. Council of City of Emporia, 442 F. 2d 570 (1971).

165. Wright v. School Board of Greensville County, 252 F. Supp. 378 (1966).

166. *Ibid.*, 309 F. Supp. 671 (1970).

167. Wright v. Council of City of Emporia, 407 U.S. 470 (1973).

168. United States v. Scotland Neck City Board of Education, 407 U.S. 484 (1972).

169. *Ibid.*, 314 F. Supp. 65 (1970).

170. United States v. Scotland Neck City Board of Education, 442 F. 2d 575 (1971).

171. Bradley v. School Board of City of Richmond, Va., 345 F. 2d 310 (1965) and Gilliam v. School Board of Hopewell, Va., 345 F. 2d 325 (1965).

172. *Ibid.*, 382 U.S. 103 (1965).

173. Rogers v. Paul, 382 U.S. 198 (1965).

174. United States v. Montgomery County Board of Education, 395 U.S. 231 (1969).

175. Carr v. Montgomery County Board of Education, 253 F. Supp. 306 (1966).

176. *Ibid.*, 289 F. Supp. 647 (1968).

177. Montgomery County Board of Education v. Carr, 400 F. 2d 1 (1968).

178. United States v. Montgomery County Board of Education, 395 U.S. 231 (1969).

179. Jackson Municipal Separate School District v. Singleton, 396 U.S. 1032 (1970).

180. Singleton v. Jackson Municipal Separate School District, 419 F. 2d 1211 (1969).

181. *Ibid.*, p. 1218.

182. Porcelli v. Titus, 402 U.S. 944 (1971).

183. *Ibid.*, 431 F. 2d 1254 (1970).

184. *Ibid.*, p. 1257.

185. Northcross v. Board of Education, 37 L. Ed. 2d 48 (1973).

Selected Bibliography

Alexander, Kern, and Solomon, Erwin. *College and University Law.* Charlottesville, Va.: Michie Co., 1972.

Allen, Hollis P. *The Federal Government and Education.* New York: McGraw-Hill Book Co., 1950.

Antieau, Chester A.; Downey, Arthur T.; and Roberts, Edward C. *Freedom From Federal Establishment: Formation and Early History of the First Amendment Religion Clauses.* Milwaukee: Bruce, 1964.

Babbidge, Homer D., and Rosenzweig, Robert M. *The Federal Interest in Higher Education.* New York: McGraw-Hill Book Co., 1962.

Blackman, Francis W. *The History of Federal and State Aid to Higher Education in the United States.* Washington: Government Printing Office, 1890.

Bloustein, Albert P., and Ferguson, Jr., Clarence Clyde. *Desegregation and the Law: The Meaning and Effect of the School Segregation Cases.* New Brunswick, N.J.: Rutgers University Press, 1957.

Boles, Donald E. *The Two Swords.* Ames, Iowa: Iowa State University Press, 1957.

Bolmeier, Edward C. *The School in the Legal Structure.* Cincinnati, Ohio: W.H. Anderson Co., 1968.

Buis, Anne Gibson. "An Historical Study of the Role of the Federal Government in the Financial Support of Education, with Special Reference to Legislative Proposals and Action." Ph.D. dissertation, Ohio State University, 1953.

Butts, R. Freeman and Cremin, Lawrence A. *A History of Education in American Culture.* New York: Henry Holt and Co., 1953.

Calhoun, Daniel, ed., *The Educating of Americans: A Documentary His-*

tory. Boston: Houghton Mifflin Co., 1969.

Campbell, Olan Kenneth. "An Analysis of Provisions of State Constitutions Affecting Support of Public Schools." Ed.D. dissertation, Duke University, 1954.

Chambers, M. M. *The Colleges and the Courts: The Developing Law of the Student and the College.* Danville, Ill.: Interstate Printers and Publishers, 1972.

Cohen, Felix S. *Handbook of Federal Indian Law.* Albuquerque, N.M.: University of New Mexico, 1972.

Costanzo, Joseph F. *This Nation Under God: Church, State and Schools in America.* New York: Herder and Herder, 1964.

Cubberly, Elwood P. *Public Education in the United States.* Boston: Houghton Mifflin Co., 1934.

Cubberly, Elwood P. *State School Administration.* Boston: Houghton Mifflin Co., 1927.

Edwards, Newton. *The Courts and the Public Schools.* Chicago: University of Chicago Press, 1958.

Fellman, David, *The Supreme Court and Education.* New York: Teachers College, Columbia University, 1969.

Fraser, Stewart. *Governmental Policy and International Education.* New York: John Wiley and Sons, 1965.

Gabel, Richard J. *Public Funds for Church and Private Schools.* Washington: Catholic University of America Press, 1937.

Good, Harry G., and James D. Teller. *A History of American Education.* New York: Macmillan Co., 1973.

Gutek, Gerald Lee, *An Historical Introduction to American Education.* New York: Thomas Y. Crowell Co., 1970.

Hamilton, Robert R., and Mort, Paul R., *The Law and Public Education.* Chicago: Foundation Press, 1941.

Hazard, William R. *Education and the Law.* New York: The Free Press, 1971.

Hinsdale, B. A., "Documents Illustrative of American Educational History," *Annual Report of the U. S. Commissioner of Education, 1892–1893.* Washington: Government Printing Office, 1895. II, 1225–1414.

Keppel, Francis. *The Necessary Revolution in American Education.* New York: Harper & Row, 1966.

Knight, Edgar W. *A Documentary History of Education in the South Before 1860.* Chapel Hill, N.C.: University of North Carolina Press, 1950.

Knight, Edgar W. *Public Education in the South.* Boston: Ginn & Co., 1922.

Knight, Edgar W., and Hall, Clifton L., *Readings in American Educational History.* New York: Appleton-Century-Crofts, 1951.

Lee, Gordon C., *The Struggle for Federal Aid: First Phase.* New York: Teachers College, Columbia University, 1949.

Lu, Hsien. *Federal Role in Education.* New York: American Press, 1965.

McLaughlin, Sr. Raymond. *A History of State Legislation Affecting Private Elementary and Secondary Schools in the United States, 1870–1945.* Washington: Catholic University of America Press, 1946.

Meranto, Philip. *The Politics of Federal Aid to Education in 1965.* Syracuse, N.Y.: Syracuse University Press, 1967.

Miller, Helen A., and Shea, Andrew J. *Federal Assistance for Educational Purposes.* Washington: Government Printing Office, 1963.

Morgan, Richard E. *The Supreme Court and Religion.* New York: The Free Press, 1972.

Pierce, Truman M. *Federal, State, and Local Government in Education.* New York: Center for Applied Research in Education, 1964.

Quattlebaum, Charles A. *Federal Educational Policies, Programs and Proposals.* Washington: Government Printing Office, 1968.

Rainsford, George N. *Congress and Higher Education in the Nineteenth Century.* Knoxville, Tenn.: University of Tennessee Press, 1972.

Roberts, Roy W. *Vocational and Practical Arts Education: History, Development, and Principles.* New York: Harper & Row, 1971.

Ross, Earle D. *Democracy's College: the Land-Grant Movement in the Formative Stage.* Ames, Iowa: Iowa State College Press, 1942.

Sorgen, Michael S.; Duffy, Patrick S.; Kaplin, William A.; and Margolin, Ephraim. *State, School, and Family.* New York: Matthew Bender & Co., 1973.

Spurlock, Clark. *Education and the Supreme Court.* Urbana, Ill.: University of Illinois Press, 1955.

Strahan, Richard Dobbs. *The Courts and the Schools.* Lincoln, Neb.: Professional Educators Publications, 1973.

Suffrin, Sidney C. *Issues in Federal Aid to Education.* Syracuse, N.Y.: Syracuse University Press, 1962.

Swift, F. H. *Federal Aid to Public Schools.* Washington: Government
    Printing Office, 1922.
Taylor, Howard Cromwell. *The Educational Significance of the Early
    Federal Land Grant Ordinances.* New York: Columbia Univer-
    sity Press, 1922.
Tiedt, Sidney W. *The Role of the Federal Government in Education.* New
    York: Oxford University Press, 1966.
True, A. C. *History of Agricultural Education in the United States, 1785–
    1925.* Washington: Government Printing Office, 1928.

Index

Abington School District v. *Schempp* 208
Academic freedom 230, 234
ACTION 135
Adams Amendment (1906) 63
Adams, John 50
Adams, John Quincey 52
Adams v. *Richardson* 317 (n 96), 31
Adler v. *Board of Education* 234, 238, 239, 240, 242
Admissions
  reverse discrimination in student 263
Affirmative action employment programs 265
Age discrimination 228
Agency for International Development 130
Agricultural Act of 1949 23
Agricultural education 58, 96
Agricultural Experimental Stations Act (1887) 62, 97
Agricultural extension 101
Agriculture, Department of 22, 61, 63, 64, 97, 109
Air Force Academy 56
Alabama 277, 279, 280, 292, 307
Alaska 9
Alexander, Kern 276, 280
Alexander v. *Holmes* 31, 291, 292
Allen case 168, 180, 191

Allen, Hollis P. 4
Allgood v. *Brewer* 369 (n 136), 299
Alston v. *School Board* 224
Amendments: *see* Constitutional amendments
American Association of University Professors (AAUP) 83, 223
American Association of University Women 126
American Bar Association Journal 264
American Civil Liberties Union, 206
American Institute of Instruction 7
American Library Association 24, 79
American Printing House for the Blind 124
Amish and public schools 159
Appalachian Regional Development Act of 1965 112
Area Redevelopment Act (1961) 109
Arizona 233
Arkansas 216, 240, 281
Arts
  aid for study 71
Association for the Advancement of Education 7

Babbidge, Homer D. 4
Baggett v. *Bullitt* 358 (n 54), 232, 234
Bailyn, Bernard 17

Bankhead-Flanagan Act (1945) 102
Bankhead-Jones Act (1935) 62, 64, 101
Barenblatt v. *United States* 358 (n 70), 239
Barlow, Joel 51
Barnard, Henry 2, 7, 8, 17, 126
Barnette case 248
Barnett, Ross 279
Barrera v. *Wheeler* 319 (n 125), 39; 350 (n 153), 193
Beilan v. *Board of Education* 238
Berea College Case 153, 269
Bible reading in public schools 20, 204, 206
Bilingual education 37, 261
Black, Hugo L. 148, 169, 173, 178, 181, 198, 202, 204, 205, 232, 236, 251, 291
Blackman, Harry A. 262
Blaine Amendment, 18
Blair proposals 61
Board of Foreign Scholarships 129, 132
Boles, Donald E. 165
Bolling v. *Sharpe* 274, 275
Bolmeier, Edmund 141
Brademas, John 136, 137
Bradfield v. *Roberts* 199
Bradley v. *Milliken* 370 (n 152), 303
Bradley v. *State Board of Education* 370 (n 141), 300
Brameld, Theodore 159
Brand case 221, 222
Breen v. *Kahl* 362 (n 47), 256
Brennan, William J., Jr. 145, 181, 210, 264, 301
Briggs v. *Elliott* 274
Brown v. *Board of Education* (Brown I) 28, 30, 154, 274, 278, 280, 282, 286, 289, 303
Brown II, 275, 281, 287, 288
Browning, Stephen 145

Brusca v. *Missouri* 184
Buchanan, James 59, 61
Burger, Warren 176, 180, 234, 242, 256, 293, 299, 303
Burstyn v. *Wilson* 354 (n 79), 214
Burton, Harold H. 174, 199
Bush, Vannevar 68
Busing for desegregation 30, 31, 292
Bus transportation for nonpublic school children 171

Calhoun v. *Latimer* 366 (n 70), 283
California 143, 257, 261
Campus organizations 254
Capper-Ketcham Act (1928) 101
Carter v. *West Feliciana School Board* 291
Caswell, Hollis P. 159
Chamberlain v. *Dade County Board of Public Instruction* 354 (n 73), 213
Chapel attendance at service academies 218
Child-benefit theory 22, 38, 164, 165, 169, 172, 198
Childs, John L. 158
Chinese children
    school segregation 269, 276
    special English classes 261
Chipman, Nathaniel 16
Civil Rights Act of 1875 267
Civil Rights Act of 1964 12, 28, 42, 94, 261, 288, 295, 296
Clark, Tom 209, 214, 231, 242
Coast Guard Academy 55
Cochran v. *Louisiana* 164, 169, 172, 199, 345 (n 50), 165
Cohen maternity case 228
Coleman Report 142, 146
Colmer, William M. 207
Colorado 300
Columbia Institution of the Deaf, Dumb, and Blind 121

Commerce, Department of 109
Communications media
   aid 73, 82
Communist party membership 236,
   240
Community colleges
   aid 78, 91, 108
Comprehensive Employment and
   Training Act of 1973 110, 111,
   117
Conant, James B. 158
Congressional pages
   education 23
Congress, Powers of 2, 59
Connecticut 176, 258
Connell v. *Higgenbotham* 358 (n 57),
   234
Constitution and education 2, 48,
   51, 52, 59
Continental Congress 2, 14, 54
Continuing education
   aid 80
Coons, John E. 143, 145
Cooperative Research Act of 1954
   36, 67
Cooper v. *Aaron* 281
Coram, Robert 16
Corporal punishment 260
Correspondence schools 154
Corwin, Edwin 200
Costanzo, Joseph F. 168, 344 (n 39,
   41)
Counseling services
   aid 23, 36, 73, 100
Cramp v. *Board of Public Instruction*
   358 (n 53), 232
Cubberly, Ellwood P. 45, 151, 334
   (n 96), 342 (n 6)
Cumming v. *Board of Education* 364 (n
   16), 268

Dandridge v. *Jefferson School Board* 369
   (n 138), 299

Dartmouth College case 150, 152, 153
Davis v. *County School Board* 274
Davis v. *School Commissioners* 368 (n
   114), 295
Davis v. *School District of the City of
   Pontiac* 369 (n 124), 296
De Funis v. *Odegard* 263
Delaware 171
Denver school case 300
Desegregation
   busing as a means 30, 31, 292
   elementary and secondary educa-
      tion 274, 280
   evaluation of progress 275
   higher education 268
   payment of litigation fees 308
   teaching staffs 307
Detroit school case 303
Di Censo case: *see Robinson* v. *Di Censo*
Dickman case 167
Dirksen, Everret M. 207
Discrimination: *see* Equality of edu-
   cational opportunity, Reverse
   discrimination
District of Columbia 274, 275
Dixon v. *Alabama State Board of Educa-
   tion* 361 (n 23), 249
Dodge v. *Board of Education* 356 (n
   19), 223
Dolliver, Jonathan P. 97
Donahue v. *Richards* 353 (n 48), 207
Doremus v. *Board of Education* 207
Douglas, William O. 145, 161, 170,
   178, 181, 186, 195, 201, 209,
   235, 256, 264, 276, 302, 304,
   305
Dowell v. *Board of Education* 291
Dred Scott case 266
Drinan, Robert M. 207
Drug Abuse Education Act (1970)
   40
Due Process Clause: *see* Fourteenth
   Amendment

Economic Opportunity Act of 1964 27, 82, 86, 110, 118, 146
Economics, aid for teaching 82
Education Amendments of 1972 12, 43, 45, 68, 138, 298
Education of the Handicapped Act (1970) 124
Education Professions Development Act (1967) 83, 87, 91
Educational materials offensive to religious conscience 214
Educational opportunity grants 81, 85, 90
Eisenhower, Dwight D. 72, 128, 282
Elementary and Secondary Education Act of 1965 (ESEA) 21, 32, 43, 46, 68, 123, 146, 171, 185, 193, 233
Elementary and Secondary Education Amendments (1966) 37, 42
Elfbrandt v. *Russell* 358 (n 55), 233
Emergency Employment Act (1972) 117, 118
Emergency Insured Student Loan Act (1969) 89
Emergency School Aid Act of 1972 41, 308
Enabling Act of 1802 14
Engel v. *Vitale* 170, 204, 208, 213, 214
Environmental Education Act (1970) 39
Epperson v. *Arkansas* 216
Epworth League 245
Equality of educational opportunity 43, 62, 143, 144, 146, 260, 266
Equal Pay Act of 1963 94
Equal Protection Clause: *see* Fourteenth Amendment
Eskimo children 9
Essex v. *Wolman* 184

Establishment Clause: *see* First Amendment
Esteban v. *Central Missouri State College* 361 (n 36), 253
Ethnic Heritage Program 43
Everson v. *Board of Education* 33, 169, 171, 180, 185, 188, 199, 200, 214
Evolution, Teaching of public schools 216

Farrington v. *Tokushige* 343 (n 21), 156
Faubus, Orville 281
Federal aid to education 2, 14, 20
Federal control of education 1, 15
Federal Security Agency vocational rehabilitation 118
Federal Surplus Commodities Corporation 22
Federal Vocational Rehabilitation Act (1920) 118
Feinberg Law 234, 240
Fellowships 73, 84, 88, 91
see also scholarships
Fifteenth Amendment 267
Fifth Amendment 156, 236, 238, 274, 282
Financial aid to nonpublic schools 18, 22, 33, 35, 36, 38, 57, 79, 88
Finnish Exchange Act of 1949 129, 131
First Amendment 152, 158, 159, 168, 169, 170, 171, 172, 176, 180, 184, 186, 196, 198, 205, 207, 217, 218, 236, 241, 242, 248, 250, 255
Fischer, Louis 225, 234
Fisher v. *Hurst* 364 (n 23), 271
Flag saluting compulsory 247
Flast v. *Cohen* 171
Fleishman, Charles A. 58

Florida 145, 213, 232, 234, 292
"Follow-Through" program 27
Folsom, F. G., Jr. 247
Foreign Buildings Act (1946), 128
Foreign languages
aid for teaching 23, 36, 73, 138, 261
Fortas, Abe 170, 217, 218, 250
Fourteenth Amendment 30, 143, 145, 159, 168, 169, 173, 198, 220, 222, 226, 228, 231, 239, 246, 249, 253, 256, 260, 261, 264, 267, 269, 271, 272, 274, 282, 283, 285, 296, 304, 305, 308
Frankfurter, Felix 174, 203, 231, 234, 247, 249
Frasier v. *Board of Trustees* 365 (n 45), 278
Fraternity membership 245
Freedmen's Bureau 267
Freedmen's Hospital 58
Freedom-of-choice plans for desegregation 31, 287
Free transfer plan of desegregation 289
Freund, Paul A. 170
Frothingham v. *Mellon* 346 (n 75), 171
Fulbright Act (1946) 127, 131
Fulbright-Hays Act (1961) 131
Fulbright, J. William 126, 132
Future Farmers of America 102

Gaines case 269, 273
Gallaudet College 121
Garfield, James A. 8
Gault case 244
Gebhart v. *Belton* 274
General Education Provisions Act (1968) 9, 12
George-Barden Act (1946) 73, 99
George-Deen Act (1936) 99, 100

George-Ellzey Act (1934) 99
George-Reed Act (1929) 99
Georgia 148, 268, 292
Gerende v. *Board of Supervisors* 231
G. I. Bill of Rights 66, 118, 130
Gideons International v. *Tudor* 353 (n 53), 208
Girard College case 151, 152, 154
Gobitis case 247
Goldberg, Arthur 211
Goldstein, Stephen R. 359 (n 38)
Goldwater, Barry 34
Gong Lum v. *Rice* 269
Goss v. *Board of Education* 366 (n 68), 283
Grant, Ulysses S. 18, 53
Green, Edith 80
Green v. *Connally* 287, 293
Green v. *County School Board* 287, 291
Griffin case 284, 291
Grit v. *Wolman* 192
Guey Heung Lee v. *Johnson* 365 (n 37), 276
Guidance and counseling services aid 23, 36, 73, 100

Hadley v. *Junior College District* 342 (n 38), 148
Hair styles of male students 256
Hall v. *St. Helena Parish School Board* 286
Hamilton, Alexander 50, 55
Hamilton v. *Regents of University of California* 246
Handicapped Children's Early Education Assistance Act (1968) 123
Handicapped, Education for 24, 37, 86, 115, 121
Hansen, Allen Oscar 51
Hargrave v. *Askew* 145
Harlan, John Marshall 169, 211, 366 (n 67)

Hatch Act (1887) 62, 97
Hawaii142, 156
Hawkins v. *Board of Control of Florida* 278
Head v. *University of Missouri* 221
Health, Education and Welfare, Department of (HEW) 8, 9, 12, 25, 40, 84, 95, 109, 110, 120, 122, 137, 176, 261, 262, 291, 295, 296
Healy v. *James* 361 (n 41), 254
Henderson v. *United States* 273
Higher Education Act of 1965 76, 79, 83, 85, 86, 87, 89, 112
Higher Education Amendments of 1966 76, 83
Higher Education Amendments of 1968 76, 85, 112, 138
Higher Education Facilities Act of 1963 76, 83, 85, 91, 112, 175
Hinsdale, Burke A. 49
Hoar proposals 61
Hobsen v. *Hansen* 142
Holmes decision 31, 291, 292
Hoover, Herbert 127
Howard University 9, 57
Hoyt, John W. 53
Hughes, Charles Evans 49, 165, 270
Humanities
aid for study 71
Humphrey-Thompson Act (1956) 129
Hunt v. *McNair* 186

Illinois 145, 197, 223, 282
Impact Laws (1950) 20, 45
India Emergency Food Act of 1951 129
Indiana 222
Indian education 9, 44, 162
Information and Educational Exchange Act of 1948 129

Interior, Department of 8, 44
International affairs institutes 126, 138
International Cultural Exchange and Trade Fair Participations Act of 1956 129, 131
International education 126
International Education Act of 1966 76, 136
International Text-Book Company v. *Pigg* 154
Itz v. *Penick* 360 (n 7), 244

Jackson, Andrew 52
Jackson, Robert 174, 199, 200, 203
Jacobson v. *Massachusetts* 244
James v. *Board of Education* 359 (n 85), 243
Javits, Jacob 305
Jefferson School Board v. *Dandridge* 369 (n 138), 299
Jefferson, Thomas 17, 50, 151, 163, 200
Jehovah Witnesses 247
Jenks, Christopher 146
Job Corps 111, 118
Johnson, Andrew 8
Johnson, Lyndon B. 29, 35, 78, 79, 107, 110, 112, 114, 136
Johnson-O'Malley Act of 1934 45
Johnson v. *Branch* 357 (n 25), 224
Johnson v. *New York State Education Department* 362 (n 61), 260

Kansas 274
Keith, Damon J. 297
Kendall School 121, 122
Kennedy, John F. 28, 29, 32, 74, 76, 103, 105, 131, 132, 167
Kentucky 153, 171, 269
Keyes v. *Denver School District* 367 (n 97), 290
Keyishian v. *Board of Regents* 240

Kirk v. *Board of Regents* 362 (n 50), 257, 259
Kirp, David L. 146
Kline v. *Vlandis* 362 (n 55), 257
Koob, Albert J. 182
Kosydar v. *Wolman* 350 (n 151), 192
Kurland, Philip B. 146

Labor, Department of 95, 100, 109, 110
La Fleur maternity case 228
Land-Grant College Act of 1862: *see* Morrill Acts
Land grants to education 2, 14, 59
Lanham Act (1941) 20
Laski, Harold 1
Lau v. *Nichols* 362 (n 63), 261
Law schools
federal aid to 88
Lemon v. *Kurtzman* 175, 178, 185, 190
Lerner v. *Casey* 358 (n 68), 239
Leupp, Charles E. 163
Levitt case 187, 189
Libraries
financial aid 24, 36, 81, 87, 89
Library Services and Construction Act (1956) 24, 112
Lichtenberger, Arthur 213
Lincoln, Abraham 59, 266, 267
Litigation fees
payment of desegregation 308
Loans to college students 65, 73, 81, 89, 90, 104, 112
Local communities 2, 141, 144
Louisiana 164, 279, 286, 292
Loyalty oaths 74, 230
Lu, Hsien 4
Lucy v. *Adams* 277, 279, 280

Madison, James 48, 49, 51, 200
Maine 207

Mann, Horace 17, 127, 207
Manpower Development and Training Act (1962) 106, 108
Maritain, Jacques 1
Marshall, John 150
Marshall, Thurgood 145, 178, 181, 186, 261, 304
Maryland 171, 231, 233, 299, 300
Massachusetts 219
Maternity leaves for teachers 228
Mathematics education
aid 23, 69, 72
McCarthy, Joseph R. 128, 241
McCollum case 198, 202
McDaniel v. *Barresi* 369 (n 116), 295
McGowan v. *Maryland* 214
McInnis v. *Ogilvie* 145
McLaurin v. *Oklahoma State Regents* 270, 272, 279
McMurrin, Sterling M. 75
McNeese v. *Board of Education* 366 (n 66), 282
Medical education 103
Mental Retardation Facilities act (1963) 122, 124
Merchant Marine Academy 55
Meredith v. *Fair* 279
Mexican-American children
English language 263, 301
Meyer v. *Nebraska* 151, 154, 155, 156, 157, 219
Michigan 147, 304
Military Academy 54
Military training in colleges
compulsory 245
Millage Rollback Act 146
Milliken v. *Bradley* 370 (n 152), 303
Minersville School District v. *Gobitis* 360 (n 16), 247
Minorities 42, 261
see also Equality of educational opportunity

Minton, Sherman 235
Mississippi 166, 191, 269, 292
Missouri 147, 184, 193, 270
Monroe, James 52
Monroe v. Board of Commissioners 289,
   293
Morgan, Richard E. 216, 217
Morrill Acts (1862, 1890) 2, 8, 54,
   56, 58, 97, 151, 246
Morrill, Justine S. 59, 61
Morse, Wayne 33, 80, 137, 167
Murray, John Courtney 200
Murray v. Curlett 354 (n 56), 209
Mutual Educational and Cultural
   Exchange Act of 1961 131,
   138
Mutual Security Act of 1952 128

National Commission on Libraries
   and Information Science Act
   (1970) 25
National Council of Churches 213
National Deaf-Mute College 121
National Defense Act of 1916 56
National Defense Act of 1920 57
National Defense Education Act of
   1958 (NDEA) 25, 35, 70, 72,
   81, 83, 85, 87, 88, 101, 108,
   110, 130, 138
National Educational Association
   53, 54
National Education Improvement
   Act of 1963 77, 106
National Foundation on the Acts
   and the Humanities Act (1965)
   71
National Institute of Education 12
National School Lunch Act (1946)
   21
National Science Foundation Act
   (1950) 68, 74, 87, 130
National Sea Grant College and
   Program Act (1966) 70

National system of education, Plans
   for 15
National Teachers Corps 82, 84
National Teachers' Association 7,
   53
National Technical Institute for the
   Deaf 122
National Vocational Student Loan
   Insurance Act of 1965 85,
   112
National university 16, 48
National Voluntary Action Program
   135
National Youth Administration
   (NYA) 21, 65
Naval Academy 55
Nebraska 155, 185
Nelson Amendment (1907) 62
New Hampshire 150, 237
New Jersey 172, 207, 220
New York, state 147, 168, 171, 187,
   190, 204, 234, 260
Nixon, Richard M. 47, 135, 297,
   298, 301
Nonpublic schools: *see* Private
   schools
North Carolina 295, 300
Northcross v. Board of Education 371
   (n 185), 308
Northwest Ordinances (1785, 1787)
   14, 162
Norwood v. Harrison 287, 350 (n
   148), 191
Nursing education
   aid 103
Nyquist case 187, 189

Odessa College 227
Ohio 162, 164, 184
Oklahoma 171, 230
Oregon 157, 167
Oregon School Case 151, 154, 156,
   157, 159

Packel, Israel 162
Pages
  education expenses for congressional and Supreme Court 23
Parker v. *Board of Education* 357 (n 23), 224
Peace Corps 86, 90, 132
Pearson v. *Coale* 245
Pennsylvania 152, 162, 178, 179, 187, 190, 207, 238
Penny Milk Program 22
Pfeffer, Leo 347 (n 93)
Phelps v. *Board of Education* 356 (n 12), 220
Pickering v. *Board of Education* 242
Pickncy, Charles C. 48
Pierce, Truman M. 4
Plessy v. *Ferguson* 153, 154, 268, 269, 270, 272, 273, 274, 304
Poindexter case 367 (n 82), 286
Pollak, Louis H. 276
Pontiac (Michigan) busing case 296
Poor 27, 35, 144, 146, 193
Porcelli v. *Titus* 371 (n 182), 308
Porter, John A. 96
Powell, Adam Clayton 33, 35, 77, 106, 137
Powell, Lewis F., Jr. 144, 186, 255, 300, 302
Prayers in public schools 204, 208
Pregnant teachers, Leaves for 228
Prince Edward County, Virginia 284
Prince Georges County busing case 299
Private schools
  attendance 156
  financial aid 162
  foreign language teaching 155
  right to exist 150, 184
  salaries of teachers 178
  segregation 191, 286
  textbooks for children 164, 191

"Project Headstart" 27
Property tax for support of education 142
  see also Rodriguez case
Public education
  control 1, 15, 147
  financing 1, 141
  religious activities 204, 214, 218
  religious teaching 17, 197, 214
Public Health Service Act (1963) 103
Public Law 320 (1935) 22
Public Law 461 (1936) 22
Public Law 815 (1950) 20
Public Law 874 (1950) 20, 45
Public School Assistance Act of 1961 32
Purnell Act of 1925 63

Quick Bear v. *Leupp* 163

Rabout Amendment 128
Rainey v. *Board of Education* 367 (n 91), 289
Reconstruction Finance Corporation 21
Redistricting school districts 305
Reed, Stanley 199
Rehabilitation Act of 1973 120
Rehabilitation efforts in education:
  see Vocational rehabilitation
Rehabilitation Services Administration 120
Rehnquist, William H. 256, 302
Released time programs 159, 197
Religious activities in public schools 204, 218
Religious schools
  attendance 156
  financial aid 16, 45, 162
  right to exist 150, 184
  salaries of teachers 178
  textbooks for children 164, 191

Religious teaching in public schools
  17, 197, 214
Research and Marketing Act of
  1946 64
Research, Grants for 13, 36, 69,
  75
Reserve Officers Training Corps
  (ROTC) 56, 245
Reverse discrimination
  students' admissions 263
  teachers 308
Rhode Island 23, 178
Ribicoff, Abraham 105, 167
Richardson, Elliott W. 176
Roberts v. City of Boston 364 (n 14),
  268
Robinson v. Di Censo 175, 178, 185
Rodriguez v. San Antonio Independent
  School District 143, 147, 304
Rogers v. Paul 371 (n 173), 307
Roosevelt, Franklin D. 65, 273
Root, Elihu 126
Rosenberg v. Board of Education 354 (n
  80), 214
Rosenzweig, Robert M. 4
Ross, Earl D. 61, 323 (n 79)
Roth case 225
Rotnem, Victor 247
Rush, Benjamin 15
Rutledge, Wiley 174, 199

Sailors v. Board of Education 342 (n
  36), 147
Sanborn, Edwin D. 59
Schempp case 208
Schimmel, David 225, 234
Scholarships for students 69, 81
School board membership 147
School district elections 147
School Lunch Program 21
Science clubs and fairs 26
Science education
  aid 23, 36, 68, 73, 75, 103

Science Information Service 70, 74
Scopes trial 216
Scotland Neck City school case 305
Scoville v. Board of Education 361 (n
  34), 252
Secret societies in schools 245
Serrano v. Priest 143
Service Academies 53, 218
Servicemen's Readjustment Act of
  1944: see G.I. Bill of Rights
Sex discrimination
  prohibition 93
Shelley v. Kramer 273
Shelton v. Tucker 358 (n 72), 240
Shriver, Sargent 133
Sinderman case 225
Singleton v. Jackson Municipal Separate
  School District 292, 308
Sipuel v. Oklahoma 270, 271, 273,
  279
Sloan v. Lemon 187
  see also Lemon v. Kurtzman
Slochower v. Board of Education 236
Smith-Bankhead Act (1920) 118
Smith-Hughes Act (1917) 98, 114,
  119
Smith-Lever Act (1914) 96
Smith-Mundt Act (1948) 129, 131
Smith-Sears Vocational Rehabilita-
  tion Act (1918) 118
Smithsonian Institution and be-
  quest 52, 59
Smith-Towner bill 8
Solomon, Edwin S. 276, 280
Sorgen, Michael S. 146
South Carolina 186
South Dakota 167, 171, 300
Spencer v. Kugler 370 (n 161), 305
Spurlock, Clark 4, 154, 164, 166,
  273
Sputnik
  impact on education 72
Starns v. Malkerson 362 (n 52), 257

State, Department of 127, 129, 131, 135
States and education 1, 17, 141, 144
Stewart, Potter 205, 211, 226, 229, 259
Story, Joseph 152
Student Loan Marketing Association 90
Student protest, Right of 250
Student War Loan Programs 65
Students for a Democratic Society (SDS) 254
Supplemental Appropriation Act of 1954 128
Supreme Court and education 3
Supreme Court pages 23
Surplus Property Act of 1944 127
Swann case 30, 292, 297, 299, 303, 368 (n 106)
Sweatt v. *Painter* 270, 271, 273, 279
Sweezy v. *New Hampshire* 358 (n 64), 237
Swisher, Carl Brent 363 (n 7)

"Talent Search" programs 85, 90
Tax credits
  children in religious school 184, 192
Taylor, H.C. 13, 313 (n 4)
Teacher Corps: *see* National Teacher Corps.
Teachers
  age discrimination 228
  contracts of employment 220
  desegregation of teachers 307
  freedom of expression and association 232, 234
  maternity leaves 228
  retirement laws 223
  salaries 220, 224
  viewed by the public 219
Teller, James D. 38
Tennessee 216, 283

Tenth Amendment 2
Tenure 220
Texas 143, 144, 292
Textbooks
  children in religious schools 164
  denied to children in segregated private schools 287
  poor children in nonpublic schools 260
Thirteenth Amendment 267
Thurmond, Strom 33
Tiedt, Sidney W. 4
Tilton v. *Richardson* 79, 175, 181, 187
Tinker case 243, 250
Truman, Harry S 69, 127, 273
Tuition and fees for students 257
Tuition reimbursement for nonpublic school children 188
Turner, Jonathan B. 59
Turner v. *Touche* 342 (n 42), 148

United States Commissioner of Education 8, 9, 12, 24, 26, 29, 40, 44, 46, 47, 78, 80, 81, 82, 84, 100, 116, 122, 123, 124, 126, 267
United States Office of Education 7, 26, 58, 68, 75, 81, 82, 92, 100, 103, 106, 120, 124
"Upward Bound" programs 86, 90

Vaccination of school children 244
Van Buren, Martin 53
Vaughns v. *Board of Education of Prince Georges County* 370 (n 139), 299
Veterans educational benefits: *see* G.I. Bill of Rights
Veteran's Readjustment Assistance Act of 1952 66
Vietnam War
  protest against 243, 250

Virginia 300
VISTA 86, 90, 111
Vlandis v. *Kline* 362 (n 55), 258
Vocational Education Act of 1946:
    see George-Barden Act
Vocational Educational Act of 1963
    105, 112, 116
Vocational Education Amendments
    of 1968 112
Vocational rehabilitation 118
Vocational Rehabilitation Act of
    1943 119
Voting in school elections 147

Wallace, George C. 213, 280
Walz v. *Tax Commission* 181, 287
Ware v. *Estes* 362 (n 58), 260
Warfield, Benjamin B. 334 (n 85)
War Food Administration 22
War Orphans' Educational Assis-
    tance Act 67
Warren, Charles 312 (n 15)
Warren, Earl 147, 237, 242, 274
Washington, George 17, 49, 53, 55,
    162
Washington, state 232
Wasilewski v. *Board of School Directors*
    358 (n 73), 240
Watson v. *Memphis* 284
Waugh v. *Mississippi University* 245
Webster, Daniel 150
Webster, Noah 16
Weinberger, Caspar 277

Weiss v. *Walsh* 228
Wentworth, John 59
West Virginia 300
West Virginia State Board of Education
    v. *Barnette* 248
Wheeler v. *Barrera: see Barrera* v.
    Wheeler
Wheelock, John 150
Whelan, Charles M. 182, 195
White, Byron 145, 169, 176, 181,
    191
Whitehill v. *Elkins* 233
White House Conference on Educa-
    tion (1955) 72
White House Conference on Educa-
    tion (1965) 35
Wieman v. *Updegraf* 358 (n 49), 230
*Winston-Salem/Forsyth Board of Educa-
    tion* v. *Scott* 369 (n 133), 299
Wilson, Woodrow 96, 98
Wisconsin 159, 171, 207, 225, 256
Wolman v. *Essex* 184, 192
Wong v. *Hayakawa* 361 (n 39), 254
Works Progress Administration
    (WPA) 21
Work-study program 82, 86, 116
Wright v. *Council of City of Emporia*
    371 (n 164), 305

Yoder v. *Wisconsin* 159

Zorach case 201
Zucht v. *King* 244